| modality | | | | | concurrent |
Other	Inpatient	Outpatient			problems
		X		21	Marital; occupational
		X	Abstinence	6	Assertiveness; stress; depression; marital
Biblio-therapy		X	Nonproblem drinking	24	Depression; marital
		X		24	Tension; depression
Antabuse		X	Abstinence	30	Financial; vocational
Antabuse		X	Nonproblem drinking	6	Financial; vocational
Antabuse		X	Abstinence	30	Marital; financial
Antabuse		X	Abstinence	5	Weight; interpersonal
		X	Nonproblem drinking	6	Assertiveness; vocational
		X	Nonproblem drinking	18	Insomnia; tension: marital; assertiveness
		X	Abstinence	10	Marital; depression; spouse behaviors
		X	Nonproblem drinking	12	Marital
		X	Nonproblem drinking	15	Marital; assertiveness
	X	X	Nonproblem drinking	72	Marital; sexual; depression; dyslexia
	X	X	Nonproblem drinking	9	Marital
		X	Nonproblem drinking	42	Marital; vocational

Clinical Case Studies in the Behavioral Treatment of Alcoholism

Clinical Case Studies in the Behavioral Treatment of Alcoholism

Edited by
WILLIAM M. HAY
and
PETER E. NATHAN

Rutgers University
New Brunswick, New Jersey

PLENUM PRESS • NEW YORK AND LONDON

Library of Congress Cataloging in Publication Data

Main entry under title:

Clinical case studies in the behavioral treatment of alcoholism.

Includes bibliographical references and index.
Contents: Behavioral treatment of binge drinking / Peter M. Miller—Behavioral
treatment of alcoholism / Mark S. Goldman and Diane K. Klisz—When is a book a
treatment?: bibliography for problem drinkers / William R. Miller—[etc.]
1. Alcoholism—Treatment—Case studies. 2. Behavior therapy—Case studies. I.
Hay, William M., 1947.   . II. Nathan, Peter E. [DNLM: 1. Behavior therapy—Case
studies. 2. Alcoholism—Therapy—Case studies. WM 274 C644]
RC565.C487   1982   616.86'106   82-18048
ISBN 0-306-40940-2

RC
565
C487
1982

©1982 Plenum Press, New York
A Division of Plenum Publishing Corporation
233 Spring Street, New York, N.Y. 10013

Printed in the United States of America

For our fathers

WILLIAM G. HAY, Jr.

EMIL NATHAN, Jr.

Contributors

Glenn R. Caddy, *Department of Psychology, Nova University, Fort Lauderdale, Florida*

Tony Cellucci, *North Carolina Weslyan College, Rocky Mount, North Carolina*

Mark S. Goldman, *Department of Psychology, Wayne State University, Detroit, Michigan*

William M. Hay, *Alcohol Behavior Research Laboratory, Rutgers—The State University, New Brunswick, New Jersey*

Ray J. Hodgson, *Addiction Research Unit, Institute of Psychiatry, Maudsley Hospital, London England*

Diane K. Klisz, *Department of Psychology, Wayne State University, Detroit, Michigan*

Barbara S. McCrady, *Problem Drinkers Project, Butler Hospital, Providence, Rhode Island*

Peter M. Miller, *Sea Pines Behavioral Institute, Hilton Head Island, South Carolina*

William R. Miller, *Department of Psychology, University of New Mexico, Albuquerque, New Mexico*

Peter E. Nathan, *Alcohol Behavior Research Laboratory, Rutgers—The State University, New Brunswick, New Jersey*

Ted D. Nirenberg, *Veterans Administration Medical Center, Davis Park, Providence, Rhode Island*

Nora E. Noel, *Problem Drinkers Project, Butler Hospital, Providence, Rhode Island*

E. Mansell Pattison, *Department of Psychiatry, Medical College of Georgia, Augusta, Georgia*

Howard J. Rankin, *Addiction Research Unit, Institute of Psychiatry, Maudsley Hospital, London England*

Linda C. Sobell, *Clinical Institute, Addiction Research Foundation, and University of Toronto, Toronto, Ontario, Canada*

Mark B. Sobell, *Clinical Institute, Addiction Research Foundation, and University of Toronto, Toronto, Ontario, Canada*

Roger E. Vogler, *Department of Psychology, Pomona College, Pomona, California*

Preface

There is no shortage of books on behavioral research, on behavioral research on alcoholism, or on behavioral research on alcoholism treatment. Most of the authors of chapters in this book have been involved in the writing of these books. The books and their authors have played an important role in the dramatic increase in the influence of behavioral approaches to one of our society's most troubling human problems.

There are not many books, though, which detail the longitudinal course of the behavioral therapies, none doing so for behavior therapy with alcoholics and problem drinkers. That this book now appears, then, is a first, made more valuable by the fact that the chapter's authors are both researchers and clinicians, willing and able to combine respect for empirical data with clinical sensitivity and compassion, concern, and commitment for their patients.

The chapters in this book reveal important commonalities and telling divergencies in technique, strategy, and treatment tactics. Despite a common perspective on etiology and treatment, the authors of the chapters in this book diverge in criteria for deciding on treatment goal, choice of initial intervention target, the specifics of techniques used, and follow-up procedures. Common to all, though, is an openness to innovation, a pragmatic appreciation of approaches that work, and a sincere respect for the patient and his or her fundamental desire for a healthy, happier, and more productive life.

Our major debt, then, is to our colleagues and friends who have joined us in preparing this book. As on other occasions, we owe them our thanks for participating with us in an enterprise we all feel is a worthwhile one. As well, we would like to thank our colleagues at the Alcohol Behavior Research Laboratory and the Graduate School of Applied and Professional Psycholo-

gy, who continue to offer us the kind of intellectual and emotional suste-
nance that makes this kind of work so enjoyable as well. Barbara Honig
typed much of this book with her usual mixture of gentle grumbling and
good grace. And the National Institute on Alcohol Abuse and Alcoholism
supported salaries, supplies, and scribes for a number of those whose chapters appear in this book, including its editors.

Peter E. Nathan
William M. Hay

Contents

Clinical Case Studies in the Behavioral Treatment of Alcoholism

I
Contemporary Behavioral Assessment and Treatment Procedures

Part I includes four chapters. Chapter 1, by Peter M. Miller, describes the behavioral treatment of a binge drinker. In Chapter 2, Mark S. Goldman and Diane K. Klisz trace the course of one client through an abstinence-oriented behavioral treatment program. Chapter 3, by William R. Miller, evaluates the effectiveness of bibliotherapy as a treatment procedure for two clients who wish to become nonproblem drinkers. And Chapter 4, by Linda and Mark Sobell, Nora E. Noel, Tony Cellucci, and Ted D. Nirenberg, details step-by-step procedures for developing both abstinent and nonproblem-drinking treatment programs. Taken together, these four chapters represent a comprehensive overview of contemporary, multifaceted behavioral approaches to the assessment and treatment of alcoholism.

Behavioral Treatment of Binge Drinking

PETER M. MILLER

1. INTRODUCTION

Periodic or binge drinking presents special problems in clinical assessment and treatment. The following case is somewhat unusual in that the majority of reports of behavioral treatments focus on alcoholics whose drinking is fairly continuous. There are, however, a category of alcohol abusers who exhibit brief binge-drinking episodes interspersed with periods of either moderate alcohol intake or complete abstinence. These cases do not easily fit into the traditional diagnostic classifications. For example, the third edition of the *Diagnostic and Statistical Manual of Mental Disorders* (American Psychiatric Association, 1980) describes three main patterns of chronic pathological alcohol use: (1) regular daily intake of large amounts, (2) regular heavy drinking limited to weekends, and (3) long periods of sobriety interspersed with binges of daily heavy drinking lasting for weeks or months. In the present case excessive drinking occurred only under one circumscribed situation (during business trips), on a very irregular basis (i.e., during only *some* business trips), and with a brief duration (1 to 5 days). This brief episodic drinking pattern, which is highly situationally specific, has been noted in successful, hard-driving business executives who travel a great deal in their jobs (Miller, 1976). These problem drinkers present unique treatment difficulties.

PETER M. MILLER • Sea Pines Behavioral Institute, Hilton Head Island, South Carolina 29928.

2. REASON FOR REFERRAL

The client was a 52-year-old married male who was self-employed as a free-lance business consultant. Immediately after a drinking binge of four days duration he referred himself for outpatient treatment to a local behavioral medicine center. His periodic binges were causing decreases in work efficiency and a progressively worsening relationship with his wife. His self-referral was precipitated by (1) guilt and concern over his inability to control his binge drinking, (2) concern over the integrity of his consulting firm, and (3) the encouragement of his wife.

3. HISTORY OF DRINKING PROBLEM

The client began drinking in the military service at the age of 18 years. He described his early drinking as predominately "moderate" (two to three beers, two to three times per week) with excessive drinking occurring on an average of once or twice per month. Heavy alcohol intake was limited to one evening's duration and was social in nature (i.e., in the company of his Army buddies). After military service he attended college, and his drinking decreased. He drank only moderately on social occasions and rarely became intoxicated. After college he married and worked for several years with a large management consulting firm. He was a diligent, hard-working employee, who rose quickly in the company. His drinking remained moderate during this time. When he was 43, the client and an associate in his company decided to resign and start their own consulting firm. The client valued independence in his work and had long dreamed of owning his own business. The next few years were marked by extremely difficult times. The client worked long hours to build up his new business, which was slow in developing. His partner proved to be inefficient and left the struggling business. The client, who had previously been earning a substantial corporate salary, developed financial problems. His long hours and financial worries led to conflict with his wife. During this period the client's drinking increased markedly, although it was limited to his business life. Typically, he drank after work with clients and after stressful business dealings. At this point he began a pattern of having two to three drinks almost every night during the workweek, becoming intoxicated on an average of one evening per week. He never drank on weekends or during work.

Over the next few years his consulting business improved and began to prosper. His total devotion to his work led to further marital difficulties and eventual divorce. He remarried soon after. His drinking decreased for a few months after his new marriage but gradually increased once again. He became intoxicated two to three evenings per week. He consulted a psychiatrist who conducted weekly outpatient psychotherapy for 4 months. The client's drinking problem did not change during this time, and he discontinued treatment.

He and his wife then decided to make major changes in their lives in an attempt to reduce stress. They moved to a small resort community, which allowed them more time with each other and more recreational activities, but which necessitated traveling for him. He traveled to the New York area to consult with business firms approximately once or twice per month for 2 to 5 days at a time. At this point his drinking pattern changed. He abstained completely from alcohol at home and drank only during business trips with clients. He never drank to excess until his business was concluded. However, he would often arrive home in an intoxicated state. One of these episodes, involving four days of constant drinking, necessitated a brief hospitalization in a local general medical hospital. It was then the client was put in contact with Alcoholics Anonymous by his physician. He attended AA meetings twice per week and seemed to profit from this experience. He went for 3 months without drinking, although his binge episodes began again. He continued to attend AA meetings regularly at home and periodically on business trips. His drinking bouts continued. Worries about the effects of his drinking on his marriage and on his business efficiency led him to contact the author for outpatient treatment.

In terms of family history the client's parents were both light drinkers who consumed one or two drinks only very occasionally at social functions. No blood relative exhibited a problem-drinking pattern.

4. CURRENT STATUS

At the initiation of treatment the client's drinking bouts were causing increased marital discord. Arguments over his drinking were especially severe both prior to business trips and upon his arrival home, especially if he had been drinking. His business was not severely affected, since the client drank heavily only after his business dealings were concluded. He was, however, becoming more anxious about the eventual effect of increased drinking on his productivity. This increased stress led to chronic worrying about his performance and the stability of his business.

At the time of treatment the client's drinking was limited to binges during business trips lasting 3 to 5 days. When drinking began it was continuous until he arrived home. No drinking ever occurred in his home community. No evidence of delirium tremens or blackouts existed. A medical examination revealed essentially negative findings. Liver function studies and glucose tolerance tests were normal. There was no past or present history of psychiatric problems.

5. ASSESSMENT PROCEDURES

As an initial screening assessment the client was administered the Michigan Alcohol Screening Test (Selzer, 1971). He obtained a score of 27, well above the alcoholism cutoff score of 6. The MAST seems to be an appropriate screening instrument for an episodic drinker, since it focuses on problems associated with drinking as opposed to sole emphasis on quantity of alcohol consumption.

To obtain a more detailed analysis of drinking behavior, self-monitoring procedures are often used in the assessment of alcohol abuse. However, this method poses a considerable problem when assessing low-frequency behaviors. Daily monitoring of cravings was useless for this client, since he rarely experienced an impulse to drink at home.

Two self-reporting procedures were followed. First, a calendar approach (Sobell, Maisto, Sobell, Cooper, Cooper, & Sanders, 1980) was used to obtain a detailed drinking history of binges over the past 21 months. Using a yearly calendar to determine reference points, the client was able to provide information on specific binge episodes and their durations. A month-by-month journal that the client kept of the time, location, purpose, and outcome of his out-of-town business meetings proved invaluable in this regard. The reliability of his reports was checked against his wife's reports. Since these episodes occurred relatively infrequently (approximately two every 3 months) few discrepancies were reported. Binges were calculated in blocks of 3-month intervals. It is interesting to note that the client found this quarterly assessment system intriguing, since his financial and tax statements were prepared on the same quarterly basis. Clinicians would do well to take into account the ways in which self-assessment procedures fit into a client's lifestyle. This calendar assessment method indicated that the client had approximately one binge per month, with each lasting about 4 days.

In addition, the client was requested to keep records of binge episodes. He did so by recording these instances in his business journal and appointment book. He was requested specifically to make note of (1) the date, (2) time of first drink, (3) circumstances of first drink, (4) events leading up to first drink, (5) total amount of alcohol comsumed per day, (6) type of alcoholic beverages consumed, (7) duration of drinking episode in days. Details of business trips in which temptations occurred but drinks were avoided were also recorded by the client. The client's wife was also asked to keep records on occasions in which her husband arrived home from a trip in an intoxicated state or in which he telephoned her from another city while intoxicated. This monitoring was used to analyze drinking episodes during treatment and to evaluate progress during and after treatment.

The historical drinking information was used within an interview format to obtain a functional analysis of the client's drinking behavior. Information was sought on five major categories of antecedents and consequences: situational, social, emotional, cognitive, and physiological. In examining precursors to the client's binges it was apparent that a combination of social, emotional, and cognitive factors were the most influential elements in triggering a drinking episode. A typical episode illustrates these influences in the client's self-description of events leading up to one of his binges:

> I had been at the Hilton in New York City for 2 days conducting a time management seminar for executives of a large publishing firm. I felt under a great deal of stress, since the quality of my seminar might determine potential consulting business from companies of those in attendance. I put a great deal of physical and psychological energy into my presentation and felt relieved and fatigued when it was over.
>
> We finished about 4:00 in the afternoon. My presentation apparently went well, since several participants were interested in talking with me further. Three executives from the XYZ Company wanted me to have a drink with them at the bar to discuss my doing more consulting for their firm. They all wanted to unwind after the meeting. I hesitated at first but they were very insistent. I remember thinking to myself, "It's very important that they like me. I must make a good impression." I planned on going into the bar but ordering plain club soda. Once we sat down all three were quite insistent that I join them in a drink. At this point I remember thinking, "Oh, well, one won't hurt me. I'll just have one and stop there. Besides, I deserve to relax. I owe it to myself." After one drink my thinking started to change. As I started to feel the effects of the drink, I felt that a couple more wouldn't hurt me. My companions turned out to be heavy drinkers. I really felt relaxed and congenial. Finally, they had to leave but I remained in the bar drinking for the rest of the evening.

Thus, the major antecedents for drinking appeared to be business-related anxiety, social pressure, and detrimental cognitive patterns. Immediate positive reinforcers of alcohol intake included pleasant taste sensations, reduction in tension, avoidance of expected negative evaluations from others for not joining in, avoidance of expected loss of business from potential clients.

Additionally, the client's marital adjustment and social skills were assessed. Both husband and wife were asked to complete the Marital Happiness Scale (Azrin, Naster, & Jones, 1973), a 10-item rating scale on marital satisfaction. With the exception of their communication, the couple reported that they were relatively satisfied with the marriage. No major difficulties in the areas of responsibilities, social activities, or sex were reported. The wife's major concern was with her husband's drinking and his increased tendency to avoid personal conversations with her (e.g., regarding his feelings). She viewed his drinking problem as worsening and was concerned that he would become incapacitated. The client reported that he was most bothered by his wife's comments regarding past drinking episodes and threats regarding future ones. He reported a general increase in what he termed "controlling" behavior from his wife. Generally, this control referred to advice about his work such as, "You shouldn't do business with ABC Company because they're a bunch of alcoholics," or "You should be more organized and then you wouldn't worry so much." Such comments aggravated him and if they occurred immediately before a trip or in a telephone conversation during a trip, they increased the likelihood of his drinking. Concomitantly, his drinking episodes increased the probability of such comments from his wife.

6. TREATMENT GOALS

The goals of treatment involved several elements. First, the issue of controlled, moderate drinking versus total abstinence was discussed. While the client had no medical contraindications for a controlled-drinking goal, both he and his wife definitely preferred total abstinence. Their reasoning for this was threefold: (1) he had no difficulty in maintaining total abstinence when not on business trips, (2) his past association with Alcoholics Anonymous had convinced him that total abstinence was the only viable goal for him, and (3) his wife drank very infrequently and was willing to become totally abstinent to support her husband.

Second, more detailed clinical goals were established, based primarily on the historical reports of drinking episodes. The functional analysis indicated that business trips were the major stimulus cue for drinking and that drinking was further triggered by job stress, inappropriate cognitive monologues, and social pressure. Role playing also emphasized the importance of the client's inability to handle encouragement to drink by others. Marital problems appeared to be specifically related to the abuse of alcohol in terms of the wife's critical comments and threats and the husband's emotional withdrawal from his wife.

Thus, based on the assessments, treatment goals included the following:

6.1. Drinking Goals

1. To eliminate all alcohol consumption
2. To increase self-management skills in order to better identify and control thoughts and environmental circumstances leading to drinking

6.2. Social-Emotional Goals

1. To decrease job-related stress
2. To increase refusal skills necessary to cope with social pressure to drink

6.3. Marital Goals

1. To decrease his wife's negative comments and threats regarding alcohol
2. To increase more positive, goal-oriented interactions
3. To increase the client's personal-emotional conversations with his wife

7. TREATMENT IMPLEMENTATION

Treatment progressed over a period of 18 months, with sessions gradually being reduced in frequency. The client was seen once per week during the first 6 months, once every other week during the second 6 months, and once per month during the final 6 months.

During the first two sessions the husband and wife were seen together for two reasons. First, assessment data as described earlier were accumulated from both, and details of past and present drinking and marital problems were discussed. Second, the couple was in an immediate state of crisis at the initiation of treatment, and two joint sessions were needed to calm them down and develop positive outcome expectancies. These sessions focused on pinpointing problems, setting goals, and describing the elements and sequence of the behavioral treatment strategies. Since the client's next business trip was not scheduled for 2 months, emphasis was initially placed on reducing stress and improving marital relations.

7.1. Stress-Management Training

Stress-management training was initiated with the client and consisted of three elements. These included (1) relaxation training, (2) anxiety-management training, and (3) lifestyle evaluation and reinforcement sampling.

Personal Relaxation Training (Miller, 1978), a three-phased method, was completed over four sessions. It consisted of muscle, cardiorespiratory, and cognitive relaxation. In the first phase the client was taught muscle relaxation by means of tightening and then relaxing several muscle groups in the body. This was accompanied by the client's silent repetition of such phrases as "Relax," "I am feeling totally relaxed," and "I am calm and relaxed." Relaxation of the cardiorespiratory system was accomplished by instructing the client to focus on his breathing and heart rate. Deep breathing was used to induce slow, shallow breaths. Again, emphasis was placed on the repetition of phrases such as "My breathing is slowing down," and "My heart rate is becoming slow and steady." Cognitive relaxation was induced by imagery techniques. The client was instructed to imagine pleasant scenes (e.g., a quiet walk in the woods) and to concentrate on total cognitive and physical relaxation. The client was instructed to practice these techniques at least three times per week for a duration of 20 minutes each time. After 4 weeks he was instructed to use relaxation at times when stress was likely. For example, he was instructed to stop at least twice during his work when he was writing a consulting report for a client and, for a period of 2 minutes, concentrate on relaxation. The aim was to provide him with a method of either avoiding or escaping stress induced during periods of work. The client became quite adept at this technique and found 1 or 2 minutes of relaxation spaced throughout his workday more beneficial than two or three longer periods of relaxation each week.

Anxiety-management training, developed by Suinn and Richardson (1971) was also utilized. This method required the client to systematically induce and then control stress in his imagination. The client was relaxed and then instructed to imagine a stressful business situation. For example, during one session he imagined giving a seminar to a group of high-level executives on a relatively unfamiliar topic. He was instructed to focus on his stress reactions (e.g., increased respiration, increased forehead-muscle tightness) and reduce them by means of muscle relaxation, deep breathing, or cognitive self-instructions (e.g., "I have the ability to control my tension," "The tension is slowly going away," or "I am in complete control over my body"). This procedure was repeated, using several different stressful scenes. The client was advised to practice this anxiety-management routine frequently in an attempt to "innoculate" himself against the effects of stressors in his environment. Prior to each business trip potential stressful business encounters were rehearsed in this manner.

Finally, the client's time schedule was examined to increase the number and duration of reinforcing and relaxing activities. The client spent an inordinate amount of time either engaged in business activities or worrying about these activities. He was a very orderly, time-oriented individual, whose business and performance worries infiltrated his leisure time. A lifestyle analysis and scheduling procedure was used to break this pattern. The client was asked to list as many pleasant activities as he had either enjoyed in the past or always wanted to do. To encourage a list of adequate length the client was asked to imagine activities in which he would engage if he had unlimited time and resources and none of his present family or business responsibilities. Such activities as jogging, tennis, piano lessons, flying lessons, and physical fitness endeavors were included on his list. A typical week's schedule was then constructed in which leisure-time activities were scheduled in whatever time remained. Even so, leisure-time activities comprised only a small portion of the client's time, with more than adequate time being allowed for business activities. Time was allocated each day for a 30-minute exercise and jogging routine, twice weekly for tennis, and once weekly for flying lessons. Time for family and business activities was scheduled next. The client was instructed to follow this schedule strictly, with no deviations.

His self-employed status fostered the implementation of this schedule. Although the client initially expressed doubts, he slowly began to enjoy his leisure activities. Also the quality of his work time increased, and worrying about business decreased.

7.2. Marital-Skills Training

Only a few sessions were spent on marital-skills training, since the couple's marital difficulties seemed directly related to drinking binges and not to major interpersonal excesses or deficits. As described in the section on treatment goals the couple expressed very straightforward objectives needed to improve the marriage. In addition to refraining from drinking alcohol, the wife wanted her husband to share his personal thoughts and feelings with her more often. Such behavior was modeled by the therapist and rehearsed in treatment session. Since both partners desired more positive interactions with each other, they agreed to schedule a 30-minute session per day to discuss positive aspects of their relationship along with personal thoughts and feelings. The progress of this method was discussed and reinforced in treatment sessions. Since the client's wife wanted to lose weight it was decided that she would accompany him in his exercise activities each day, and they arranged for joint tennis lessons. The rationale of this approach consisted of an attempt to encourage positive alternatives to replace discussion of drinking episodes and to increase marital satisfaction.

The wife was instructed to refrain from all comments regarding past drinking episodes or the possibility of future episodes. Threats regarding drinking behavior were also to be discontinued. After several violations of this agreement, leading to arguments, the wife was taught a form of brief relaxation to avoid the urge to mention drinking. Also, the therapist modeled various responses which the client was to use when his wife violated these agreements. He was to calmly remind her of her agreement in a nonthreatening, nonsarcastic tone. During treatment sessions the couple received guided practice at role-playing their interactions regarding such contract violations. The client was prompted to reinforce his wife's refraining from negative, threatening comments with positive, personal remarks. Such comments as "Honey, it really gives me more confidence in my progress when you don't mention my past drinking. Thanks a lot for trying so hard" were encouraged. During role playing of such remarks the client noted that personal reactions of this nature, even toward his wife, were difficult for him to express and were accompanied by mild anxiety. Repeated behavioral rehearsal of such statements, together with relaxation training, resulted in less anxiety. As training progressed the client's wife reported a dramatic increase in positive comments from her husband at home.

7.3. Environmental Manipulation

Prior to each business trip treatment sessions focused on environmental manipulation, drink-refusal training, and craving-control strategies. In terms of modifying the client's environment, a detailed schedule of his trip was planned. The client and clinician mapped out an hour-by-hour structured schedule of activities. While ample time was scheduled for relaxation and recreation between meetings, "unstructured" time was kept to a minimum. Careful attention was given to structuring activities at times when drinking was most likely (e.g., at the end of a day of meetings and prior to dinner). A sample schedule is indicated below:

7:00 A.M.	Wake up
7:00–7:20 A.M.	Calisthenics
7:20–8:00 A.M.	Shower and dress
8:00–9:00 A.M.	Breakfast with clients
9:00–12:00 P.M.	Meetings
12:00–1:30 P.M.	Lunch with clients
1:30–2:00 P.M.	Stress-management routine in hotel room
2:00–5:00 P.M.	Meetings
5:00–5:45 P.M.	Jog, walk, or swim
5:45–6:30 P.M.	Shower and change
6:30–7:00 P.M.	Relaxation routine and craving-control training
7:00–8:00 P.M.	Dinner
8:30–10:00 P.M.	Alcoholics Anonymous meeting
10:30–11:30 P.M.	Read, prepare for tomorrow's meetings, call home promptly at 11:30 P.M., retire for the evening

The client was instructed to stick to this schedule religiously. Business associates who wished to schedule business discussions during the cocktail hour or at dinner were asked to meet instead at a breakfast or luncheon meeting the next day. At the end of the afternoon meetings the client was instructed to talk briefly with associates and then to excuse himself for the remainder of the evening. All offers of drinks were to be refused without hesitation. The client was advised to discuss his jogging and physical-fitness interests in an attempt to find companions for this activity. Such people might be more likely to be light drinkers or abstainers and could provide "safe" dinner companionship.

The client was also advised to plan his airplane reservations to and from business meetings in such a way that little spare time was available. Since he was especially vulnerable at the end of business trips, his transportation home was planned very carefully. For example, if his meetings ended at 6:00 in the evening he was to fly home late that evening rather than wait until the next day. This plan was to be followed even if the flight was quite late (e.g., midnight).

Since the client enjoyed the camaraderie at Alcoholics Anonymous meetings, and since these meetings appeared to deter drinking, he prepared a list of AA meetings in various cities on the East Coast. Thus, if need be, he could attend a meeting almost every evening on all business trips.

7.4. Drink-Refusal Training

Since hesitancy in refusing offers of alcoholic beverages presented a problem for the client, drink-refusal training (Foy, Miller, Eisler, & O'Toole, 1976) was conducted before each trip. Prior to training sessions several discussions revolved around the client's reasons for succumbing to social pressure to drink. Apparently, he felt that his refusal might affect his business relationships with clients. In addition, he felt a need for companionship after business meetings. To alleviate these concerns several alternatives were discussed. For example, as was indicated previously, the client was instructed to schedule business appointments at "safe" times, such as breakfast. In addition, "safe" companionship was encouraged via AA attendance and physical-fitness activities with others with similar interests.

Drink-refusal training was initiated by constructing scenes depicting typical encounters with drink "pushers." Two sample scenes are listed below:

Scene 1. You have just completed conducting a workshop on company mergers. The president and the general manager of a large conglomerate were in attendance and were very impressed by your performance. They approach you and say, "That's just the kind of information our company needs. How about joining us in the bar? I'd like to discuss the possibility of your consulting with our firm."

Scene 2. You have just signed a very large consultation contract with an important and influential company. The president invites you to his home for cocktails and dinner along with a few others from the company. You arrive and meet a few other guests that are present. The host turns to you and says, "I've got a fine batch of martinis made up. What can I get you to drink?"

These and other scenes were role-played, with the clinician serving as the business associate. It was apparent that the client felt very awkward and hesitant in refusing offers of drinks. During the initial role-playing sessions he spoke hesitantly with such comments as, "Well, ah, I really don't think so. Ah, perhaps we could get together later." The client reported a moderate degree of anxiety during these role-playing encounters.

Training consisted of using a combination of specific instructions, modeling by the therapist, rehearsal, and verbal feedback. Components of the refusal response that were discussed and rehearsed included: (1) eye contact, (2) voice tone and affect, (3) direct refusal, and (4) offering alternatives. These components were rehearsed one at a time, with performance feedback provided after each practice scene. The final goal response for Scene 1 involved the following: In a firm, assured, and serious tone of voice the client was to look directly at the business associate and say, "I'm sorry, Paul, but I have something else scheduled right now. I'm very interested in discussing this with you. Let's get together for a breakfast meeting at 8:00 in the morning." Responses were practiced for several encounters of this type until the client felt comfortable with his response and until his response included the necessary verbal and nonverbal components.

Upon his return home from each business trip, actual encounters of this nature were discussed, with additional feedback provided. Difficult scenes were reenacted through role playing. For example, if the encounter was particularly problematic (e.g., an insistent, important client who is unable to meet at other times or in other circumstances), alternatives were discussed and rehearsed.

7.5. Craving-Control Training

Occasionally, the client found himself in business situations in which alcohol was present and the opportunity for him to drink presented itself. Prior to and during these circumstances the client was instructed to use craving-control training (Miller & Sims, 1981). This training is similar to anxiety-management training, except that it focuses on alcohol-craving sensations as opposed to stress reactions.

Craving-control training consists of the following sequence: (1) relaxation, (2) craving induction, (3) focused attention to craving reactions (4) control of these reactions, and (5) positive-consequences imagery. During training sessions the client was instructed to relax, using the focused-muscle exercises, deep breathing, and self-instructions described previously. This was a very brief relaxation, lasting no more than two minutes. While relaxed the client was instructed to imagine a situation likely to induce cravings for alcohol. The therapist guided the imagery at first by describing a typical scene and enhancing the craving through vivid descriptions of possible sensations. For example, the therapist might say:

> You're sitting in the hotel bar with some colleagues and friends. You haven't seen them for a long time and the atmosphere is congenial. You just finished a very tense meeting and have nothing more scheduled before your departure for home. Your plane has been delayed until tomorrow morning because of the weather.
> All of your friends are enjoying their drinks. You can see and smell the liquor very clearly. The friend next to you is enjoying your favorite drink—a vodka martini. You can almost taste it as you watch him drink. The craving for a drink is getting stronger and stronger.

The client was advised to imagine the scene as vividly as possible, as if it were actually happening. Once the image and craving were clear, he was to focus on the physical and cognitive sensations associated with craving. The therapist assisted in this process by providing an inventory of possible reactions.

> As you think about your craving, focus on specific sensations. Are any of your muscles tense? Do the muscles in your forehead, jaws, or neck feel any less relaxed than they did a minute ago? Is your mouth watering? Have your breathing and heart rate increased ever so slightly? What are you thinking about? What specific things are you saying to yourself about the craving?

The client then focused on these reactions and described them. A typical description follows:

> My breathing was definitely increased. The muscles around my mouth and jaws are a bit less relaxed. I can feel slight movements in them. I also notice increased salivation in my mouth.
> My thoughts are jumping around. I'm thinking, "One drink won't hurt you. Besides, you deserve it. You just had a rough meeting, and you need a drink to calm your nerves."

The client was then given specific instructions on controlling each element of his craving response. For example, he was to practice deep breathing, together with thoughts of "My breathing is slowing down," to control increased respiration rate. He was instructed to clench his teeth and then relax his jaw muscles several times. Five or six exaggerated swallows helped alleviate increased salivation. In addition, he was instructed to challenge negative thoughts and to repeat such challenges several times. For example, he might think "One drink *will* hurt me. I should know by now that I can't handle alcohol. I must learn to relax in other ways. Besides, I feel so miserable after drinking, it really doesn't calm me down anyway." The client rehearsed these craving control techniques until he was able to induce a craving and then completely eliminate it. The therapist continuously reinforced the notion that cravings were under his control and that cravings were nothing more than the physical and cognitive reactions he experienced.

The final phase of craving-control training consisted of imagery focusing on positive outcomes and expectancies. In the scene described above the client was instructed to imagine his complete and successful control over the craving. He might imagine the following:

> Now you have complete control over your cravings. You see your friends drinking, but all of your cravings are gone. Completely and totally gone! *You* have controlled them and eliminated them.
> Now imagine yourself leaving your friends after an enjoyable evening. You did not even have one drink. You feel great. You take a brisk walk and feel a new strength in you. You feel a real sense of accomplishment and control.
> Now imagine yourself 5 years from now. You haven't had a drink in 5 years! Your business is prospering. Your marriage is a happy one. Everything is going well for you. Imagine all this as clearly and as vividly as possible . . . as if it's really happening right now.

This training was repeated over six consecutive sessions and prior to each business trip. The client was instructed to use craving-control training in several ways. First, he was to practice the technique twice per week to "innoculate" himself against the effects of cravings. Second, he was to use the training sequence prior to any situation that would constitute a temptation. For example, prior to a business cocktail party at someone's house he was to practice the craving-control routine several times. Essentially, he would repeatedly rehearse a positive outcome. Third, he was to use a shortened modified version of the procedure when experiencing cravings in tempting situations.

8. TREATMENT RESULTS

Figure 1 illustrates the number and duration of binge episodes expressed in 3-month intervals from January 1976 through December 1980. Pretreatment data included the 21 months immediately preceding the initiation of treatment in October 1977. These data were obtained from reports by

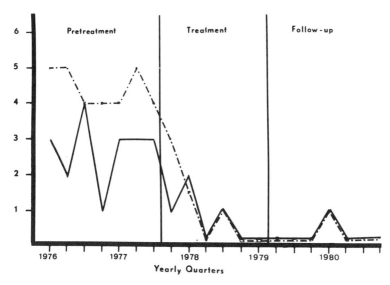

Figure 1. The number and duration of binge episodes expressed in three-month intervals from January 1976 to December 1980. The solid line represents the number of binges, while the dashed line represents the duration of each binge.

the client and his wife as mentioned previously. Percentage of agreement between husband and wife was 100% for the occurrance of binges and 86% for number of days involved. Prior to treatment the client averaged 2.7 binges per 3-month interval, with the range varying from 1 to 4 per quarter. Mean duration of binges for the entire pretreatment period was 4.4 days.

During treatment, binges decreased in frequency to .66, or fewer than one per 3-month interval. During the 18 months of treatment the client experienced a total of 4 binges, as opposed to 16 binges in the 18 months prior to treatment. Figure 1 illustrates a steady decline in binges over the treatment period, so that no binges occurred during the final 6 months of treatment. At that time the client was seen by the therapist only on a monthly basis.

Duration of binges during treatment also decreased markedly. Binges during treatment lasted a mean of 1.3 days, as compared to 4.4 days after treatment. Thus, the client was exhibiting more control over binges as treatment progressed.

As indicated in Figure 1 the client experienced a binge during December 1977, soon after treatment began. Since the first few sessions focused on stress reduction and marital intervention, the client's drink-refusal skills and thought-control abilities had not as yet been developed. He succumbed to social pressure and the added temptation of Christmas parties as part of his business dealings. This early slip, however, provided an opportunity to functionally analyze the drinking episode and rehearse alternative methods of coping with the antecedents.

During February and March 1978 the client experienced two binges, one lasting 2 days and the other 1 day. Both episodes occurred in very high-stress situations in which the client was attempting to gain new consultation contracts. He was dealing with insistent clients, who were heavy drinkers themselves. In each case the client gained control of his drinking quickly with the help of an Alcoholics Anonymous meeting on one occasion and a telephone conversation with the therapist on the other.

The client then went for 4 consecutive months without a drinking episode. In September 1978 he evidenced a brief binge on a trip to Chicago. Apparently, the client had "let his guard down," feeling that he could drink moderately if need be. He consciously avoided any self-management strategies during the trip. He reported that he was testing himself. One drink led to another, and after eight martinis he returned to his room and, luckily, fell asleep. He awoke the next morning full of remorse and convinced that he must remain vigilant. Prior to each business trip thereafter the client and therapist planned alternative strategies, structured the client's time schedule, rehearsed drink refusal, and practiced craving-control training. During the final 6 months of treatment the client remained completely abstinent.

The client also reported that throughout treatment he continued his use of the stress-management techniques and experienced significantly less tension, particularly in business situations. Both he and his wife reported a much-improved marital relationship. Total score on the Marital Happiness Scale for the client increased from 70 at the beginning of treatment to 82 at the termination of the treatment. His spouse who was less satisfied with the marriage initially increased from 63 to 79.

He reported a steady decline in negative, threatening comments regarding alcohol from his wife, with none at all during the final 7 months of treatment. She reported a significant increase in "close, emotional" conversations. Both felt that they had a more personally satisfying relationship with one another.

After treatment was discontinued, follow-up contact was maintained at 3-month intervals for 21 months. For the first 3 months the client called the therapist before and after each business trip to discuss his plans and progress. In the 8th follow-up month the client and his wife reported a very brief drinking episode. The client had been under a great deal of stress at the time. His brother, whom he was extremely close to, suffered a stroke a week before his scheduled business trip. Two days before the trip a big account of his went out of business and terminated his services. He reported attempting to relax at this meeting but was unable to do so. At the time he felt that nothing but a drink could calm him down. After three drinks he experienced increased anxiety and guilt over his drinking. He voluntarily discontinued drinking and has remained abstinent for the 13 months since.

9. DISCUSSION

Treatment of an episodic drinker can present advantages and disadvantages to the clinician. Since this client was at home and therefore abstinent, the pace of assessment and treatment could be structured and controlled easily by the therapist. Clients who drink on a regular daily basis present special clinical difficulties at the beginning of treatment. Unless they are detoxified and hospitalized, both they and their spouse often desire a rush into treatment to prevent further drinking quickly. If clinicians succumb to this strategy they may risk a hurried and incomplete assessment of the problem. In addition, a client's daily drinking during initial treatment sessions interferes with the ability to cooperate fully with the implementation of treatment strategies. In the present case, since a business trip was not planned for 5 weeks, a full assessment was completed, with ample time to institute treatment strategies on a step-by-step basis.

The disadvantage in treating an episodic drinker is that the client must wait several weeks to implement and practice self-management techniques. Thus, experience in behavior-change strategies in naturalistic settings is limited, although role playing compensates somewhat for this deficit. In addition, evaluation of treatment efficacy is prolonged, since occasions for drinking occur only on a periodic basis.

Overall, the client was motivated and cooperative. The self-monitoring procedures, together with the systematic nature of the behavioral treatment plan, proved to be quite compatible with the client's own approach to problems. In fact, he reported that the behavioral approach made sense and fit in well with his business-oriented style.

It might be noted that this client's wife's cooperation was positively affected by her enrollment in a behavioral weight-control program soon after her husband's treatment began. During the first two sessions of the client's treatment the wife was skeptical of the behavioral approach, arguing that a search for underlying emotional causes of her husband's drinking was needed. After entering the weight-management program she became noticeably more cooperative and enthusiastic. For example, she developed a better understanding of the role-playing procedures and even used a similar approach in refusing offers of high calorie foods. The couple also developed mutual interests in a wide range of physical-fitness and recreational activities as part of each of their behavior-change programs. This togetherness enhanced both personal and marital satisfaction. In addition, by confronting her weight problem the wife developed a better understanding of her husband's difficulty in dealing with situations triggering alcohol consumption.

COMMENTARY

William M. Hay

The episodic or binge drinker presents a number of special challenges to the behavioral clinician. Peter Miller provides the reader with a systematic overview of the behavioral assessment and treatment procedures that can be employed with this difficult client population. Miller's clinical approach to this case highlights a number of the basic tenets of behavioral assessment and treatment of alcoholism. One tenet is that comprehensive assessment of the individual is the nucleus of behavioral treatment. As Miller mentions, his client's drinking pattern does not lend itself readily to one of the three diagnostic patterns of excessive alcohol use listed in DSM-III. A comprehensive behavioral assessment, however, results in a striking picture of the highly situational nature of this client's drinking behavior. Behavioral assessment procedures also identified job-related, marital, and lifestyle problems that were contributing to excessive drinking behavior. The behavioral approach to alcoholism treatment, therefore, does not view drinking behavior in isolation from other life areas. Also, the behavioral clinician is aware of the situational aspects of drinking behavior. Constructs such as "loss of control" or diagnostic classifications do not provide the behavioral clinician with a detailed enough picture of the variety of determinants that affect drinking behavior.

A second tenet of the behavioral approach concerns the close relationship existing among assessment, the specification of treatment goals, and the selection of treatment procedures. In this case, assessment results indicated that three areas should be targeted for treatment intervention. Separate treatment goals were then established in each target area: drinking, social-emotional, and marital. This chapter clearly describes the evolution from the assessment process through the establishment of treatment goals to the selection of specific treatment procedures. In addition, a variety of clinical examples demonstrate how a skillful behavioral clinician integrates assessment data into the treatment process. By drawing on actual situations encountered by the client, the behavioral clinician enhances the relevance of treatment and increases the probability of treatment procedures generalizing to the client's extratherapy environments.

Another tenet is that behavioral assessment and treatment procedures must be tailored to the individual client. Consequently, each case represents unique challenges to the behavioral clinician's ingenuity. In this case, for example, the low frequency of the binge-drinking behavior called for a flexible and creative approach to data collection. Miller instructed the client to use his date book for self-monitoring and structured the self-monitoring procedures to be compatible with his client's lifestyle. By adapting the data-collection procedures to the client, the clinician increases the chances of gathering reliable information, as well as enhancing the reactive impact of the self-assessment process.

The treatment program for the binge drinker in this case called for the full armamentarium of behavioral treatment procedures. Environmental manipulation was stressed in order to restructure the client's time (e.g., to eliminate open time slots that may provide drinking opportunities). To provide constructive and creative alternatives to drinking, time-management procedures were used to increase the frequency of reinforcing nonbusiness activities. In addition the client was trained in specialized coping strategies, including stress-management and innoculation procedures, drink-refusal training, and craving-control training. Marital treatment sessions focused on altering spouse behaviors that may have served as antecedents to drinking behavior in the past. This comprehensive treatment program provides an excellent example of one further tenet of the behavioral approach. Specifically, while the establishment of control over drinking behavior is an essential ingredient of behavioral treatment, the development of positive nondrinking alternatives is just as important.

10. REFERENCES

American Psychiatric Association. *Diagnostic and statistical manual of mental disorders* (3rd ed.). Washington, D.C.: Author, 1980.

Azrin, N. H., Naster, B. J., & Jones, R. Reciprocity counseling: A rapid-learning-based procedure for marital counseling. *Behavior Research and Therapy,* 1973, *11,* 365–382.

Foy, D. W., Miller, P. M., Eisler, R. M., & O'Toole, D. Social-skills training to teach alcoholics to refuse drinks effectively. *Journal of Alcohol Studies,* 1976, *37,* 1340–1345.

Miller, P. M. *Behavioral treatment of alcoholism.* New York: Pergamon Press, 1976.

Miller, P. M., & Sims, K. Evaluation and component analysis of a comprehensive weight control program. *International Journal of Obesity,* 1981, *5,* 57–65.

Miller, P. M. *Personal habit control.* New York: Simon & Schuster, 1978.

Selzer, M. L. The Michigan alcoholism screening test: The quest for a new diagnostic instrument. *American Journal of Psychiatry,* 1971, *127,* 1653–1658.

Sobell, M. B., Maisto, S. A., Sobell, L. C., Cooper, A. M., Cooper, T. C., & Sanders, B. Developing a prototype for evaluating alcohol treatment effectiveness. In L. C. Sobell, M. B. Sobell, & E. Ward (Eds.), *Evaluating alcohol and drug abuse treatment effectiveness: Recent advances.* New York: Pergamon Press, 1980.

Suinn, R., & Richardson, F. Anxiety management training: A non-specific behavior therapy program for anxiety control. *Behavior Therapy,* 1971, *2,* 398–510.

2

Behavioral Treatment of Alcoholism
The Unvarnished Story

MARK S. GOLDMAN and DIANE K. KLISZ

1. INTRODUCTION

The reporting of a case history presents an immediate dilemma. Does one start from scratch with a new case and attempt to follow an ideal prescription, so as to achieve a model instance of assessment and treatment? Or does one report, with flaws included, an already completed case which was seen in routine fashion? Both approaches have merit. The former may serve as an unblemished treatment prototype, while the latter is probably closer to the reality of how clinicians actually work.

The present report opts for the second approach. We made this choice because we feel that the behavioral treatment literature is frequently intimidating to students. They are intimidated because published reports, in an effort to demonstrate rigor and precision, often convey the impression that all the procedures and strategies utilized have been planned to the finest detail before the case was ever begun. They cannot imagine being so perfect in their own work. Also, many reported cases have been undertaken in settings subsidized by research funds, low-cost labor from student-assistants, social-service agency support, and so forth. If treatment programs are to have widespread application, they must be self-supporting. The program in the present case report requires only two to three therapists for

MARK S. GOLDMAN and DIANE K. KLISZ • Department of Psychology, Wayne State University, Detroit, Michigan 48202. Portions of this work were supported by National Institute on Alcohol Abuse and Alcoholism. Grants AA 02898 and AA 07200.

two groups per week of about 15 patients each and can support itself fully using customary levels of medical-insurance reinbursement. If carried out in a subsidized setting, it affords the advantage of low cost per patient.

Finally, the treatment methodology in highly polished case study reports may appear more potent and generalizable than is warranted by a critical reading of the treatment outcome literature. While the literature on the behavioral treatment of alcoholism has been extremely innovative and strongly suggestive of the directions that successful treatment must take, it has not been unequivocally substantiated as the definitive prescription (see Goldman, 1980). It is not that behavioral approaches have failed systematic tests of their effectiveness. To the contrary, the empirical literature on the effectiveness of behavioral treatment is at least as convincing as any existing treatment literature. It is instead that the critical tests have not yet been completed. The heterogeneity of the group called "alcoholics" is only just coming to be appreciated. Critical tests of therapeutic effectiveness therefore require studies on more homogeneous subgroupings within the alcoholic population. Empirical tests on undifferentiated groups of alcoholics are difficult to evaluate because pretreatment subject characteristics typically account for so much of the outcome variance that any particular instance of success may reflect subject selection factors rather than actual success of a particular treatment procedure (Baekeland, 1977; Goldman, 1980; Vogler, Weissbach, Compton, & Martin, 1977).

For these reasons, the present report is of a 43-year-old woman who was seen before we planned this chapter. A number of significant characteristics of the patient are heavily disguised to preclude identification of the real individual. We chose to present this particular case for four reasons. First, case reports on the treatment of women with drinking problems are still infrequent in the literature. Second, based on the demographic descriptions of those individuals who are most likely to profit from treatment, this woman was a good risk. Although she had a very severe drinking problem, she still remained within the context of a supportive family and social environment. Our treatment program tries to reach individuals who retain a high probability of successful treatment before a marked deterioration has occurred in their lives. Since we do not demand self-identification as an alcoholic, we hope to reach individuals early in the drinking process. Third, this woman was one of the first patients in our recently opened Drinking Problems Clinic. Her case, therefore, was among those with the longest follow-up period. Last but not least, this particular woman turned out to be a treatment success. Despite the fact that we were willing to expose some treatment flaws, our egos (there, we said it) were not prepared to present a treatment failure.

This report is in two parts. First, we attempt to convey an understanding of the conceptual *and* practical concerns that shaped our overall treatment approach. Then, we describe a play-by-play overview of the ongoing treatment process by presenting case material chronologically.

1.1. Preliminary Program Considerations

The Drinking Problems Clinic operates as a subsection of the Psychology Service Center within a Wayne State University-affiliated outpatient medical center. Our treatment is performed exclusively on an outpatient basis, since the success of outpatient treatment has been comparable to inpatient treatment except for skid row alcoholics (Baekeland, 1977). Outpatient treatment is also cheaper and affords the behavioral clinician the chance to study controlling factors directly within the actual environmental context. Because we operate within a general-service psychology center, which in turn operates within a general-service outpatient medical center, we can refer patients to many backup services and supplemental procedures which are advantageous to the overall conduct of the treatment.

Each patient in our program is exposed to a preplanned treatment package, plus other treatment options which are tailored to the needs of the individual patient. We feel it is particularly important that a portion of the program is unstructured, so that patients can discuss the ongoing vissicitudes of their lives. We have found at times that patients feel lost (and thus drop-out) when their behavior and verbal reports are confined to a rigid, preexisting treatment plan. While a variety of treatment options are possible in our program, economic and practical considerations make it necessary to limit the number of specific interventions applied in any particular case. Because we cannot do everything that might be done, we make decisions to utilize treatments that seem to be the most central to a particular individual's needs.

The prepackaged portion of the program employs procedures which have shown promise in the recent behavioral treatment literature on problem drinking. (For a discussion of our views see Goldman, 1980.) We emphasize self-management procedures that can be performed easily at low cost, with a minimum of apparatus, on an outpatient basis (Chaney, O'Leary, & Marlatt, 1978; Marlatt, 1978; P. M. Miller, 1978; W. R. Miller & Muñoz, 1976). We also incorporate additional methods which derive from current research in our laboratories at Wayne State.

Foremost among these methods is an assessment-and-treatment methodology deriving from research on alcohol expectancy (placebo) effects. A host of recent studies have clearly demonstrated that many of the behavioral effects of alcohol are heavily influenced by individuals' beliefs about how alcohol makes them behave rather than the actual pharmacological effect on the physical system (Marlatt & Rohsenow, 1980). In an effort to establish the domain of these alcohol expectancies we have carried out a series of factor-analytic studies (Brown, Goldman, Inn, & Anderson, 1980; Christiansen, 1980). The instrument derived from Brown *et al.* has applicability for both assessment of the alcoholic and treatment planning.

Our research on neuropsychological recovery in alcoholics has also contributed. Over the course of a series of studies in which we have assessed alcoholics' ability to learn and perform a variety of behaviors once they have ceased drinking (Ellenberg, Rosenbaum, Goldman, & Whitman, 1980; Goldman, 1982; Goldman, Williams, Dickey, & Weintraub, 1980; Sharp, Rosenbaum, Goldman, & Whitman, 1977), we have arrived at a few general conclusions which guide our treatment planning. First, we have found that in the days immediately following their last drink, alcoholics' psychological capacities are severely restricted. They have difficulty learning new information and their psychomotor performance capabilities are curtailed. This finding suggests that any procedure which requires alcoholics to learn new knowledge and skills should be delayed at least 1 to 2 weeks after the cessation of drinking. While the initiation of treatment clearly cannot be delayed for this period—the alcoholic would return to problem drinking—the requirements of the treatment program should be graded in difficulty and repeated so that information which might escape the alcoholic during the first 1 to 2 weeks may be acquired later. The second finding of our studies has been that alcoholics over the age of 40 may take even longer for neuropsychological recovery and, in fact, may show lasting impairment of visual-spatial performance. While this observation has not been systematically incorporated into our treatment program, we do presently make some allowance for the age of the alcoholic. A cognitive-rehabilitation program which trains older alcoholics to compensate for lasting deficits may become feasible in the future.

An additional integral feature of our treatment package is relapse training, that is, the preparation of the patient for instances of relapse that might otherwise lead to treatment dropout and uncontrolled deterioration. This portion of the program derives from recent work by Marlatt and his colleagues. Marlatt correctly points out (Marlatt, 1978; Marlatt & Gordon, 1979) that the treatment of any repetitive problem behavior may fail, not because of an insufficiently broad-spectrum initial approach but rather because of insufficient attention to inevitable recurrences of the behavior in question. We suggest to our patients that statistical evidence and clinical experience indicate that some type of limited relapse is quite possible. (To avoid discussion of relapse, so that patients will not be "suggested" or encouraged to drink, is probably futile.) The occurrence of relapse, therefore, should not be taken as a sign of treatment failure but rather as an event to be anticipated and dealt with as a part of treatment itself.

In contrast to some of the recent behavioral treatments of alcoholism, our program is targeted exclusively at achieving abstinence. Abstinence is our goal not because controlled drinking is impossible but rather because ways to select alcoholics remain imprecise—although they are improving (Sobell, 1978). In any case, abstinence is always the safest course for anyone who has had a problem with alcohol. Abstinence requires fewer concerns for the physical well-being of an individual who may already have had subtle physical changes as a consequence of excessive drinking, and the maintainence of abstinence does not require an individual to continually make the difficult discrimination as to what constitutes safe and controlled levels of drinking.

It is very important to note, however, that from a practical standpoint we have not felt we had to wrestle with the pros and cons of offering controlled drinking. In a self-management approach, controlled drinking is merely the end point of the drinking continuum. Our explicit goal is abstinence; our actual procedure, however, aims toward drinking patterns that represent increasing restraint and self-regulation. We suggest to patients that a more controlled drinking pattern indicates that we have begun to identify and manage some of the critical stimuli and reinforcers for drinking. Using this initial level of control as a preliminary marker of the important drinking cues, the individual can go on to achieve even more restrained drinking and, ultimately, abstinence. We have found that by not openly advocating controlled drinking, we are much more compatible with alcohol treatment programs that surround us in the community. Since many alcoholics typically have contact with more than one drinking program, it is advantageous to maintain mutual accommodation with other local agencies.

A number of structural details that must be faced by any *outpatient* program for alcoholism also are pertinent here: It goes without saying that a backup system for *inpatient* treatment is necessary. Two contingencies warrant referral to an impatient program: the existence of related medical conditions that demand hospital evaluation and treatment; and the presence, at the time of initial contact with the patient, of a drinking episode that is unlikely to cease without 24-hour supervision. The first contingency requires hospitalization, while the second requires only a live-in arrangement with medical supervision. Unfortunately, availability of the latter, less expensive alternative is all too limited.

It is obvious that medical evaluation is necessary as soon as possible after initial contact. In addition to assessing the need for inpatient hospitalization, it is advisable to have a medical judgment as to the likelihood of an uneventful withdrawal if the patient is currently consuming alcohol. While no one can say for certain whether life-threatening delirium tremens with convulsions will occur (probably the best predictor is past episodes of DTs), a physician can assess the physical and nutritional well-being of the patient and make an informed judgment. In any case, a physician should be involved during the drying-out phase.

An ever-present danger during outpatient treatment is that the time period between contacts is too long for patients to effectively exercise self-control of their drinking. While it is always difficult to ascertain how long is "too long," our program has two mechanisms for maintaining frequent contact and thus minimizing this pitfall. First, the multiple aspects of the program are deliberately spaced throughout each week so that patients must attend sessions that are at most 2 to 3 days apart. Second, efforts are made to assign each patient to another, more advanced patient as a "buddy." The buddy can be used as an alternative resource to members of the treatment team in the event of a crisis. It is obvious that the success of the system depends on the newer patient's willingness to contact the buddy. Unfortunately, the limited size of our program does not always make for a ready match between patients for the purposes of the system.

While designing the prepackaged portion of the program, it became obvious that a particular sequencing of program elements was most logical. At the same time, it was impractical for us to admit only new patients at a recycling point of the sequence, for example, every 6 to 8 weeks. Our solution was to use a one-session orientation meeting, which could be held biweekly, in addition to the regularly programmed portion of the treatment. The orientation session outlines the rationale and sequencing of the entire program so that no matter which regular session the patient attends first, they will not feel "out of it."

To ensure that patients have not missed program content because of the 1 to 2-week information-processing debility during the initial weeks of the program when they may still be drinking or detoxifying, patients are encouraged to repeat portions of the program until the information is acquired. In this way, patients also do not encounter any clear-cut termination point when they might feel too much on their own. The core program is thus gradually faded as patients are shifted into our follow-up procedures.

1.2. Program Components

1.2.1. Program Sequence

The program sequence is as follows:

1.2.1a. Step 1. At the initial phone contact a judgment is made as to whether the patient requires immediate care. If not, an appointment is made for intake in the Drinking Problems Clinic.

1.2.1b. Step 2. The intake session is held a maximum of 3 days from the phone contact. There are three facets to this initial assessment. First is the intake interview itself, which is based upon a modified version of Marlatt's Drinking Profile Questionnaire (Marlatt, 1976). In addition to determining basic history and drinking information, this interview identifies on a preliminary basis the antecedents and consequences of alcohol consumption. An effort is made to identify the circumstances in which alcohol consumption typically occurs, and those situational and internal cues which precede drinking. We also attempt to identify the circumstances immediately following the consumption of each drink—particularly for drinks early in the sequence—and the drinking episode as a whole. We focus on both subjective internal experiences that result after alcohol is consumed and situational events that may play some reinforcing role in maintaining drinking.

In an effort to screen for other forms of psychopathology which may complicate the treatment picture, we administer a standard Minnesota Multiphasic Personality Inventory. The MMPI is scored by computer; computerized interpretation is carried out following the rules of Lachar (1974).

Finally, we administer the Alcohol Expectancy Questionnaire designed by Brown, Goldman, Inn, and Anderson (1980). The AEQ is a factor-analytically derived 90-item questionnaire which represents an exhaustive range of statements regarding subjects' expectations of positive reinforcement from consuming moderate amounts of alcohol. The 90 items can be grouped into six empirically determined factors: alcohol (1) transforms experiences in a positive way, (2) enhances social and physical pleasure, (3) enhances sexual performance and experience, (4) increases power and aggression, (5) increases social assertiveness, and (6) reduces tension. Details of the development of this questionnaire can be found in Brown *et al.* (1980). Although this questionnaire is still in the development phase in relation to its validity in discriminating between subgroups of drinkers, it does have an immediate utility for treatment planning. It can be used to identify an individual's range of expectations of reinforcement from alcohol. Treatment personnel can thus aim at debunking the pharmacological basis of the drinker's specific expectancies and devise self-control procedures which permit the individual to achieve some alcohol-like effects without the use of alcohol.

At the end of the intake procedure the patient is assigned to a support group of other members in the clinic who meet on a regular basis with only limited intervention of a therapist. Assignment is dependent on scheduling and availability. The patient is also referred for medical evaluation at this point.

1.2.1c. Step 3. Appointment reminders are phoned and mailed to the patients to alert them to the upcoming orientation meeting. These reminders also include an appeal for family members to attend with the patients. At the biweekly orientation meeting the patient and (if feasible) his or her family are introduced to the treatment components. Each patient attends eight weekly structured treatment sessions in addition to brief individual therapy and an unstructured support group. The support group has a therapist who gradually becomes less active so that the group may evolve into a peer support group. If family members are involved they attend the educational portion of the structured sessions with the patient. They also attend family sessions, in which the handling of problems attendant to living with the problem drinker is discussed.

1.2.2. Structured Treatment Session Content

Each of the eight sessions consists of both an educational and a skills-training component. The need to introduce effective control over drinking determined the sequencing of these sessions. Thus, record keeping, alternative skills, and anxiety management come early in the sequence, while the effects of alcohol on the body are covered later. Relapse training rounds out the sequence to prepare patients for fading the program.

   1.2.2a. Orientation Session. At the orientation, the etiology of problem drinking from the biological, sociological, and psychological (including behavioral) viewpoints is briefly discussed. We emphasize that a definitive etiology has not been established and therefore this program takes a pragmatic point of view and trains self-control of drinking regardless of the cause. We then explain that drinking often occurs within repetitive situational and psychological contexts. By studying the context for the individual patient one can pinpoint cues which may alert the individual to the likelihood of drinking and thereby signal him or her to make appropriate responses to curtail or avoid drinking. Patients at this point are given a brief introduction to recording procedures. Record cards are handed out. The notion that "slips" (episodes of drinking after the program begins) may occur either during or subsequent to the program is introduced. It is explained that these slips are not unpredictable accidents but events that may be anticipated and controlled. Slips are not viewed as failure but as an instance of drinking for which self-control strategies have yet to be planned. "Slip cards" are handed out to be carried in the patients wallet. The slip card is structured in the following manner:

   In case of a slip:
   1. STOP drinking and THINK, "Why did this happen?" Call Buddy if necessary. Phone Number _____.

2. REMEMBER, slips can happen to anyone—you and your treatment have *not* failed.
3. UNDERSTANDING of a slip can be an important part of treatment, so note: time, place, how much, and what led up to it.
4. CALL your counselor. Phone Number _____.

Finally, the sequence of the entire program is outlined. It is pointed out that the program attends to many aspects of the individual's life because cessation of drinking will not cause all problems to evaporate.

1.2.2b. Session 1. Record keeping is thoroughly reviewed in the educational portion of Session 1. Record cards include a scale rating the urge to drink from 1 to 10. Verbal descriptors are included at reference points: 0–1 describes "little need" to drink, 2–5 describes "uncomfortable," 6–7 describes "bad," and 8–10 describes "bad as I can stand." In addition, each card has room for listing the date, the time of the drinking urge or episode, a box listing "what you are doing," "what you are thinking," "who is with you," and "where are you." Since patients are encouraged not to drink at all, recording urges permits contextual analysis even in the absence of drinking. Of course, instances of actual drinking are recorded as well.

In the skills-training portion of Session 1, patients are taught to develop social activities which do not require alcohol. Alternative activities such as a health club, adult education courses, political groups, sports, church socials, and so on are suggested, and other possible activities are solicited from patients. Behavioral rehearsal to prepare patients for participating in these alternative activities is undertaken. The avoidance of large amounts of unstructured spare time is emphasized.

1.2.2c. Session 2. The educational portion of this session includes a thorough discussion of how dysphoric affect, especially anxiety and depression, originates and is maintained. Emphasis is placed on managing psychological distress. We point out that not all uncomfortable emotions *can* or *should* be eliminated. In the skills-training portion standard techniques of cognitive restructuring of anxiety and depression-producing self-statements are taught (Goldfried & Goldfried, 1980; Mahoney & Arnkoff, 1978). Progressive muscle relaxation is also begun.

1.2.2d. Session 3. The six alcohol-reinforcement expectancy factors established in Brown, Goldman, Inn, and Anderson (1980) are discussed in the educational portion of Session 3, with the aim of debunking patients' concepts of the "magical" effects of alcohol. It is explained that in other parts of the program, they are being taught to achieve some of these effects, such as anxiety reduction and increased social skillfulness, without alcohol. Progressive-relaxation training continues in the skills-training portion.

1.2.2e. Session 4. A standard discussion of the short- and long-term effects of alcohol on the nervous system and other body organs is carried out as the educational aspect of this session.

In the skills-training portion, estimation of blood-alcohol level (BAL) is taught using a standard format (e.g., Miller & Muñoz, 1976). BAL estimation is taught even though we encourage abstention in order to prepare patients for possible slips and their control. A cognitive approach to BAL estimation is used because BAL biofeedback is apparently ineffective with alcoholics (Nathan, 1978).

1.2.2f. Session 5. Physical addiction to alcohol, that is, increased tolerance and the occurrence of withdrawal symptoms, is discussed as the educational components of this session. Efforts are made to separate the concept of physical addiction from psychological dependence. Patients are taught that "craving" has *not* been demonstrated to be an irresistible biologically induced need and, thus, can be managed.

In skills training, patients are taught to develop a list of rewards that can be used as alternatives to drinking and as reinforcers for other behaviors that help an individual cope with problem drinking. They are also taught how to time self-reward to maximize its effectiveness.

1.2.2g. Sessions 6 and 7. In Sessions 6 and 7, the anticipation and handling of slips is discussed. As Marlatt and Gordon (1979) point out, slips rarely occur in a context that cannot be anticipated. Certain situations, such as being at a party, leaving work with co-workers who go to a bar, marital frustration, and so forth, increase the likelihood of slips. Individuals can anticipate most of these occasions and either avoid them or prepare for them. Preparation includes developing a list of self-statements to guide one through the situation and statements to help handle social pressure to drink. We emphasize that guilt as a result of a slip is counterproductive and can interfere with continued treatment. During skills training, the group generates a list of the situations that are most likely to tempt them to drink and methods for best dealing with them. Suggested methods are rehearsed.

1.2.2h. Session 8. Session 8 is a complete review of the programmed components. Subsequent to Session 8, the program recycles.

2. MRS. J.

2.1. Chronological Report

2.1.1. Initial Contact

We first received a phone call from a 20-year-old student nurse at Wayne State University. She had heard of our service through the university grapevine. Her interest was piqued by our *outpatient* alcohol treatment, and she had heard we used an innovative treatment not directly rooted in Alcoholics Anonymous principles (although we made no explicit advertisement to that effect). She was inquiring for her mother, who had been through an AA-based inpatient treatment for alcoholism approximately 1½ years earlier. Apparently the drinking problem was continuing, and her mother was no longer willing to participate in an AA-style program. Mrs. J. (the mother) felt that her "real" problems had not been approached in the prior treatment. When Mrs. J.'s daughter confirmed that AA participation was not required she had her mother call to set up an appointment.

2.1.2. Week 1—Intake

Mrs. J. came alone for the intake interview. She was a conservatively dressed middle-aged woman with a sallow, somewhat sickly appearance. She was friendly and cooperative with the intake process but did not initiate conversation. In fact, in early sessions she was consistently quiet and reserved, responding only to questioning. (Later in the program, her spontaneous speech increased dramatically.)

She was 43 years old, married, and had two grown children. Besides her daughter, she had a son, age 27, who was married and had been out of the home for a period of five years. To build rapport, Mrs. J. was first interviewed, and then completed our paper-and-pencil questionnaires.

Although a regular alcohol user for most of her adult life, Mrs. J. traced her drinking problem to the birth of her daughter in 1960. At that time, she developed a chronic fatigue which made housework and daily activities very difficult. As a result, a physician prescribed stimulant medication (she did not remember which). She rapidly began to use this medication to excess, requiring repeated dosages to make it through each day. Because she began to worry about overusing this medication, and because it became difficult to get frequent prescriptions, she switched to alcohol after about 1 year. At that time, she required one to two shots of gin a few times each day to increase her energy level so that she might continue with her chores. In 1971 she increased the frequency of her alcohol use by an amount that was difficult for her to remember. Also, in 1971 she developed angina pectoris and began using alcohol for pain relief. The final escalation to severe problem drinking occurred in 1973 when her family moved next door to her in-laws because of their increasing age and failing health. She began to feel taken advantage of by her in-laws and ignored by her husband, who became increasingly concerned with the care of his parents. She found herself frustrated and angry on a daily basis. For relief of this emotional distress she drank one to two pints of gin over a 1- to 2-hour period, usually in the evening. On the average, these drinking bouts occurred 3 to 4 days per week, but there were many times when she drank continuously for a few days. The immediate consequence of beginning drinking was an increase in her energy level and a decrease in tension and anxiety. On many occasions she had memory blackouts for the period of time that passed after she began to drink.

The amount consumed was entirely determined by the amount available in the house. She had only limited amounts of gin available because her husband, who had become disturbed by her drinking, had taken away her control of the family checkbook and severely curtailed her allowance. He also restricted her use of the family automobile. Her funds only permitted her to purchase one pint of gin each day. Because she was an "old-fashioned" wife, she was not inclined to challenge her husband on these matters.

This drinking pattern was interrupted only once since 1973, during a 4-week period of residential treatment for alcoholism. This period occurred approximately $1\frac{1}{2}$ years prior to our intake and was followed by an outpatient alcohol program on a once-a-week basis. Mrs. J. returned, however, to her normal drinking pattern, even before ceasing to attend the outpatient program after approximately 1 month.

Although Mrs. J. was no longer willing to undergo AA-related treatment, she was quite pleased that her husband began at that time to attend Al-Anon meetings where he first came to view alcoholism as a disease. He was consequently no longer planning to break up the marriage owing to his marital obligation to help his wife through a period of disease. However, since her drinking resumed after treatment, Mr. J. still intended to seek a divorce once her "disease" had been effectively treated, or when there was no further hope.

Drinking had gradually narrowed the scope of Mrs. J.'s everyday functioning. She had become a virtual prisoner of her house, leaving only to buy food and alcohol. Shortly after residential treatment, Mrs. J. took a waitress job to help her rehabilitation. She left this job by her own choice after a short period of time, however, because she claimed it was too fatiguing. She acknowledged that excessive alcohol consumption made functioning on the job difficult.

Mrs. J. also had medical conditions, including angina pectoris and arthritis, which may have been related to her excessive alcohol intake. These conditions clearly warranted an abstinence-oriented program because alcohol abuse may exacerbate these disorders. Mrs. J. denied ever experiencing DTs after alcohol use but did report frequent blackouts. She also frequently awakened with a severe feeling of illness, including some tremulousness in the morning after a binge. At times, she drank to relieve these "shakes." Occasionally, she was even awakened during the night by shaking and tremors.

One event stood out in the life history of Mrs. J. When she was 15, her father died, and she fell into a significant depression. She lost interest in her school work, lost her appetite, and had some difficulty sleeping. Social ties with friends were cut off. Two years after the death of her father, her mother remarried. She was unable to relate comfortably to her stepfather and from that time on felt like an outsider in her own home. She reports that her marriage was in part a vehicle for her to leave home. Even after her marriage she had been chronically depressed. In fact, one wonders if the fatigue she experienced following the birth of her second child was due to depression. Despite psychiatric treatment four years prior to our intake, her affect was markedly depressed at the time of the intake interview, and she cried a number of times during the course of the session.

To conclude the intake interview, we discussed with Mrs. J. a very sensitive, yet absolutely essential topic, namely, the consumption of alcoholic beverages during the treatment program. We include this discussion as a standard part of all intake interviews. We strongly emphasize our preference that patients cease drinking for the duration of their treatment. We explain that their use of alcohol on a continual basis before coming to us has left their clarity of thinking reduced. We further explain that if they continue to drink, their unclear thinking may continue, and they may consequently be unable to benefit from the treatment program. We try to walk a very fine line, however, since we also understand that there is a very high probability of at least a minimal amount of drinking after actually starting the program. While we wish to discourage drinking, we do not wish to set up a situation in which episodes of drinking will cause rejection of the program. Therefore, we also explained to Mrs. J. that we would not be shocked if she did have drinking episodes as she had done in the past, nor would we condemn her for these episodes. In fact, what we intended to do if these episodes occurred was to actually use them as part of treatment. We explained that by studying each drinking episode we could more successfully arrive at an understanding of the exact conditions that preceded and followed such episodes. We also told Mrs. J. that we were so interested in finding out what led to her drinking that we wanted her to keep a record of any drinking "urges" she might have, even if she chose at that moment not to drink. The use of the record cards was explained to Mrs. J. The last part of the intake process was the administration of our two paper-and-pencil assessment instruments.

No explicit contract was drawn up with Mrs. J. to regulate either abstention or a particular level of consumption. Before accepting any patients, we had decided against explicit contracting for two reasons. First, the usual form of contracting for limiting self-injurious behavior has patients put up money as insurance for keeping the contract. Many of the patients we anticipated treating were not in a position to put up any sort of monetary insurance, and requesting such amounts would likely drive patients away. Second, we did not wish to set up a condition at the beginning of treatment which might make patients feel they had quickly failed the program. We first wanted to prepare patients for a failure experience via our relapse-training process.

2.1.2a. Preliminary Formulation. To summarize the information gathered by the intake interview and the paper-and-pencil devices: Mrs. J. was a 43-year-old woman who had been a regular and serious binge drinker for at least 7 years. She clearly demonstrated a strong psychological dependence on alcohol, and on a number of occasions she may have been physically addicted. Based on self-report, the stimulus complex most likely to precede a drinking episode was the failure of Mrs. J. to assert herself in family interactions. In these interactions, she felt that members of her family, particularly her husband and her husband's parents, made excessive demands or tended to disregard her feelings and her importance to the family. The internal and subjective stimuli that immediately preceded drinking binges were anger at being disregarded and imposed upon and frustration over an inability to assert her own needs. In addition, she frequently began drinking when she felt fatigue or physical pain. There was some suggestion in her history that her fatigue was related to depression and internal tension when demands on her increased, as after the birth of second child. The most immediate consequence of alcohol intake was a subjective increase in energy level and decreased pain. In recent years, an added reinforcer seemed to be impaired awareness. Family members told her that during a binge she continued on with household activities with apparent disregard for those around her.

The MMPI showed no significant psychopathology. The behavioral correlates of her profile (6328–47019/5KLF/) are depression, anxiety, and a tendency to make physical complaints when suffering from internal tension states. Individuals with this profile are also guarded and suspicious with people and thus are not able to interact freely. On the AEQ she responded primarily to items from the first factor and last two factors. She expected alcohol to transform her experiences in a positive way, to increase her social assertiveness, and to reduce tension. For example, she felt that "drinking makes the future seem brighter," that "if I have a couple of drinks it is easier to express my feelings," and "alcohol decreases muscular tension."

Based on our assessment information we formulated a preliminary hypothesis that Mrs. J. was a woman who, due to early training, had come to believe that her role as a successful woman demanded that she be the consummate housekeeper, wife, and mother. She consequently placed excessive demands upon herself for keeping her household in tiptop shape and for complying with family demands. She was also unable to assert her own needs. Owing to prior medical and psychological experiences, she used alcohol as a self-medication, that is, as a means of modifying her own emotional state.

A more speculative hypothesis was that her father's death was also connected to her inability to assert herself with family members. She may have viewed family arguments as intolerable because life is tenuous and should be an entirely positive experience; or because one may be rejected by family members (as her mother seemed to do) when disagreements occur. Approaching this issue in treatment was difficult, however, because she reported complete resolution of this problem during her psychiatric treatment. She remained resistant to discussing what transpired during that earlier psychotherapy throughout our contact with her.

A number of treatment techniques in addition to the prepackaged elements of the program were suggested by the above formulation. Apparently, Mrs. J.'s alcohol use was frequently in response to tension states. While the prepackaged program practiced tension reduction, ancillary tension-reduction training was deemed advisable. Second, the external stimulus that most often led to excessive drinking was her feelings of being ignored and taken advantage of. Consequently, assertiveness training was warranted. Third, many of the demands upon her resulted from her own internal irrational belief system regarding appropriate female behavior when fulfilling the roles of wife and mother. She also apparently believed that successful relationships with other people should never involve conflict. She thus needed cognitive restructuring of her irrational beliefs. As this aspect of treatment was explored it was also considered advisable (if possible) to evaluate how much her father's death and the ensuing disruption in her family of origin had to do with the development of her belief system and unwillingness to engage in interpersonal conflict within her family. If necessary, extinction procedures might be introduced to decrease emotional reactivity in this connection. Finally, many of her reported difficulties centered within the marital relationship itself. Marital therapy was thus strongly advised.

The first three strategies for ancillary treatment were, in fact, used with Mrs. J. Cognitive restructuring and ancillary training in tension reduction were included as components of her individual therapy. Assertiveness training was included in individual therapy and a separate assertiveness-training group. Despite its advisability, Mrs. J. was unwilling to engage in marital therapy or even to have her husband and children participate in our treatment program. She felt that they had participated in the prior program, and she was unwilling to expose herself to having them directly engage in another failure experience. Furthermore, she felt that her husband remained with her because he continued to view her alcohol problem as a disease. She was very afraid that if he were to participate in our treatment, his belief in alcoholism as an uncontrollable disease might be disrupted and her marriage might be lost.

2.1.3. Week 2

During her second week of attendance, Mrs. J. participated in an orientation session and individual therapy. Due to scheduling conflicts, we were forced to have her attend all individual-therapy sessions during the same visit as the drinking-problems group. This is not the optimal scheduling plan because it allows too many days to pass between visits. However, the availability of our therapists just did not coincide with Mrs. J.'s availability. We might note that scheduling also prevented her attendance at the assertiveness and social-skills group until the fourth week of the treatment program. Sometimes, practical considerations just do not match the optimal treatment procedure.

2.1.3a. Orientation. The content of this session was outlined earlier. It turned out that Mrs. J. had a drinking episode the previous night. She had recorded consumption of one pint of gin after a frustrating experience with her father-in-law. We were consequently able to relate the discussion of drinking stimuli to her own particular drinking situation. She was thereby able to gain some understanding of stimulus control of drinking. Her drinking episode also provided the perfect basis for discussing the handling of slips.

2.1.3b. Individual Session. During the first individual session, Mrs. J. elaborated upon her drinking episode. She began the evening with a plan to finish her work and then relax. As she finished her work and put aside a book to read, her father-in-law unexpectedly stopped by. He proceeded to complain about how unwell he was feeling. She immediately resented that he had disrupted her plans without prior notice. However, she was unable to refuse to listen and sat with him for about 1½ hours while feeling more resentful as time proceeded. As soon as he left, she felt very exhausted and angry with herself for not asking him to leave. In addition, she began to mull over her continuing distress with her husband in regard to sharing financial responsibilities. As she obsessed, she felt more tired and decided the only solution was to drink.

Although the initial individual-therapy session was primarily intended to gather further information and develop rapport, the serendipitous occurrence of a drinking episode made a perfect opportunity to begin intervening in the pattern. Note that these interventions were not preplanned; they were developed spontaneously during the session. While relating the prior night's experience, Mrs. J. explained that it was impossible to alter her father-in-law's habit of stopping by unexpectedly because a good daughter-in-law and wife should accommodate her in-laws at any time. To begin restructuring this impossible-to-meet expectation the therapist attempted an alternative rationale. It was explained that if Mrs. J. could play a greater role in scheduling visits, not only would her in-laws be losing nothing, they might have much to gain: if they came at more agreeable times, Mrs. J. would be better prepared and would not be distracted by irritation at their visits; consequently, the relationship might be enhanced. A brief discussion ensued of appropriate wording for conveying a schedule to her in-laws. It was decided that, in a joking tone, she might escort her father-in-law to the door after a few minutes, while saying that he should return for coffee in about an hour when she would be finished with the job she was doing. Furthermore, she might head off the problem situation by phoning them in the morning and suggesting a time they might stop by for coffee. In this way, she might regulate their visits without hurting their feelings. Mrs. J. was given the opportunity to practice these plans with the therapist. She was then instructed to attempt at least one of the interactions before the next session.

At this session, restructuring of her expectation of perfect housekeeping was also begun. In a lighthearted fashion, the therapist mentioned that Mrs. J. seemed intent to win the Betty Crocker White-Gloves Award. This referred to passing a test where the judges run white gloves across counters and windowsills to check for dust. By making light of this comment, the therapist was able to convey the idea that her self-demands might be excessive, without undermining Mrs. J.'s value system in an offensive way. As a finale to this initial session Mrs. J. was assigned to read *Stand Up, Speak Out, Talk Back!* (Alberti & Emmons, 1975) as bibliotherapy in self-assertion.

2.1.4. Week 3

2.1.4a. Drinking-Problems Group. As planned, the educational portion of Session 1 reviewed record keeping and instructed patients in how to select social activities which do not involve the use of alcohol. Record keeping was reviewed not merely to guide recording of the details relating to drinking urges and drinking episodes but to introduce the notion that drinking episodes can be anticipated. Anticipation is accomplished by noting typical circumstances when the drinking urge increases and by looking ahead to likely times for those circumstances to recur. It is impressed upon the patient that they do not have to feel at the mercy of the impulse to drink. Instead, they could have a good deal of forewarning if they learned to read the signals.

The skills-training component of Session 1 was somewhat irrelevant to the characteristic drinking style of Mrs. J., since she tended to be a solitary drinker. The therapist therefore noted that a modified discussion of alternative practices to drinking would have to be undertaken with Mrs. J. during her individual treatment session.

2.1.4b. Individual Session. Discussion of alternative strategies to be used to replace drinking for Mrs. J. ensued. Two alternate behaviors were planned for those times when Mrs. J. felt particularly fatigued or frustrated with family interactions. The first called for her to cease all housework activities, set a place at the table, and drink a cup of tea slowly, over at least half an hour. The second strategy was a warm bath. The bath was particularly appropriate when she was feeling angry and frustrated with the treatment she had received from family members because it removed her from the problem stimuli and relaxed her. She was also told that she would begin relaxation training, which could be used as an additional alternative behavior.

Also discussed was the tremendous demand Mrs. J. placed on herself for having a spotless home and perfectly prepared meals. A list was made of the activities she felt she needed to complete during the course of a single day. This turned out to be an extremely lengthy list which would require almost superhuman effort to complete. After discussion, the list was shortened by eliminating low-priority activities. A new work schedule which included rest periods, was prepared. If this new schedule were followed, Mrs. J. would have less cause to feel that an interruption would prevent her from completing essential tasks. She would also have a chance to relieve tension by relaxing at the scheduled intervals.

Mrs. J. also wished to discuss how her husband had kept her out of the family finances by withholding the checkbook. During this discussion, Mrs. J. revealed that she had failed to raise this issue for a few years, owing to her guilt about drinking. She thus had no way of knowing if he would still insist on these arrangements. The therapist then planned and rehearsed statements she might use to discuss the situation with her husband. Finally, she was assigned the initiation of this discussion as homework.

2.1.5. Week 4

2.1.5a. Drinking-Problem Group. The drinking-problems group proceeded as planned.

2.1.5b. Individual Session. It was apparent that Mrs. J. was a bit disheveled and shaky the morning of her session. As it turned out, Mrs. J. had consumed over 1 pint of alcohol the prior evening and had a memory blackout. She attributed her drinking to the following: Mr. J. was next door with his parents and two other couples who were friends of his parents. To show the group their newly purchased furniture, Mr. J. brought them into Mrs. J.'s home without warning. At this time, Mrs. J. was baking a cake and her kitchen was in disarray. As a result, she was angry that these people had been brought over without notice, and she was embarrassed that outsiders had a chance to observe her home in a nonperfect state. She felt in considerable emotional turmoil and began to drink as soon as everyone left.

Despite this particular event, Mrs. J. felt that the overall situation at home had improved. Mr. J. was more accommodating about the finances than she had anticipated and was willing to share the checkbook. He said the only reason he had not shared the checkbook in the recent past was because he thought she did not want financial burdens.

Two specific procedures were instituted in response to the drinking episode. First, since Mrs. J. felt particularly unassertive with strangers, a classical assertiveness-training procedure was used to reduce her fear of offending strangers: she was to go to a store each day, select an item, bring the item to the register, question the salesperson about the item, and then finally return the item to the shelf while stating it was not precisely to her liking. Although at first Mrs. J. thought this task was too difficult, the procedure was practiced a few times, and she went off to try it with enthusiasm. Second, relaxation was extensively practiced so that she could use it to interrupt her pattern of emotional upset and drinking.

2.1.5c. Assertiveness-Training Group. Later that week, Mrs. J. also attended the first of four sessions of a standard assertiveness-training group. It began with a discussion of assertiveness versus aggression and an elaboration of what types of situations require assertiveness. Modeling, coaching, and behavioral rehearsal (McFall & Lillesand, 1971) were carried out within the group setting. (Videotape recording and feedback were used in this instance, although the assertiveness-training program did not require this procedure.) The group first practiced giving and receiving compliments and expressing affection and went on to making and refusing requests. Mrs. J. was initially reserved in this group but quickly became one of the more active participants.

2.1.6. Week 5

2.1.6a. Drinking-Problems Group. The educational portion of the drinking-problems group elaborated upon expectancy effects. It was explained that many of the effects individuals attribute to alcohol may not be due to alcohol or may be due to alcohol only at certain doses. At times, an individual's beliefs may produce the effects instead. Therefore, these effects can occur independent of alcohol consumption. For Mrs. J., tension-reduction effects could be achieved through relaxation, and energizing effects might be achieved through proper pacing of her activities. The skills-training portion of the session practiced progressive relaxation.

2.1.6b. Individual Session. In the individual session, Mrs. J.'s record keeping was reviewed. During the previous week she had three different occasions where her drinking urges became quite strong. However, instead of drinking, she was able to relax and employ alternative behaviors, particularly the half-hour of tea drinking. She had also continued discussing financial arrangements with her husband, and he agreed to set aside three times per week for reviewing finances. Her affect was markedly improved, and she seemed quite proud of herself. She no longer cried repeatedly, as she had during earlier sessions.

2.1.6c. *Assertiveness-Training Group.* Mrs. J.'s two main goals were to refuse inconvenient requests without feeling guilty and delay responding to questions until she could decide what she actually wanted. The group practiced making and refusing requests.

2.1.7. Weeks 6, 7, and 8

Treatment during Weeks 6, 7, and 8 was generally unremarkable. Mrs. J. completed drinking-problem group sessions 4, 5, and 6, and had one individual-therapy session per week. During Weeks 6 and 7 she also completed the final two sessions of assertiveness training.

One notable event occurred during Week 6. Although only low-level drinking urges were reported each week, Mrs. J. consumed one glass of beer with a meal on two occasions during Week 6. None of the antecedent conditions of earlier binges had occurred. Instead, Mrs. J. felt renewed confidence in controlling drinking, since she had no further inclination to drink at either occasion. We refrained from criticizing her decision to drink these beers, but we pointed out that anyone who ever had drinking problems should never take drinking lightly. Although any single instance of alcohol use does not necessarily lead to further drinking, there may be preexisting habits that have not been thoroughly extinguished even after months of abstention. If any of the previous reinforcing circumstances are accidently recreated, problem drinking may easily redevelop. While panic because of an instance of drinking is unnecessary, the circumstances and consequences must be considered.

2.1.8. Termination

Mrs. J. phoned after the sixth session and informed us that she had taken a job that conflicted with our meeting times. Therefore, she was unable to continue regular sessions even though the first cycle of our program included two more sessions. We were elated with this very assertive step (which included both job seeking and new financial responsibilities), but we were also concerned. While Sessions 7 and 8 were not sacrosanct, we believed longer involvement meant better outcomes. Old habit patterns might easily recur when contact discontinued. Therefore, telephone contact was maintained with Mrs. J. twice during the month following termination and monthly thereafter.

2.1.9. Six-Month Follow-up

When telephoned 6 months after her last session, Mrs. J. reported that all was going well, except that she had to leave her job. The economic hard times had deprived her husband of overtime pay. Since the reduced income made the maintainance of two cars impossible, she no longer had a car to use for work. Public transportation was not feasible. She was therefore seeking a job at a different location.

Mrs. J. declined to come for a 6-month follow-up session, also because of lack of access to a car. We became concerned and suspicious because very often people who have returned to problem drinking do not wish to appear and make their drinking obvious. However, she also sounded enthusiastic and articulate on the phone, quite unlike her manner when she drank. When questioned further, she hinted at another reason for her reluctance to come. Without our awareness, she had received a bill from the medical center of which we are a part. It had been our understanding that treatment was covered entirely by health insurance, which was paid directly by the insurer, requiring no supplemental payments from her. The bill from the medical center turned out to be in error. She (and more so, her husband) was, however, quite distressed by the bill because of the dire financial condition of her family. To make matters worse, straightening out the bill had required some effort because the insurance company insisted that aspects of treatment were not covered. She was therefore reluctant to come in and possibly subject herself to a charge.

Although somewhat reassured, we were not completely comfortable with our inability to make direct personal contact. We therefore planned to continue follow-up calls.

2.2. Treatment Results Summarized

Figure 1 graphs the weekly parameters of drinking and drinking urges for Mrs. J. Note that while the number of days per week that Mrs. J. consumed alcohol dropped rapidly upon admission to our treatment program, the average self-report of drinking urge was probably a more accurate reflection of treatment effects. In fact, Figure 1 also shows that the average drinking urge bore a strong negative relationship to the number of assertive responses performed each week. Assertive responses were recorded by Mrs. J.,

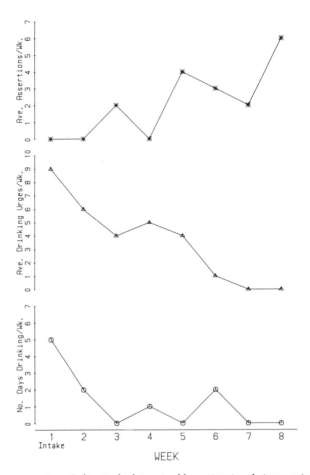

Figure 1. Average assertions (subjectively determined by patient in relation to prior behavior), average subjective drinking urges, and number of days drinking during each of the eight weeks of the treatment program. Averages were computed as means. The point recorded for each week refers to the previous week's activities.

based upon her subjective judgment of those interpersonal interactions where she asserted her wishes rather than passively conforming to the demands of others. This inverse relationship suggests that the target behavior initially selected, interpersonal assertive responses, was indeed central to her drinking problem. When a relationship between drinking behavior and some other response can be observed, the presumption of the importance of the targeted responses to the drinking problem is strengthened even before treatment ends. When such a relationship is not observed, doubts remain that critical relationships have been discerned.

While we have had monthly phone contacts since Mrs. J. stopped attending sessions regularly, we have not had any direct means of corroborating her drinking reports. We did not phone her family because at the beginning of treatment Mrs. J. explicitly requested they not be involved. Because of the content and articulation of her responses to extensive telephone interviewing, we were cautiously optimistic of treatment success. We did, however, view any long-lasting and powerful behavioral habit to be easily prone to reinitiation. We did not naively assume that every aspect of the habit complex related to her problem drinking had been extinguished or replaced by new habits. Some circumstance for which she had been unprepared could undoubtedly still occur and rekindle problem drinking, particularly in the absence of regular visits. Hopefully, continuing phone calls, coupled with a noncritical attitude on our part, would afford quick access to booster treatment if problems recurred. We were also aware, however, that the guilt which is a part of the Abstinence Violation Effect described by Marlatt (1978) might make self-disclosure difficult for her regardless of our approach.

2.3. Final Comment

We have tried to demonstrate how an operating treatment program amalgamates the best procedures from the current treatment literature with pragmatic solutions to the problems of a specific environment and specific case. Some of these latter components can be preplanned, but many are necessarily "seat-of-the-pants" decisions to be made quickly while therapy is ongoing. We also hope we have shown that one had better be flexible; it never goes exactly as planned.

By now we expect you have found us out. Are we "behavioristic," or even "cognitive behavioristic"? It is hard to say, and the labels no longer truly apply. We are active, yes; systematic, yes; empirical, yes; based as much as possible on observable and clearly describable procedures, yes. But in practice we also make many inferences and try to capitalize upon therapist variables and nonspecific therapeutic effects in the manner described recently by Garfield (1980). Maybe differentiating the clinicians who want to base their art upon science from the "fad" therapists and therapists who persevere in old methods without concern for new developments still requires the use of labels. We prefer to think that a common ground of rational, empirical practice is developing that will make the need for labels obsolete.

ACKNOWLEDGMENTS

We would like to express appreciation to Douglas Snyder and Andrew

Weintraub for reviewing earlier manuscripts and to Mark Filippi, Rex Kline, Anthony Stringer, and Michael Vredevoogd for their participation in the planning of the treatment program.

COMMENTARY

William M. Hay

A major driving force behind the conception and planning of this text was our desire to give each reader a thorough understanding of the complexities involved in the behavioral treatment of alcoholism. As we see throughout this book, a variety of clinical procedures fall under the rubric, behavioral treatment. It should be evident to the reader, then, that behavioral treatment does not simply mean the implementation of a set of prescribed treatment techniques, applied without consideration for the individual client. Rather, the individualized nature of the behavioral assessment process allows the clinician to select and modify the various available treatment components according to the individual client's needs. This case study by Mark Goldman and Diane Klisz provides an excellent example of how a structured treatment program may be adapted to the special require- ments of each client. The case of Mrs. J. is also important because descriptions of successful programs for the female problem drinker are rare in both the behavioral and other treatment literatures.

The outpatient treatment format utilized by Goldman and Klisz integrates group and individual sessions. Behavioral groups provide a cost-effective modality for teach- ing self-management skills. The group aids each individual in the identification of antecedents to drinking and in the development of alternative responses when faced with a high-probability drinking situation. Group members provide feedback and reinforcement for behavior change. In addition to the group sessions, Mrs. J. received assertiveness training and intensive training in muscle-relaxation procedures as non- drinking alternatives for high-probability drinking situations. Individualized home- work assignments gave Mrs. J. the opportunity to practice her new skills. This combination of structured group sessions and individualized treatment components appeared to be effective for this client.

In this chapter, the authors describe how the Alcohol Expectancy Questionnaire, developed originally for experimental use, aided in the assessment of Mrs. J.'s expecta- tions concerning the positive consequences to be derived from alcohol ingestion. As we will see in a number of chapters, behavioral clinicians frequently integrate their research findings with their clinical work. The authors' interesting findings concerning neurop- sychological impairment have also been incorporated into their treatment program. Research studies have shown that alcoholics experience varying degrees of neuropsycho- logical impairment during the recovery phase following the cessation of drinking. There-

fore, the early sessions of this treatment program are paced slowly, with frequent repetition of important information.

For health reasons, the abstinence goal was deemed most appropriate for Mrs. J. The authors' commitment to the abstinence goal for most clients is steadfast. Goldman and Klisz remind us that while behavioral approaches may be successful, the youth of our treatment-outcome literature suggests a conservative use of alternative-treatment goals. It is especially important that we do not convey conflicting messages concerning the availability of an alternative-treatment goal to clients where abstinence is appropriate.

The reader should take special note of how the clinicians in this case deal with the issue of drinking during treatment. As Goldman and Klisz note, the clinician must, of necessity, walk a fine line. Clinical skill must be used so that the client is not encouraged to drink but, if drinking does occur, to integrate the episode into the treatment as a learning experience, an experience that can lead to a better understanding of the factors impinging on the drinking response, and an opportunity to learn how to anticipate and deal with the situation in the future. Likewise, the discussion of slip cards, which specify a set of procedures to handle slips or urges, is presented as another self-management tool for the client. The introduction of the cards in the group context appears to maximize the opportunity for feedback and group support. The analysis of urges can also be a useful method to verify clinical hunches. In this case, the average number of drinking urges was found to be highly negatively correlated to the number of assertive responses recorded each week. This relationship lends support to the clinical hypothesis that Mrs. J.'s assertiveness problems increased the chances of a drinking episode.

3. REFERENCES

Alberti, R. E., & Emmons, M. L. *Stand up, speak out, talk back!* New York: Pocket Books, 1975.

Baekeland, F. Evaluation of treatment methods in chronic alcoholism. In B. Kissen & H. Begleiter (Eds.), *The biology of alcoholism* (Vol. 5), *Treatment and rehabilitation of the chronic alcoholic.* New York: Plenum Press, 1977.

Brown, S. A., Goldman, M. S., Inn, A., & Anderson, L. Expectations of reinforcement from alcohol: Their domain and relation to drinking patterns. *Journal of Consulting and Clinical Psychology,* 1980, *48,* 419–426.

Chaney, E. F., O'Leary, M. R., & Marlatt, G. A. *Skill training with alcoholics.* Unpublished manuscript, University of Washington School of Medicine, 1977.

Christiansen, B. A. *Adolescent cognitive attributions regarding alcohol.* Unpublished masters' thesis, Wayne State University, 1980.

Ellenberg, L., Rosenbaum, G., Goldman, M. S., & Whitman, R. D. Recoverability of psychological functioning following alcohol abuse: Lateralization effects. *Journal of Consulting and Clinical Psychology,*1980, *48,* 503–510.

Garfield, S. L. *Psychotherapy, an eclectic approach.* New York: Wiley Interscience, 1980.

Goldman, M. S. Alcoholism: Empirical foundations and behavioral treatment approaches. In R. J. Daitzman (Ed.), *Clinical behavior therapy and behavior modification.* New York: Garland STPM Publishing, Inc., 1980.

Goldman, M. S. Reversibility of psychological deficits in alcoholic: The interaction of aging with alcohol. In A. Wilkinson, (Ed.), *Symposium on cerebral deficits in alcoholism.* Toronto: Addiction Research Foundation, in press.

Goldman, M. S., Williams, D. L., Dickey, J. H., & Weintraub, A. L. *Recoverability of psychological functioning following alcohol abuse: Lasting visual dysfunction in older alcoholics.* Unpublished manuscript, Wayne State University, 1980.

Goldfried, M. R., & Goldfried, A. P. Cognitive Change Methods. In F. Kanfer & A. Goldstein (Eds.), *Helping people change* (2nd ed.). New York: Pergamon Press, 1980.

Lachar, D. *The MMPI: Clinical assessment and automated interpretation.* Los Angeles: Western Psychological Services, 1974.

Mahoney, M. J., & Arnkoff, D. Cognitive and self-control therapies. In S. Garfield & A. Bergin (Eds.), *Handbook of psychotherapy and behavioral change.* New York: Wiley, 1978.

Marlatt, G. A. The Drinking profile: A questionnaire for the behavioral assessment of alcoholism. In E. J. Mash & L. G. Terdal (Eds.), *Behavioral therapy assessment: Diagnosis, design, and evaluation.* New York: Springer, 1976.

Marlatt, G. A. Alcohol, stress, and cognitive control. In P. E. Nathan, G. A. Marlatt, & T. Løberg (Eds.), *Alcoholism: New directions in behavioral research and treatment.* New York: Plenum Press, 1978.

Marlatt, G. A., & Gordon, J. R. Determinants of relapse: Implications for the maintenance of behavior change. In P. Davidson (Ed.), *Behavioral medicine: Changing health lifestyles.* New York: Brunner/Mazel, 1979.

Marlatt, G. A., & Rohsenow, D. J. Cognitive processes in alcohol use: Expectancy and the balanced placebo design. In N. K. Mello (Ed.), *Advances in substance abuse: Behavioral and biological research.* Greenwich, Conn.: JAI Press, 1980.

McFall, R. M., & Lillesand, D. B. Behavioral rehearsal with modeling and coaching in assertion training. *Journal of Abnormal Psychology,* 1971, *77,* 313–323.

Miller, P. M. Alternative skills training in alcoholism treatment. In P. E. Nathan, G. A. Marlatt, & T. Løberg, (Eds.), *Alcoholism: New directions in behavioral research and treatment.* New York: Plenum Press, 1978.

Miller, W. R., & Muñoz, R. F. *How to control your drinking.* Engelwood Cliffs, N.J.: Prentice-Hall, 1976.

Nathan, P. E. Studies in blood alcohol level discrimination. In P. E. Nathan, G. A. Marlatt, & T. Løberg, (Eds.), *Alcoholism: New directions in behavioral research and treatment.* New York: Plenum Press, 1978.

Sharp, J. R., Rosenbaum, G., Goldman, M. S., & Whitman, R. D. Recoverability of psychological functioning following alcohol abuse: Acquisition of meaningful synonyms. *Journal of Consulting and Clinical Psychology,* 1977, *45,* 1023–1028.

Sobell, L. C. A critique of alcoholism treatment evaluation. In G. A. Marlatt & P. E. Nathan (Eds.), *Behavioral assessment and treatment of alcoholism.* New Brunswick, N.J.: Rutgers Center of Alcohol Studies, 1978.

Vogler, R. E., Weissbach, T. A., Compton, J. V., & Martin, G. T. Integrated behavior change techniques for problem drinkers in the community. *Journal of Consulting and Clinical Psychology, 45,* 267–279.

3

When Is a Book a Treatment?
Bibliotherapy for Problem Drinkers

WILLIAM R. MILLER

1. INTRODUCTION

Over the course of the past 50 years a wide variety of methods have been proposed for dealing with problem drinking. Until recently, social ostracism and legal sanctions such as fines and imprisonment were far and away the most likely results of public identification as an inebriate. Within the realm of therapeutic interventions a broad array of alternative approaches have appeared, including aversion therapies, drug treatments, surgical procedures, Alcoholics Anonymous and group therapies, hypnosis and psychotherapy, halfway houses and family therapies (Miller & Hester, 1980). The one goal that these approaches all have in common has been to produce total and permanent abstention from alcohol.

2. CONTROLLED DRINKING

An important departure from previous treatment methods was introduced in 1970 by Lovibond and Caddy, who used a multimodal training program to teach problem drinkers how to drink moderately. They reported an 85% success rate in this endeavor. Since this report, many other researchers have evaluated the effectiveness of multimodal controlled-drinking treatment programs

WILLIAM R. MILLER ● Department of Psychology, University of New Mexico, Albuquerque, New Mexico 87106.

(Alden, 1978; Baker, Udin, & Vogler, 1975; Brown, 1980; Caddy & Lovibond, 1976; Caddy, Addington, & Perkins, 1978; Hedberg & Campbell, 1974; Lovibond, 1975; Schaefer, 1972; Vogler, Compton, & Weissbach, 1975; Vogler, Weissbach, & Compton, 1977a,b). The methodology and outcome of these studies have been reviewed elsewhere (Miller & Hester, 1980), but in general their findings have been quite positive, with success rates at 1-year follow-up averaging between 60% and 70%. It should be noted that in these studies the methodology (which has in most cases included longer-term follow-ups reaching over 80–90% of clients, random assignment to treatments, appropriate control and comparison groups, and corroboration of clients, self-reports) has been among the most meticulous in the current outcome literature.

There are, however, some important practical disadvantages to these multimodal approaches. They are time-consuming, requiring up to 45 hours per individual client. They have also included the use of potentially objectionable electric-shock aversion procedures and the serving of alcohol to clients within treatment sessions (Caddy & Lovibond, 1976; Lovibond & Caddy, 1970; Sobell & Sobell, 1973; Vogler et al., 1975, 1977a,b). These represent substantial obstacles to the application of such therapeutic methods within the average treatment setting.

An alternative approach to teaching moderation is behavioral self-control training (BSCT). This is an educational counseling method that can be offered on an outpatient basis in either group or individual formats. BSCT typically requires about 10 sessions and includes the following elements: (1) specific behavioral goal setting, (2) self-monitoring, (3) external cue training in blood-alcohol concentration discrimination, (4) training in self-control of consumption rate, (5) functional analysis of drinking behavior, (6) self-reinforcement training, and (7) training in alternative behavioral competencies to substitute for previous functions of drinking (Miller & Muñoz, 1976). Controlled evaluations of BSCT approaches have yielded rates of successful outcome comparable to those for the multimodal programs discussed above (Alden, 1978; Miller, 1978a,b; Miller, Pechacek, & Hamburg, 1981; Pomerleau, Pertschuk, Adkins, & D'Aquili, 1978; Vogler et al., 1977b). Summarizing data from 17 controlled studies, Miller and Hester (1980) reported average success rates of 70% for both multimodal and BSCT treatment programs at 12-month follow-ups, with 97% of clients located. Direct-controlled comparisons of BSCT and multimodal approaches have found a modest advantage at best for the more extensive approaches (Alden, 1978; Miller, 1978; Vogler et al., 1975, 1977a,b).

3. BIBLIOTHERAPY

Our use of bibliotherapy in treating problem drinkers arose as a serendipitous byproduct of our outcome research on BSCT. In our initial study (Miller, 1978) we provided a self-control manual to half of our clients (randomly selected) at the end of their treatment. Those who received the manual showed significantly greater continued gains than did those not given the manual. We further identified a group of clients who had received the manual and had not read it. In general, this group had been doing quite well at the point the manual was given and reported that they felt no need to read it. Those who *did* read the manual had higher alcohol consumption rates at the point the manual was given to them but showed significant improvement over the subsequent 3 months. Whether or not the nonreaders were included, the group given the manual was significantly more improved at 3-month follow-up than the group who had not received it.

This finding surprised us and led to a second study, in which we randomly assigned clients either to receive the manual alone (with standard intake assessment and self-monitoring procedures) or to be given the full BSCT program within 10 sessions with a paraprofessional therapist (Miller, Gribskov, & Mortell, 1981). The *content* of treatment was the same in both groups, but the latter group received therapist attention, whereas the former did not. To our surprise the 3-month success rates were 80% and 88% respectively. No advantage was found for therapist-administered over self-administered approaches, with both showing very promising response to treatment. This finding was replicated in another controlled study, for which we have now completed 24-month follow-up (Miller & Taylor, 1980). A third study (Miller, Taylor, & West, 1980) has yielded similar results, with perhaps a modest advantage for the therapist-treated group. Research now in progress in our laboratory (Buck & Miller, 1981) indicates that both bibliotherapy and therapist-administered BSCT produce significantly greater gains than either a waiting-list control group or a group using self-monitoring alone.

The results of these 6 years of research have led us to regard bibliotherapy with a good deal more respect than we once afforded it. We strongly share Rosen's (1976; Glasgow & Rosen, 1978) caveats regarding the risks of unevaluated self-help manuals and his call for careful evaluation research on bibliotherapy. With the completion of the studies described above, however, we are satisfied that bibliotherapy can be an effective intervention for at least some problem drinkers whose goal is moderation. We did not set out to find what we found and have been surprised and even chagrined at various points along the way. Nevertheless, our findings have been quite consistent across populations varying widely in socioeconomic, educational, and psychometric properties and ranging across three states, Oregon, California, and New Mexico. As research has begun to accumulate, limited data have been reported to support the cost effectiveness of bibliotherapy with other problem areas including anxiety (Glasgow & Rosen, 1978), depression (Schmidt,

1981), sexual dysfunction (McMullen & Rosen, 1979; Zeiss, 1978), and weight control (Dilley, Balch, & Balch, 1979).

4. DIFFERENTIAL DIAGNOSIS

An important question now is this: For whom are these approaches appropriate? The conventional belief among professionals working with problem drinkers is that a controlled-drinking approach is taboo for the alcoholic. This has led to a heated controversy over the usefulness, if not the morality, of moderation-oriented methods. This debate reached a peak with the publication of the first Rand report (Armor, Polich, & Stambul, 1978). The popular press misrepresented this report as advocating a return to drinking for abstinent alcoholics, and a storm of emotional protest followed. In fact the Rand report found only what many previous and subsequent studies have shown: In a systematic follow-up of a population treated for alcoholism, a small percentage, usually about 12%, are found to be drinking alcohol moderately and without problems (Miller & Hester, 1980). This finding could be surprising only to someone unfamiliar with alcohol treatment outcome research. The controversy revolved around the belief that an alcoholic can *never* drink again without relapsing to full-blown addiction and progressive deterioration. Even if we were to ignore the mountains of experimental and clinical data that now question this universal assumption (Pattison, Sobell, & Sobell, 1977), the Rand findings would not be controversial except for another important historical error: the confusion of *all* problem drinking with gamma alcoholism. Unless one assumes that every person treated for alcoholism must be a gamma alcoholic it should not be surprising that some establish or reestablish moderate drinking patterns. Jellinek (1960), to whom the disease model is attributed, clearly recognized the existence of numerous varieties of alcoholism, only *two* of which (gamma and delta) involved true addiction and thereby deserved disease status. In alpha, beta, epsilon, and other types of alcoholism, Jellinek recognized the existence of nonaddictive problem drinking. Through historical circumstances, however, both the public and treatment agents have forgotten this distinction. Just 2 years after Jellinek's landmark work, alcohol professionals were protesting the publication of Davies's (1962) documentation of controlled-drinking outcomes in a population treated for alcoholism. This confusion highlights all the more our need for data to answer the question: For whom are moderation-oriented approaches most likely to work?

In a retrospective analysis of data from four of our studies (Miller & Joyce, 1979; Ogborne, Annis, & Miller, 1981) we attempted to provide such data by contrasting clients falling into three categories at follow-up: moderate drinkers, abstainers, and uncontrolled drinkers. We found that, relative to successful abstainers, successful controlled drinkers had less severe drinking problems, higher incomes, and less of a family history of alcoholism; were more likely to be married and female; and were less likely to regard themselves as alcoholics. Similar findings have been reported by Popham and Schmidt (1976) and Vogler *et al.* (1977a). Strikingly similar findings have also been reported in studies comparing controlled drinkers and abstainers following *abstinence*-oriented treatment (Armor *et al.*, 1978; Levinson, 1977; Orford, 1973; Orford, Oppenheimer, & Edwards, 1976; Polich, Armor, & Braiker, 1980; Smart, 1978). Thus the trend in the data seems quite clear: Whether the initial goal was abstinence or moderation, the same kind of client tends to become a controlled drinker. This is the client with significant but less severe problem drinking. Abstainers, on the other hand, tend to have had more severe drinking problems, approximating those usually associated with the term "alcoholism." Data from the second Rand report (Polich *et al.*, 1980) suggest, in fact, that early-stage problem drinkers are *less* likely to relapse from moderation than from abstinence, whereas for previously addicted individuals the reverse is true. There are exceptions on both sides, of course. Some early-stage problem drinkers do very well with abstinence, and some gamma alcoholics have become documented controlled drinkers beyond any reasonable scientific doubt. Nevertheless the trend remains. Miller and Caddy (1977) have described a set of differential diagnostic criteria for selecting moderation versus abstinence goals in individual cases. Although these criteria were proposed before many of the above-described data were published, they seem to remain sound in light of subsequent research.

To date we have not accumulated enough cases to make meaningful statistical predictions regarding the success of bibliotherapy as a moderation approach, but the trend appears to be the same: Early-stage problem drinkers seem to do best with this minimal-intervention approach. This is consistent with findings from the major treatment outcome study conducted by Edwards and his colleagues (1977).

The two cases that follow were treated at the Alcohol Research and Treatment Project located in the Department of Psychology at the University of New Mexico. Both responded to newspaper announcements of the availability of an experimental program to teach moderation to problem drinkers. The media publicity included the clear statement that these programs were not intended for alcoholics or for people who were currently abstinent. Both were treated as part of our ongoing program of clinical-outcome research. Richard L. was treated in our fourth clinical study (Miller & Taylor, 1980), and Leah M. a year later in our fifth study (Miller, Taylor, & West, 1980). Although clients' names and other critical identifying details have been altered to protect anonymity, none of these changes would substantially influence interpretation of outcome.

5. CASE ONE: LEAH

5.1. Background

Leah M. was a 60-year-old housewife and grandmother. She had worked for 20 years as a receptionist-secretary but was now retired and living with her 62-year-old husband, who worked as a night watchman. She responded promptly to a newspaper article describing our research clinic for problem drinkers.

To Leah's knowledge none of her relatives had been problem drinkers. Both of her parents had been lifelong teetotalers. Her first drinking episode occurred at age 16 and resulted in intoxication, which she found somewhat unpleasant. She became a social drinker and drank moderately and occasionally throughout her 20s and 30s (one or two mixed drinks once every week or two). During her 40s her drinking increased to one or two drinks daily, in part, she reported, because a doctor advised her to drink a beer daily in order to decrease her depression. Drinking posed no problem for her during this time. During her 50s Leah's drinking gradually increased to the level that she reported at the time she entered our program: 8 oz. of bourbon three nights a week, 4 to 5 oz. on all other nights except Sundays, when she abstained for religious reasons. Converted into our Standard Ethanol Content (SEC) units, this totaled approximately 32 SECs per week. (One SEC equals 0.5 oz. [15 ml] of absolute ethanol; for commonsense purposes 1 SEC equals one normal drink of beer, 4-oz. glass of wine, or 1-oz. shot of 100-proof distilled spirits.) From the reported spacing of her drink's (8 oz. over 5 to 6 hours) and her sex and weight (125 lb.), we estimate that her peak blood-alcohol concentration (BAC) during a typical week of drinking was about 156 mg%. This estimate was made via a computer program for calculating BAC (Matthews & Miller, 1979). Collateral interviews were conducted with her husband and her two children (now living away from home). All reported that they believed her to be an occasional and moderate drinker, estimating her weekly drinking at about 2 SECs per week. This was consistent with Leah's own report that she did almost all her drinking alone.

Leah's medical history revealed a lifelong thyroid deficiency that had been successfully treated with medication, a history of moderately elevated blood pressure, but no other major health problems. Six years earlier a physician had informed her that her liver function values were elevated, suggesting mild liver damage. He asked her to stop drinking for 3 months, which she did. The physician also prescribed Valium for her on an as-required basis, which she had used subsequently on occasions when she felt tense (one or two tablets about once every 2 weeks in addition to her usual drinking pattern). Among the drinking-related symptoms that she reported were several blackouts, feelings of craving for alcohol (more an inability to abstain than an inability to stop once started, thus resembling Jellinek's delta type more than his gamma type), and mild to moderate tremor on mornings following heavier drinking episodes. She had never experienced withdrawal hallucinations, seizures, or delirium. She restricted all of her drinking to the evening, never drinking before 5:00 P.M.

Asked about situations or feelings that typically precipitated heavier drinking, Leah pointed to family arguments and feelings of anger, depression, frustration, loneliness, and tension. Regarding her motivations for seeking help at this time she said, "I realize that I can't wait for 5:00 to arrive so that I can start drinking. I can't go out to dinner or social situations and just have one drink—I want to have more. I don't want this to get any worse." She expressed the belief that alcoholism is a disease rather than a bad habit and opined, "I don't think that I'm an alcoholic, but I do have a drinking problem. If this doesn't work for me, then I guess I'll quit drinking altogether, but I would like to be able to have one or two drinks on social occasions without having to have more." She described her husband as a light social drinker and indicated that most people would probably describe her in the same way. She had never sought help for her drinking before.

All of the above information was collected via a standardized interview format modified from Marlatt's (1976) Drinking Profile Questionnaire, which we have used as our intake interview for the past 5 years. With Leah we also employed a modified method of goal attainment scaling (Kiresuk, 1972) to determine other life problem areas. She identified her three most important life problems other than drinking as (in order of importance to her) feelings of tension and anxiety, depression, and inability to express her feelings.

A serum sample was drawn and assayed for two indicators of liver function (Reyes & Miller, 1980). Her serum glutamic-oxalacetic transaminase (SGOT) level was 29.0, a mild elevation, falling within the borderline normal range. Her serum gamma-glutamyl transpeptidase (GGTP) level was found to be 24.8, falling within normal limits.

5.2. Psychometric Data

On the Michigan Alcoholism Screening Test, Leah scored 14, placing her well into the "alcoholic" range according to the criteria proposed by the scale's author (Selzer, 1971). On Rotter's (1966) Internal-External Locus of

Control Scale, her score was 11 at intake, indicating a moderate tendency to view her life as being controlled by external forces. On the Personality Research Form (Jackson, 1974), the only need state score that exceeded normative data by 1 standard deviation was need for Harmavoidance. On the Profile of Mood States, however, Leah reported herself to be quite tense ($t = 66$), depressed ($t = 70$), fatigued ($t = 60$), and confused ($t = 69$), as compared with the authors' normative data for outpatient samples (McNair, Lorr, & Droppelman, 1971).

5.3. Diagnostic Summary

Leah posed a mixed diagnostic picture that is typical of clients who have presented themselves to our moderate-drinking program. If one were to use the MAST or the diagnostic criteria of the National Council on Alcoholism (1972), she would unquestionably be diagnosed as alcoholic. Neither of these diagnostic standards allows for an intermediate category of "nonalcoholic problem drinker," however, an error that has been corrected in the newest edition of DSM-III (American Psychiatric Association, 1980).

Was Leah addicted to ethanol? Certainly the occurrence of morning tremors suggested that the process of pharmacologic dependence had reached early stages, and this would be sufficient to place her within the "alcohol dependence" category of DSM-III. Yet her drinking pattern was not one of maintenance consumption. Her blood-alcohol concentration fell to 0 every day, remaining there for at least 36 hours once a week because of her Sunday abstinence. Tremors did not normally occur during this time, in spite of abstinence from alcohol and Valium. She had no history of more advanced withdrawal signs. She did report blackouts, which some diagnosticians regard as conclusive evidence of alcoholism. Blackouts, however, occur as early symptoms of problem drinking and do not differentiate alcohol dependence in particular from alcohol abuse in general. Medical data in this case suggested mild physical impact of ethanol on the liver. Her ability to abstain Sundays and for longer periods of time on occasion was not wholly consistent with Jellinek's delta category, and her consistent ability to constrain her drinking to certain times and amounts was not indicative of gamma alcoholism. Thus she appeared to fail to meet criteria for a variety of "disease" or "addiction" categories, yet it was clear that she was a problem drinker and may have developed more serious problems related to alcohol unless intervention was begun.

5.4. Treatment

Leah was accepted as a candidate for our experimental controlled-drinking program. She showed none of the major contraindications to a moderation goal (Miller & Caddy, 1977) and, as an early-stage female problem drinker without family history of alcoholism, fit some of the predictors for successful outcome in moderation (Miller & Joyce, 1979; Ogborne, Annis, & Miller, 1981). Because she was a participant in a controlled treatment outcome study, Leah's treatment modality was chosen at random. She was assigned to the bibliotherapy condition and was provided with a copy of our self-help manual (Miller & Muñoz, 1976) and a supply of self-monitoring cards and mailers. She was encouraged to believe that she would be able to control her drinking if she followed the instructions provided in the manual, and she was asked to mail in self-monitoring data to the project weekly. We had no further personal or telephone contact with her until the first follow-up interview 6 months later.

5.5. Results

Leah's reported weekly alcohol consumption in SECs is shown in Figure 1. Data from intake and from 6-, 12-, and 24-month follow-ups were based on personal structured interviews with the client. (The follow-up point designated as "6 months" occurred 6 months after Week 18 of self-monitoring, the formal end of the treatment phase, and thus came approximately 12 months after intake. Similarly, the 12- and 24-month follow-ups were sched-

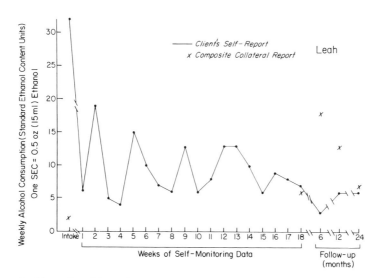

Figure 1. Leah's total weekly alcohol consumption during treatment and follow-up, expressed in Standard Ethanol Content (SEC) units.

uled for 18 and 30 months after intake, respectively.) At each follow-up point the three collateral sources were interviewed by telephone and a composite collateral estimate of alcohol consumption was constructed using the most accurate information from each. In Figure 1 the Xs indicate the collateral estimates of consumption. Finally data points during weeks of self-monitoring are based upon daily records of drinking, with summary data prepared by our ALCOMP computer program for processing self-monitoring data (Matthews & Miller, 1979).

Leah's drinking showed a marked drop between the intake interview and her first week of self-monitoring. This might be attributed to a discrepancy owing to different methods of estimation (interview vs. record keeping), but Leah also reported in retrospect that "The first week of keeping cards was a real shock. I had no idea how much I was drinking, and it really made me cut down. Every time I went to pour a drink I looked at the card and thought, 'I'll have to write this one down.' It made me aware of just how much I was drinking." This is a common report among our clients, who normally show about a 33% reduction in drinking between intake and the 1st week of self-monitoring. Our present data suggest, however, that this reduction is ephemeral unless other self-control methods are also taught.

Following her first week of record keeping, Leah showed a rebound in drinking, followed by a gradual decline in weekly consumption, with the usual peaks and valleys representing heavy and lighter weeks. By the end of 18 weeks of keeping records, which she faithfully mailed to the project each week, her drinking had stabilized at about 7 SECs per week. This level of consumption was confirmed by her collaterals. (Note that this represents an *increase* in drinking as reported by collaterals!)

At 6-month follow-up Leah reported an average of 3 SECs per week. She now was drinking on only 2 days per week. Interestingly, her collaterals now estimated a consumption level of 18 SECs per week. Several reasons for this discrepancy emerged. The family had now become sensitized to the fact that Leah drank alone and had begun to correct for this by guessing. Leah also reported one episode during the previous 3 months in which she had openly consumed 3 oz. of bourbon daily for about 2 weeks, an amount corresponding very closely to what collaterals reported to be her regular consumption rate. Finally it is possible that Leah was underestimating her own alcohol consumption. Improvement on other dimensions was apparent. She reported that her smoking rate had declined from 18 to 6 cigarettes per day. The Profile of Mood States reflected improvement on every scale, with all six scales now well within normal limits. Decreases in anxiety and depression were particularly marked. Finally her Locus of Control score had declined to 6, slightly on the "internal control" side.

At both 12- and 24-month follow-up Leah reported drinking six drinks per week, or about 1.5 SECs on each of 4 drinking days per week. Collateral estimates declined to 13 and then to 7 SECs per week. Her decreased-smoking level was maintained at both follow-ups, and a weight gain of 7 lb. that she associated with decreased smoking had reversed itself by 12 months. Improvement on the Profile of Mood States was maintained through 24 months. Goal attainment scaling reflected substantial improvement in all three of her major reported life problems: anxiety, depression, and unassertiveness. The only change in her Personality Research Form that exceeded one standard deviation was an increase in Dominance from $t = 30$ to $t = 48$.

Figure 2 reflects Leah's weekly peak BAC as estimated by our ALCOMP program from her alcohol consumption data. The pattern of change closely parallels that seen in alcohol consumption. From an intake high of 156 mg%, her BAC declines to about 45mg% at the end of self-monitoring, well within the range of normal social drinking. This level is maintained throughout follow-up and is well confirmed by collaterals. Thus Leah not only decreased her total alcohol consumption but also changed the level of intoxication reached. Because Leah was not a rapid drinker to begin with, most of the decline in BAC is attributable to decreased alcohol consumption rather than to increased spacing of her drinks. This is somewhat different from the pattern we normally observe, in which the first gains are made in BAC improvement

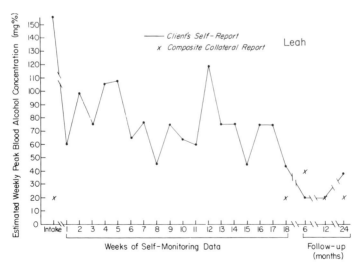

Figure 2. Leah's estimated weekly peak blood-alcohol concentration (BAC) during treatment and follow-up.

owing to wider spacing of drinks, followed by a more gradual decrease in total consumption over the later weeks in treatment.

6. CASE TWO: RICHARD

6.1. Background

Richard L. was a 43-year-old manager of a retail store and the father of two teenagers. He came to the clinic in response to reading a newspaper article describing the controlled-drinking research program. "I don't think I'm an alcoholic, and I don't think that I have to stop drinking," he said, "but my drinking is getting to be a problem for me." He had begun to experience regular hangovers, insomnia, nausea, and vomiting in association with his drinking, and his blackouts were becoming more frequent. He also reported feeling a craving for alcohol at times, as well as occasions on which he seemed to be unable to stop drinking once he had started. He had been having an increasing number of arguments with his wife (usually about drinking) and had been separated from her for several months. In addition to these marital stresses he reported that his increased drinking had lost him a few friends, mostly because he had said offensive things while intoxicated. He reported that about once a month he would stop drinking for 2 to 3 days. He had experienced no signs of withdrawal other than hangovers and reported no marked change in his tolerance for alcohol.

Richard did not have his first drink until age 20, at which time he became quite intoxicated. His father had been a heavy social drinker, his mother a lifelong abstainer. He reported that his drinking began to increase to problem proportions when he was around age 37 as a result of increased pressures at work when he was promoted to manager. His pattern of drinking was quite consistent when he came to the clinic. Each weekday after work he would stop at a bar with friends and have 3 or 4 drinks—usually martinis or double scotches. Then he would drive home and have another 3 or 4 drinks of the same type. On Saturdays and Sundays he tended to drink less than this. From our reconstruction of his typical drinking week, we estimated that he was consuming about 98 SECs each week, with a peak BAC of about 295 mg% at the end of his usual weekday night drinking.

Asked about his main motivations for drinking, Richard pointed to relaxation, release from social inhibitions, and forgetting his problems. After drinking, he said, he felt secure, relaxed, outgoing, and friendly. He also enumerated some negative aspects of his excessive drinking: his tendency to become depressed, to say offensive things to people, and to get into arguments with his wife. He indicated that he wanted to get back together with his wife, who refused to do so as long as he continued his heavy drinking. Herself an occasional light drinker, she wanted him either to stop drinking or to cut down substantially. Both agreed that he was a problem drinker, although most of his friends saw him as a heavy but nonproblem drinker. He indicated that he thought of alcoholism as a bad habit rather than as a disease and repeated that he did not think his own drinking was serious enough to qualify him as an alcoholic. Two years before coming to the clinic he had attended about 20 weekly meetings of Alcoholics Anonymous at the urging of his wife, but finally stopped going because, "I didn't think I was that bad off." He had never sought other help for his drinking problem. His medical history was unremarkable, with no major illnesses or health problems reported during the past 10 years. A serum assay, however, revealed liver function values elevated substantially above normal, with an SGOT value of 60 and a GGTP value of 176. These values were judged by our medical consultants to be indicative of early liver pathology but not of major or irreversible disease such as cirrhosis. (We have used a value of 200 on either scale as the absolute cutoff for acceptance into our program. In a borderline case like Richard's we require a physician's examination and clearance before beginning treatment.)

6.2. Psychometric Data

On the MAST, Richard scored 28, well above the mean score ($\overline{X} = 18$) for problem drinkers accepted into our research program. This reflected the large number of life problems that Richard had incurred in relation to drinking. On the Profile of Mood States he showed significantly elevated levels of tension and anxiety, depression, anger and hostility, and fatigue. His Locus of Control score was 7, close to the normative mean for the Rotter scale. Goal attainment scaling revealed his three most significant life problems other than drinking to be marital problems, boredom, and tension.

6.3. Diagnostic Summary

Richard's overall diagnostic picture was one of moderate to severe problem drinking. Relative to Leah, he had incurred more life problems and showed higher liver function elevations, indicative of the beginnings of physical damage. His drinking clearly had begun to affect the quality of his life in general. His blackouts signaled the beginnings of impairment to the central nervous system (Miller & Saucedo, in press). The very volume of his alcohol consumption bespoke a developed tolerance to ethanol. By almost any traditional diagnostic criteria, Richard would have been classified as an alcoholic.

Yet again there was the total absence of a history of withdrawal syndrome, even of early-withdrawal symptoms such as tremor. Extended periods of abstinence from alcohol without substitution drugs evoked no marked discomfort. In this sense Richard was not an alcohol addict, and fit neither the gamma nor the delta type of alcoholism in Jellinek's schema. Rather he qualified for either the alpha or the beta type, with his life problems and medical signs. We have observed successful outcomes with clients similar to Richard in our moderation-oriented programs, although the probability of achieving controlled drinking is somewhat reduced (Ogborne et al., 1981).

Because of his avowed refusal to consider himself an alcoholic or to pursue abstinence and because he showed no signs of pharmacologic addiction or other important contraindication to moderation as a treatment goal (Miller & Caddy, 1977), Richard was accepted into our controlled-drinking research program. He was assigned at random to the bibliotherapy condition and received treatment identical to that described above for Leah.

6.4. Results

Figure 3 shows Richard's weekly alcohol consumption from intake until the 24-month follow-up. He kept self-monitoring cards for 15 weeks, mailing them to the clinic on a weekly basis. From his high point of 98 SECs per

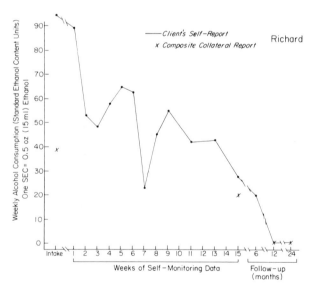

Figure 3. Richard's total weekly alcohol consumption during treatment and follow-up, expressed in Standard Ethanol Content (SEC) units.

week at intake his consumption declined rapidly over early weeks, then increased somewhat before resuming the final decrease to about 28 drinks per week at the program's end. Note that as in the case of Leah, Richard's three collaterals were unaware of the full extent of his drinking. Nevertheless his decreased consumption is reflected in their subsequent reports. Parallel decrements in Richard's weekly peak BAC are shown in Figure 4.

At the end of the self-monitoring period Richard had been reunited with his wife and reported marked improvement in their relationship. He still complained of boredom and high tension levels, with no improvement in these problems. Likewise his Profile of Mood States reflected slightly more depression than before and little improvement on other dimensions.

Six months later Richard reported a further decrease in his drinking to about 20 SECs per week, and his peak BAC level had declined to about 50 mg%, a normal social-drinking level. Both he and his wife reported continued improvement in their marriage. Nevertheless Richard remained dissatisfied with his sense of control over his drinking and worried that he could relapse and ruin his now-happy marriage. His tension and depression levels remained high. His liver function values reflected substantial improvement, with a normal SGOT value of 16 and a mildly elevated GGTP of 59.

Three months later Richard did have his relapse, returning to his pretreatment level of drinking for 1 full week. With his wife's encouragement

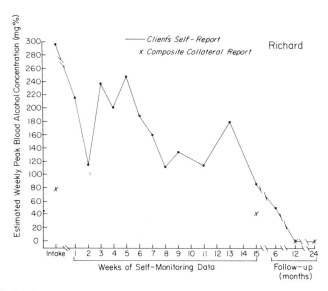

Figure 4. Richard's estimated weakly peak blood-alcohol concentration (BAC) during treatment and follow-up.

he decided to admit himself at the end of this week to an inpatient alcoholism treatment program, where he spent the next 3 weeks. When we next interviewed Richard (at 12-month follow-up) he had been abstinent for 3 months except for one slip 2 months earlier, in which he had drunk about 8 oz. of scotch over a period of 2 days. He reported that he had felt encouraged by the fact that he did not lose control over his drinking at that time, and feeling confident in his self-control, he again resumed his abstinence. His marriage remained happy, and he showed marked improvement in general mood states as well. He reported good improvement in his boredom and tension problems when we repeated the goal attainment scaling procedure, and his Profile of Mood States reflected improvement on all scales to near-normal levels. His abstinence was confirmed by all three collaterals, although none of them (including his wife) had been aware of his slip. Richard had also begun regular attendance at AA meetings. His liver function values remained at approximately the same levels as before (SGOT = 19, GGTP = 53).

At our final follow-up interview 24 months after the end of self-monitoring, Richard reported continuous abstinence for 14 months, again confirmed by all three collaterals. He was still attending weekly AA meetings, and his marital and mood gains were being maintained nicely. His Locus of Control score (6), smoking rate (2 packs per day), and overweight condition (200 lb. at 5 ft. 10 in.) remained unchanged from pretreatment levels. His liver function values again were found to be improved, with both now within normal limits (SGOT = 18, GGTP = 37).

7. DISCUSSION

These two cases represent two typical kinds of outcome that we have observed in our applications of behavioral self-control training with problem drinkers. Leah represents a successful moderation case. Her pattern of progressive reduction in alcohol consumption and peak BAC over weeks of treatment followed by good maintenance during follow-up is perhaps the typical pattern or response to BSCT. Her individual pattern, in fact, resembles the mean data for groups treated with BSCT in our research (Miller & Taylor, 1980; Miller et al., 1980). We have found that the client's status at the end of the treatment period is quite predictive of longer-term outcome, and Leah illustrates this. A client who has successfully moderated his or her drinking by the end of treatment has, by our calculations, about a 90% chance of maintaining a successful outcome at 24-month follow-up.

Richard, on the other hand, represents a different kind of successful outcome: total abstinence. Paradoxical though it may seem, abstinence is not an unusual outcome following controlled-drinking training. In some studies, in fact, abstinence rates following moderation training have rivaled or exceeded those resulting from abstinence-oriented comparison treatment (Caddy et al., 1978; Sanchez-Craig, 1980). We have observed at least two patterns by which such "paradoxical abstinence" occurs. The first is a pattern of gradual reduction in drinking until finally abstinence is achieved. This is approximately what occurred in Richard's case. His self-control was coming along nicely and even his slip was controlled by comparison with his pretreatment drinking level, but he opted for abstinence as a surer and safer way. A similar outcome was popularized in Davis's 1976 novel *The Pilot.* The other course toward abstinence is one of total failure at controlled drinking, which seems to serve as a kind of self-confrontation of the necessity of abstinence and impossibility of moderation (Miller & Caddy, 1977). In the latter case in particular, it is not unusual for the individual to seek abstinence-oriented treatment prior to beginning his or her period of abstinence. In a way an abstinent outcome following controlled-drinking training may be a kind of supersuccess. Of the cases we have studied over our 6 years of research, *not one* who has achieved abstinence has relapsed to uncontrolled drinking, although about half have returned to moderate drinking for various (usually brief) periods of time. The process of testing self-control is not unusual and is exemplified by Richard's private slip. The availability of modulated drinking as an alternative to full-blown relapse may be an important safeguard which we can provide clients who desire secure abstinence, a possibility that Marlatt has discussed in his model of relapse prevention (Cummings, Gordon, & Marlatt, 1980).

What is most interesting about these cases, however, is not that they show successful control over drinking. As indicated above, such outcomes are not unusual (Miller & Hester, 1980). Rather, the interesting aspect of these cases is that they were not treated in any conventional sense. They received a comprehensive intake assessment, a self-help manual, and a set of self-monitoring cards. From there they were on their own, given the encouragement that they could succeed if they followed the program. These two cases have been replicated again and again in our research on bibliotherapy and behavioral self-control training.

These findings have several important implications for clinical practice. First there is the potential application of minimal-therapist-contact interventions in treating problem drinkers (Christensen, Miller, & Muñoz, 1978). The use of *effective* adjunctive interventions can improve both the scope and the impact of treatment systems. Elsewhere I have described four possible applications of bibliotherapy in treatment: Self-help manuals may be used as *replacements* for therapist-directed treatment or as *concomitant* aids to the therapist's efforts in treating a problem. Manuals may also *complement* therapist time by focusing on one problem area while formal treatment is directed toward others. Finally manuals may be provided as a *supplement* after formal therapy has ended in order to improve maintenance of gains (Miller, 1978b). In our research we have used our self-help manual as replacement, concomitant, and supplement and have found it to be effective in all three applications. In my own practice I have also used it in complementary fashion, with good results.

If a self-help manual is a sufficient intervention for successful outcome in many cases, this fact can be used to the advantage of both client and therapist, in that direct therapy time can be reserved for those clients who really need it. Our data suggest that the manual is a sufficient intervention for about 60% of our early-stage problem-drinking clients. This has resulted in the following levels-of-care model, which has come to represent our standard procedure for treatment delivery.

7.1. Levels-of-Care Model

The first step is a careful differential diagnostic interview to determine whether our moderation approach is a suitable goal for the individual. This follows the process described above (Marlatt, 1976; Miller & Caddy, 1977). If no major contraindication is identified the client is eligible for moderation-oriented treatment. Our initial inclination, then, is to assign him or her to bibliotherapy—unless there is a particular crisis or other clear reason for immediate therapist attention. Our reasoning here is that clients' initial chances for attaining moderation are just as good in bibliotherapy as in individual or group treatment sessions. We schedule a 2-week visit to check on the client's progress in implementing the program (to be sure that self-monitoring is underway, etc.) and a second visit at 6 weeks to monitor progress. Usually self-monitoring cards are mailed weekly and are tabulated and processed via ALCOMP (Matthews & Miller, 1979) prior to the client's return visit. If at the 6-week visit he or she seems to be making satisfactory progress the next visit is scheduled for 12 weeks after initial contact. This is because our data suggest that good progress at 6 weeks is prognostic of longer-term improvement. If, on the other hand, no progress has been made by 6 weeks, our data suggest that further weeks in the same treatment modality would be unlikely to yield additional gains. In this event we take the client into treatment for either individual sessions or group training, both of which have been validated in our previous research. In this way the effort and expense of professional treatment are devoted to those clients who most need this kind of direction.

From both a clinical and a research viewpoint this seems to represent an optimal approach to treating early-stage problems drinkers. Our current data suggest that minimal treatment interventions are at least as effective with *early-stage* problem drinkers as are more extensive therapist-directed efforts (Buck & Miller, 1981; Edwards *et al.*, 1977; Miller & Hester, 1980). Early-stage problem drinkers as a group may even be *less* likely to improve with extensive than with self-directed interventions. Needless to say, bibliotherapy is also one of the least expensive treatments. Thus with proper differential diagnosis this approach may be in the best interests of the problem drinkers in terms of both absolute and cost effectiveness. Because most alcohol treatment agencies are faced with an overwhelming case load, a differential levels-of-care model may also be in the best interests of the staff and may extend total service delivery far beyond what can be provided under traditional models of treatment (Christensen *et al.*, 1978).

What are the risks? We believe that they are minimal. Proper differential diagnosis will identify clients in need of more intensive services, but even if a case is misdiagnosed and placed into bibliotherapy, the 2- and 6-week safeguard visits quickly pick up the error. We find that clients are not alienated by our introduction of bibliotherapy as an alternative. To the contrary, they often find it attractive because of its emphasis on self-control and are encouraged by our optimistic research findings. Further, clients seem to perceive us as being quite committed to their best interests in not routinely requiring extensive, expensive, and potentially unnecessary treatments. Our message is basically this: "We'll stick with you and provide whatever treatment it seems to take for you to reach your goals. Often the self-help program is enough, and if so, that's great. If not, then together we'll work out what you need instead." This is a very positive message. Certainly bibliotherapy should not be used in lieu of adequate diagnosis or without some ongoing follow-up and safeguards. Within these limits of professional care, however, bibliotherapy seems to be an effective treatment approach for many early-stage problem drinkers.

COMMENTARY

William M. Hay

As we can see throughout this book, a variety of clinical procedures fall under the rubric of behavioral treatment. Before treatment begins, as a consequence, the behavioral clinician must address a number of questions including: What treatment goal has the highest probability of success for this client (abstinence or controlled drinking)? Which treatment procedures should be incorporated into the treatment plan? How should treatment be delivered (e.g., group, individual, or a combination)? Who should be involved in the treatment process (the client only, the client and the spouse, the client and family, etc.)? Historically, there has been only one answer to the question concerning treatment goal; that answer has been total abstinence from alcohol. The guiding belief in alcoholism treatment has been that the alcoholic can never drink again without becoming progressively debilitated.

The number of chapters in this text that describe cases in which controlled drinking was the treatment goal stands in sharp contrast to this historical precedent. The development of alternatives to the abstinence treatment goal is not surprising, given the accumulating evidence that a consistent proportion of clients treated for alcohol-related problems return to some level of controlled consumption. As clinicians, however, we are faced with a difficult diagnostic issue, how to identify clients who are appropriate for the controlled-drinking goal, and with the reality that abstinence remains the practical as well as the emotional choice of the overwhelming majority of treatment programs.

The chapter by Bill Miller summarizes the treatment outcome literature concerning controlled-drinking programs. The two cases presented give the reader guidelines for the identification of clients who may be appropriate for controlled-drinking treatment plans. In addition, Miller's clinical research program has provided us with some preliminary answers about clients who are able to maintain controlled-drinking status. Miller has found that successful controlled drinkers versus successful abstainers report less severe drinking problems, have higher incomes, have a minimal family history of alcoholism, are more likely to be married and female, and are less likely to describe themselves as alcoholics. If we were to place these successful controlled drinkers on a continuum ranging from "no alcohol-related problems" to "severe problems," therefore, these clients would best be described as early-stage problem drinkers with above-average social-support systems and resources.

The first case Miller describes fits this profile: the client was a 60-year-old female in the early stages of problem drinking. The onset of this client's alcohol problems occurred late in life, following a history as a social drinker. The client's family system was intact, with no family history of alcoholism. The second client, however, was consuming substantial amounts of alcohol, experiencing marital problems, and reporting high levels of tension and depression. This client did achieve his controlled-drinking goal but eventually sought inpatient treatment and, at follow-up, reported 14 months of abstinence. Mr. D., the client who is described by Barbara McCrady in Chapter 6, followed a similar treatment course. In Mr. D.'s case, the behavioral treatment was abstinence-oriented, and he subsequently became actively involved in Alcoholic Anonymous. McCrady and Peter Nathan, in his commentary, suggest that Mr. D.'s involvement in behavioral treatment played a crucial role in his subsequent treatment success. The ultimate success of Richard, the second client described by Miller in this chapter, may also be related to his involvement in behavioral treatment. My own feeling is that clients entering treatment have different levels of preparedness or commitment. In some cases, clients will participate in a number of treatment programs before attaining control over their consumption of alcohol. A behavioral treatment program does seem to facili-

tate this process because the functional analysis of drinking behavior clearly presents the negative consequences of continued drinking to the alcohol abuser.

In both cases the major treatment procedure consisted of giving each client a detailed self-control manual, which specified how they could gain control over their drinking. While this may be considered a minimal intervention strategy, the procedures were actually quite elaborate. Each client underwent a comprehensive assessment which covered the full range of physical, personal, and psychological factors and pinpointed their consumption levels at intake. All of these data were considered before treatment began, to ensure that there were no contraindications to pursuing a controlled-drinking goal. (The interested reader can review these contraindications in Miller and Caddy, 1977, or in Chapter 12 of this text.) Both clients were given the self-control manual and were seen at scheduled follow-up times. Collateral sources were also interviewed at intake and during follow-up in an attempt to verify drinking status. In both cases, however, collaterals initially underrated consumption. This pattern subsequently reversed as the collaterals became sensitized to consumption. The specialized bibliotherapy treatment procedures operated with a system of checks and balances. The system allowed for the careful monitoring of clients in the bibliotherapy modality, with lack of progress resulting in an early shift to another treatment strategy.

The contrast in outcomes for these two cases should alert the reader to the fact that much more work needs to be done before we will be able to answer questions concerning the optimal behavioral treatment goal for a particular client. This is especially true for Richard L. in this chapter. During his attempt at controlled drinking this client reported substantial improvement in his marital relationship but also experienced high levels of tension and depression related to the stress-provoking aspects of constantly monitoring his alcohol intake. When the client opted for abstinence, these stress indicators subsided. Miller's work, therefore, provides a further example of how an empirically-based research program can complement the work of practicing clinician and, perhaps, eventually generate some answers to these questions.

8. REFERENCES

Alden, L. Evaluation of a preventive self-management programme for problem drinkers. *Canadian Journal of Behavioural Science*, 1978, 10, 258–263.

American Psychiatric Association. *Diagnostic and Statistical Manual of Mental Disorders* (3rd ed.). Washington, D.C.: Author, 1980.

Armor, D. J., Polich, J. M., & Stambul, H. B. *Alcoholism and treatment.* New York: Wiley, 1978.

Baker, T. B., Udin, H., & Vogler, R. E. The effects of videotaped modeling and self-confrontation on the drinking behavior of alcoholics. *International Journal of the Addictions*, 1975, 10, 779–793.

Brown, R. A. Conventional education and controlled drinking education Courses with convicted drunken drivers. *Behavior Therapy*, 1980, 11, 632–642.

Buck, K., & Miller, W. R. *Why does bibliotherapy work? A controlled study.* Paper presented at the annual meeting of the Association for Advancement of Behavior Therapy, Toronto, November 1981.

Caddy, G. R., Addington, H. J., Jr., & Perkins, D. Individualized behavior therapy for alcoholics: A third-year independent double-blind follow-up.*Behaviour Research and Therapy*, 1978, *16*, 345–362.

Caddy, G. R., & Lovibond, S. H. Self-regulation and discriminated aversive conditioning in the modification of alcoholics' drinking behavior. *Behavior Therapy*, 1976, *7*, 223–230.

Christensen, A., Miller, W. R., & Muñoz, R. F. Paraprofessionals, partners, peers, paraphernalia, and print: Expanding mental health service delivery. *Professional Psychology*, 1978, *9*, 249–270.

Cummings, C., Gordon, J. R., & Marlatt, G. A. Relapse: Prevention and prediction. In W. R. Miller (Ed.), *The addictive behaviors: Treatment of alcoholism, drug abuse, smoking, and obesity*. Oxford: Pergamon Press, 1980.

Davies, D. L. Normal drinking by recovered alcohol addicts. *Quarterly Journal of Studies on Alcohol*, 1962, *23*, 94–104.

Davis, R. P. *The pilot*. New York: Morrow, 1976.

Dilley, D., Balch, P., & Balch, K. A comparison of strategies for behavioral obesity treatment. *Journal of Behaviour Therapy and Experimental Psychiatry*, 1979, *10*, 193–197.

Edwards, G., Orford, J., Egert, S., Guthrie, S., Hawker, A., Hensman, C. Mitcheson, M., Oppenheimer, E., & Taylor, C. Alcoholism: A controlled trial of "treatment" and "advice." *Journal of Studies on Alcohol*, 1977, *38*, 1004–1031.

Glasgow, R. E., & Rosen, G. M. Behavioral bibliotherapy: A review of self-help behavior therapy manuals. *Psychological Bulletin*, 1978, *85*, 1–23.

Hedberg, A. G., & Campbell, L. M. A comparison of four behavioral treatment approaches to alcoholism. *Journal of Behaviour Therapy and Experimental Psychiatry*, 1974, *5*, 251–256.

Jackson, D. M. *Personality research form manual*. New York: Research Psychologists Press, 1974.

Jellinek, E. M. *The disease concept of alcoholism*. Highland Park, N.J.: Hillhouse Press, 1960.

Kiresuk, T. J. *Measuring treatment outcome with goal attainment scaling*. Paper presented at the annual meeting of the American Psychological Association, Honolulu, September 1972.

Levinson, T. Controlled drinking in the alcoholic—a search for common features. In J. S. Madden, R. Walker, & W. H. Kenyon (Ed.), *Alcoholism and drug dependence: A multidisciplinary approach*. New York: Plenum Press, 1977.

Lovibond, S. H. Use of behavior modification in the reduction of alcohol-related road accidents. In T. Thompson & W. S. Dockens, 3rd. (Ed.), *Applications of behavior modification*. New York: Academic Press, 1975.

Lovibond, S. H., & Caddy, G. Discriminated aversive control in the moderation of alcoholics' drinking behavior. *Behavior Therapy*, 1970, *1*, 437–444.

Marlatt, G. A. The Drinking Profile: A questionnaire for the behavioral assessment of alcoholism. In E. J. Mash & L. G. Terdal (Ed.), *Behavior therapy assessment: Diagnosis, design, and evaluation*. New York: Springer, 1976.

Matthews, D. B., & Miller, W. R. Estimating blood alcohol concentration: Two computer programs and their applications in therapy and research. *Addictive Behaviors*, 1979, *4*, 55–60.

McMullen, S., & Rosen, R. C. Self-administered masturbation training in the treatment of primary orgasmic dysfunction. *Journal of Consulting and Clinical Psychology*, 1979, *47*, 912–918.

McNair, D. M., Lorr, M., & Droppelman, L. F. *Manual for the Profile of Mood States*. San Diego, Calif.: Educational and Industrial Testing Service, 1971.

Miller, W. R. Behavioral treatment of problem drinkers: A comparative outcome study of three controlled drinking therapies. *Journal of Consulting and Clinical Psychology*, 1978, *46*, 74–86. (a)

Miller, W. R. *Effectiveness of nonprescription therapies for problem drinkers*. Paper presented at the annual meeting of the American Psychological Association, Toronto, August 1978. (ERIC Document Reproduction Service No. ED 166 612) (b)

Miller, W. R., & Caddy, G. R. Abstinence and controlled drinking in the treatment of problem drinkers. *Journal of Studies on Alcohol,* 1977, *38,* 986–1003.

Miller, W. R., Gribskov, C. J., & Mortell, R. L. Effectiveness of a self-control manual for problem drinkers with and without therapist contact. *International Journal of the Addictions,* 1981, *16,* 1247–1254.

Miller, W. R., & Hester, R. K. Treating the problem drinker: Modern approaches. In W. R. Miller (Ed.), *The addictive behaviors: Treatment of alcoholism, drug abuse, smoking, and obesity.* Oxford: Pergamon Press, 1980.

Miller, W. R., & Joyce, M. A. Prediction of abstinence, controlled drinking, and heavy drinking outcomes following behavioral self-control training. *Journal of Consulting and Clinical Psychology,* 1979, *47,* 773–775.

Miller, W. R., & Muñoz, R. F. *How to control your drinking.* Englewood Cliffs, N.J.: Prentice-Hall, 1976.

Miller, W. R., Pechacek, R. F., & Hamburg, S. Group behavior therapy for problem drinkers. *International Journal of the Addictions,* 1981, *16,* 827–837.

Miller, W. R., & Saucedo, C. F. Neuropsychological impairment and brain damage in problem drinkers: A critical review. In C. J. Golden, J. A. Mosts, Jr., J. A. Coffman, W. R. Miller, F. Strider, & B. Graber (Ed.), *Behavioral effects of neurological disorders.* New York: Grune & Stratton, in press.

Miller, W. R., & Taylor, C. A. Relative effectiveness of bibliotherapy, individual and group self-control training in the treatment of problem drinkers. *Addictive Behaviors,* 1980, *5,* 13–24.

Miller, W. R., Taylor, C. A., & West, J. C. Focused versus broad-spectrum behavior therapy for problem drinkers. *Journal of Consulting and Clinical Psychology,* 1980, *48,* 590–601.

National Council on Alcoholism, Criteria Committee. Criteria for the diagnosis of alcoholism. *American Journal of Psychiatry,* 1972, *129,* 127–135.

Ogborne, A. C., Annis, H. M., & Miller, W. R. Discriminant analysis and the selection of patients for controlled drinking programs: A methodological note. *Journal of Clinical Psychology,* 1981, *38,* 213–216.

Orford. J. A comparison of alcoholics whose drinking is totally uncontrolled and those whose drinking is mainly controlled. *Behaviour Research and Therapy,* 1973, *11,* 565–576.

Orford, J., Oppenheimer, E., & Edwards, G. Abstinence or control: The outcome for excessive drinkers two years after consultation. *Behaviour Research and Therapy,* 1976, *14,* 409–418.

Pattison, E. M., Sobell, M. B., & Sobell, L. C. *Emerging concepts of alcohol dependence.* New York: Springer, 1977.

Polich, J. M., Armor, D. L., & Braiker, H. B. *The course of alcoholism: Four years after treatment.* Santa Monica, Calif.: Rand Corporation, 1980.

Pomerleau, O., Pertschuk, M., Adkins, D., & d'Aquili, E. Treatment for middle-income problem drinkers, In P. E. Nathan, G. A. Marlatt, & T. Løberg (Eds.), *Alcoholism: New directions in behavioral research and treatment.* New York: Plenum Press, 1978.

Popham, R. E., & Schmidt, W. Some factors affecting the likelihood of moderate drinking by treated alcoholics. *Journal of Studies on Alcohol,* 1976, *37,* 868–882.

Reyes, E., & Miller, W. R. Serum gamma-glutamyl transpeptidase as a diagnostic aid in problem drinkers. *Addictive Behaviors,* 1980, *5,* 59–65.

Rosen, G. M. The development and use of nonprescription behavior therapies. *American Psychologist,* 1976, *31,* 139–141.

Rotter, J. B. Generalized expectancies for internal versus external control of reinforcement. *Psychological Monographs,* 1966, *80,* (1, Whole No. 609).

Sanchez-Craig, M. Random assignment to abstinence or controlled drinking in a cognitive-behavioral program: Short-term effects on drinking behavior. *Addictive Behaviors*, 1980, 5, 35–39.

Schaefer, H. H. Twelve-month follow-up of behaviorally trained ex-alcoholic social drinkers. *Behavior Therapy*, 1972, 3, 286–289.

Schmidt. M. M. *Amount of therapist contact and outcome in a multimodal depression treatment program.* Unpublished doctoral dissertation, University of New Mexico, 1981.

Selzer, M. L. The Michigan Alcoholism Screening Test: The quest for a new diagnostic instrument. *American Journal of Psychiatry*, 1971, *127*, 1653–1658.

Smart, R. G. Characteristics of alcoholics who drink socially after treatment. *Alcoholism: Clinical and Experimental Research*, 1978, 2, 49–52.

Sobell, M. B., & Sobell, L. C. Individualized behavior therapy for alcoholics. *Behavior Therapy*, 1973, 4, 49–72.

Vogler, R. E., Compton, J. V., & Weissbach, T. A. Integrated behavior change techniques for alcoholism. *Journal of Consulting and Clinical Psychology*, 1975, *43*, 233–243.

Vogler, R. E., Weissbach, T. A., & Compton, J. V. Learning techniques for alcohol abuse. *Behaviour Research and Therapy*, 1977, *15*, 31–38. (a)

Vogler, R. E., Weissbach, T. A., Compton, J. V., & Martin, G. T. Integrated behavior change techniques for problem drinkers in the community. *Journal of Consulting and Clinical Psychology*, 1977, *45*, 267–279. (b)

Zeiss, R. A. Self-directed treatment for premature ejaculation. *Journal of Consulting and Clinical Psychology*, 1978, *46*, 1234–1241.

4

Behavioral Treatment of Outpatient Problem Drinkers
Five Clinical Case Studies

NORA E. NOEL, LINDA C. SOBELL,
TONY CELLUCCI, TED D. NIRENBERG,
and MARK B. SOBELL

1. INTRODUCTION

For years the field of alcoholism has been influenced by traditional concepts of alcohol dependence (Pattison, Sobell, & Sobell, 1977). Consequently, treatment interventions have focused primarily on alcohol abusers who are physically dependent on alcohol (gamma alcoholics). Most treatment has also been of an inpatient or residential nature and has focused exclusively on abstinence, rarely addressing other areas of life or health functioning. In the last decade, however, epidemiologic studies have suggested that chronic alcoholics represent only a small proportion of those who have serious drinking problems, and that the number of individuals whose drinking behavior is

NORA E. NOEL • Problem Drinkers Project, Butler Hospital, Providence, Rhode Island 02906.   LINDA C. SOBELL • Clinical Institute, Addiction Research Foundation, and University of Toronto, Toronto, Ontario, Canada M5S 2S1.   TONY CELLUCCI • North Carolina Wesleyan College, Rocky Mount, North Carolina 27801.   TED D. NIRENBERG • Veterans Administration Medical Center, Davis Park, Providence, Rhode Island 02908.   MARK B. SOBELL • Clinical Institute, Addiction Research Foundation, and University of Toronto, Toronto, Ontario, Canada M5S 2S1.

problematic and high risk, but who are not physically addicted, is quite large (Cahalan & Room, 1974).

While outpatient alcohol treatment programs offer several advantages over inpatient settings (Sobell & Sobell, 1978), until recently there have been few such programs. Further, despite the large number of problem drinkers, little has been written about this population, probably because relevant treatment services have been seriously lacking. This chapter presents several short but comprehensive case descriptions of the clinical treatment of outpatient problem drinkers. Multiple clinical case studies are included to allow description of a variety of behavioral treatment strategies and interventions which can be used with this population. The five cases presented were selected from the clinical experiences of each of the five authors, although all of the treatment was conducted at one facility.

Since several cases are presented, readers will be provided with a generic description of the admission, assessment, and treatment planning and development processes that were used. The five clients described in this chapter participated in voluntary outpatient treatment at the Dede Wallace Center Alcohol Program in Nashville, Tennessee. The program, which was part of a comprehensive community mental health center, was developed in 1975 and had a multimodal assessment and treatment orientation (Sobell & Sobell, 1980).

Compared to clients in most alcohol treatment programs, the clients in our program generally had less overall health impairment. Fully 70% lacked sufficient clinical symptomatology to warrant a diagnosis of alcohol dependence as described in DSM-III (American Psychiatric Association, 1980); rather, they were diagnosed as alcohol abusers (Sobell & Sobell, 1980). In fact, only one case in this chapter has a diagnosis of alcohol-dependence. Typically, the majority of clients in the program were younger, had more intact families and careers, and had less severe alcohol-related dysfunction than chronic alcoholics. There are several advantages in working with this population: (1) Significant others can be involved in treatment; (2) Maintaining one's intactness—social, physical, or economic—can be an important source of motivation for changing behavior; (3) Clients have more available resources; and hence, (4) clients have sources of reinforcement other than just drinking-related experiences. Thus, a greater variety of treatment alternatives can be generated.

Since alcohol abuse frequently pervades many aspects of a drinker's life, a comprehensive assessment of each client's overall situation was conducted. In most assessment processes therapists are dependent on clients' self-reports. In general, the evidence suggests that when alcohol abusers are interviewed in a clinical setting and when alcohol free, we can have confidence in their self-reports of drinking and related behaviors (Sobell &

Sobell, 1981). In addition to self-reports the clinical assessment was based on a convergence of evidence: the client's self-reports, report from significant others, therapist's observations of the client, clinical and official records, and such physical and mental health indices at intake as liver functioning, cognitive functioning, and medical problems. Examples of the detail and thoroughness of the assessment procedures are reflected in the treatment plan descriptions for each case presentation.

For all clients a functional analysis was performed to identify antecedents and consequences of their drinking. The following information was also obtained:

1. Specific quantities of alcohol consumed on a regular basis
2. Usual and unusual drinking patterns
3. Where and with whom drinking occurred
4. Predominant mood states and circumstances antecedent and consequent to the drinking
5. Indicators of tolerance and dependence—the most alcohol ever consumed in one 24-hour period, highest recorded blood-alcohol concentration
6. History of alcohol withdrawal symptoms
7. Past or present indications of acute or chronic liver dysfunction
8. Possible difficulties clients might encounter in initially refraining from problem drinking while in treatment (e.g., clients who have never experienced more than a few days of abstinence or whose present environment is extremely conducive to excessive drinking might find it very difficult to abstain initially from alcohol, and consequently their compliance with other aspects of treatment may be jeopardized)
9. The risk the client's present environment posed for problem drinking (e.g., drinking occurs on the job; most of one's weekend social activities involve drinking; all of one's friends drink heavily; the primary social activity is meeting with friends at the neighborhood tavern)

Part of the initial assessment also included an in-depth health screening and evaluation. The main components of the health assessment were (1) a breath test at admission to determine the client's BAC, (2) a blood pressure check at admission and continuous monitoring of abnormalities, (3) a general health history questionnaire, (4) a profile of past and present use of prescribed and nonprescribed drugs, and (5) a blood test to assess general physical health and liver function (SGOT and GGTP levels). All significant past medical and psychiatric treatment records were requested, and the entire health assessment was reviewed by a physician. When appropriate, and with physician approval, medication and treatment of significant medical problems were included in the overall plan (see Case No. 2). Clients were referred for further medical assessment as indicated.

Based on the assessment, an individualized treatment plan was developed for each client. The treatment plan contained both long-term and short-term goals, with all goals and interventions operationally defined. Long-term goals typically represented the aim and ultimate purpose of therapy. Since long-term goals often required a significant investment of effort by the client, they were partitioned into several short-term goals defining more immediate treatment objectives. Short-term goals are usually objectives that are easily operationalized, measureable, and relate in a step-wise progression to the long-term goal. Short-term goals allow progress to be evaluated more frequently and provide more opportunities to reinforce clients for behavior changes. As reflected in the treatment plans of Case Nos. 1 and 4, minimally demanding and easily accomplished goals were initially deliniated, and only after these small goals were accomplished were larger goals considered.

In all cases, client involvement in the treatment planning process was stressed. The process of treatment planning and development was continuous and dynamic involving frequent updating and revision. Case No. 1 is an example of a treatment plan that evolved as the client's problems and abilities changed. (For further discussion of the differential treatment planning approach, see Sobell, Sobell, & Nirenberg, 1982.)

As illustrated in Case No. 3, the principle of shaping can also be used to facilitate the termination of treatment. If a client is compliant with treatment and is making progress, then the therapeutic relationship is probably positively reinforcing to the client. In this regard, two questions arise. First, will terminating the relationship engender difficulties for the client? Second, can the client adequately function without treatment? While empirical evidence is lacking, one way of diminishing the reward value of the therapeutic relationship without impairing client functioning is to terminate treatment gradually. Phasing clients out of treatment also allows for resumption of more frequent scheduling should problems arise, as well as providing a performance-based criterion for ending treatment.

Different treatment strategies obviously necessitate different costs for clients, depending on their lifestyle, values, and resources. Consequently, whenever possible, effective and least restrictive treatment goals (Sobell & Sobell, 1978; Sobell *et al.*, 1982) were chosen (i.e., goals which required the least total change in the client's life). For example, while an effective treatment might be forever avoiding drinking situations, learning to say no to offers of alcoholic beverages is certainly a much less restrictive treatment strategy.

A final but crucial aspect of treatment planning concerned developing strategies for dealing with future problems. While new problems cannot be addressed until they arise, consideration was given to the general idea of recognizing and dealing with potential problems. With drinking behavior in particular, it was stressed that a serious relapse might be avoided if the client could identify the onset of abusive drinking. Throughout treatment we discussed with our clients the likelihood that problems would arise in the future and stressed that the critical factor was how those problems were managed. As noted in the treatment description section for Case Nos. 1, 2, and 4, such planning and discussion of problem areas and possible relapses helped prevent full-blown relapses and consequently provided for early intervention. Self-monitoring of drinking behavior (Pomerleau & Adkins, 1980; Sobell & Sobell, 1973), a commonly used treatment technique with our clients, also provided an opportunity for the client and therapist to discuss *any* ongoing drinking and to further identify early in treatment possible high-risk drinking problems.

The above description provides a general account of the clinical assessment and treatment planning processes that were used with all clients in the treatment program, and thus with the five cases in this chapter. Any additional or different processes are noted in the respective case descriptions. Each case presentation contains (a) a short clinical history of alcohol and nonalcohol related aspects of the case; (b) the diagnosis as determined by the DSM III (APA, 1980); (c) a detailed treatment plan listing all the goals and interventions associated with the case; and (d) a detailed description of the course of clinical treatment. Since the five cases were purposely selected for each to have a distinct clinical import, the treatment descriptions have a primary focus on the unique aspects(s) of each case. Following the case studies, concluding comments on the cases are presented.

2. CASE NO. 1 (THERAPIST L.C.S.)

2.1. Case History

In November 1977, this 29-year-old white male was referred by his employer for treatment of a drinking problem. At the time of referral, the client's wife of 2 years was divorcing him. An earlier marriage had lasted a similarly short time. The second marriage was being dissolved because of the client's drinking problem, his general irresponsibility, and, as he described it, his passivity within the relationship. He had a child from each marriage. The client acknowledged a serious drinking problem dating back 9 years to when he was in the Navy. Prior to entering treatment, he had received his first drunk-driving (DUI) arrest. Indications of high tolerance to ethanol included a self-reported consumption of 1 quart of spirits in a 24-hour period and a BAC of 290 mg% at the time of his arrest. The client reported two hospitalizations for drinking: In 1968 he spent 10 days in a Naval hospital, and just prior to his present treatment he was hospitalized for alcohol-related withdrawal symptoms—hallucinations and severe psychomotor agitation. Prior alcohol-related treatment included sporadic attendance at AA meetings for 6 months in 1973 and one visit to a marriage counselor in 1977. In the year prior to this treatment, the client reported daily consumption of about a dozen 12-oz. beers and use of antianxiety drugs.

The client had done poorly in school and after 1 year of college withdrew to work full-time. His longest period of continuous employment was the 2 years on his present job. Even so, he had been absent from work 10 days in the last year because of drinking. His job as a file clerk was minimally demanding and did not pay well. While the client was not satisfied with his occupation, he had no alternative vocational preferences or skills, He described his childhood as happy and his three siblings as fairly successful in their careers; however, he referred to himself as the black sheep in the family. At intake, he was in good health, with no significant health problems.

2.2. Diagnosis

Alcohol dependence, continuous (DSM-III: 303.91)

2.3. Treatment Plan: Goals and Interventions

1. Reduce drinking to a nonproblem level (abstinence)
   A. Functional analysis of drinking and related behaviors.
   B. Disulfiram (250 mg QD) as needed: self-monitored and program-monitored (at the client's request).
   C. Self-monitoring of urges and thoughts of drinking via written cards.
   D. Self-monitoring of *any* drinking via weekly reports to the therapist at each session.
   E. Relapse-prevention training.
2. Avoid drunk-driving arrests. Use portable breath alcohol testers when considering driving after any alcohol consumption; if reading indicates a level of legal intoxication, then (a) walk home, if possible, (b) get a friend to drive you home, or (c) take a taxi.
3. Improved self-efficacy: Decrease self-expectancies of failure

A. Functional analysis of failure experiences—real or imagined.
   (1) Delineate antecedents and consequences of past failure experiences.
   (2) Delineate possible behaviors the client avoids as a result of labeling something a failure.
B. Functional analysis of past risk-taking behaviors.
C. Cognitive restructuring.
   (1) Set up and test hypotheses about one's self-efficacy. (To promote a sense of accomplishment and competence, first identify and accomplish small, easily attainable goals, and then gradually deal with more difficult goals.)
   (2) Shape in desired success experiences (undertake tasks likely to lead to successful outcomes): At each therapy session monitor accomplishments and gains from the previous session, and set new goals for the next session.
   (3) Decrease negative self-statements.
       (a) Therapist will monitor negative self-statements in therapy sessions.
       (b) Client will monitor the number of negative self-statements he makes via self-monitoring cards.
       (c) Self-reinforcement and therapist reinforcement for positive self-statements.
D. Skills training to deal with daily problem situations as they develop in therapy.
   (1) Role playing, *in vivo* rehearsal, therapeutic instructions, modeling, problem solving, assertiveness training.
   (2) Extend learned skills to novel situations outside of therapy.
E. Bibliotherapy for assertive training: *I Can If I Want To* (by A. A. Lazarus).
   (1) Read one to two sections of the book each week; discuss sections relevant to the client's problems at the next therapy session.
   (2) For relevant sections, the client will complete homework assignments in the book.

4. Attain financial stability and independence
   A. Prior to each therapy session, pay all bills due each week, and handle other related financial matters (e.g., respond to past-due notices from credit companies, call creditors regarding payment status).
      (1) Maintain a monthly ledger of all bills, their due dates, payment schedule, and current balance.
      (2) At each therapy session, review all bills paid; if bills are

unpaid, the client agrees to write out checks at the end of the therapy session and mail the payments immediately thereafter.

B. Balance checkbook monthly.

C. Cancel credit cards.

D. Work overtime to pay off outstanding debts more quickly.

E. Use next year's income tax refund to pay off additional bills, especially those where interest accrues on the unpaid balance.

F. Have telephone disconnected until back telephone bill is paid; when telephone is in service, make no long distance calls.

G. Open a savings account and deposit $25 per month; this money will be used for personal reinforcement (e.g., dinner at a restaurant, clothes) each time a major bill is paid off.

5. Evaluate and develop career opportunities

   A. Evaluate interests, potential, and feasibility of pursuing another career.

      (1) Complete the Strong Vocational Interest Test.

      (2) Vocational counseling at the Veterans Administration Center.

      (3) Career planning and counseling at a local state college.

      (4) Check with employer about feasibility of taking a course during working hours.

      (5) Pursue VA educational benefits.

   B. Enroll and perform satisfactorily in a technical training program at a state college (after first determining the appropriateness of the program).

      (1) Attend all classes.

      (2) Complete all class assignments promptly.

      (3) Schedule an adequate amount of weekly study time.

      (4) Pass all courses with a minimum grade of C.

      (5) After 1 year, client and the college's career counseling staff will evaluate his status and satisfaction with the program.

   C. Complete 2-year training program.

      (1) Decrease work from full-time to part-time to complete the training program.

      (2) Get a part-time job on weekends to supplement income.

      (3) Attend all classes, complete all assignments promptly, and schedule study time.

6. Reduce dependence on therapy without disrupting treatment gains

   A. Gradually lengthen intersession interval while monitoring the client's progress.

   B. Client will telephone the therapist if a crisis develops.

2.4. Treatment Description

This client attended 93 individual outpatient therapy sessions over a 30-month period, missing only two appointments without prior notice. The unique aspect of this case is the length of time this client was seen in outpatient treatment and the comprehensiveness of the treatment plan. Treatment goals and interventions for this client were modified over time; as therapy progressed, new interventions were developed and implemented as necessary. Further, as the therapist gained additional knowledge about the client, and as the client successfully accomplished initial short-term goals, more elaborate treatment interventions were incorporated into the plan.

Initially the client reported "a general feeling of inadequacy and lack of accomplishment." However, the initial clinical assessment of the client suggested he was competent both verbally and intellectually but had very few positive experiences after high school. Also, his completion of various tasks had often been retarded due to drinking. The client was generally impatient and disorganized in his daily affairs, had no plan for paying off accumulated financial obligations, and was dissatisfied with his present job but had given no thought to alternative careers.

A shaping strategy, reinforcing incremental approximations to the long-term goal, was used to accomplish several of the treatment goals. Since the client described himself as generally inadequate and ineffective in managing his daily activities, early in treatment *very small* but highly attainable short-term goals were used to provide the client a history of "success" experiences. As the client accomplished these goals, and was thus reinforced for his behavior changes, new and more difficult—but *attainable*—goals were pursued. Since space does not permit a description of how each goal was accomplished, two of the goals will be used to illustrate the procedure of shaping. The other treatment goals and interventions for this client are outlined in the treatment plan.

Prior to therapy the client had repeatedly dropped in and out of college but had never completed much course work. The initial assessment suggested that the client's heavy drinking usually precluded regular attendance at classes and the completion of courses. Further assessment (i.e., career counseling, the Strong Vocational Interest Test, available funds and time) indicated that the client could probably successfully complete a technical training program. The client's interests and testing suggested that he train to be a medical records librarian. Before the client could enroll in a training program, it seemed necessary that he first demonstrate to himself that he could successfully compete in school. Thus, the first incremental goal was to attend all classes for a given course. A nonthreatening course—typing—was chosen. The goal was not achieving a certain grade but simply *attending all classes.*

Although this took several months, eventually the client was convinced that he could finish a course and even receive a good grade. (The client took disulfiram during this time.) Next, the client enrolled in two courses related to his training program. At this point, besides attending all classes, the goal was to set aside a specific amount of study time each week. The client did this, and while he had some trepidation about his grades, he finished the semester with an A and a B in the two courses. Through these successive experiences, the client came to evaluate himself as able to complete course work successfully and get above-average grades. After his 1st year in the program, the client independently decided to enroll in college full-time and work part-time. The remainder of the vocational goals and treatment interventions are specified in the aforementioned treatment plan.

Through similar shaping procedures, the client became financially stable by paying off nearly $1,000 indebtedness. Using the interventions listed in the treatment plan, it took nearly $1\frac{1}{2}$ years to achieve the goal of financial stability. However, smaller accomplishments (i.e., reducing the amount owed on each bill, paying off bills with interest charges first, seeing one or two of the small bills paid off, obviating calls by creditors) were evident from week to week. Lastly, one of the clearest ways that the client received incremental reinforcement for behavior changes was through maintaining a ledger which showed the amount of the original debt, the amount owing at the beginning of the month, the amount paid each month, and the amount due the following month. When last seen in treatment (months after paying off all of his outstanding debts), the client had continued to be financially responsible. With this client the process of shaping in success experiences was accomplished by asking the client to generate and test hypotheses about himself. In this regard, structuring initial goals so that they are easily achieved is critical to the successful testing of hypotheses about oneself.

Another major treatment focus was the client's lack of assertiveness in situations in which he felt inadequate (e.g., talking with bill collectors about past-due bills; asking his employer for a long-overdue raise; dealing with an insurance adjuster on a claim where he felt more money was due). The treatment involved repeated role playing and role reversal. Over time, the client became quite proficient at demonstrating assertive behavior when necessary; consequently, he came to view himself as capable of handling situations which he had previously avoided.

As the client successfully accomplished treatment goals, it was further expected that the skills learned within the treatment context would generalize to other situations. This, in fact, occurred. Decision making and handling of routine life problems became easier for the client, so that near the end of treatment he was handling situations without clinical intervention or discussion (e.g., deciding to enroll in school full-time; discussing with his employer the need to work part-time; contacting the VA when his benefit check did not arrive as expected; not drinking after someone damaged his car; ending a relationship with a girlfriend without adverse consequences).

One further aspect of treatment involved repeated discussions with the client about ways he could cope with relapses. More specifically, he had previously interpreted the onset of drinking as a personal failure and an additional reason for continued drinking. However, during treatment he came to realize that while a return to drinking was regrettable, he could minimize the impact of an episode by terminating the drinking as early as possible. Throughout the 2½ years of treatment the client never approached his pretreatment level of dysfunctional daily drinking; he also stopped using antianxiety drugs after entering treatment. There were, however, several isolated single evenings of heavy drinking (five to eight 12-oz. beers). On several occasions throughout treatment the client requested and used disulfiram, once taking it for 6 months. When not using disulfiram, the client self-monitored and reported all drinking to the therapist at the next session.

In summary, treatment concentrated on increasing the client's self-efficacy through a carefully designed incremental-success approach to goal attainment. While cognitive behavior therapy is a relatively new approach and still difficult to operationalize, this case reflects some aspects of cognitive restructuring. Through purposeful and agreed-upon behavioral changes, the client's self-efficacy improved. Changes in novel situations outside of the treatment setting were also observed.

3. CASE NO. 2 (THERAPIST T.D.N.)

3.1. Case History

This 19-year-old single white male was court-referred for treatment following his fourth DUI arrest (at last arrest, BAC was 250 mg%). He also reported several prior arrests for public drunkenness and for disturbing the peace. He reported a 3-year history of daily problem drinking (averaging six 12-oz. beers daily on weekdays and up to a case of 12-oz. beers daily on the weekend) with occasional periods of abstinence (longest period was the 30 days following his last DUI arrest). He had several alcohol-related car accidents and frequent (biweekly) blackouts but reported no prior alcohol withdrawal symptoms. Previous treatment had included a brief contact with AA and outpatient counseling at a local hospital.

Although the client was enrolled in a technical school for computer programming, when he began treatment his school attendance was sporadic. Although he worked occasionally, his parents assisted him financially while he attended school. They also consistently bailed him out of various difficulties. The client's family history was unremarkable. His parents' marriage was described as good, although his father had been seriously ill for about 1 year. He reported that his childhood had been happy. His married sister (age 26) and unmarried brother (age 28) had successful careers and no alcohol problems. His father, a moderately successful builder, and his mother, a part-time secretary, frequently criticized the client for his excessive drinking, his performance in school, and his social relationships. While in treatment, the client lived with two male roommates.

3.2. Diagnosis

Alcohol abuse, continuous (DSM-III: 305.01)

3.3. Treatment Plan: Goals and Interventions

1. Reduce drinking to a nonproblem level
   A. Enforced abstinence.
      (1) Written contract specifying self-administered use of disulfiram for 60 days and general rules of treatment compliance (i.e., attendance, completion of homework assignments).
      (2) Functional analysis of drinking and related behaviors.
         (a) Self-monitoring of cravings for alcohol and their situational determinants via written daily logs.
         (b) Develop effective alcohol-refusal skills and general assertiveness training (via role playing, modeling, *in vivo* practice, and therapeutic instruction).
         (c) Increase knowledge of the effects of alcohol on behavior (e.g., driving, talking, tolerance, socializing).
      (3) Blood test to assess acute liver function.
   B. Self-imposed abstinence.
      (1) Written contract specifying no drinking for 30 days.
      (2) Continued functional anaiysis of drinking behavior.
      (3) Continue drink-refusal skills and training and general assertiveness skills training.
   C. Nonproblem drinking.
      (1) Written contract specifying drinking limits for 60 days.
      (2) Self-monitoring of drinking, cravings, and their situational determinants via written daily logs.
      (3) Modification of the topography of the client's drinking re-

sponses (e.g., decrease tendency to gulp drinks, the need to finish all drinks, drinking alone).

    (4) Introduce and encourage use of portable breath-alcohol testers when considering whether to drive after drinking.

D. Follow-up and evaluation.

    (1) Gradually increase the interval between treatment sessions (from weekly to biweekly, then from biweekly to monthly).

    (2) Monthly phone contacts for 6 months to obtain information on client's drinking behavior.

    (3) Availability of phone contacts or additional treatment if problems begin to develop.

2. Life-planning and problem-solving skills training

A. Problem-solving skills training to teach client effective behaviors to deal with daily, routine life problems.

B. Training in effective decision making: Outline projected short- and long-term consequences to make effective major life decisions so as to maximize present and future reinforcement.

3. Financial and vocational stability and independence

A. Decrease financial dependence on parents.

    (1) Learn basic budgeting skills.

    (2) Finish school and get a full-time job.

B. Clarify employment interests and job options.

    (1) Take Strong Vocational Interest Test.

    (2) Brief counseling at a local vocational technical school.

C. Job training at a vocational technical school.

D. Training in preparing a résumé and job interviewing (via modeling, role playing, therapeutic instruction, and homework assignments).

4. Improve interpersonal skills related to dating

A. Reduce anxiety in dating situations.

B. Improve the quality of heterosexual conversations via social-skills training (role playing, therapeutic instruction, *in vivo* desensitization).

3.5. Treatment Description

When the client first entered treatment, he was disillusioned with therapy because of a previous unsuccessful counseling experience at a local community hospital. Moreover, while the client disliked being court-referred to treatment because of a drunk-driving arrest (his fourth), he preferred treatment to jail. When the therapist explained the nature of the program and its orientation toward treating problem drinkers the client was particularly responsive to the possibility of nonproblem-drinking training, since he had difficulty imagining himself being abstinent for the rest of his life. Considering the client's youth and his attitude toward abstinence, it was decided to evaluate his suitability for a nonproblem-drinking treatment goal.

This case is unique because it used the principle of shaping to evaluate and accomplish a treatment goal of nonproblem drinking. Unlike reports in the literature, where nonproblem drinking has been the immediate goal of treatment, this client was asked to maintain abstinence for 3 months before considering the nonproblem-drinking training. In addition, three other major treatment goals were identified (see treatment plan). A functional analysis of the client's drinking behavior revealed that his excessive use of alcohol was associated with (1) inadequate interpersonal skills, primarily poor heterosexual skills (e.g., difficulty communicating with females, poor dating skills), and associated excessive anxiety when interacting with females, (2) a lack of adequate problem-solving skills to deal with daily problems (e.g., unable to manage his time and money and maintain his car), and (3) lack of self-direction and inadequate life-planning skills. Related problems included his unstable employment history, financial dependence on his parents, and lack of knowledge of the physical and behavioral effects of alcohol.

Based on the assessment information, the client and therapist devised a treatment plan in four phases:

1. Drug-enforced abstinence: The client would self-administer disulfiram for 2 months.
2. Self-enforced abstinence: The client would abstain from all drinking on his own (without disulfiram) for 1 month.
3. Nonproblem-drinking training: The client would receive training and feedback about appropriate nonproblem-drinking behaviors for 2 months.
4. Follow-up and evaluation: A 6-month follow-up and evaluation of the client's abilities to maintain and generalize nonproblem-drinking behaviors to his extratreatment environment.

The specific strategies used to accomplish these goals are described in the treatment plan.

Drug-enforced abstinence was used first because it gave the therapist an opportunity to observe and evaluate how the client functioned without alcohol, and to conduct problem-solving and social-skills training while the client was deprived of his most salient coping behavior, drinking. It also gave the client an opportunity to practice these skills without the interference of alcohol. In this context, disulfiram served as a time-out mechanism from the pressures of having to make decisions about drinking. This initial phase also served as an opportunity for self-reinforcement, as the client was engaging in behaviors that he enjoyed but heretofore had avoided because of drinking. During this 2-month period of weekly therapy sessions the client reported taking his disulfiram daily. In-session assessment (through role playing) and self-report measures of interpersonal skills indicated gradual improvement over sessions. Specifically, the client began socializing without drinking and exhibited improved drink-refusal skills. Additionally, during this phase the client began a new job, which led to an improved financial situation.

The self-enforced abstinence phase was intended to extend the abstinence period and demonstrate to the client that he could abstain from alcohol on his own, without disulfiram. During this phase the client reported total abstinence and exhibited continued improvement. He also reported that he felt comfortable while socializing without alcohol and proud that he could abstain from alcohol on his own, and that he had begun dating without much anxiety.

During the third phase, which lasted 2 months, the client was seen once every other week for nonproblem-drinking training and evaluation. Throughout this phase the client continued to self-monitor all drinking behavior and cravings to drink. The client was instructed to drink no more than $\frac{1}{2}$ oz. of pure ethanol a day for the first 2 weeks to a total weekly maximum of 1 oz. pure ethanol. The drink limit was increased to a maximum of 1 oz. of pure ethanol per day over the next 4 weeks (to a total weekly maximum of 2 oz. pure ethanol), and no more than 2 oz. pure ethanol per day thereafter (to a total weekly maximum of 4 oz. pure ethanol). During this last period the client twice exceeded his daily limit; he drank $2\frac{1}{2}$ and 3 oz. of pure ethanol, respectively. The therapist did not censure the client when he reported exceeding the drinking limits; instead these reports were viewed as providing an opportunity for further functional analysis of problem-drinking situations followed by a general review of problem solving, social skills, and nonproblem-drinking skills training. They also promoted discussion of relapse to problem drinking, including the early identification of relapse and techniques to limit its severity.

For clients who successfully engage in a target behavior during treatment, the critical question is whether the behaviors are maintained and generalized after formal treatment. In this case, a 6-month follow-up was used to evaluate how successfully the behavior of nonproblem drinking had generalized to the client's extratreatment environment. During this phase the client was seen on three occasions and was also contacted monthly by telephone to check on his progress. The client reported continued improvement and no episodes of drinking beyond the agreed-upon goals. He was dating weekly, with only occasional feelings of anxiety, and although he had not yet found a steady girlfriend, he was satisfied with his heterosexual relationship skills and situation. Finally, he continued to work, and when last contacted he was about to begin vocational training to improve his present employment status.

4. CASE NO. 3 (THERAPIST M.B.S.)

4.1. Case History

The client, a 49-year-old white male with 2 years of college, entered treatment voluntarily. He reported a 4-year history of problems with alcohol and had been hospitalized briefly on two occasions at the VA hospital during the year prior to treatment. He felt that the VA program was designed to benefit physically addicted alcoholics and only stayed for 5 days each time. He reported one arrest for public drunkenness and no history of alcohol-related withdrawal symptoms. He had attended a few AA meetings but felt they "didn't really help me." His wife of 32 years, however, regularly attended Al-Anon meetings. The client's wife had recently threatened divorce if he did not stop drinking.

The client had not been able to work for the last 11 years because of a permanently disabling back injury resulting from an industrial accident. Because of the injury, pain medication (usually Darvon) was prescribed. While the client's drinking was episodic and limited to several beers on any given day, the alcohol was synergistic with the medication and consequently impaired his functioning when he drank. The amount of his disability pension was directly related to the number of dependents he supported, and his pension was about to be substantially reduced because his youngest daughter was getting married and would be leaving home. Three major problems were identified at the initial assessment: (1) episodic drinking related to chronic back pain, (2) pending financial difficulties, and (3) marital disharmony related to the drinking.

4.2. Diagnosis

Alcohol abuse, episodic (DSM-III: 305.02), and marital problem (V61.10)

4.3. Treatment Plan: Goals and Interventions

1. Reduce drinking to a nonproblem level (abstinence)
   A. Disulfiram (250 mg QD) until marital problems are resolved to mutual satisfaction.
   B. Couples therapy.

       (1) Functional analysis of drinking behavior.

       (2) Functional analysis of how drinking relates to the couple's relationship.

   C. After marital relationship problems are resolved, discontinue disulfiram in favor of self-enforced abstinence.

2. Evaluate and develop ways of assuring financial stability after the pension is reduced

   A. Couples therapy: Itemize financial assets and liabilities in order of importance.

   B. Reciprocal contracting for specific behavior changes.

   C. Structured home discussions with mutual agreement on all major purchases and debt repayment.

3. Increase number of conjoint activities

   A. Structured home discussions on planning mutually agreeable activities.

   B. Couples therapy: Discuss planned and completed activities.

4. Increase sensitivity of client and spouse to each other's perceived needs and problems

   A. Structured home discussions on assigned topics (e.g., each other's strengths).

   B. Couples therapy: Examine inaccurate perceptions and inferences, and negotiate reciprocally rewarding resolutions to disagreements, using therapist feedback and supervision.

5. Decrease significance of therapy without disrupting treatment gains

   A. Gradually increase emphasis on home assignments and self-scheduled structured home discussions.

   B. Gradually lengthen intersession interval while monitoring marital relationship and client's drinking behavior.

4.4. Treatment Description

When the client first entered treatment, disulfiram was prescribed and he was assigned to a social-skills training group which he attended nine times. He requested additional therapy, and after four assessment sessions (three individual and one conjoint) he was assigned to a new primary therapist for couples therapy. The course of the couples therapy, amounting to 41 sessions over $2\frac{1}{2}$ years, is the focus of this case report. The treatment goal of abstinence from alcohol was selected because of the danger of drinking while taking analgesic medication, and the client's wife's emphatic assertion that *any* drinking by her husband was highly objectionable. There are four noteworthy aspects of this case: (1) the use of marital contracting, (2) the use of structured discussions to facilitate meaningful couples interactions, (3) the design of behavioral interventions to be compatible with the spouse's continuing involvement in Al-Anon, and (4) the application of shaping principles in the termination of treatment.

Early in therapy, two major problems required immediate attention. The first was financial—the client's disability pension was to be reduced by $300 per month because of their youngest daughter's forthcoming marriage. When they entered treatment the couple used the client's disability pension check to pay for all routine expenses (e.g., house payments, car insurance). His wife operated a small day-care business in their home and put most of her limited profits into a savings account. She steadfastly refused to help her husband with their basic expenses, attributing her stance to the Al-Anon philosophy that she should make provisions for her own financial independence should her husband continue to drink. She did acknowledge, however, that the pending financial crisis was not related to her husband's behavior, and she knew that if he pursued other means of obtaining funds he might lose his disability pension.

The second major problem was the couple's inability to discuss family problems. Their communication deficiency was evident early in therapy (based on observations of their interactions in therapy sessions and tape recordings of discussions held at home). In particular, each partner tended to blame the other for current problems or claim the other was unwilling to make any changes.

A basic issue was how the client's wife could help meet their living expenses while maintaining an independent financial base for herself. The problem was further complicated when the client, claiming to be frustrated by his wife's failure to help with their financial obligations, stopped taking his disulfiram, drank several beers, and was arrested for driving under the influence of alcohol (his BAC was 110 mg%, slightly above the legal limit of 100 mg%). His wife refused to pay his bail or help get their car out of impoundment. In therapy, this situation (clearly a consequence of his drinking) was contrasted with their financial needs (mostly not related to his drinking), and his wife came to recognize that certain problems would exist even if the client had never had a drinking problem. Thus, she was able to differentiate concerns about her husband's drinking from concerns about other aspects of their relationship. Further, she agreed that while she needed to protect her own welfare, responsibility for their routine living expenses was a mutual obligation.

Shortly after the client was released from jail and resumed use of disulfiram, his pension check was reduced—a month earlier than anticipated. Consequently, there was an immediate need for action. However, in light of the client's recent intoxicated escapade (which had increased their indebtedness), his wife was extremely apprehensive about making financial concessions, since she felt it was possible that she would file for divorce. A success-ful resolution of this issue was suggested by the wife, who stated that she would be willing to contribute to family expenses if their house (their major capital asset) was transferred to her sole ownership. Both parties agreed to this course of action, and the following contract was negotiated.

CONTRACTED BEHAVIORS

1. The client agrees to immediately file a quit-claim deed in order to transfer title of the house to his wife, thus providing her with more financial security.
2. The wife agrees to provide her husband with her day-care profits, minus a mutually agreed-upon 10% donation to her church.
3. The client agrees to maintain a written family budget, itemizing all income and expenditures; the wife would have regular access to these records.
4. Both parties agree to make no further purchases on credit.
5. The client agrees to seek opportunities to generate extra income, provided that such activities would not jeopardize his pension.

CONSEQUENCES FOR CONTRACT VIOLATIONS

1. The client agrees that his wife would have no further obligation to provide him with any revenue if he violates the contract.
2. Both parties recognize that a family financial crisis would ensue if the client's wife violates the contract.

The financial contract produced an immediate resolution to the im-pending crisis. In fact, the couple later reported that in the past each tended to ventilate financial frustrations on the other, despite knowing that the problems were beyond either's control. The couple also agreed to engage in structured discussions, which were practiced during therapy sessions and at home and basically involved agreeing, by contract, to schedule explicit time-limited periods (e.g., 15 minutes) when designated topics would be discussed without interruption and in accordance with specified guidelines. In particu-lar, each party agreed not to engage in certain specific behaviors (e.g., raising irrelevant past problems, grimacing when the other spoke) so that the discus-sion would remain calm, focused, and oriented toward a mutual resolution. If none was forthcoming, the topic was addressed at the next therapy session. The guidelines for interactions were largely based on their suggestions and on observations of their interaction styles during therapy sessions.

As the intersession intervals were lengthened, the couple not only re-vised and initiated new contracts themselves but also held several unplanned structured discussions. Throughout this time the client continued to take disulfiram. Approximately 1 year into the couples therapy, the client an-nounced at a therapy session that he had not taken disulfiram in the last month and wished now to assume full responsibility for his abstinence. He further stated that he had not informed his wife that he had stopped taking disulfiram because he felt her reaction would have created additional stresses for him and he wished to minimize stresses while learning to be abstinent on his own. His wife agreed that she would have been quite upset had she known, and she reluctantly agreed to accept his self imposed abstinence, making clear that if he resumed drinking their relationship would deteriorate rapidly. The client, however, did not resume drinking, and their relationship continued to improve.

Initially, couples therapy was conducted weekly: After 3 months the interval was lengthened to biweekly, then monthly for 6 months, and finally, once every 4 months. Mutually agreed-upon changes in the intersession intervals were designed to gradually eliminate the role of therapy without disrupting treatment gains. Approximately $2\frac{1}{2}$ years after beginning treatment the couple forgot a scheduled session, later saying that it was probably because they had so little to discuss in therapy. At the next session, which also was agreed would be their last session, the couple announced that they had just paid off their last remaining financial debt and had initiated a revised contract regulating how their extra revenues would be used to renovate their house. They also felt that they had no further need for structured discussions because they were now meaningfully and routinely interacting with one another.

5. CASE NO. 4 (THERAPIST N.E.N.)

5.1. Case History

This 26-year-old white unmarried male was referred by the courts following his third DUI arrest (BAC was 270 mg%). He was the youngest of seven children and a high school graduate. The client reported a 3-year history of problem drinking, with no prior history of alcohol-related withdrawal symptoms. His drinking pattern prior to treatment involved consuming 7 to 8 oz. of whiskey on weekdays and up to 1 quart of whiskey on weekends. He also reported that his drinking had never interfered with his job as a construction worker. Although he had taken disulfiram for 3 months the year prior to treatment, he resumed drinking following the deaths of his parents and a friend. He reported two major reasons for drinking: to relieve depression and to socialize at bars. The initial health history screening and evaluation identified four major health risks: (1) obesity—5 ft. 10 in. and 240 lb.; (2) uncontrolled high blood pressure and a fairly high level of serum triglycerides; (3) suspected acute liver dysfunction, as indicated by elevated SGOT and GGTP levels, possibly associated with recent heavy ethanol consumption; and (4) a family history of diabetes, heart disease, and alcohol problems.

5.2. Diagnosis

Alcohol abuse, continuous (DSM-III: 305.01)

5.3. Treatment Plan: Goals and Interventions

1. Reduce drinking to a nonproblem level (abstinence)
    A. Functional analysis of drinking and related behaviors.
    B. Disulfiram (250 mg QD) for 6 months.
        (1) Evaluate client's ability to maintain self-enforced abstinence.
        (2) Develop plans for discontinuing disulfiram.
    C. Assess high-risk situations for relapse to drinking by self-monitoring of thoughts and urges.
        (1) Evaluate and develop strategies to cope with high-risk situations.
        (2) Relapse prevention training.
2. Improved physical health
    A. Physical examination by family physician.
    B. Establish communication between therapist and client's physician regarding medical management of the client.
    C. Lower blood pressure to normal range: Take prescribed medication, stop drinking, control diet, monitor blood pressure regularly at therapy sessions, learn relaxation skills.
    D. Repeat blood test to check for continued or new abnormalities.
    E. Lose weight: Diet, exercise, stop drinking.
3. Discuss feelings related to the recent deaths of family and friend
    A. Encourage expression of grief in therapy sessions.
    B. Focus attention on bereavement as a normal reaction to death of loved ones.
4. Improve social adjustment and satisfaction
    A. Learn to share feelings with others, ask for and give support: Role playing, role reversal, modeling.
    B. Learn to express anger appropriately.
        (1) Functional analysis of the expression of anger in past and future situations.
        (2) Practice expressing anger when deemed appropriate through skills training.
    C. Evaluate relationship with women, especially current girlfriend.

5.4. Treatment Description

At the time of this writing, the client has been in treatment for 5 months and has attended 18 individual therapy sessions. Although treatment has not been completed, this case is included because it illustrates the use and importance of health screening assessment information in treatment planning.

As with many alcohol abusers, this client had incurred serious health problems, which were further exacerbated by the drinking. The identified health problems—obesity, hypertension, acute liver dysfunction, a family history of related medical problems—clearly suggested that treatment initially focus on health problems as they related (directly or indirectly) to drinking. The client's physical problems were unusually severe for his age and potentially life-threatening. Also, the client was deeply depressed about the recent deaths of his parents (his father had died from a heart attack, and his mother from a stroke and the effects of diabetes), and this highlighted the importance of his own health problems.

Although he was court-referred for treatment because of a DUI arrest, the client was not enthusiastic about being treated for a drinking problem. By focusing on the relationship between the client's health problems and his drinking behavior, the therapist was able to stimulate the client's interest and involvement in treatment. Direct and concrete feedback (i.e., blood pressure readings, laboratory results, weight) was provided to the client to stress the seriousness of his present health problems. It was hoped that if the client made health-related behavior changes, his involvement in therapy might generalize to other significant clinical problems, such as social adjustment, death of family members, and relationships with others.

Because the client was unable to abstain from alcohol, he was asked to monitor any drinking that occurred. (Daily monitoring consisted of recording on 4 × 6 index cards the date, time, place, size, and number of each drink.) Despite the fact that the therapist carefully explained the importance of self-monitoring certain behaviors, the client had great difficulty from the beginning in complying with requests for self-monitoring and self-regulating specific target behaviors. Since he was unable to maintain continued abstinence on his own, disulfiram was prescribed for 6 months. During this time the client was also asked to monitor thoughts and urges to drink. However, despite acknowledging that this information could identify possible antecedents to his drinking, he reported that such monitoring was "impossible." As a result of repeated failures to self-monitor most behaviors, the simple goal of *learning to self-monitor* was introduced. Initially, the therapist supplied all of the cards, labeling one for each day of the week. Then, through role playing and participant modeling, the client was taught how to use the cards, and even where to put them (in a shirt pocket with a pencil) so that he would not forget them.

Training this client to take his hypertension medication on a daily basis also involved elaborate procedures. Since hypertension often does not produce discernible symptoms, the client had very few reminders of his condition; consequently he often left his medication at home and was hence unable to take it during the day. The client further failed to understand that the medication controls, but does not cure, hypertension, and thus discontinued the medication after the first few normal blood pressure readings. The client's physician also needed frequent blood pressure checks on the client before a proper course of medication could be prescribed. Frequent contacts between the therapist, physician, and client resulted in the establishment of a system whereby the client associated taking the medication with brushing his teeth (disulfiram was added to this routine too). Blood pressure readings, which became a regular part of the client's therapy sessions, served as reinforcers for his successful self-regulation. Although the client lost 30 pounds during the first 5 months of treatment, no systematic attempts were made to effect weight loss.

Early in treatment, when a breach of confidentially was averted, the client developed a strong sense of trust in the therapeutic relationship. Perhaps as a result, he felt comfortable discussing more personally troubling topics (i.e., the death of his parents, relationships with women) during the therapy sessions. The supportive nature of the therapeutic relationship may also have helped the client minimize the seriousness and duration of the one drinking relapse that occurred. When the client's brother died quite suddenly (because of alcohol-related complications), the client purposely discontinued his disulfiram for 3 days to drink. However, within a few hours of taking the first drink, he called the therapist and expressed a need to talk rather than continue drinking. Rather than being interpreted as a failure experience, this drinking incident was used as a springboard for discussion of the client's need for others and for increased social contact and support.

In summary, the original focus on the client's health problems served as a vehicle for stimulating interest and involvement in therapy as well as improving the client's health. During the 5 months of treatment, the client has been abstinent, except for the single relapse noted above. He has also become quite proficient at administering his disulfiram and hypertension medication. After the first 2 months of treatment his blood pressure readings were within the normal range, and his second blood test—taken 3 months after his entry into treatment—revealed no abnormalities. According to the client, the repeated feedback of his normal blood pressure readings, normal blood test results, and weight loss served as a major reinforcer for his behavior changes. After 5 months in therapy, he is making progress in monitoring various behaviors. Since the client continues in treatment and his health problems have abated, the therapeutic focus has shifted to dealing with interpersonal issues related to drinking. A final long-term goal will be to discontinue disulfiram in favor of self-enforced abstinence.

6. CASE NO. 5 (THERAPIST T.C.)

6.1. Case History

This 32-year-old white male was court-referred for treatment after receiving his fifth DUI arrest; the last three arrests had occurred within a 2-week period. (BACs were 240 mg%, 330 mg% and 140 mg%, respectively.) This client reported a 3-year history of excessive drinking, consuming an average of six to eight 12-oz. beers daily and greater amounts on occasion (up to a case of 12-oz. beers). No alcohol-related hospitalizations or withdrawal symptoms were reported. The client reported that his drinking was associated with socializing at a particular bar, and that it helped him to reduce "nervous tension."

The client had completed college. He had once worked as an elementary school teacher, but when he entered treatment he was employed by his uncle's construction company. The client had been married once for 2 years and had one son but had been divorced for the 9 years prior to treatment.

6.2. Diagnosis

Alcohol abuse, continuous (DSM-III: 305.01)

6.3. Treatment Plan: Goals and Interventions

1. Reduce drinking to a nonproblem level
   A. Do a functional analysis of drinking and related behaviors, and assess high-risk situations for relapse to excessive drinking, with emphasis on potential consequences of such drinking.
   B. Self-monitor drinking via written daily logs.
   C. Establish drinking limits (i.e., BAC < 100 mg%; no more than 8 oz. pure ethanol per week).
   D. Increase knowledge of alcohol and its effects on behavior (e.g., BAC determination, drunk driving, tolerance).
   E. Use portable breath alcohol testers when considering driving after any alcohol consumption.
   F. Develop nondrinking social and recreational activities.
   G. Review social learning history with emphasis on the development of drinking behavior.
2. Modify maladaptive self-statements
   A. Do a functional analysis of cognitive-behavioral patterns (e.g., response style, self-defeating statements, implicit assumptions).

    B. Identify and challenge irrational beliefs (e.g., "I'm not worth any-
        thing." "It is better to avoid anything that makes me anxious').
    C. Homework assignments designed to increase the frequency of
        positive self-statements and reduce the frequency of defeating
        self-statements.
3. Increase assertiveness and problem-solving at work
    A. Assess response deficits via situation-difficulty questionnaire
        and role playing.
    B. Develop assertive belief system (e.g., discuss advantages of ex-
        pressing feelings, disadvantages of continued nonassertiveness,
        and how the appropriate expression of one's feelings can some-
        times be helpful to others).
    C. Behavioral rehearsal (e.g., request that his uncle establish a set
        pay schedule and not interfere in the client's personal life).

6.4. Treatment Description

The major clinical focus of this case revolves around the client's drinking behavior and the variables maintaining that behavior. Self-monitoring of
drinking behavior was also used to develop drinking limits and evaluate the
success of a nonproblem-drinking goal.

Over the course of 8 months this client was seen for 28 individual
therapy sessions. When the client first entered treatment he did not feel he
had a drinking problem, stating that "I can stop drinking whenever I want."
Considering the client's age, his previous lack of success with short-term
abstinence, and initial reluctance to commit to an abstinence goal, it was
important early in treatment to focus the client's attention on his drinking
behavior and its consequences. Also, there was some concern that until the
client developed and integrated alternative positive reinforcement activities
in his behavioral repertoire, his dependence on the bar environment for
social reinforcement would make total abstinence quite difficult. Thus, it
was stressed from the beginning of treatment that nonproblem drinking
would involve more than simply reducing the quantity and frequency of
drinking. The client was told that there would be considerable therapeutic
emphasis on the functions of his drinking and also on identifying the high-
risk nature of his drinking.

Given the above, the client was asked to monitor his daily drinking via
written cards. For convenience and to be unobtrusive, each card was small
enough to fit into a shirt pocket. The client was asked to record the date and
time of any drinking that occurred. To further assess cognitive and situational antecedents to drinking, feeling states associated with the drinking were
also recorded. At each session client and therapist reviewed the previous

week's drinking data, discussing and evaluating any drinking and related behaviors. The client monitored his drinking behavior for the first 25 weeks of therapy; thereafter he provided the therapist with verbal reports of his drinking. He was very compliant with therapy, as reflected in the completeness of his self-monitoring records and the length of time that he maintained written records.

The therapist reinforced the client for frank and accurate reporting of drinking. During the first 2 months of treatment, the client twice exceeded the agreed-upon drinking limits. These two incidents provided an opportunity to explore the situational determinants associated with the client's noncompliance. Following these two occasions, the client agreed to a week of self-imposed abstinence as a consequence of exceeding the limits. After the second drinking-limits violation (which occurred during a holiday period), the client successfully maintained a nonproblem-drinking pattern (i.e., adhered to the original drinking limits). These two situations were also explicitly used to help the client recognize that drinking was more of a problem than he had acknowledged at the beginning of treatment.

This case also illustrates how a detailed social-learning history can be used to develop hypotheses about variables maintaining drinking behavior. Treatment involved taking a developmental view of the client's cognitive response style, and how he *learned* to incorporate alcohol into his life. This client reported never really committing himself (cognitively) to any goals throughout his life. While this lack of commitment was most evident in terms of educational and vocational functioning, such behavior was a pervasive factor relating to a lack of self-efficacy. The following anecdote is relevant in this regard:

> The client reported that when he was a member of his high school swim team, he was evaluated as an excellent competitive swimmer. However, in examining the functions of his early drinking history, the client reported that prior to some meets he would sneak a drink so he could subsequently rationalize a failure—"I would have done better if I hadn't had that drink."

During the course of treatment the client reported experiencing several problems at work. Specifically, he was paid irregularly, there was no system for assigning jobs, and there were misunderstandings between his uncle and him about what customers had been told. Because the client was evaluated as deficient in problem-solving and assertiveness skills, especially at work, behavioral rehearsal and role playing were used to enable him to assert himself in interactions with his uncle. With practice, the client was successful in acquiring assertiveness skills.

Finally, using current life situations, the client identified and questioned the rationale of apparent self-defeating thoughts (e.g., "I'm not worth anything"; "This work should be perfect"; "There is something drastically wrong with me"). The objective was to help the client recognize occasions where such automatic conclusions led him to inaction or feelings of worthlessness and then have him actively challenge these implicit negative self-statements. In addition, the client was given homework assignments that involved making positive self-statements.

As of this writing, the client had resolved many of his past job problems. During the last 6 months of treatment, the client reported spending considerably more time socializing in places other than bars. Also during this time, he successfully maintained nonproblem drinking (adhering to the drinking limits agreed to early in treatment) and incurred no further adverse consequences as a result of his drinking.

7. CONCLUDING COMMENTS

It is worthwhile to examine the similarities and differences among the case examples described in this chapter. One notable similarity across all five cases was the detailed functional analysis of drinking and related behaviors conducted at assessment and the subsequent use of this information in the development of treatment goals and interventions. The functional analysis of drinking continued throughout therapy and often led to changes in the treatment plan.

All five cases shared one long-term goal—the reduction of drinking to a nonproblem level. However, for three clients, this goal was operationalized as abstinence from alcohol, while for two it was defined as a moderate level of alcohol consumption. Sometime during their course of treatment, four of the five clients used disulfiram on a short-term basis. In fact, in Case No. 2, use of disulfiram constituted one step in shaping toward a long-term goal of nonproblem drinking.

Beyond the common drinking goal, the diversity of the other goals reflects the variety of behavioral interventions and techniques that can be used with outpatient problem drinkers. For example, self-monitoring of drinking and related behaviors was used with four of the five clients. This information often helped to delineate antecedents of problem drinking. Other behavioral techniques included contracting, cognitive restructuring, and various skill-training methods.

An important unifying factor in all five cases was an emphasis on shaping new behaviors within the client's natural environment over an extended period of time. Outpatient treatment provides opportunities to change behaviors gradually through the use of multiple short-term goals without causing abrupt disruptions in the client's life. Moreover, it promotes generalization within the client's normal environment and enhances maintenance of behavior change, since frequent self- and other-administered reinforcement can be provided when short-term goals are achieved. In four of the cases, shaping was also used to facilitate treatment termination. Based on the assumption that after participating in treatment for several months, therapy often becomes positively reinforcing for clients, sessions were gradually spaced further apart to allow clients to learn to function with less therapeutic support and to allow the therapist to assess further the clients' independent functioning. If clients experienced dysfunction, then more frequent scheduling of sessions was resumed.

The five cases illustrate the use of outpatient behavior therapy as both an effective and a least restrictive mode of treatment for many problem drinkers. It is clear from the authors' clinical experience that services for problem drinkers need to be designed so as to appeal to that population. Problem drinkers usually have relatively intact personal, social, and economic resources and are unlikely to make the personal sacrifices prerequisite to inpatient treatment. Moreover, in most cases it is neither necessary nor desirable that they be removed from their everyday environments. Problem drinkers are also unlikely to embrace treatment orientations that demand massive changes in lifestyle, and such demands are not ethically warranted unless less intensive approaches have failed. Most notably, treatment has to be flexible enough to consider nonproblem drinking as well as abstinence goals, and both assessment and treatment planning must consider other aspects of life and health functioning in addition to drinking behavior.

COMMENTARY

Peter E. Nathan

Much has been made, in the past decade, of the potentially favorable cost-benefit ratio of prevention of the substance-use disorders, including alcoholism. Yet few clinicians have focused their efforts on persons whose substance-use problems have not yet assumed malignant proportions. Two individuals who have taken the promise of prevention seriously have been Linda and Mark Sobell, who—with their colleagues Nora Noel, Tony Cellucci, and Ted Nirenberg—have detailed the treatment of four problem drinkers and one alcoholic. All five were voluntary outpatients at the Nashville community mental health center, whose alcoholism unit Linda Sobell directed. In earlier papers and books, as well as in their introduction to these case reports, the Sobell group has stressed the advantages of getting individuals to treatment before their drinking problems have totally destroyed the fabric of their lives. The advantages of this early intervention include maintenance of family, social network, and employment—all indicators for suc-

cessful alcoholism treatment. The cost advantages of treatment on an outpatient basis are also obvious, when they are contrasted to the costs of hospitalization. Notable too is the fact that with persons whose problem drinking has not yet reached crisis proportions, greater flexibility in treatment, including nonproblem-drinking goals, is possible. Few clinicians nowadays would recommend a controlled-drinking goal for an alcoholic. The data do suggest, though, that a nonproblem-drinking goal for a problem drinker who will not abstain from drinking, whose denial of problems with alcohol cannot be breached, and whose drinking promises only to become more and more dangerous, may be the most immediate and, perhaps, the most appropriate.

The behavioral treatment of each of the five persons chronicled here was implemented only after extensive functional analysis, centering on the familiar SOR assessment formula. Detailed assessment of the abusive drinking and its behavioral accompaniments in the individual (organism) was accompanied by an equally thorough analysis of the environmental and personal stimuli associated with the abusive drinking and its reinforcing and punishing consequences (responses). This earnest effort to define functional relationships among drinking, its antecedents, and its consequences permits targeted and, hence, maximally effective behavioral treatment. The detail in which the authors of this chapter describe treatment goals, establish their priorities, then further separate them into more discrete elements illustrates the conviction that in this way patient and therapist can best approach a multivariate treatment goal—small steps, gradually building self-esteem, with modest successes.

The Sobells and their coworkers and Glenn Caddy share many approaches to treatment. One is the requirement that problem drinkers who aspire to nonproblem-drinking goals reach and maintain abstinence for a month or more. This requirement is discussed further in the commentary on chapter 12. Another commonality is the thorough functional analysis that all undertake. Still another is their conviction that the etiology and treatment of alcoholism are best conceptualized as multivariate.

Linda Sobell and Glenn Caddy diverge in one crucial treatment decision. Caddy chose to treat the troubled-relationship component of an alcoholic marriage, while Linda Sobell chose, in Case No. 1 of this chapter, to attack the drinking problem first. Sobell's patient was a very heavy drinker, whose abuse of alcohol involved physical dependence and tolerance and whose associated marital problems were serious enough that they could not be dealt with before the tremendously disruptive impact of the abusive drinking could be tempered. Nonetheless, this clinical decision is instructive, for it provides us with some important guidelines for decisions on the priorities to be applied to interventions when a multiproblem couple is is to be treated.

Throughout the five cases described in this chapter are numerous references to the importance of self-efficacy interventions in alcoholism treatment. Every patient seen here was provided with "success experiences" in the form of graded tasks designed to yield positive consequences. Even interventions designed to modify maladaptive vocational, academic, and financial self-management skills were structured to affect self-efficacy. "Self-efficacy" is Albert Bandura's term to describe a person's view of the predicted *outcome of a behavior. Therapy, so far as Bandura is concerned, is an endeavor whose focal point is a change in the patient's sense of self-efficacy. The decision by this group to focus treatment on self-efficacy makes especially good sense, in view of the well-known sense of failure and incompetence that interferes so often with treatment of problem drinkers and alcoholics. Even with persons like those the Sobell group describes who have not reached "bottom," self-efficacy is impaired and the will to make hard changes in life functioning is correspondingly difficult.*

Interwoven with efforts to enhance self-efficacy (in small but predictable steps) is the recognition that attention to less dramatic issues, to freedom from debt and better financial management, to more effective vocational adjustment, to considerations of status and self-respect, add as well to a positive treatment outcome, both by an indirect enhancement of self-efficacy and by providing something tangible to justify the loss of alcohol in one's daily life.

Readers critical of this group's decision to support patients who choose nonproblem-drinking goals will note that an abstinence goal was chosen for three of the five patients (Case Nos. 1, 3, and 4). Other features of the Sobell's approach to behavioral intervention are present, including thorough SOR exploration, detailed list of goals in order of importance, focus on efforts to enhance self-efficacy, and so on.

Throughout this group of case descriptions, efforts are made to share with the reader some of the thinking that went into outcome decisions. Mansell Pattison also devotes substantial space in his chapter in this book to the same issue, since valid criteria for choosing among alternative treatment strategies are of enormous potential importance. This chapter and others in this book suggest that behavior therapists devote considerable time and effort to these decisions, in the continuing absence of wholly valid predictors of successful outcome.

8. REFERENCES

American Psychiatric Association. *Diagnostic and statistical manual of mental disorders* (3rd ed.). Washington, D.C.: Author, 1980.

Cahalan, D., & Room, R. Problem drinking among American men. *Monograph of the Rutgers Center of Alcohol Studies,* No. 7, 1974.

Pattison, E. M., Sobell, M. B., & Sobell, L. C. *Emerging concepts of alcohol dependence.* New York: Springer, 1977.

Pomerleau, O., & Adkins, D. Evaluating behavioral and traditional treatment for problem drinkers. In L. C. Sobell, M. B. Sobell, & E. Ward (Eds.), *Evaluating alcohol and drug abuse treatment effectiveness: Recent advances.* New York: Pergamon Press, 1980.

Sobell, L. C., & Sobell, M. B. A self-feedback technique to monitor drinking behavior in alcoholics. *Behaviour Research and Therapy,* 1973, *11,* 237–238.

Sobell, L. C., & Sobell, M. B. *Clinical aspects of a behavioral treatment program for problem drinkers.* Paper presented at the 14th annual meeting of the Association for the Advancement of Behavior Therapy, New York, November 1980.

Sobell, L. C., & Sobell, M. B. Outcome criteria and the assessment of alcohol treatment efficacy.

In National Institute of Alcohol Abuse and Alcoholism Research Monograph, *Evaluation of the alcoholic: Implications for research, theory and treatment.* Washington, D.C.: U.S. Government Printing Office, 1981.

Sobell, L. C., Sobell, M. B., & Nirenberg, T. Differential treatment planning. In E. M. Pattison & E. Kaufman (Eds.), *The American handbook of alcoholism.* New York: Gardner Press, 1982.

Sobell, M. B., & Sobell, L. C. *Behavioral treatment of alcohol problems: Individualized therapy and controlled drinking.* New York: Plenum Press, 1978.

II

Relationships between Marital Discord and Alcohol Abuse

The three chapters in Part II consider the complex interrelationships of marital problems and abusive drinking behavior. Chapter 5, by Peter E. Nathan, and Chapter 6, by Barbara S. McCrady, consider the diverse factors in dysfunctional marital relationships that contribute to excessive alcohol consumption; these authors also suggest methods to address these factors in treatment. Chapter 7, by William M. Hay, alerts us to the fact that marital discord and excessive alcohol consumption can be independent and, consequently, may require successive rather than concurrent treatment.

5

Louise: The Real and the Ideal

PETER E. NATHAN

1. THE SETTING

In central New Jersey there are many persons, groups, and institutions that offer help to alcoholics who wish to stop drinking. Though they vary in competence, cost, and commitment, they are in abundance and they make themselves visible. Local community mental health centers will make room for the alcoholic who truly wants to achieve abstinence, even if they prefer other kinds of patients, who are generally more interesting. The state hospitals have outpatient clinics where alcohol problems are addressed. Several private psychiatric hospitals provide both detoxification and treatment services of varying lengths, depending on the patient's ability to pay and motivation to stop drinking. Some general hospitals also have detoxification facilities; a few offer outpatient treatment as well. Central New Jersey is also blessed with a multitude of psychologists and psychiatrists who provide treatment to alcoholics on a private basis. Other professionals with varying degrees and kinds of training offer marital, family, and pastoral counseling, social casework, and other services to alcoholics and their families. In addition, the State of New Jersey has organized a network of facilities, where alcoholism counselors focus directly (and, usually, first) on cessation of drinking. Several Alcoholics Anonymous groups also meet regularly in the region, making it possible for a well-motivated alcoholic to spend practically every waking hour at one AA meeting or another if he or she so desires.

PETER E. NATHAN ● Alcohol Behavior Research Laboratory, Rutgers—The State University, New Brunswick, New Jersey 08903.

Given this richness of treatment resources for alcoholics, problem drinkers, and their families in central New Jersey, it is natural to ask whether any gaps in the range of services exist in this area. I think such a gap does exist—and I undertook to fill it for Louise and Morris.

It was Morris, Louise's husband, who called to ask whether I would agree to see Louise. Morris and Louise had heard about the clinical services I offered from a colleague in another state, whose writings on controlled-drinking treatment for alcohol problems had come to Louise's attention. Since my office was within an hour's ride of their home in central New Jersey, and because Louise was interested in some of my writings on controlled drinking, she decided that I was what she was looking for—someone who could help her control her heavy drinking so that it would no longer represent a threat to her marriage. Although Louise had made up her mind, it took me a good deal longer to determine that Louise was suitable for my specialized practice.

My practice reflects both my belief in the promise of controlled-drinking treatment and my recognition of the perils it offers in the hands of those unaware of its limitations (Nathan & Lansky, 1978; Nathan & Lipscomb, 1979). Since I am thoroughly familiar with the field of nonproblem-drinking treatment, and since I want my very limited private practice to be stimulating and interesting, I have decided to restrict it to persons who want to control their drinking and have the resources to do so.

I have no trouble keeping my practice filled, yet I am not overwhelmed by numbers of persons I cannot accommodate; a relatively small number of persons meet my criteria for selection for this treatment. Those who do not are almost always chronic alcoholics who have been unable to control their drinking for any substantial period of time, use alcohol to deal with profound psychological dysfunction, and have inadequate personal, family, or vocational resources to sustain a pattern of nonproblem drinking. I have directed such people to inpatient detox centers and local AA groups, which are far better equipped than I to help persons who ought to achieve immediate abstinence.

2. BEHAVIORAL ASSESSMENT, INCLUDING DRINKING HISTORY

Louise shows her 45 years: Her complexion is a bit too ruddy, her body fuller and rounder than it once was, her gait a trifle unsteady, her hands are tremulous when she fails to exercise her usually rigid control over them. She inclines to sudden shifts in mood, laughing gaily one minute, breaking into sobs the next, when she reflects on an interesting life full of ups and, more recently, downs.

Directly on meeting Louise, I told her that we had to get to know each other better before we could decide whether the therapy I had to offer was for her; I stressed the reciprocal nature of this process—that we both had to be sure that I could help her for the treatment to work. We agreed to devote two or three sessions to this mutual assessment process.

Another matter we took up at our first meeting reflected my resolve to give no consideration to a nonproblem-drinking treatment program if continued drinking would pose a threat to a patient's health. Accordingly, I asked Louise to arrange for a thorough physical examination, including a comprehensive liver profile. During the same session, we talked about why she wanted to change her drinking pattern and how supportive her husband Morris would be of a nonproblem-drinking pattern rather than abstinence. I concluded that Louise was highly motivated to control her drinking, both out of fear of losing her husband and because she was convinced continued heavy drinking would destroy her skills as a journalist. Morris, a light drinker himself, was skeptical of Louise's chances for success, in part because the two of them had previously consulted another mental health professional without much success for marital problems tangentially related to Louise's drinking. Morris was, however, willing to help, though he believed that most of the effort ought to be Louise's, an observation with which Louise agreed. Morris's views on the legitimacy of a controlled-drinking outcome were heavily influenced by his own light drinking pattern; since he had never felt a strong urge to drink, he found it hard to empathize with someone who reported her drinking to be out of control. Still, Morris did say he would do what was asked of him; his apparent lack of enthusiasm for direct involvement in Louise's treatment unhappily foreshadowed his role as treatment progressed.

The final issue addressed at our first meeting was Louise's drinking history. Drinking history is of crucial interest, since heavy drinkers who have had no success controlling their drinking in any way—who have never maintained periods of sobriety or of nonproblem drinking—are unlikely to be good candidates for a nonabstinence-oriented treatment program (Nathan & Hay, in press; Sobell, Sobell, & Nirenberg, 1982).

Louise described a drinking pattern characterized by both rigid control and generous license. For the past several years, she had confined her drinking to a 4-hour period daily, from 8:00 in the evening to midnight. During that time, however, she downed between a pint and a fifth of vodka, mixed evenly with tonic water or Marguerita mix. Her drinks were generally consumed in front of the television set, in the company of Morris, with neither person doing much communicating.

Toward the end of an evening, when Louise felt like going to bed, she would persist in efforts to force Morris to join her, even though he was rarely ready to do so. And almost invariably a violent argument would ensue; it usually ended only when Morris acquiesced to Louise's demand. Louise blamed these encounters on both an undemonstrative spouse and her drinking, "which gives me the courage to say things to Morris I'd never say when I was sober." These "things" related to Morris's emotional inattentiveness, his preoccupation with his successful business, and his unwillingness to talk to Louise about her sense of isolation, feelings of worthlessness, and depression.

Louise's earlier drinking had been somewhat less controlled. As a child, she recalled, she had gotten used to a father who drank very heavily at home; he was almost certainly an alcoholic. He died in late middle age of a heart attack associated with an alcoholic cardiomyopathy. Because alcohol was a constant accompaniment of life at home (her mother also drank heavily, though with more restraint), Louise herself began to drink as an early adolescent, first with her parents and siblings, later at parties and on dates. Her drinking was not a problem during those years, in part because "I resolved never to let alcohol ruin my life as it did my father's." Drinking did become a problem once she graduated from college, though, and became a stringer for a small Midwestern newspaper. The job meant lots of good experience; it also entailed a good deal of solitude, strange towns, lonely hotel rooms, and empty weekends. She took to bringing a bottle back to her room to help while away the lonely hours until bedtime.

Even though she did exert enough control over her drinking to confine it to the evening and to the hotel rooms in which she spent them, Louise did less well at controlling her intake. It was the rare evening that she didn't finish off a pint of vodka; on lonely weekends, a fifth wouldn't last through Saturday and Sunday.

Gradually, Louise's drinking began to take its toll. At first she simply postponed beginning her day because of the hangover; later, more and more often, the day simply never began. It was after Louise lost an important story, the verdict following a sensational trial in a small town in the Corn Belt—missed because she couldn't get up one morning—that Louise and her editor realized how serious things had become.

Louise was given a leave of absence for treatment. She entered a private alcoholism treatment facility in another state, underwent 5 painful days of detoxification, then remained for several weeks of treatment, which was strongly disease-model, AA-oriented. For the next several years, Louise remained abstinent by throwing herself into her work, successfully fighting loneliness by long hours of dedicated labor. Toward the end of that time, when she was approaching her 30th birthday, she married Bill, a man from her home city, and quit her job at the paper.

A year of marriage was all it took to convince Louise that the life of a homemaker was not for her. She found a job with a local department store as publicist and advertising manager. While the job did not require that she spend days away from home, it did force her to do a good deal of entertaining of potential clients at lunch and to attend numerous evening receptions; in both situations alcohol was plentiful. Gradually, "because it was expected," Louise began to drink again, at first a drink when others were drinking, later, more than that during lengthy social gatherings, and finally, back to a pattern of heavy and solitary drinking at home at night.

Not long afterward, Louise's drinking cost her both her job and her husband. The nub of the problem was the sudden rages into which Louise would fly after a few drinks, compounded by the remorse and self-pity she experienced on the days following the increasingly predictable explosions. When Louise was hospitalized for a suicidal gesture directly linked to the aftermath of an angry encounter with Bill, he decided that he had had enough. He filed for divorce while Louise was in hospital; they saw each other only once thereafter, at the final divorce hearing.

Following her separation, Louise surprised everyone by remaining sober and refusing to wallow in self-pity. She threw herself into local AA activities, becoming an unpaid publicist for one group and gradually assuming sponsorship responsibilities for another after she had been dry a year. She also found a job, after a long search, as reporter for a weekly newspaper on the Atlantic Coast. Things were looking up after a long down period.

Louise stayed with the weekly for 10 years, working her way up to a position as feature editor and columnist. While her drinking started again after a couple of years of sobriety, under the pressures of a deadline job, Louise kept it successfully under rigid control for several years. Never one to enjoy drinking to intoxication at parties or business functions, Louise now exercised even greater control over her drinking in social situations, to the extent that she usually refused any alcoholic beverage, even wine, when with co-workers or interviewees. And instead of beginning to drink as soon as she arrived home after a day's work, and drinking all evening to unconsciousness or close to it, Louise limited her drinking to 2 or 3 hours in the middle of the evening. During those hours, though, she gradually increased her drinking to between a pint and a fifth of vodka, with a mixer. She needed the alcohol, Louise said, to get to sleep after an overstimulating day. Without it, she was convinced, she would not be able to sleep and would be unable to function effectively the following day.

Although she was drinking very heavily, Louise got to work on time and did what she and her boss, the paper's editor, both felt was a good job. She saw a local physician periodically, and he confirmed that her health was good, although from time to time she had a tendency to add a few more pounds than was good for her.

Table 1. Louise's Drinking History

Age	Behavior
12–14	First drink
14–22	Moderate social drinking, first with parents, later with peers
22–27	Problem drinking as a daily newspaper stringer[a]
27	Inpatient treatment for problem drinking
27–30	Abstinent; work as journalist continues; marriage
30–32	Gradually increasing consumption to problem-drinking levels; marriage and new job not working out
32	Hospitalization for suicide attempt
32–34	Abstinent while working for weekly newspaper; intensive Alcoholics Anonymous involvement
34–37	Nonproblem drinking while at weekly newspaper
37–42	Problem drinking at weekly newspaper
42	Louise meets, then marries, Morris; quits weekly
42–44	Problem drinking with Morris; no job; brief marital therapy
44–46	Behavioral controlled-drinking treatment begins; a nonproblem-drinking pattern was resumed toward the end of this period

[a] Problem drinking almost always involved daily consumption of between 16 and 28 oz. of vodka in a mixer during the middle and late evening hours.

Louise first met Morris, her present husband, when she interviewed him for her paper. He was a small businessman with a valuable patent on an industrial process that promised to revolutionize the manufacture of machine tools. At the end of the interview Morris, divorced many years, asked Louise to join him for a drink. Instead, she had coffee. They sat mutually entranced for several hours and talked about politics (they were both state committeepersons at the time), the world situation (both had traveled extensively), their failed marriages (both took on most of the responsibility for them), and their loneliness. The relationship flourished, and after a few months of intense courtship, Louise and Morris married and moved into his very large antebellum mansion, purchased with his former wife but never restored as the two had planned. Louise quit her job because it now required a commute of about an hour and a half.

Louise's drinking was not a problem for Morris during their courtship, since she drank nothing at the parties to which they were frequently invited (both were "social animals," something neither of their previous partners had been) and little more on quiet evenings along together. In fact, through their courtship and the early months of their marriage, Louise had been able to preserve much of her old heavy-drinking pattern. This was possible because Morris was in the midst of introducing a new technology to his industry at the time and had so much traveling to do that their schedules were irregular and unpredictable (Louise went with him to many of his marketing engagements). As a result, Louise got her pint or so of vodka a day in but not always at the precise time she might have chosen. Then, on the heels of Morris's great marketing effort, a local political campaign developed, and Louise and Morris threw themselves into it. As before, all sorts of people were in their landmark home at odd hours, and the two of them were often out for meetings and rallies, so that Louise's drinking still did not become obvious.

When things calmed down a bit and Morris began working a more regular schedule, Louise was left at home with little to do. The excitement of their courtship wore off a bit—and Louise returned to her old drinking pattern with a vengeance. Despite Louise's elaborate rationalizations, efforts to hide the evidence, and pleas for understanding, Morris quickly recognized that Louise had a problem of long-standing and that it was likely to affect their relationship. In particular, Morris reported, Louise soon began to confront Morris angrily and aggressively when she was drunk about issues she did not raise when she was sober.

So unhappy did Morris become at Louise's drinking and its effect on their relationship that he began to actively contemplate dissolving their relationship within a few months of their marriage, even though he knew it would mean a return to the desperate loneliness from which he had so recently escaped. But before Morris could make more than vaguely threatening noises about leaving Louise, she brought up the possibility of marital therapy. Despairing of the outcome of a direct attack on her drinking, Louise felt that therapy which would help Morris see his role in their troubled marriage would also give Louise less reason to drink so heavily. The dynamically oriented marital therapy which followed was doomed shortly after it began, largely because Morris correctly perceived that the therapist did not plan to focus exclusively on Louise's responsibility for their bad marriage. Morris's sarcasm, intellectualisms, and obfuscations led all three participants to give up the effort after a futile few months.

Six months passed and things got no better. Morris began more actively to pursue options in living that did not include Louise. Louise, drinking even more heavily and convinced that therapy requiring Morris to share some responsibility for her plight was unlikely to succeed, began reading about treatment specifically for alcoholism. She found behavioral treatment approaches to be most intriguing because of their specificity and focus—and because she could not imagine herself attending AA meetings for the rest of her life.

If Louise found behavioral treatments for alcoholism to be of interest because they focused so narrowly on so many of the problems associated with her alcoholism, she found nonproblem-drinking treatments that much more fascinating because they seemed to offer the opportunity to "have one's cake and eat it too," as she and so many others have put it. Typically, Louise read much of what has been written on controlled drinking, pro and con, then called the author of the book that most impressed her.

3. LOUISE AT THE BEGINNING OF TREATMENT

Louise came to the initial exploratory session with Morris, who joined Louise and me for the first half of the session and then sat in a separate waiting room for the other half. Louise was tearful, apprehensive, and depressed. She thought her marriage might very well fail, she believed she was drinking too much, and she worried that the alcohol might be responsible for sundry physical problems she was experiencing. She blamed Morris for the "excessive" part of the drinking she was doing. She also believed that controlled-drinking treatment was a panacea and that she would simply have to conform to a rigid treatment protocol to get the desired result—which was to reduce her drinking to levels acceptable to Morris without having to forsake it entirely. While unclear about whether she was an alcoholic, a problem drinker, or a heavy social drinker, Louise did know that her drinking was getting her into trouble now; she also recalled that it had done so in the past. Above all, Louise was scared to death of being alone again. She was prepared, she said, to do practically anything to get Morris to stay with her.

Louise's drinking had assumed formidable dimensions. Though she admitted that her decision to seek treatment had precipitated a reduction in her consumption (a rather common phenomenon), she was still drinking a pint or more of vodka each evening. Since she was a smallish woman (though 20% or so overweight), my calculations indicated that Louise was reaching a blood-alcohol level close to 300 mg% virtually every evening! (It is the rare social drinker whose BAL exceeds 80 mg%; BALs beyond 100 mg% mark the drunk driver in most states.)

Beyond its ultimate impact on her health and its more immediate effect on her eating and sleeping habits, Louise's drinking most affected her interactions with Morris. As Louise and Morris told it, together and singly, Louise's drinking was often follo·ved, within 60 to 90 minutes, by an increasing crescendo of critical comments and complaints on Morris's past, present, and future behavior. Since Louise and Morris generally ate dinner in silence, then sat silently in front of the television set the rest of the evening, Louise's angry outbursts tended to reflect the fact that the couple rarely communicated about anything more intimate than the progress of their home's renovation or local politics.

I told Louise and Morris at that initial session that I could not make an immediate decision about Louise's appropriateness for controlled-drinking treatment. I also stressed the fact that abstinence is far easier to achieve for most alcoholics and problem drinkers than nonproblem drinking, and that it must be seriously considered along with alternative goals. I offered to make a referral to a high-quality inpatient program where detoxification would precede abstinence-oriented threatment. Louise would have none of this and said that if she could not continue to drink at least moderately, she saw no reason to keep living. She had tried abstinence-oriented treatment several times in the past, she recalled, and had been unable to consistently maintain abstinence, largely because she needed a drink or two to get to sleep at night.

Louise anticipated most of the caveats I shared with her from my writings on controlled-drinking treatment. Specifically, she responded to questions designed to establish her readiness and appropriateness for controlled-drinking treatment by referring to detailed notes proving (1) a history of control over drinking behavior for lengthy time periods, (2) current drinking that showed evidence of control, (3) repeated failure to achieve abstinence following treatment with that goal, (4) presence of a significant other in her environment willing to help her maintain control over drinking, and (5) absence of physical findings to contraindicate moderate drinking. So intent was Louise on believing that controlled drinking was a scientifically defensible alternative to abstinence-oriented treatment that she delighted in correcting me when I made statements about it that were not supported fully by the available data!

A 3-week period of daily self-monitoring of alcohol intake revealed that Louise consumed, on average, 12 oz. of vodka in a mixer between the hours of 9:00 P.M. and midnight 7 days a week. Range of beverage alcohol consumed ranged from 10 to 15 oz. (This amount was down somewhat from the pint or more Louise had reported she was consuming before treatment began; the decrease in consumption reflected the well-known reactive effects of self-monitoring; Nelson, 1977; Nelson & Barlow, 1981.)

At the end of three assessment sessions, Louise, Morris, and I agreed on an eight-session trial contract that required a marked reduction in drinking by Louise and an equally marked increase in prosocial behavior on both Louise and Morris's parts. My reasons for agreeing to this plan included the conviction that Louise would continue to drink immoderately without treatment, the belief that she was highly motivated to control her drinking, and the observation that Morris was as desirous as Louise of a new, more moderate consumption pattern. As well, Louise possessed no physical contraindications to continued drinking, surprising in view of her lengthy history of very heavy drinking. And while Louise had failed repeatedly to achieve abstinence, she had maintained a controlled, if excessive, intake pattern for many years.

4. THE EIGHT-SESSION CONTRACT

In connection with the eight-session agreement, Louise and I agreed on an initial drinking target: reduction of 2 oz. of beverage alcohol in daily intake and reduction of half an hour in the consumption period, the 30 minutes between 11:30 P.M. and midnight. These choices of target were made (1) because it seemed likely that they could be complied with easily, in that way giving the patient an early, significant success experience, (2) because they would both reduce consumption level and limit its impact on surrounding life circumstances, and (3) because they would be tangible signs of progress to a spouse who had begun to despair of real changes in his wife's behavior.

At the same time, because Louise's drinking had assumed such a central role in her continuing psychological battle with her husband, I asked Louise and Morris to join together to examine their relationship in a marital therapy effort. Like most couples caught in the web of alcoholism, Louise and Morris focused exclusively on the role the alcoholic partner's drinking played in bringing their relationship to its precarious state. But Louise's abusive drinking could also be viewed as a desperate, largely ineffective effort to maintain her marriage—since alcohol gave Louise the courage to confront basic relationship problems with Morris that neither would face otherwise.

In order to determine more precisely the reciprocal roles alcohol and their deteriorating relationship played in their lives, Louise and Morris were asked to record, independently, the interpersonal course of two consecutive weeks, day by day and hour by hour: how much time the two spent together, the circumstances of their interaction, whether an interaction of a particular kind occurred during a specific time of the day or under specific circumstances, and what the emotional correlates of the interactions were.

The results of this exercise surprised Morris and Louise. Though the two shared the same house, bedroom and bed, and though Morris spent most of his nonworking time at home, Louise and Morris actually communicated very little about anything other than (1) what they were having for dinner, (2) what they would have for dinner the following evening, (3) what was to be done to the house the next days and weeks during its renovation, and (4) how each felt about whatever political campaign he or she was currently involved in. Neither spent time exploring the other's feelings, memories, or aspirations, and neither lent support to the other in times of emotional need. Louise felt that every effort to enlist Morris's interest in her hopes for the future (which included getting out of the house and back into writing and publishing) or to get him to appreciate her feelings of failure at having remained in the house without working for so long was met with efforts to change the subject. From Morris's point of view, it was not a matter of wishing to avoid dealing with Louise's feelings; rather, it was a desire to avoid the inevitable hassles, recriminations, and crying that accompanied every discussion of Louise's needs, plans, and desires. So Morris touched only on "neutral" subjects with Louise, preferring to sit before the television set in silence, to read alone, or, occasionally, to visit old friends alone.

Morris's inattention, in turn, led Louise to continued heavy drinking; with enough alcohol coursing through her veins, she could muster the courage to *demand* that Morris listen to her, to *force* him to take seriously the immensity of her unhappiness and the depths of her despair. And so things went, from bad to worse, in the downward spiral of alcoholism.

Predictably, Louise found it a good deal easier than she had expected to reduce her drinking by 2 oz. an evening and to end it half an hour earlier. Early in the process of implementing these changes, she realized more clearly than before that some of her motivation for drinking centered on fear of not falling asleep. Like many alcohol abusers, Louise drank heavily in part because she believed that she had to self-medicate in order to sleep. She now found to her surprise and pleasure, though, that sleep onset did not increase with reduced alcohol consumption. I chose, at this point, to share with Louise my views on the relationship between drinking and sleeping, based on a growing body of research data suggesting that while heavy drinking at bedtime often makes going to sleep a bit easier, it almost invariably makes sleep more fitful and the likelihood of early awakening much greater. I gave Louise some references to this work because the written word at times more effectively shaped her behavior than the spoken one.

Midway through the eight-session mark, Louise had consolidated the initial drinking changes. She reported that her sleep pattern was unchanged, which meant that she continued to experience moderate difficulty falling asleep and to awaken once or twice a night. As a consequence, she generally slept late, sometimes well into the morning, to compensate for sleep missed during the night. Louise's sleep problems, causing virtually a sleep phobia, impacted directly as well as indirectly on her relationship with Morris: indirectly because she drank, at least in part, to ensure access to sleep, and that drinking led to angry outbursts at Morris; directly because her demands that Morris turn out his reading light when he would have preferred reading himself to sleep stemmed from her own need for sleep. Morris often commented on how much he enjoyed reading late into the night and how much he resented having to stop reading because Louise wanted the light extinguished. Yet whenever Morris would offer to go to another room to read in order not to disturb her, Louise would remind him of her inability to sleep without him beside her. So the light would be turned off—and Morris would again have compromised in order to avoid another angry confrontation.

These observations on my part influenced an assessment strategy I introduced during the fifth contract session. Another reduction in consumption—from 10 to 8 oz. of beverage alcohol an evening—was programmed at that time; it was to be effected during the ensuing 4 weeks. I also told Louise that I expected the additional reduction, like the first, to have no adverse effect on sleep because it would be accompanied by a reduction in tolerance so that the alcohol's net effect would remain roughly the same. Because the consumption reduction would also reduce alcohol's impact on sleep maintenance, early and frequent awakening might even decrease somewhat.

I introduced an assessment strategy at this session that required Morris and Louise, during the ensuing 2 weeks, to pinpoint the five behaviors in the other they most liked and the five they least liked. The two were asked to track the frequency of those 10 behaviors as they were emitted during the 2-week period by the other person. The aim of this assessment was to help develop a contingency package that would permit a reinforcement-based behavior change plan to be implemented in the future. Simply reducing Louise's drinking was not sufficient treatment. To the extent that Louise's drinking served important functions beyond the pharmacologic one, she would not give it up—unless those functions could be assumed by other, more constructive behaviors.

At the next session, Louise reported she had had no real problem reducing her consumption to the target level. Morris disputed this positive evaluation by observing that twice during the week Louise had staggered and fallen and once had become incoherent during her drinking period. Though Louise earnestly denied breaking the consumption contract, Morris was insistent that no other explanation for this behavior would suffice. I did not side with either person, though I did observe that Louise's target consumption was at the point where behavioral disruption solely because of alcohol was unlikely.

Louise's bedtime outbursts at Morris began to diminish somewhat. From most nights, the outbursts decreased to two or three a week, still unpleasant but more bearable than before, according to Morris. In the effort to work more directly on controlling the outbursts, in contract session six Louise, Morris, and I turned to the results of the self-assessment of Louise and Morris's relationship. Most reinforcing of Morris's behaviors, for Louise, were those which led her to feel wanted, needed, and loved, behaviors like touching her arm in conversation, complimenting her on her appearance or competence, or calling her from the office during the day "just to talk"; least reinforcing were behaviors which suggested that Morris had little or no need for or interest in her. Morris disliked Louise's interruptions of his reading, her insistence on knowing more about his business or what was going on inside his head than he felt was her due, and her inability or unwillingness to act independent of him. What Morris liked most about

Louise were her spunkiness, intelligence, writing skill, and concern for him, though none but the latter had been enough in evidence during the preceding several years to convince him they were still part of Louise's behavioral repertoire.

A contingency management package was established in accordance with these findings. It focused on Louise's behavior at bedtime, since that behavior appeared to all concerned to be more resistant to change than her drinking, which appeared to be changing under less strict management. All agreed that both the frequency and the intensity of Louise's angry outbursts at Morris needed to be reduced, ultimately to zero. To effect this change, it was agreed that every night that Louise went to bed without expressing anger at Morris would be followed, the next day, by a comment from Morris recognizing this accomplishment. As well, Morris was to set aside at least 15 minutes twice a week to sit with Louise, share his feelings, and listen to her talk of her own.

For a few nights, this simple set of contingencies appeared to work, until one night the old pattern returned in even greater intensity. On describing the evening a few days later, Louise could not recount the events fully without dissolving into torrents of tears. So threatening and angry was Morris's response to her entreaties that he accompany her to bed, that he stop watching television so she would not have to be alone, that Louise feared he would attack her physically. For his part, Morris was able, with little trouble, to reexperience the intense anger he had felt and to repeat his pledge that one or two more episodes of this kind would mean the end of the marriage. "Nobody should have to spend his life awaiting these kinds of outbursts, these kinds of frantic efforts at control," was his comment. It was clear that a focus on Louise's drinking problem at this point was essentially irrelevant; instead, what was required was strong, effective behavioral intervention to bring the disruptive behavior under control long enough for other behavioral changes, including those affecting drinking, to have a chance to take place.

A jointly developed plan drew enthusiastic support from both Louise and Morris—Louise because she believed that Morris had reached the end of his rope, and Morris because he really didn't want to have to leave his home. The agreement began with the statement that reciprocity in two-person relationships contributes importantly to the long-term maintenance of such relationships. It went on to set forth a series of mutual agreements to ensure the reciprocity that had been lacking in Louise and Morris's relationship. In return for Morris's agreement to spend more time with Louise and to devote some of that time to a sharing of more than pedantries, Louise agreed that Morris could watch television or read at bedtime without pressure from her to come to bed. Louise also agreed to postpone discussion of complaints about Morris's behavior until the daytime, when she was sober. In return for the luxury of an unencumbered bedtime, Morris agreed to set aside at least half an hour a day, at a predetermined time, to discuss feelings, thoughts, and mutual plans with Louise. He also agreed to consider Louise's complaints about his behavior the day following her registering a bedtime complaint.

This reciprocal agreement was tried for a week. It coincided with a third consumption reduction of 2 oz. by Louise. Unhappily, the successful reduction in consumption was not accompanied by successful implementation of the contingency contract. Although Louise and Morris maintained their reciprocal agreements for the first 3 days of the 1-week trial period, Morris began to find it difficult to set aside 30 minutes a day to talk to Louise just about the time Louise found herself unable to suppress her anger at Morris for forgetting the anniversary of their first meeting. She spent much of the evening of that day excoriating Morris for his thoughtlessness and lack of sensitivity. Morris reported getting almost no sleep that night and conse-

Table 2. Louise's Behavioral Treatment

Week	Treatment events
1	Evaluation for controlled-drinking treatment; asked to self-monitor intake for 3 weeks; therapist advocacy of abstinence-oriented treatment; elicitation of drinking and marital history (drinking: 1 pint or more an evening)
2–3	Continued behavioral assessment, including drinking and personal history (drinking: about 12 oz. per evening)
4	Establishment of eight-session contract and initial consumption reduction to 10 oz. per evening; consideration of solutions for marital conflict, especially at bedtime (drinking: about 12 oz. per evening)
5	Request for a record of the interpersonal course of two consecutive weeks; discussion of details of marital interaction (drinking: about 10 oz. per evening)
6–7	Continued detailed analysis of interaction patterns and of Louise's vocational goals; discussion of relationships between drinking and sleeping (drinking: about 10 oz. per evening)
8	Second consumption reduction; assessment strategy asking for frequency of five most and five least desired behaviors from other person (drinking: about 10 oz. per evening)
9–10	Consideration of results of new assessment; discussion of diverse perceptions of second consumption reduction; establishment and discussion of first contingency-management package; discussion of improved functioning at bedtime (drinking: about 8 oz. per evening)
11–12	Establishment of second contingency-management package; third consumption reduction (drinking: about 8 oz. per evening)
13	Establishment of third, effective, contingency-management package (drinking: about 6 oz. per evening)
14–32	Management and modification of contingency-management package; continued reduction in targeted consumption; individual behavior therapy techniques for troublesome target behaviors (drinking: about 5 oz. per evening, 6 evenings per week)

quently being unable to function at work the following day. The events of this day and evening so colored the remainder of the trial week that Louise and Morris were convinced contingency contracting would never work when they returned to my office at the end of the week. Neither could explain the apparent success of the drinking manipulation, nor could either easily see a relationship between Louise's drinking and her overwhelming anger at Morris.

I was convinced that a major function of Louise's abusive drinking was that it gave her license—provided her with an excuse—to express angry feelings at Morris that she could not express when she was sober. In turn, Morris was presumably more "understanding" of her anger when she was drunk because he, like she, believed that alcohol essentially destroyed her self-control. But I was convinced that Louise *could* control herself if she wished at her present blood-alcohol levels, since I believed that her expectations about alcohol's disinhibiting effects, not the pharmacologic impact of 6 oz. of beverage alcohol, were responsible for her uncontrolled behavior (Mendelson & Mello, 1979; Wilson, 1978).

5. THE CONTRACT THAT WORKED

What was required was a new contingency contract that would assure (1) that Louise could express her justifiable anger at Morris's avoidance of her, but only when she was sober, and (2) that Morris could make his own decisions about bedtime unencumbered by Louise's nagging and angry outbursts. The contingency contract that was agreed upon established the following sequence of steps to which both parties agreed: (1) When Louise was ready for bed, she would go upstairs to the bedroom; she could ask Morris to join her but could not force him to do so. (2) When in bed, Louise could not require Morris to turn off the light if he wished to continue reading; if he did wish to continue reading and Louise wanted to go to sleep, Morris could go into an adjoining bedroom to continue his reading. (3) If Louise became angry at Morris, she could not engage him in an angry discussion of the issue in question. Instead, she would give Morris a card on which she would note the issue about which she had become angry; that card guaranteed that she and Morris would meet the following day to discuss the issue during a time Louise was sober. (4) If Louise persisted in expressing her anger, Morris could retreat to a nearby room, a predetermined "refuge," where Louise could not follow him; if she did so, she would forfeit her next appointment with her therapist. (5) In return for these concessions, Morris promised (1) that he would establish and keep a regular meeting time at least three times a week for at least 30 minutes at a time to discuss mutual concerns, needs, and wishes, and (2) that he would meet at any time with Louise to discuss reasons for her anger the day following a successfully aborted expression of anger.

Despite Morris's great reservations about this plan, which he felt sure Louise would sabotage ("When she has too much to drink, she simply can't help herself"), reports during the following few weeks revealed a reduction in troublesome bedtime encounters from approximately three a week to less than one every fortnight. And that reduced frequency has continued to this point in the treatment, some 6 months after implementation of the final contract. Louise has followed agreed-upon procedures to the letter. When deviations from the contract occur, they are Morris's, for Morris is not above subtle sabotage of the system, in part because he is not pleased to follow anyone else's prescription, in part because he does not like being wrong about a prediction.

With the issues surrounding Louise's behavioral excesses at bedtime under better stimulus control and her needs for a sense of greater closeness with Morris more adequately and appropriately met, Louise has found it even easier than before to continue to decrease her drinking. Successive decreases have brought her, at the date of writing, to a 30/5/6 consumption formula (no more than 30 oz. of beverage alcohol a week, no more than 5 oz. a day, drinking on no more than 6 days a week) from a 150/20/7 situation when she entered therapy. Our ultimate goal is 20/4/5, since 20 oz. of beverage alcohol have been widely cited as differentiating heavy social drinkers from those who are problem drinkers (Pattison, Sobell, & Sobell, 1977). Two "dry" days a week may have a greater impact on tolerance, moreover, than slightly lighter consumption through the week.

Louise has also begun to explore new career paths more seriously. No longer content simply to oversee the renovation of her historical home, she has spoken of various options, including the purchase and management of a local newspaper, freelance writing, a series of articles on a trip to the Soviet Union a year ago, and proprietorship of a small retail business.

6. LOUISE: THE REAL AND THE IDEAL

Viewed from the perspective of our initial goals, Louise's treatment has been successful. Over the course of 18 months, she has regularized and, most important, reduced her alcohol consumption dramatically, to the point where it no longer represents an immediate threat to health and happiness. Whether her continued drinking represents a continued threat, though, is also beyond question; Louise almost certainly continues to drink too much. While she plans to reduce her consumption further, her resolve on this question has diminished as reasons for continued change decrease. Louise is getting along much better with Morris, and both are much happier living together than they were 18 months ago. Both the reduced drinking and the improved interpersonal habits appear to be stable.

Viewed from the perspective of an ideal existence, however, Louise continues to drink more than is good for her, has remained an isolated woman who is not realizing her considerable potential for contributing to society, and is not really terribly satisfied either with herself or with her lot in life. Would abstinence have brought her closer to her ideals? The question is almost certainly moot, since Louise absolutely refused to consider that treatment option. It seems reasonable to assume, however, that Louise would not have changed her habitual ways of interacting with the world even if she had been able to stop drinking. Relevant literature suggests that happiness and abstinence are not invariably linked (Miller, 1976; see also Chapter 11).

In a very real way this therapeutic compromise epitomizes the conflicts confronting the therapist who would do what seems best and most reasonable for his or her alcoholic client. While not a perfect outcome, Louise's current life and level of functioning may be about as good as one could expect—but no one could consider them ideal.

COMMENTARY

William M. Hay

Those of us who have treated individuals with drinking problems will recognize Louise. The case description is a realistic portrayal of the course of treatment for many middle-aged married women who seek treatment. Such clients confront their therapists with a variety of interrelated problems. In Louise's case, she was consuming excessive amounts of alcohol, and the future of her marriage was tenuous at best. She was no stranger to adversity, however, given her hospitalization record and previous marital discord. The narrative style of this case gives us a strong sense of the gradual but unceasingly negative impact of Louise's alcohol consumption on her personal and professional life.

Faced with this cluster of problems, a critical issue for Nathan became which problem to consider as the initial focus of treatment. The "clinical rule of thumb" apparently subscribed to by the majority of contributors to this text is to make the establishment of control over alcohol consumption the initial goal of treatment. Glenn Caddy's chapter is a successful exception to this "rule of thumb." In most treatment programs, this means that abstinence from alcohol would be the number one treatment priority. In the case of Louise, client and therapist opted for a gradual reduction to a mutually conceived controlled-drinking level. Even though the initial focus of a number of the clinicians in this text is the reduction of excessive alcohol consumption, all of us have remained committed to a broadly based assessment strategy. The necessity of this strategy of assessing and monitoring multiple life areas in addition to alcohol intake is apparent from the description of Louise's course of treatment. Even after the "official" assessment period was over, Peter Nathan continued to probe, in an effort to clarify the functional relationships among Louise's drinking, marital problems, and difficulties asserting herself with her husband. The view of assessment as an ongoing process, modeled by Nathan and the other contributors to this text, provides the behavioral clinician with a flexible clinical model. On a number of occasions, Nathan redirected Louise's treatment based on assessment data. The most notable examples were a shift to marital issues at a critical time in treatment and the consideration of the relationship between reductions in Louise's alcohol consumption and expectations concerning her purported sleep problems.

It is interesting to note that substantial changes in the relationship between Louise and her spouse, Morris, did not automatically follow reductions in Louise's drinking. The improvements in the relationship that did occur awaited the implementation of contingency management procedures aimed at bringing Louise's disruptive behavior under control and at establishing more reciprocity in the relationship. In my own chapter (Chapter 7), changes in the marital relationship were also independent of changes in drinking status. The relationship between change in drinking status and changes in the status of other problem areas is difficult to predict if the cases in this text are representative—and I feel they are. The cases appear to be just about evenly divided between instances where positive changes in drinking status resulted in concurrent improvements in other areas and instances where changes in other areas were independent and required specialized intervention.

Part of the folklore of traditional alcoholism treatment programs has been that the achievement of abstinence will result, by definition, in positive changes in other life areas. As Nathan notes, however, happiness and abstinence are not inextricably related. It appears that the same caveat applies to situations in which controlled drinking is the treatment goal. Nathan's title, "Louise: The Real and the Ideal," therefore, is quite apt. To be sure, further reductions in drinking were seen as desirable by the therapist at the end of treatment; however, I share his doubts that further reductions or total abstinence would have altered the outcome significantly.

One final comment concerns the relationship of the behavioral clinician to the other alcoholism treatment providers in the area. Nathan provides the behavioral clinician with some basic "survival" skills. The reader will likely be aware that the majority of treatment programs remain abstinence-oriented, with strong emphasis on AA involvement. Alternative treatment programs, whether directed towards abstinent or controlled-drinking goals, are suspect and may never be accepted by local agencies such as AA. The resourceful behavioral clinician, however, can provide a number of important clinical services. As Peter Nathan suggests, a positive relationship with various agencies must be cultivated. In my own clinical and research work, I have made it a point to visit my referral resources to clearly define the type of client I deal with and the services I can provide. Since my work in both areas focuses on couples and families, I have become a *useful resource for a number of private and public agencies. This relationship is a reciprocal one, however, and I frequently refer appropriate clients to agencies such as Alcoholics Anonymous for an abstinence program. Given a substantial proportion of problem drinkers like Louise who would not enter treatment unless alternatives to abstinence existed, one of the behavioral clinician's most important contributions is in the area of prevention.*

7. REFERENCES

Mendelson, J. H., & Mello, N. K. Diagnostic criteria for alcoholism and alcohol abuse. In J. H. Mendelson & N. K. Mello (Eds.), *The diagnosis and treatment of alcoholism.* New York: Mc-Graw-Hill, 1979.

Miller, P. M. *Behavioral treatment of alcoholism.* New York: Pergamon Press, 1976.

Nathan, P. E., & Hay, W. M. Alcoholism: Psychopathology, etiology and treatment. In H. E. Adams & P. B. Sutker (Eds.), *Comprehensive handbook of psychopathology.* New York: Plenum Press, in press.

Nathan, P. E., & Lansky, D. Management of the chronic alcoholic: A behavioral viewpoint. In J. P. Brady & H. K. H. Brodie (Eds.), *Controversy in psychiatry.* Philadelphia: Saunders, 1978.

Nathan, P. E., & Lipscomb, T. R. Behavior therapy and behavior modification in the treatment of alcoholism. In J. H. Mendelson & N. K. Mello (Eds.), *Diagnosis and treatment of alcoholism.* New York: McGraw-Hill, 1979.

Nelson, R. O. Assessment and therapeutic functions of self-monitoring. In M. Hersen, R. M. Eisler, & P. M. Miller (Eds.), *Progress in behavior modification* (Vol. 5). New York: Academic Press, 1977.

Nelson, R. O., & Barlow, D. H. Behavioral assessment: Basic strategies and initial procedures. In D. H. Barlow (Ed.), *Behavioral assessment of adult disorders.* New York: Guilford Press, 1981.

Pattison, E. M., Sobell, M. B., & Sobell, L. C. *Emerging concepts of alcohol dependence.* New York: Springer, 1977.

Sobell, L. C., Sobell, M. B., & Nirenberg, T. Differential treatment planning. In E. M. Pattison & E. Kaufman (Eds.), *The American handbook of alcoholism.* New York: Gardner Press, 1982.

Wilson, G. T. Booze, beliefs, and behavior: Cognitive factors in alcohol use and abuse. In P. E. Nathan, G. A. Marlatt, & T. Løberg (Eds.), *Alcoholism: New directions in behavioral research and treatment.* New York: Plenum Press, 1978.

6

Conjoint Behavioral Treatment of an Alcoholic and His Spouse

The Case of Mr. and Mrs. D.

BARBARA S. McCRADY

1. INTRODUCTION

The role of the spouse in the treatment of alcohol abuse and alcoholism has been a controversial one. Early models, based on psychodynamic conceptualizations of alcoholic marriages, suggested that spouses of alcoholics were conflicted, needy, neurotic people, who needed intensive individual treatment in order to resolve their own neurotic conflicts (e.g., Price, 1945). Later, sociologically oriented theories suggested that wives of alcoholics were coping with an acute stress. Organizations such as Al-Anon were seen as an excellent modality to provide supportive intervention (e.g., Jackson, 1954). In the 1970s, general systems therapists and behavior therapists both suggested that alcohol problems and marital discord were integrally related, and that modifications of the marital system were perhaps necessary to effect change in an alcoholic's drinking behavior (e.g., Miller, 1976; Ward & Faillace, 1970).

A number of treatment outcome studies (reviewed in Paolino & Mc-Crady, 1977) have found that involving the spouse in the treatment of alcoholism leads to a slightly more successful treatment outcome than

BARBARA S. McCRADY ● Problem Drinkers Project, Butler Hospital and Brown University, Providence, Rhode Island 02906. Preparation of this chapter was supported in part by NIAAA grant 5ROIAA03984.

treatment without the spouse involved. However, in these studies, the mode of involvement of the spouse has ranged widely from education about the disease concept of alcoholism, to spouse group therapy, to conjoint hospitalizations for alcoholics and their spouses, to intensive marital therapy. Thus, the literature says little about what type of spouse involvement is the most effective and economical, and for whom. Because of this state of the couples treatment literature, a 3½-year, NIAAA-funded research program was begun in order to study components of spouse involvement in the treatment of alcoholism.* In this study, three modes of spouse involvement are compared: (1) minimal spouse involvement, (2) teaching the spouse how to effectively respond to drinking behavior and reinforce nondrinking, and (3) marital therapy. All couples receive individualized behavior therapy for the drinking behavior, and all receive treatment as couples. Each subject is being followed for 18 months after the termination of treatment.

In the present chapter, one of the couples treated through this study will be presented. This particular couple was selected because they were randomly assigned to the experimental group which included marital interventions. Thus, the role of marital interventions with alcoholic couples is well illustrated through their treatment. Ways of teaching the spouse how to cope with drinking behavior are also illustrated through this case. Finally, and most importantly, this couple was exceedingly difficult to treat, and the discussion will demonstrate some rather unconventional techniques for involving the couple in treatment and maintaining a therapeutic relationship with them.

2. IDENTIFYING INFORMATION

Mr. and Mrs. D. were referred for outpatient treatment for Mr. D.'s alcohol abuse by their therapist from a community mental health clinic. Mr. D. is a 52-year-old white man; he has a 10th-grade education and is employed as a factory worker. Mrs. D. is 50 years old, and at the time of treatment was a homemaker, although she had intermittently worked outside of her home. They had been married for 28 years, and had 5 children. The oldest child, a daughter, was currently separated from her husband. The other four children, boys who ranged in age from 18 to 24 years, all lived at home. Several of the sons had had problems with the police, and one had made a suicide attempt as a teenager.

Nine days prior to contacting us for treatment, Mr. D. had begun to

* NIAAA research 5R01 AA-03984, "Marital, spouse and self-control treatment of alcoholism," B. McCrady, principal investigator.

drink beer and hard liquor in combination. He felt that he had lost control of his drinking that particular evening and called a hotline to talk. He also drove to a private psychiatric hospital in the middle of that same night but was not admitted to the hospital. He did not go to work the next day and later that morning went to the state hospital alcohol detoxification unit. He stayed in the hospital for two days and then signed himself out of the hospital on the third morning. He found the experience of the state hospital frightening, especially seeing patients who had had 20 to 30 previous hospitalizations, with severe physical consequences of drinking. After his discharge, he contacted his outpatient counselor, who referred him to our couples treatment program.

3. HISTORY OF DRINKING PROBLEMS AND CURRENT STATUS

Mr. D. reported problems with alcohol for the last 36 years. He previously had been a bar-room drinker but for the past several years had confined all of his drinking to the home. He reported a number of consequences of his drinking that were of concern to him; he also reported that his wife, parents, relatives, and friends and all expressed concerns about his drinking. He had begun to miss work because of his drinking and in the last year had missed 8 days. He had been arrested for DWI in 1953 and was charged with leaving the scene of an accident in 1949. He reported that he felt that he needed alcohol to function, because he often felt jittery and irritable. He had experienced blackouts in the past because of his drinking, and his wife had sought help through Al-Anon approximately two years prior to this treatment. He also complained of chronic feelings of depression, having "no ambition," and lack of interest. He was not sure if these problems were a consequence of his alcohol-use pattern.

However, prior to his hospitalization at the state hospital, Mr. D. had never received treatment for his drinking. He had had one successful period of abstinence since his drinking had become a problem. At the time of their 25th wedding anniversary, Mrs. D. told her husband that she did not want to spend the second 25 years of marriage like the first 25 years and asked her husband to stop drinking. He stopped drinking for 43 days, returning to the use of alcohol at a Christmas party. After that one drinking day, he immediately returned to his pattern of daily drinking. She reported that his drinking had seriously affected their relationship, citing communication problems and a lack of mutually shared interests as being the most significant consequences. In the past, she reported that they had frequently argued about his drinking, but that in the last few years she had stopped commenting about it, so the arguments had ceased.

In the year prior to seeking treatment, Mr. D. reported that he drank some alcohol every single day. About half of the time (176 days), he reported that he drank 3 to 6 drinks in the day (see Figure 1). His heavy drinking typically occurred on weekends, holidays, and vacations. On those days, he would begin drinking in the morning and drink throughout the day, mostly at home. He drank an average of one case of beer per weekend. During the week, he usually consumed three beers as soon as he returned home after work and would then have three more beers after dinner. He never drank in the morning or during the day on work days, and he showed no overt signs of alcohol withdrawal. He also reported no withdrawal symptoms when he had stopped drinking at his wife's request or when he was in the state hospital. However, both he and his wife reported that they believed that he needed beer at night to avoid being irritable. He reported no medical consequences as a result of his drinking. Liver function studies (including Total Bilirubin, SGOT, SGPT, LDH, and Alkaline Phosphatase) were all within normal limits at the beginning of treatment, and his family doctor, who had examined him 6 months prior to treatment, stated that he was in good health.

4. PSYCHOLOGICAL-PSYCHIATRIC HISTORY

At the time that he presented for treatment, concerns were raised about

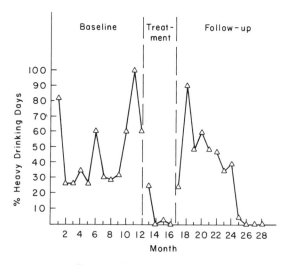

Figure 1. Drinking behavior.

the possibility of other psychological or psychiatric problems. In May 1979, Mr. D. had sought treatment at his local mental health clinic because of problems in dealing with his sons. He and his wife were seen for three sessions of conjoint treatment, with the focus on helping them to learn to let their sons make their own decisions and to allow them to experience the consequences of their own actions. However, after this phase of treatment was completed, Mr. D. continued in individual treatment. He was seen every 2 weeks, with the focus of treatment on problems with depression and "midlife issues," including his feelings of being a failure in his life, of having failed with his children, and dissatisfaction with his job.

In the summer of the same year, he saw his family physician, who said that he was healthy medically but somewhat depressed. He was given Elavil, 75 mg, which he said calmed him but had no effect on the depressed feelings. At the time that he sought treatment in our program, he was still taking the medication and had some problems associated with depression. For example, he felt that his work was unimportant, and that his childrens' failures were a reflection on him. He also reported that he had chronic "low spirits," saying, "I've never been a happy person." He had few interests outside of his job and was unable to complete chores and responsibilities around the house. He also reported that it usually took him 2 to 3 hours to get to sleep at night, and that this had been a problem for as long as he could remember. However, he did not report any suicidal ideation, changes in appetite or weight, or a worsening of any of these symptoms in recent months or years.

He was screened for various psychotic symptoms (Wing, Cooper, & Sartorius, 1974) and given a brief screening interview (Folstein, Folstein, & McHugh, 1975) for problems commonly associated with organic brain syndromes, such as questions about orientation, memory, ability to follow instructions, copy simple figures, etc. He showed absolutely no impairment on the organicity screening and no psychotic symptomatology.

It was concluded from these initial data that alcohol was playing a major part in his current difficulties, in that he was drinking daily, it appeared to interfere with his relationship with his wife and his ability to complete responsibilities at home, and it was beginning to interfere with his work. It was hypothesized that his daily alcohol consumption might be a major contributing factor to his ennui and fatigue, and that it was possibly contributing to his depressed mood as well. However, the alternative hypothesis, that the chronic feelings of failure and self-deprecation might be independent of his alcohol use, could not be excluded. It was decided that treatment would focus on his alcohol use, and the presenting problems with depression would be monitored throughout treatment.

5. ASSESSMENT PROCEDURES

Detailed assessments were completed in three major areas: drinking behavior, spouse involvement in drinking, and marital functioning. Some of these assessments were completed prior to the initiation of treatment, some constituted the first phase of intervention, and some were utilized as a means to monitor ongoing treatment.

5.1. Measurement of Drinking Behavior

Prior to the initiation of treatment, a 365-day drinking history (Sobell, Maisto, Sobell, Cooper, Cooper, & Sanders, 1980) was obtained, in which Mr. and Mrs. D. were asked to categorize his drinking for each day as abstinent, light (1 to 2 drinks), medium (3 to 6 drinks), or heavy (more than 6 drinks). The couple was asked to recall significant events, such as birthdays, holidays, illnesses, and vacations, and to mark these on a calendar prior to obtaining the daily drinking history. Recalling these significant events assisted them in recalling Mr. D.'s drinking and also helped the therapist to identify patterns. As noted above, this history revealed that his heaviest drinking was on weekends, holidays, and vacations.

Two other procedures were used to obtain more details about the factors associated with Mr. D.'s drinking: a functional-analysis questionnaire, developed for this study, and self-recording cards. The Drinking Patterns Questionnaire (Zitter & McCrady, 1979), presents over 200 situations, feelings, and thoughts often associated with drinking. Both Mr. and Mrs. D. completed the questionnaire independently, endorsing all items which they thought were associated with his drinking. The questionnaire covers 10 major areas, including environmental, work and financial factors, physiological states, interpersonal situations, marital problems, relationships with parents, problems with children, emotional factors, and recent major life stresses. At the same time, both Mr. and Mrs. D. were introduced to the use of self-recording cards and instructed in their use. On Mr. D.'s cards, he was to record the exact time and situation for each drink which he consumed, and also any thoughts he had about wanting to have a drink which he did not fulfill by drinking. He was also to rate his marital satisfaction daily, using a 1–7 scale. As a validity check, Mrs. D. was asked to keep a daily estimate of her husband's drinking, recording it as abstinent, light, moderate, or heavy. She also made a single entry on a 1–7 scale of how strong she believed his urges were to drink during the day, and a similar scale rating her satisfaction in their relationship.

After they had completed the questionnaire and spent 1 week of self-recording, two sessions were devoted to teasing out the most important areas associated with Mr. D.'s drinking, as well as to teach Mr. and Mrs. D. how to develop behavior chains. Thus, several situations from the cards and the questionnaire were discussed. For each, the therapist and couple would discuss the environmental factors, Mr. D.'s cognitive and affective response to the situation, and both the positive and negative consequences of the drinking in that situation. Blank sheets, with boxes for each of the components of the behavior chain, were completed given to Mr. D. to complete between sessions.

Based on these assessments, four major areas were identified as related to Mr. D.'s drinking. These included environmental, habitual aspects of his drinking; certain interpersonal situations; certain cognitive or emotional events; and certain physical feelings. Some of the most salient environmental cues surrounded his return home from work each day. Coming in the door, sitting in his favorite chair at the kitchen table, and watching television in the den were all components of this particular behavioral sequence, which he strongly associated with drinking. Furthermore, he and his sons all kept their beer in a separate refrigerator, Mr. D.'s beer was always kept on the top shelf, and he described an almost automatic sequence of walking into the pantry, opening the refrigerator, and grabbing a beer. There were some other environmental antecedents which were also quite salient, although they did not occur as frequently. For example, he occasionally worked a second job delivering cars on weekends. He wanted a beer very much when he returned home. Also, returning home from church on Sunday mornings was a strong cue to drink, as were weddings or parties.

A second important area associated with his drinking was interpersonal situations. At many times, he would feel strongly that he was not as good as other persons. This feeling could be elicited when he was trying to do a project and saw someone else complete it more successfully, or when he was with someone who was better educated than he. The other interpersonal aspects of his drinking all related to actual drinking situations, such as being offered a drink, having a friend or workman over to his house and offering the other person a drink, or merely being around other people who were drinking.

The third aspect of his drinking was the strong cognitive and emotional antecedents. These included his repeated ruminations about past mistakes, feeling that he had failed the children or his wife, feeling depressed, thinking that he was not a good provider for his family. He also associated feeling bored or tired with a desire to drink.

In the fourth major area, the physiological area, Mr. D. reported that he often drank in response to aversive physical states, such as when he felt tired or fatigued, restless, jittery, or nervous. He believed that alcohol helped him to relax when he returned home from work, and that it helped him to feel more energetic when he was fatigued.

Most of the aversive consequences of his drinking were described in the history and current-problems section above. In addition to the interview, the Michigan Alcoholism Screening Test (Selzer, 1971) and a negative-consequences section of the Drinking Patterns Questionnaire were used to help identify these negative consequences. His score on the MAST was 35. The DPQ also includes a section on positive consequences of drinking, which helped him to identify some of the potentially reinforcing effects of alcohol for him, such as feeling happier and more relaxed when he drank, feeling that he could forget his problems and not follow through on responsibilities, and feeling more comfortable, outgoing, and friendly in social situations.

5.2. Measurement of Spouse Behavior

After completing this rather detailed functional analysis of Mr. D.'s drinking behavior, we turned to Mrs. D.'s role in the drinking. Both Mr. and Mrs. D. filled out a Spouse Behavior Questionnaire, modified from that developed by James and Goldman (1971) to include more positive behavioral responses to drinking, as well as adding in more items related to cuing behavior for drinking or reinforcement of drinking behavior. Both identified that Mrs. D. engaged in many behaviors that seemed to punish drinking but also cued further drinking. These particular behaviors seemed on the surface to be strong punishers for drinking, but because Mr. D. reacted to most of these actions by becoming angry and resentful or depressed, they actually served as cues for further drinking. These negative actions included threatening to leave because of his drinking, saying that the children would lose respect for him, pouring alcohol down the sink or getting rid of it in other ways, hiding alcohol, and questioning Mr. D. on where he had been. In addition to cuing further drinking directly, Mrs. D. appeared to protect her husband from the consequences of his drinking by attempting to make him comfortable when drunk, cleaning up after him when he drank, getting him to bed, bringing him up from the car if he passed out, doing his chores for him, and doing things together with him when he was drinking. Both agreed that the actions of hers which most contributed to increasing his drinking were arguing with him before he would go out, pleading with him not to drink, or pleading with him to stop.

At the same time that we identified many ways in which Mrs. D. perpetuated her husband's drinking, many positive actions of hers were apparent. She was an extremely giving, loving woman and was very attentive to him. She would arrange special treats for him when he was drinking less and would often suggest that they do something together that would relieve his boredom as well as be incompatible with drinking, such as going for a ride, to the movies, or bowling. She was very available to him if he wanted to talk about his desire to drink when he was not drinking, reported that she would compliment him in his actions or appearance when sober, and would express affection or have sexual relations with him when he was not drinking. She also would frequently reassure him that he was not a bad person and would offer practical advice to him on how to handle his feelings of depression. While some of this latter attention may have actually served to reinforce his expressions of negative thoughts, her involvement with him was apparent.

5.3. Measurement of Marital Relationship

The final area which was assessed in detail was Mr. and Mrs. D.'s marital relationship. Two main assessment approaches were used, including the Locke-Wallace Marital Adjustment Test (Locke & Wallace, 1959), and the Areas of Change Questionnaire (Birchler & Webb, 1977). In addition, observations of their interactions were made during the early assessment and treatment sessions. On the Locke-Wallace, Mr. and Mrs. D. disagreed somewhat in their assessment of the current status of their relationship. For example, Mrs. D. stated that if she had her life to live over again, she would not marry at all, while Mr. D. stated that he would marry the same person again. They both identified finances, recreation, and philosophy of life as areas of occasional disagreement between them. On the Areas of Change, Mrs. D. expressed her desire for her husband to start conversations more often, drink less, give her more attention, participate in planning their free time, and express his feelings more clearly. Mr. D., on the other hand, did not mark any items as areas in which he wanted his wife to change. Clinical observations of this couple yielded more information about their interactions. For example, it quickly became apparent that Mrs. D. often assumed that she knew what her husband was thinking and would then act as if her assumption were correct. Mr. D., in turn, would rarely correct her but would respond to her by withdrawing, sighing, and making faces. However, he also experienced her as withdrawn from him because she would often fall asleep in the evening, which he interpreted as a statement that she did not want to be with him. However, he almost never expressed this concern to her directly. The other interaction which occurred frequently in the sessions was Mrs. D.'s enthusiastic suggestions to her husband on how to change his drinking or his negative thinking. She would give him minilectures, which he would listen to, making little eye contact throughout and reacting little after she was done. Thus, it was apparent that they lacked skills in expressing feelings directly to each other, were deficient in their ability to understand and validate the other's statements, and had specific problems in the areas of finances, recreation, spending time together, and expressing affection.

In addition to the assessment procedures described above and the observations of interactions in the initial evaluation sessions, the therapist made several observations of the D.'s style of interacting with the therapist, as a way to help plan a therapeutic style of intervention which might be most effective in helping them to make changes. Two particular components of their interactions were notable at the beginning of treatment. First, Mr. D. repeatedly made reference to the authority of the therapist, making comments such as, "Well, you're the doctor, you know these things." He would also comment on his limited education, in comparison to the therapist's. Together, Mr. and Mrs. D. asked innumerable questions of the therapist in the first sessions. These questions usually were requests for advice on how to handle various problems, such as how Mrs. D. should respond if her husband had some alcohol, or how to handle problems with their children. A number of these questions usually were presented at once, and the couple usually did not wait for the therapist to reply. Later in treatment, many other interactional problems arose with the therapist and the D.'s, but these will be presented below, since they did not contribute to the original treatment planning.

6. TREATMENT GOALS AND IMPLEMENTATION STRATEGY

Since Mr. and Mrs. D. were part of a clinical research program, much of their treatment plan was prepackaged. However, the degree of emphasis on different components of the package and the appropriateness of the components had to be evaluated. In this discussion, focus will be placed on the relationship between the assessment information and the treatments utilized. Some components of the package were of limited relevance to this couple, and while they were introduced to the D.'s, these elements will not be discussed here. Table 1 summarizes the components and sequencing of the treatment package.

Interventions were planned to occur in three major areas: Mr. D.'s drinking behavior and associated problems, Mrs. D.'s response to her husband's drinking, and interventions to affect the quality and type of marital interactions and to improve communication skills. Since Mr. D. was still drinking on a daily basis at the beginning of treatment, an initial decision had to be made about whether or not he would require detoxification. Then a decision about drinking goals had to be agreed upon. Since he had stopped drinking without withdrawal symptoms on two occasions in the past, and

Table 1. Treatment Interventions

Session No.	Client interventions	Spouse interventions	Couple interventions
1	Treatment rationale	Same	Same
	Introduction to functional analysis	Same	Same
	Teaching self-recording	Same	Same
2	Client functional analysis		
3	Client functional analysis	Spouse functional analysis	
4	Stimulus control	Spouse functional analysis	
		Verbal reinforcement	
5	Stimulus control	Concrete reinforcement	Joint enjoyable activity
	Self-reinforcement		
6	Rehearsal of negative consequences of drinking	Ignoring drinking	"Love day"
		Decreasing "protection"	
7	Cognitive restructuring	Decreasing "protection"	"Love day"
8	Drink refusal and assertiveness	Spouse role in drink refusal	"Love day"
			Introduction to communication
9	Assertion	Assertion	
10	Relaxation	Relaxation	Communication I: Listening and summarizing
11	Relaxation	Relaxation	Communication II: Identify communication deficits
12			Communication III: Leveling and editing
13			Negotiating and problem solving
14			Problem solving
15	Maintenance planning	Same	Same

since his pattern of drinking did not include morning drinking or drinking to quell obvious physical withdrawal symptoms, it was decided that detoxification was not necessary. Both Mr. and Mrs. D. felt that abstinence was the appropriate drinking goal. Both believed, based on popular knowledge, that abstinence was the only appropriate goal for a person with a drinking problem. Further, Mr. D. reported that at times he felt that he was unable to control his drinking and that it would be exceedingly difficult for him to limit his alcohol intake at those times. Their subjective preference would have been enough to lead to a decision for abstinence for Mr. D. However, because of the problems which he was experiencing with his mood and his inability to complete tasks or enjoy activities, it was also decided that abstinence would be important as a tool to assess more accurately the interaction of the depressant effects of the alcohol with any possible independent depressed state. Therefore, because of their subjective preference, his experience of loss of control, and the importance of assessing his depression in a drug-free state, a treatment goal of abstinence was agreed upon.

After this treatment goal was decided upon, several interventions were seen as most important in helping Mr. D. to abstain from the use of alcohol. Rate-reduction procedures, stimulus-control procedures, and procedures to teach him to engage in activities alternative to drinking, were the primary strategies to deal with the environmental aspects of his drinking. Cognitive restructuring techniques were seen as the best modality for intervening in his negative cognitions in interpersonal situations, as well as in teaching him to respond differently when he began to ruminate about the past. Finally, relaxation training was planned to help him with the fatigue and jitteriness which he experienced.

To teach Mrs. D. new ways of responding to her husband's drinking, it was planned to teach her to reinforce his nondrinking behavior contingently, rather than providing rewards on a noncontingent basis. Second, teaching her ways to express her negative feelings about his drinking in an assertive and constructive manner was seen as important. And third, teaching her ways to decrease her protection of him was identified as an important intervention.

To intervene in the marital relationship, a two-phased plan was established. First, interventions to increase the rewarding value of the marriage were planned. These were to include structuring enjoyable activities together and increasing their rate of daily positive exchanges. The second phase of intervention was to teach them improved communication skills (e.g., Gottman, Notarius, Gonso, & Markham, 1976; Weiss, 1978).

The timing and phasing of these interventions were seen as extremely important. The first focus had to be on helping Mr. D. to reduce then stop his drinking. This was important for three major reasons: (1) If he was drinking heavily every day he probably would not be able to learn and practice new behaviors effectively. (2) If he was able to stop drinking, he would have a strong initial success in treatment, which would help him to attempt some of the later, difficult treatment tasks. (3) Teaching his wife to reinforce nondrinking, or teaching the couple to engage in mutually rewarding activities, was probably not possible when he was drinking, because the drinking resulted in so much tension, anger, and ill will between the two of them.

The second area that was to be phased into treatment was to increase the reward value of abstinence, through spouse reinforcement and mutually enjoyed activities. It was felt that his naturally occurring density of rewards was low and that increasing this density early would help him to maintain his initial gains in treatment; it might also affect his depressed mood.

Finally, after he was not drinking and was experiencing some rewards for this, interventions to teach him active coping skills and to teach the couple to improve their communication skills were seen as more feasible, since they would have built up some good feelings to draw on in learning to talk to each other more honestly and collaborate in solving problems.

In addition to these specific interventions, certain therapeutic stances of the therapist were planned. These included making it very clear to the couple that the responsibility for change lay with Mr. D. in regard to his drinking, to attempt to neutralize Mrs. D.'s attempts to control his drinking, and as a way to affect indirectly Mr. D.'s sense of self-efficacy. A second part of the therapeutic stance was to tell the couple that the goal of treatment was to teach them ways to solve their problems, rather than to provide answers to each of their specific questions. This consultant role was especially important for them, since Mr. D. so frequently would degrade his own abilities and appeal to authority for answers.

With this treatment plan in mind, the discussion will now focus on the course of treatment. The reader should refer to Table 1 for clarity about the ordering of the interventions.

6.1. Treatment of Drinking Behavior

The first several sessions were extremely difficult. As noted above, the D.'s asked innumerable questions. The goals of these first sessions were accomplished, but the therapist felt that the couple had dominated the sessions. Therefore, this concern was shared with the couple, the therapist indicating that it would be important for them to focus on topics one at a time, so that progress could be made, instead of trying to resolve all problems at once. They were amenable to this limit setting and suggested that they expected the therapist to let them know what was appropriate to talk about in the session.

Reducing the rate of Mr. D.'s drinking was the first focus of treatment. He contracted for rate reduction, with the goal being that he would be completely abstinent from alcohol by the 5th week of treatment. Mr. D. expressed concern that he would not be able to stop drinking and also said that he was afraid that if he stopped drinking he would return to even heavier drinking if he resumed it. The therapist attempted to handle these feelings in several different ways. First, the validity of the anxiety about stopping drinking was acknowledged, since he was not experienced at abstinence, and drinking was an overlearned response for him. At the same time, he was reminded about the reasons he had stated for stopping drinking, especially his concerns about his work and his not wanting to return to the state hospital. Setting goals for rate reduction were also indirectly aimed at his concerns. After the first session, the goal was set for him to reduce his nightly alcohol consumption from 6 beers per night to 3 beers and to halve his weekend consumption to 12 beers, rather than his customary 24 beers. He was successful in his weeknight consumption on 3 of 5 days but drank 4 beers on 2 evenings. On the first weekend, however, he had a great deal of trouble, drinking 9 and 20 oz. of alcohol, respectively. Since he had only partially accomplished his rate reduction the 1st week, the same goal was established for the 2nd week. He continued to have partial success, drinking above the 3 beers-a-day goal on two occasions and drinking 16 beers during this second weekend. The same goal was set for the 3rd week, with several interventions to assist him in limiting his drinking. First, he was taught how to complete behavior chains, first by completing chains on previous drinking situations and then by completing chains on urges which he experienced during the week. He was successful in analyzing drinking urges but did not find this skill helpful in controlling his drinking. We also began to introduce Mr. D. to stimulus-control procedures. While these will be described in detail below, it should be noted here that he thought that these procedures were "silly," stating that he believed that people drank because they wanted to, and that once he made a decision to stop, he would do so. Despite the functional analysis and stimulus-control skills, Mr. D. continued to drink at approximately the same level for 2 more weeks. Then, 2 days before the fifth treatment session, he stopped drinking completely, saying that he had made a commitment to treatment and to stopping drinking by the fifth session, so he had done so!

During these first five sessions, the therapist was also teaching Mr. and Mrs. D. basic concepts about alcohol use and the development of behavior chains around different drinking situations. Mr. D. repeatedly questioned the notion of antecedents and consequences of drinking, especially stating that nothing "made" him drink. The therapist attempted to discuss antecedents in terms of probabilities and suggested that a behavioral analysis would help him think about his drinking in a way that would allow him to decide how to make changes to help him abstain. He did not accept this view of drinking, but indicated a willingness to listen and try some of the interventions suggested.

By the fourth session, we began to develop self-management plans to help Mr. D. change some of the habitual aspects of his drinking. He thought that the approach was silly, and the therapist decided to attempt to use self-revelation as a way to decrease his alternately excessively compliant—excessively resistant pattern of interaction in therapy. Therefore, I talked at some length about my own struggles with binge or compulsive eating, and some of the self-management strategies that had been helpful in controlling this problem, such as taking a bath, going to bed early, always having low-calorie, attractive snacks available, etc. I also emphasized that I agreed with his assessment that a person had to make a decision to change his or her behavior, but that once the decision was made, a person could select actions that would facilitate carrying out the decision. I also frequently suggested that he should try out different approaches but that he ultimately would decide what would be most helpful to him in the long run.

With this lengthy discussion about the therapist's own attempts at self-management, and attempts to reframe his views about change, we began some self-management planning. Mrs. D. got very involved in this section of the treatment. As the notion of self-management was introduced, she eagerly indicated that she had been telling her husband for years that he should get a hobby or some interests, and that if he only did these instead of drinking, he would be fine. This created more problems, as Mr. D. was quite resistant and resentful toward his wife for making suggestions about how he should manage his life. The therapist strongly emphasized that the primary responsibility for change lay with Mr. D., that he had to decide what changes were good for him, and that even if the changes he ultimately decided on were the same as ones which his wife had suggested, it was different if he chose to do them. She was able to accept this, since it was framed in the context of her intense desire to help him, indicating that one of the ways to help was to allow Mr. D. to take responsibility for himself. He also liked this view, saying to his wife, "So what the doctor is saying is for you to butt out."

During the 1st week in which self-management planning was attempted, Mr. D. was still drinking and implemented none of his plans. However, after he stopped drinking, he began to develop and implement a number of plans, most of which he generated himself. His plans included: running errands after work instead of going straight home, taking a nap when he got home, going into the den to read the paper instead of sitting at the kitchen table, working late, or exercising. In addition, he decided to buy soda to put in his place in the refrigerator and keep the beer in the closet instead of in the refrigerator. He was, however, unwilling to entertain the notion of buying no beer at all. He was successful in implementing several of these plans, including the soda, going into the den, and reading the paper. However, he never ran errands, stating that he was too tired, never exercised, and, surprisingly, never took naps. He felt that the self-management procedures were moderately helpful but kept stating that this wasn't keeping him from drinking. The therapist agreed with him that his decision not to drink was paramount, and these were merely ways to help him follow through and reinforce the decision. It was important not to directly challenge his belief in his decision-making ability, as this man had so many beliefs about his own lack of control over his life that it was important to increase rather than challenge this sense of control.

6.2. Increasing Reinforcement for Abstinence

By the fifth session, Mrs. D. was incorporated more fully into the change process. At this point, the concept of reinforcement for desirable behavior was introduced. It was now possible to introduce this notion, as Mr. D. was not drinking and was therefore exhibiting behavior which Mrs. D. could reinforce. However, Mr. D. was resistant to the notion of reinforcement. He stated that there was nothing that his wife could say that he would like, stating instead that she could show her appreciation only through her actions. Since improving verbal communication skills was important for this couple, some time was spent on trying to help them articulate ways in which she could verbally reinforce him. He finally stated that if she were very matter-of-fact, saying something like "Gee, Gerry, you're doing good," he would like that. They practiced this interaction in the session. She had a great deal of difficulty in the role playing but finally was able to express her compliments to him. She was able to deliver these types of compliments three times during the week but said that she felt unnatural doing so, and he stated that he didn't like it when she did so.

They were, however, much more amenable to suggestions about her providing concrete positive reinforcers for him and to the idea of doing something enjoyable together, contingent on his not drinking. Thus, over the next two weeks, they went to a movie (they saw *Kramer versus Kramer*, which he found depressing), to flea markets, and spent time window shopping for furniture. They both reported enjoying these activities together, which were new for them. Also, she began to fix special dinners and snacks for him. One evening, she fed their sons, first, and then fixed his favorite dinner and dessert, so that she and her husband could eat their special dinner together. Another evening, she fixed him a hero sandwich and brought it into the den for him to eat while he watched television.

By the end of the first five sessions, several goals had been accomplished. Mr. D. was not drinking alcohol, a complete functional analysis of his drinking and his wife's involvement in his drinking had been accomplished, some assessment of their marital relationship had been done, and they had both begun to implement behavior changes. The therapist had found that a combination of self-revelation, emphasizing Mr. D.'s own control and capacity for change, and reframing Mrs. D.'s behavior as attempts at support seemed to be effective in helping Mr. and Mrs. D. to make changes in treatment.

Several goals were outlined for the next several sessions of therapy. First, it was decided that Mr. D. needed to learn several skills to help support his abstinence. These included cognitive-restructuring techniques, drink-refusal skills, and relaxation skills. Mrs. D. also needed to learn to respond more effectively to her husband's drinking. The skills targeted included learning to express her feelings about his drinking without being nagging or angry, learning to allow him to experience the negative consequences of his drinking, and learning to make her behavior contingent, rather than noncontingent, on his drinking.

6.3. Skills Training—Mr. D.

The primary focus on teaching cognitive-restructuring techniques revolved around Mr. D.'s strong and frequent negative self-statements. He was able to identify many such thoughts, stating that they came most frequently when he was sitting at his machine in the factory. He felt that such thinking was natural and impossible to change. He did not understand the notion of irrational thinking when it was presented to him abstractly, or when he was given examples of how his own thoughts could be seen as irrational and how these could be challenged. He expressed willingness to try a cognitive-restructuring homework exercise but did not complete it for 2 weeks in a row. During the introduction to cognitive restructuring, Mrs. D. would echo examples of rational thoughts presented by the therapist, giving examples of how she thought more rationally about their children than her husband did. Her comments served to denigrate him and may have increased his thoughts of himself as a failure. After Mr. D. came in the second time without completing this particular homework assignment and again stated his belief that there was no way to change his behavior or his thoughts, a decision was made that shaping, rational explanations, reframing, and reinforcement were not effectively getting through to him. Therefore, a higher intensity confrontation approach was used with him. He was told that he would never be any better or change at the rate that he was going, since he was putting all his considerable talents into thinking of reasons for not changing, instead of thinking of ways to change. Further, I stated that he was such a negative thinker that he would have to expend huge amounts of energy to be able to change these habits, and that nothing would change with his half-hearted attempts. I then went on at great length about how people have choices in how they act, no matter what the situation. The morning of that particular treatment session, my car had broken down on the way to work, and I was stranded in a local milk store for 1½ hours waiting for a tow truck to come. I told Mr. and Mrs. D. about this incident in great detail, telling him that I stood in the milk store working with my thoughts constantly, because I kept beginning to think "I'm wasting time; I could be getting work done," and every time those thoughts entered my head I began to get more tense, angry, and upset. I indicated that I had to consciously keep substituting more rational thoughts, such as "You have to stay with the car, and getting angry is only making you feel worse, so try to enjoy the break." I then said that I didn't want to see them again until he had made a decision to change, and until he had carried out his cognitive-restructuring homework *every* day for a week. I concluded by stating that I hoped that I would see them next week, but that they should just call and cancel if he hadn't completed the assignment.

This whole strategy clearly was a high-risk strategy, since he could easily interpret it as an attack on him and a confirmation of his own inadequacies, and use it as a way to discontinue treatment. However, I felt that several factors mitigated against such an outcome of the confrontation. First, by this time in treatment, I had a good relationship with them in general, in that they came regularly to sessions, listened carefully, and argued if they disagreed, instead of passively listening and then being noncomplaint. He also occasionally teased me about my eating, telling me in elaborate detail about some of his evening snacks, and then stating that he knew I would have liked it. Thus, the overall therapeutic relationship had become a positive one. Also, I had used self-revelation with them in the past and framed much of my confrontation in this session in terms of an example from my own life. I did this as a way to minimize the critical aspect of the confrontation as well as to model what I had been trying to communicate. Finally, I decided that an impassioned statement would be experienced as an indication of how much I cared about his changing and would therefore not be heard as an attack.

Fortunately, Mr. and Mrs. D. returned for their next appointment with homework completed. Mr. D. had kept careful records of his irrational and negative self-statements and ways he had countered them. He reported that during that week he was the happiest he had been in years, and he attributed this greater happiness to his being able to think more positively and rationally about himself. I greeted them with great enthusiasm, deliberately breathing an audible sigh of relief when I saw them outside, telling them that I had been holding my breath all day, hoping that they'd come in. He was visibly pleased with himself, as was his wife.

This represented a major turning point in treatment. Mr. D. became more involved in controlling his thoughts and, for the first time, began to express some optimism about his future. With this success in mind, it was decided to develop some other skills that were geared toward his staying sober. An attempt was made to begin some drink-refusal training with Mr. D. He insisted that saying no to other people was no problem. He reluctantly engaged in role playing exercises in the session but did not complete homework assignments in this area.

The final skills area introduced to Mr. and Mrs. D. was relaxation training, the rationale being recent examples which Mr. D. cited where he had become tense and had recorded urges to drink as a result. I also gave several examples of how I use relaxation, in an attempt to model the value of this particular skill. They were first taught tense-and-relax techniques. Mrs. D. was able to relax well during the instructions; Mr. D. was restless, and said that it had no effect on him. They agreed to practice, but Mr. D. practiced only once during the week, and Mrs. D. practiced three times. She was enthusiastic; he was negative. They were then introduced to relaxation without tensing; again Mrs. D. was positive, Mr. D. negative. However, they both practiced almost daily during the second week of relaxation training and said that they wanted to continue to practice. However, during the rest of treatment, when this was rechecked, neither indicated that they were continuing to practice or attempting to apply the skill in any situations.

6.4. Skills Training—Mrs. D.

Given Mr. D.'s history and Mrs. D.'s repeated examples of becoming overinvolved in what Mr. D. did, it was felt that it was extremely important to teach Mrs. D. new ways of responding to drinking situations, even though he was not currently drinking. For example, she would frequently argue with him when she was afraid that he would drink. Part of a session was devoted to thinking of other things that she could say to him that were assertive, but not so controlling. She first suggested that she could say, "You know that you shouldn't drink." He said that such a statement would make him angry and increase the probability that he would drink. He suggested that she ask him why he felt like drinking, and then remind him of the consequences of his drinking. They acted this out in the office but did not complete it as a homework assignment. They expressed embarrassment about the role playing and also doubt about how useful it would be to them. Some shaping was attempted to help them to complete the homework assignment. First, we acted this out further in the office. Then, they were asked just to talk at home about how they would handle this situation. They successfully completed this assignment; so the role playing was again assigned, and they were more successful in completing it this time.

Mrs. D. also attempted to take care of Mr. D. or protect him when he was drinking. For example, if he drove home after drinking, she would forcibly drag him in from the car and up the stairs to their second-story home. She would undress him, put him to bed, and then be angry and resentful in the morning for the effort she had expended. It took a great deal of discussion for her to be able to recognize the effects of her actions on her husband. He felt that it was desirable that she got him to bed, and she felt that it was part of her responsibility to care for him. The therapist thought that the best way for her to understand the negative effects of these actions was to point out that she was protecting her husband from really realizing that his drinking was a serious problem because he always awakened cozy and in his bed, instead of cold, cramped, and uncomfortable in his car. Thus, she understood the consequences and was finally able to see the problems in protecting her husband and generate an alternative way of handling this situation. She suggested that when she heard his car drive up, she could wait to see if he came up. If he did not, she would go down to check to be sure that he was not injured or unconscious. If he was not, she would return to the house, leaving him there, and not check him again. She would also go to bed at her regular time. To practice this, she used covert rehearsal, imagining this sequence twice in the office, and then rehearsing it several times per day for a week. They both seemed satisfied that her approach was an acceptable compromise between ignoring him completely and being overinvolved in his drinking.

6.5. Marital Interventions

As described in the treatment goals section, three areas were targeted for marital interventions: increasing their enjoyable activities together, increasing the daily rate of positive exchanges, and teaching them better communication skills. Mr. and Mrs. D. spent very little time together prior to treatment, rarely went out except to visit family, and had very abbreviated conversations with each other. Initially, the couple had some difficulty in thinking of mutually pleasurable activities, with Mrs. D. generating most of the ideas. She suggested several possibilities, such as going to Cape Cod together, going window shopping, visiting a fishing town in the southern part of the state and eating at a favorite restaurant there, seeing a movie, going to the zoo or out for pizza on Friday night. As noted in the section above on reinforcement for sobriety, they began to go to the movies and to flea markets and enjoyed themselves. They continued such activities throughout treatment and eventually decided to redecorate their bedroom and buy new furniture, goals which they accomplished together, much to their mutual satisfaction.

We then began to focus on ways in which they could interact more positively at home. Initially a "love day," in which each did as many positive things for the other as possible, was suggested. Both were very negative about this idea. Mr. D. reported that there was little that he could do for his wife, since she really did not want anything, and also said that his wife already did everything nice for him, so there was no more that she could do. Mrs. D., however, suggested some things that her husband could do for her with no trouble. Compliance with this exercise was shaped by first suggesting that they each attempt to do at least four nice things for the other during the week. They were able to agree to this modified homework and were quite successful. Mr. D. took his wife out for lunch one day, cleared the dinner dishes one night, opened the car door for his wife several times, and helped her on with her coat. She was very pleased with these attentions. She in turn fixed him some special snacks, served his dinner in the living room one night when he wanted to watch a special program on television, fixed tea for him in the evenings, and reminded him that there would be wine at Communion, which he appreciated. Following this successful exchange, they continued to set goals for giving to each other, keeping these goals limited to four to six exchanges per week. They were comfortable with this arrangement and seemed to become increasingly pleased with each other during this part of treatment. Of course, these changes were paralleled by his not drinking, which also contributed to Mrs. D.'s positive feeling about their relationship. They also reported that their sexual relationship was more enjoyable, and that Mrs. D. was initiating sexual contact at times, which she had not done in the past.

Since Mr. D. had stopped drinking, and the couple was enjoying a generally more rewarding relationship, the final treatment sessions could be focused exclusively on communication skills training and maintenance planning. At first, Mr. and Mrs. D. were reluctant to discuss their marital relationship and problems and often diverted the content of the sessions to discussions of Mr. D.'s drinking. He had two slips during these sessions, which tended to change the focus of the session to his drinking. One of the most effective interventions at this point was to focus on the positive, supportive, caring relationship which they already had and to give them feedback about the clear improvements in their relationship since the start of treatment. Telling them that they had a good marriage seemed to decrease their defensiveness. Also, giving short attention to the slips, and continuing to focus the sessions primarily on the marital assignments increased their compliance with this phase of treatment.

The D.'s were initially introduced to the Gottman *et al.* (1976) intent-impact notion of communication. They acted out a discussion of a recent problem—trying to decide whether or not to buy a lamp—letting the other person finish sentences and then summarizing their comments before proceeding. As expected, they had some difficulty with this role playing, but with therapist modeling, they were able to grasp the idea of validating understanding of the partner's comment before proceeding. Two other communication problems were noted at this time: Mr. D. often made faces while his wife was talking, and Mrs. D. would make the same point over and over, as if she wanted her husband to agree, rather than to just understand. For homework, they were assigned two more conversations in which they would practice listening and summarizing and carried out both of these successfully. In fact, they recorded the conversations after they had finished and brought their notes to the session. In the following session, time was spent in helping the D.'s to identify other communication deficits. They decided that Mr. D. tended not to validate his wife's comments, interrupted frequently, and would not really agree with his wife's statements. They decided that Mrs. D. also tended not to validate her husband's comments and talk at length without letting her husband have a chance to comment. They then thought of some positive alternatives to these deficits and repeated the summarizing and checking exercise during the session and for homework during the week.

In the next session, the communication topic was on "leveling" and "editing." Since both of the D.'s tended to understate, or not express their feelings to each other at all, the primary focus was to teach them to express their feelings more directly and honestly to each other. Mrs. D. quickly identified a situation where she had successfully expressed her feelings to her husband about his wanting to bring a friend along for her Mother's Day dinner and was pleased that she had been able to do so. However, it was difficult for them to identify other such situations. Since they had already been introduced to some assertiveness training in previous sessions, for homework they were each to identify at least one situation in which they had some unexpressed feelings, and to try to express them directly. Mrs. D. was quite successful in carrying out this assignment; Mr. D. said that he hadn't had any negative feelings toward his wife during the week.

The last sessions taught the D.'s problem-solving skills. They were taught how to identify problems and generate possible solutions. They turned out to be very good at this part of the communication program. They found time to sit down and generate a list of problems that had come up during the week. For example, during this first week of this homework, they identified three problems—Mr. D. not putting things where they belonged in the house, Mrs. D.'s sister parking her car in their driveway, and Mrs. D. taking long breaks from her housework on Mondays, resulting in dinner being late. They decided to work on the problem of Mr. D. leaving things

around the house, came up with a possible solution, and successfully implemented it. They repeated this homework again the next week, continued to
be successful in it, and felt that it was helpful.

6.6. Maintenance Planning

Maintenance planning was unusually important for this couple. As
part of the evaluation, they were to be contacted monthly by a research
assistant for data collection. However, they were also instructed to think of
these contacts as a way of helping them to review their progress and
maintain the gains which they had made in treatment. At the same time,
the importance of the follow-up contacts was emphasized, and they were
told that it was equally important for the research team to know if they
were having difficulties as if they were doing well, so that more could be
learned about the effectiveness of the treatments. It was important to incul-
cate this positive expectancy about honesty rather than "success," since
they were so eager to please that there was concern that they would discontinue follow-up if they began to have difficulties again. Mr. D. also
expressed an interest in attending AA meetings, saying that he felt that AA
members would understand him, and that it would help him to continue to
be abstinent. He attended several meetings while in treatment and was
encouraged to continue after his termination. He and his wife also began to
seek out activities that were both enjoyable and incompatible with drinking. For example, he noted in the local paper that a halfway house for
alcoholics was having a dance and suggested that he and his wife attend.
They went and had a good time, and he reported feeling comfortable
because, "I knew that they were all drunks like me." He also was becoming increasingly active around the house and began a fairly large house
project. He was able to control his thinking so that he could feel successful
about being involved in the project and make progress, rather than being
negative about mistakes or the lengthiness of the project. He realized that
such projects were important to his continued abstinence, and planned
several more, to begin after he completed the current project. He also
worked hard to counter negative and irrational thoughts and reported that
he felt less depressed when he did so, thus, he also identified this as a
crucial skill to work on. They were less enthusiastic about the reinforcement techniques attempted early in treatment but indicated a desire to
continue in engaging in a wide range of activities together. Mrs. D. also felt
that her beginning skills in coping with drinking behavior were important
to continue.

Thus, they identified several areas which were especially helpful to
them in treatment and wrote these down. They also had handouts from the

different treatment components and were planning to review these handouts at least every other month. Finally, some time was spent discussing how to manage a drinking episode, including many of the techniques suggested by Marlatt (1978), such as creating a time delay after the first drink; calling his wife, AA member, or therapist; and focusing on engaging in realistic and rational thinking were such a slip to occur.

7. RESULTS

Figures 2 and 3 summarize the drinking, drinking urges, and marital-satisfaction data which were collected during treatment.

As can be seen in Figure 2, Mr. D. decreased his drinking from a peak of 49 standard drinks in Week 2 to zero drinks in all but 3 of the weeks after Week 5. Each of the drinking episodes later in treatment represented one day of drinking, so Mr. D. decreased his drinking from daily drinking prior to treatment and during the first 4 weeks to 3 drinking days over the next 12 weeks. As can be seen in the same figure, he experienced a dramatic increase in the number or urges to drink after he stopped drinking, but these urges decreased over the weeks of abstinence. From Figure 3, it is apparent that there was little variability in the marital-satisfaction ratings which Mr. D. reported. However, his wife reported increased marital satisfaction after her husband stopped drinking and a further increase in her satisfaction at the conclusion of treatment.

The couple has now been followed for 10 months. As can be seen in

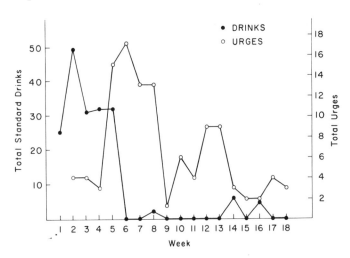

Figure 2. Drinking and drinking urges during treatment.

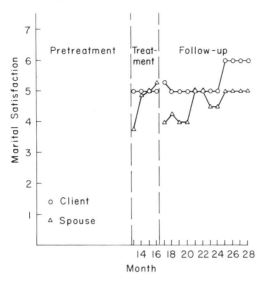

Figure 3. Marital satisfaction.

Figure 1, the gains which Mr. D. made during treatment were not sustained following the termination of treatment. Mr. D. returned to the daily use of alcohol approximately 2 weeks after he completed treatment and drank for 7½ months. At that time, he became heavily involved with Alcoholics Anonymous and has been attending AA meetings 5 days per week for the last 2 months. Figure 3 illustrates the correlation between his drinking and their marital relationship. Mrs. D.'s marital satisfaction decreased concomitant with her husband's return to the daily use of alcohol and only consistently began to increase when he returned to abstinence. As was true during treatment, Mr. D.'s ratings were less variable but also increased when he stopped drinking.

The story behind these follow-up data is extremely interesting. During follow-up, Mr. D. made several contacts with the research assistant, inquiring about the possibility of a referral for further treatment. He was told that he could contact his previous therapist for one scheduled follow-up session but would not do so. Finally, the research assistant was given a list of community resources which he and his wife could utilize, and he finally contacted a treatment program. He enrolled in a stress management program which they offered, continued to drink, and said that he learned nothing new in this program. He finally contacted his former therapist by telephone but would not come in for a meeting. Then, the D.'s therapist gave a public information lecture on alcoholism, which Mr. D. attended. He said hello to the therapist after the lecture but made no further comments. However, immediately after this lecture, he began to attend AA on a daily basis.

8. DISCUSSION

This couple presented many interesting aspects in their treatment which are illustrated in this chapter. First, the art of applying treatment packages to individual clients or couples is rarely discussed. The treatment followed a standardized treatment regime, which could not undergo significant modifications to meet individual treatment needs. This limitation may have been one of the factors contributing to the D.'s limited success with the treatment program. The D.'s apparently needed more time than was allowed to be able to understand, accept, and learn many of the skills presented in the treatment package. While as much time was allocated for each skill as in other similar treatment packages (e.g., Miller, 1978), for this couple two sessions teaching relaxation skills or two sessions on cognitive restructuring did not appear to be enough. Furthermore, there was a great deal of material covered in the treatment package, which may have been overwhelming and confusing to the couple. It is not clear how many of the strategies they were able to utilize after the completion of treatment, but it would appear that these attempts were limited. Another limitation of the package was the necessity of covering a broad range of skill areas. Since one of Mr. D.'s most salient problem areas was his depression and self-deprecatory thinking, in an individualized program more attention could have been paid to this area.

With this couple, the therapeutic relationship became very important in treatment. Several approaches were attempted to engage them in treatment and to obtain compliance with therapeutic interventions. Therapist self-revelation, shaping, and limit setting seemed to be an effective combination. In addition, specific attempts were made to increase Mr. D.'s sense of self-efficacy. However, it may be that this approach was a mistake. Mr. D. clearly appealed to authority to solve his problems. It was felt that this strategy was maladaptive for him, and that it was important to help him learn skills to solve his own problems. These attempts were of limited success, and he currently appears to be more successfully involved in a highly authoritarian treatment—AA. Therefore, it may be with some clients like Mr. D., that capitalizing on this appeal to authority, rather than minimizing it, may be an effective strategy.

A third important element in the treatment was the timing of the drinking and marital interventions. Clearly, it would not have been possible to effect changes in their marital relationship when he was still drinking. She was still angry and hurt, and neither had skills to change these behaviors or feelings. Thus, timing the first interventions to deal with drinking and helping the spouse to begin to learn how to effectively respond to drinking set the stage for them to be more interested in and able to effect changes in their relationship.

The fourth important point illustrated through this couple is the process of treatment and change that goes on after treatment has ended. Perhaps without the treatment package the therapist could have resumed treatment for a limited period of time and shortened the length of Mr. D.'s posttreatment heavy drinking. However, the monthly reminders provided by the follow-up calls may have supported his belief that he still needed to change his drinking behavior and enabled him to recognize it as a continuing problem. The interventions with Mrs. D. may also have played an important role in helping Mr. D. to get back to treatment. Her subjective reports during follow-up suggest that she has managed his drinking much more effectively than she did prior to treatment; she has not nagged him or gotten angry but has given him feedback at sober times about the impact of his drinking on her and reminded him of the positive relationship which they had when he was not drinking during treatment.

Thus, in the long run we do not yet know if Mr. and Mrs. D. are treatment successes or treatment failures. If he does continue to abstain from use of alcohol, and if the improvements in the relationship are sustained, it will be difficult to attribute their success either to our program or to AA. It would appear that a combination of the two, as well as his previous counseling experience may result in improved functioning for this couple. Too often, the therapist who sees a client last is the one to claim success or to be blamed for failure, and the more complicated picture which the D.s leave us with may be one of the most important lessons learned from this discussion and from their treatment and follow-up.

COMMENTARY

Peter E. Nathan

Planning and implementing the assessment of this couple was extensive, as was the assessment of most individuals and couples whose treatment is summarized in this volume.

Especially notable in Barbara McCrady's assessment of Mr. and Mrs. D. were two elements: functional analysis of "spouse involvement in drinking and marital functioning," and periodic validity checks on Mr. D.'s drinking by reports from Mrs. D. on her perceptions of his drinking.

Although virtually every case in this book involving a distressed couple required concurrent assessment of drinking behavior and marital dysfunction and their interaction, none gives the prominence to the latter, most important assessment that McCrady does. Perhaps this attention derived from her special interest in the behavioral treatment of alcoholic couples, a clinical phenomenon on which she is widely published. Perhaps, as well, this felicitous assessment decision derived from inclusion of the D.'s in an empirical study whose protocol required thorough, continuing assessment of both marital dysfunction and alcohol consumption. Whatever the reasons, we believe that the focus given the reciprocity inherent in marriages which are bedeviled by alcohol and disharmony by this design decision is well taken.

Checking out the truthfulness of a patient's self-reports of drinking behavior with an informed other is not new. Making it standard research practice to validate estimates of ingestion over discrete time intervals with a nonalcoholic spouse is not, however, a common one; it requires discussion and prior agreement among alcoholic spouse, nonalcoholic spouse, and therapist. It appears to have generated more valid information than otherwise in this instance and might even have been the vehicle by which spouse-spouse therapeutic cooperation was fostered. On balance, then, it seems to have worked well here—though its potential to disrupt a marital contract has to be taken into account as well.

I found myself wondering, during my reading of the fascinating chronicle of the D.'s, to what extent their participation in a formal research project affected their prospects for beneficial behavior change. On the one hand, subjects in the study's active intervention groups (like the D.'s) benefitted from carefully developed, expertly dispensed behavioral treatment; on the other, by the principal investigator's admission, the design of the intervention had to ensure comparability of treatment for each group's experimental subjects as well as differences in treatment between intervention groups. To one who has only read a brief summary of what was done (the case report on which this commentary was written), it appears that prohibitions against more time being spent on certain procedures (for example, relaxation training and cognitive restructuring) and failure to continue beyond 18 weekly sessions until a better prognosis could be envisaged diminished the outcome. On the other hand, it is difficult to argue with ultimate success—and I cannot help thinking that Mr. D.'s experience of behavioral treatment was crucial to his ultimate acceptance of the fellowship of Alcoholics Anonymous. I have written elsewhere to propose a plan whereby a short course of behavior therapy might be provided alcoholics and problem drinkers to make the interpersonal rigors of AA easier to cope with. In that way, my reasoning goes, they can derive full benefits from the AA experience, an effective treatment for many. Perhaps Barbara McCrady (and Mr. D.) have demonstrated for us that such a proposal has real merit!

One can speculate, as well, on the behavioral effects of the therapist's self-revelations on controlling her eating behavior and adjusting to her recalcitrant automobile. In so doing, she is modeling a rational, relaxed, and effective response to stress that does not require the salve of alcohol. Yet the therapist notes the inordinate esteem in which both the D.'s held her. To what extent could Mr. D. feel it at all possible to learn to react to misfortune and stress like Dr. McCrady did? Although we presume that our patients model our strengths (and hope they overlook our failings), the gap between patient and therapist—sometimes great, sometimes small—is bound to interfere with our efforts to model effective behavior.

Another interesting issue on which to speculate is why Mr. D. was able to maintain abstinence with Alcoholics Anonymous when the behavior therapy package he and his wife completed induced but did not maintain sobriety. Regardless of whether the behavior therapy actually enabled Mr. D. to benefit from AA (a matter about which we speculated above), the fact remains that Mr. D. maintained abstinence only to the end of the 18-session behavior therapy contract, then lost it almost immediately afterwards. Only when Mr. D. began regular AA attendance, 8 months after the behavior therapy, did he again begin to achieve some control over his drinking. Several explanations suggest themselves. The first is that Mr. D. could only remain abstinent or control his drinking when he was actively engaged in some sort of therapy. The second is that AA provided something behavior therapy did not, a comprehensive social-recreational experience that took up much of the nonwork time Mr. D. had previously devoted to drinking.

Another of the things AA might have provided Mr. D. was "understanding," which Mr. D. did not think his therapist or, consistently, his wife provided. The comfort Mr. D. felt while around "drunks like me" was not a feeling he experienced during the behavior therapy sessions. As well, McCrady speculates that the authoritarian appeal of AA might have played an important role for Mr. D., since its program allows less latitude for individual decision making than the behavior therapy program in which Mr. D. had been engaged. With Dr. McCrady, though, I believe that AA made the most sense for Mr. D. because it took responsibility for control from him and placed it on the group; I also believe that it could not have succeeded for Mr. D. without a "priming dose" of behavior therapy, which introduced him to the ideas of self-control and introspection, the value of enhanced self-efficacy, and the benefits of making his wife happier. In sequence, then, behavior therapy and Alcoholics Anonymous made a good treatment package for Mr. D.

9. REFERENCES

Birchler, G. R., & Webb, L. J. Discriminating interaction behaviors in happy and unhappy marriages. *Journal of Consulting and Clinical Psychology, 1977, 45,* 494–495.

Folstein, M. F., Folstein, S. E., & McHugh, P. R. "Mini-mental state." A practical method for grading the cognitive state of patients for the clinician. *Journal of Psychiatric Research, 1975, 12,* 189–198.

Gottman, J., Notarius, C., Gonso, J., & Markman, H. *A couple's guide to communication.* Champaign, Ill.: Research Press, 1976.

Jackson, J. K. The adjustment of the family to the crisis of alcoholism. *Quarterly Journal of Studies on Alcohol, 1954, 15,* 562–586.

James, J. E., & Goldman, M. Behavior trends of wives of alcoholics. *Quarterly Journal of Studies on Alcohol, 1971, 32,* 373–381.

Locke, H. J., & Wallace, K. M. Short marital adjustment and prediction tests: Their reliability and validity. *Marriage and Family Living, 1959, 21,* 251–255.

Marlatt, G. A. *Craving for alcohol, loss of control, and relapse: A cognitive-behavioral analysis.* Alcoholism and Drug Abuse Institute Technical Report No. 77–05, 1978.

Miller, P. M. *Behavior treatment of alcoholism.* New York: Pergamon Press, 1976.

Miller, W. Behavioral treatment of problem drinkers: A comparative outcome study of three controlled drinking therapies. *Journal of Consulting and Clinical Psychology,* 1978, 46, 74–86.

Paolino, T. J., Jr., & McCrady, B. S. *The alcoholic marriage: Alternative perspectives.* New York: Grune & Stratton, 1977.

Price, G. M. A study of the wives of twenty alcoholics. *Quarterly Journal of Studies on Alcohol,* 1945, 5, 620–627.

Selzer, M. L. The Michigan Alcoholism Screening Test: The quest for a new diagnostic instrument. *American Journal of Psychiatry,* 1971, 127, 1653–1658.

Sobell, M. D., Maisto, S. A., Sobell, L. C., Cooper, A. M., Cooper, T. C., & Sanders, B. Developing a prototype for evaluating alcohol treatment effectiveness. In L. C. Sobell, M. B. Sobell & E. Ward (Eds.), *Evaluating alcohol and drug abuse treatment effectiveness: Recent advances.* New York: Pergamon Press, 1980.

Ward, R. F., & Faillace, L. A. The alcoholic and his helpers: A systems view. *Quarterly Journal of Studies on Alcohol,* 1970, 31, 684–691.

Wing, J. K., Cooper, J. E., & Sartorius, N. *Measurement and classification of psychiatric symptoms.* New York: Cambridge University Press, 1974.

Weiss, R. L. The conceptualization of marriage from a behavioral perspective. In T. J. Paolino, Jr., & B. S. McCrady (Eds.), *Marriage and marital therapy.* New York: Brunner/Mazel, 1978.

Zitter, R., & McCrady, B. S. *The Drinking Patterns Questionnaire.* Unpublished questionnaire, 1979.

7

The Behavioral Assessment and Treatment of an Alcoholic Marriage

The Case of Mr. and Mrs. L.

WILLIAM M. HAY

1. INTRODUCTION

This chapter describes the behavioral assessment and treatment of a couple, Mr. and Mrs. L., who were experiencing significant problems related to their alcohol consumption. The couple also had severe marital problems. The case of Mr. and Mrs. L. was chosen for inclusion in this text because it was unique in a number of ways.

Both spouses were experiencing problems related to their heavy consumption of alcohol, not an uncommon situation but one rarely recorded in the literature. The goal of treatment for both Mr. and Mrs. L. was a return to a nonproblem, controlled level of alcohol use rather than total abstinence. Mr. and Mrs. L. were a couple in transition both in terms of age and life style, and both presented some unique challenges to the behavioral procedures employed. Finally, this case provided the opportunity to chart throughout assessment, treatment, and follow-up the interaction of marital and alcohol problems.

WILLIAM M. HAY ● Alcohol Behavior Research Laboratory, Rutgers—The State University, New Brunswick, New Jersey 08903.

2. SUBJECT CHARACTERISTICS AND REASON FOR REFERRAL

Mr. and Mrs. L. had been married for 29 years; they had 4 children (3 boys and 1 girl), whose ages ranged from 18 to 28 years old. The 18-year-old daughter was the only child living at home at the time of the referral—she left for college at a point early in treatment. Mr. L. was a 51-year-old manager with a college education. Mrs. L. was a 49-year-old librarian. The couple was financially secure and reported successful professional careers.

Mr. and Mrs. L. responded to an advertisement in a local newspaper describing a treatment group for problem drinkers and their spouses. The couple described their marital relationship as having deteriorated over the previous 5 years. During that period they had been involved in marital encounter groups and two unsuccessful attempts at marital therapy. Both spouses indicated that their alcohol consumption had also increased over this 5-year period and now was "out of control." Six months prior to their self-referral, Mr. L. had sought assistance for his alcohol problem through the employee assistance program sponsored by his employer. From Mr. L.'s report, the program counselor insisted that Mr. L. was an alcoholic and that abstinence from alcohol was the only treatment. Mr. L. terminated this "treatment" after two visits. Mr. and Mrs. L. had decided to enter treatment at this time because they felt that their drinking and their marital difficulties were related. They also wished to investigate alternatives to total abstinence.

3. ASSESSMENT PROCEDURES

Mr. and Mrs. L. participated in an intake interview followed by eighteen 1-hour conjoint sessions. The first two sessions were devoted to in-depth assessment of alcohol use and marital-relationship problems. Assessment procedures included detailed and comprehensive interviewing, supplemented with standardized self-report instruments and videotape role playing.

The assessment approach was initially broad spectrum, encompassing a search for problems across a wide array of life areas (e.g., financial, sexual functioning, employment, etc.). Once problem areas were identified, the focus of assessment narrowed to a more detailed assessment of each area in subsequent sessions. The final objective of assessment was a thorough functional analysis of the interaction of drinking behavior and each relevant area (Hay, Hay, Angle, & Ellinwood, 1977; Hay, Hay, Angle, & Nelson, 1979).

3.1. Intake Procedures

The intake session had the following objectives: (1) to gather demographic information and establish the source and reason for referral; (2) to give both clients an opportunity to describe the problems from their individual perspectives; (3) to identify the range of areas that each member of the couple perceived as problems; (4) to gather information about prior psychological-psychiatric treatments; (5) to determine each client's pretreatment baseline level of alcohol intake (i.e., estimated consumption for the 3 months prior to intake); (6) to provide the couple with a brief overview of the assessment process and treatment rationale; and (7) to teach the self-monitoring procedures and assign homework projects to be completed before the next session.

The intake session lasted $1\frac{1}{2}$ hours. Semistructured interviewing procedures were utilized to identify the life areas that each member of the couple perceived as problems. Questions about alcohol consumption were drawn from three interview guides: the Drinking Profile (Marlatt, 1976); the Pretreatment Data Sheet (Sobell & Sobell, 1978), and the Behavioral Alcohol Interview (Hay, Hay, & Nelson, 1977). In addition a quantified interview procedure was used to obtain estimates of each client's weekly alcohol consumption during the prior 3 months. Each client was given a large calendar, and, with therapist prompting, daily alcohol intake over 3-month period was reconstructed.

Self-monitoring was introduced as a first step toward understanding their drinking habits and as a self-control skill. Mr. and Mrs. L. were each given a supply of daily record index cards. These 3 × 5 cards had the therapist's address and postage on one side. The other side was divided into columns. Client instructions were as follows:

1. Fill out your Daily Record completely *before* each drink.
2. Carry your recording form and a pen at all times.
3. If you decide to drink, fill and finish one standard drink at a time.
4. If you forget to fill out the form, fill it out as soon as possible.
5. Time span: Record the time at which you *start* and *stop* drinking *each* drink in Column 1.
6. Situation: Record where you are, whom you are with, your mood, and rate on a scale of 0 to 10, "How much you want this drink" (0 if you could do without it easily; 10 if you really want to have the drink). ˙
7. Type of drink: Enter the type of drink (e.g., beer, wine, fortified wine, mixed or straight drink).
8. Ounces of beverage consumed: Record exactly what you will drink (e.g., 12 oz. of beer, 4 oz. of wine).

Self-monitoring procedures were acted out to ensure that both Mr. and Mrs. L. understood the process. In addition, responses were practiced in case anyone asked about the self-monitoring procedures (e.g., "I am counting calories"). Self-monitoring data were reviewed and graphed weekly to provide the clients with feedback on their progress. Ounces of alcohol consumed were converted into Standard Ethanol Content units: 1 SEC = .5 oz. or 15 ml of absolute ethanol (Miller, 1978). A drink was defined as containing .5 oz. of absolute ethanol: the approximate amount of alcohol in 10 to 12 oz. of beer, a 4-oz. glass of table wine, 1.5 oz. of 86-proof spirits, or 2.5 oz. of fortified wine. Mr. and Mrs. L.'s response to this information was quite typical—amazement over the fact that each of these beverages contained the same amount of alcohol. Mr. and Mrs. L. were also asked to rate and record daily their respective levels of marital happiness on a scale of 1 to 7: 1 for very unhappy, displeased; 4 for reasonably happy; 7 for extremely happy.

At the end of the intake session Mr. and Mrs. L. were told that any discussion of treatment goals (i.e., abstinence versus nonproblem controlled drinking) would have to wait until the assessment process was completed. Both clients were asked to sign medical release forms, so that their family physician could be consulted to determine their current physical health. Medical clearance was sought in this case, since a nonproblem-drinking goal was being considered. With the cooperation of their family physician, blood samples were assayed for levels of SGOT, and GGTP, two indices of liver function (Reyes & Miller, 1980).

3.2. Session 1: Alcohol-Specific Assessment Procedures

At the beginning of this session and prior to every subsequent session a breath test was conducted to assess blood-alcohol level, using an Intoximeter. If at any point in treatment either client's BAL had exceeded 50 mg%, (50 mg alcohol/100 ml blood), Mr. and Mrs. L. were informed that the session would be rescheduled. Mr. and Mrs. L. did not register BALs greater than 50 mg% prior to any session. Self-monitoring data were reviewed and any recording problems clarified. During the initial portion of this session, the 3-month pretreatment baseline, begun in the intake session, was completed. To facilitate this process, Mr. and Mrs. L. had been asked to bring in their date books and fill in as many drinking days as possible on their own.

Both Mr. and Mrs. L. were asked to describe their drinking patterns from their initial experiences with alcohol, through their married life, and especially the development of their current concerns about their alcohol use. The incidence of alcohol-related problems in relatives and family was also noted. They were questioned about the presence of any symptoms of physical dependence or other sequellae of heavy alcohol use (e.g., blackouts, shakes, etc.). In addition, a functional analysis of current drinking behavior was undertaken. It drew heavily on Marlatt's the Drinking Profile and self-monitoring from the preceding week.

Antecedent conditions or triggers that increased the probability of a drinking response occurring were identified in five areas: setting-situations; social-interpersonal situations; thoughts and expectations; physiological pain; emotional (Miller, 1976). In addition to antecedents, the specific parameters of the drinking responses were assessed. Self-monitoring data provided information on the amount, frequency, duration, and type of beverage consumed (i.e., response parameters). The immediate and delayed, positive and negative, consequences of each client's respective drinking pattern were also identified.

At the end of the session the couple was told to continue self-monitoring alcohol use and marital happiness. In addition, they were asked to fill in the Precounseling Marital Inventory (Stuart & Stuart, 1973) prior to the next session. Explicit instructions were given to complete the inventory independently and not to discuss their answers.

3.3. Session 2: Marital-Assessment Procedures

Self-monitoring was reviewed, recording issues clarified, and the data were graphed with therapist assistance. Assessment in Session 2 focused on determining the severity of the couple's marital problems and on a functional analysis of relationship behaviors. Mr. and Mrs. L. completed three questionnaires: the Marital Adjustment Scale (Locke & Wallace, 1959), a widely used measure of global marital satisfaction; the Area of Change Questionnaire (Jacobson & Margolin, 1979; Weiss & Margolin, 1977), a more specific measure of marital satisfaction based on the amount of change each spouse wishes to bring about in the relationship; and the Marital Status Inventory (Weiss & Cerreto, 1975), a progressive listing of the steps that spouses can take toward the termination of their marriage. Stuart (1980) has provided a detailed and critical appraisal of these questionnaires, as well as a discussion of alternative assessment instruments. Likewise the interview format utilized in this session drew heavily from initial marital interview procedures outlined by Jacobson and Margolin (1979). Briefly, the interview established how the two spouses met, their initial attraction to each other, the circumstances surrounding their marriage, first indications of relationship problems, and the nature of their day-to-day interaction.

Mr. and Mrs. L. were then asked to act out three problem situations drawn from their assessment data. Their instructions were to take approximately 10 minutes to try to solve the problem. The problems included: their current alcohol use levels; ways to increase the number and quality of their shared activities; and ways to increase the amount of shared time they spend with friends.

3.4. Results of Assessment

Mr. and Mrs. L. met in high school and subsequently attended the same college. They had dated few other people and did not remember another serious or prolonged relationship. Both described their early relationship as based on physical attraction and a joint interest in sporting activities. They also discussed the central role drinking had in their social relationships prior to marriage.

They married following college graduation, and their first child was born 10 months later. Their reasons for marriage included peer pressure ("All our friends were getting married") and a sense of affection and respect for the other partner. Mr. and Mrs. L. both felt that the birth of their first child, followed over the next 10 years by three other children, had left little time or energy for issues or activities that were not child-related. Five years prior to treatment, the household had begun to change dramatically. Three of the four children were married and the fourth was moving out to begin college. In addition, Mrs. L. had returned to full-time employment after spending the major portion of her married life as "a traditional housewife." At the time of their self-referral, Mr. and Mrs. L. were, in their own words, "facing the prospect of life alone together . . . and we don't even know if we can talk to each other. . . . We have become independent and set in our ways." Both spouses, however, stated that they were committed to their relationship.

The results of the marital questionnaires confirmed the level of distress that Mr. and Mrs. L. reported during interviewing. Their scores on the Marital Adjustment Scale indicated a high level of marital distress and low marital satisfaction compared with other couples. The usual cutoff score for this scale between distressed and nondistressed couples is 100, with a possible range of 2 to 161; this couple scored in the low 50s (Jacobson & Margolin, 1979). Likewise a number of specific problem areas were identified from each partner's responses on the Area of Change Questionnaire. These areas included: family financial decisions; time spent with friends; time spent in "interesting conversation"; time spent together in outside activities; free-time planning; frequency of sexual interaction. Interestingly, there was a high level of agreement between partners as to which areas of their relationship needed change. The overall low level of marital happiness was reflected also in their daily marital-happiness ratings. During the first 3 weeks of self-monitoring, their daily ratings were typically 3 or below. Review of video-taped role-play scenes indicated limited problem-solving behaviors, a relatively ineffective communication pattern punctuated by silences and a general failure to remain on task. Each partner's responses on the Marital Status Inventory substantiated, however, their strong committment to the marriage.

At intake Mr. L. was consuming approximately 60 SECs or 30 oz. of absolute ethanol per week. Mrs. L. was consuming over 30 SECs or approximately 15 oz. of absolute ethanol per week. Mr. L.'s consumption declined somewhat during the first weeks of self-monitoring, rebounded to 70 SECs during Week 2, and then returned to intake levels. Mrs. L.'s consumption increased approximately 10 SECs from estimated intake levels during Week 1 and then returned to 37 SECs the next week. Self-monitoring data suggested that the number of drinks reported by Mrs. L. during the intake session was accurate but that she had underestimated the amount of alcohol in each drink.

Mr. and Mrs. L. reported that their alcohol consumption had increased dramatically over the past 5 years. As noted above, both spouses drank moderately in social situations prior to marriage. Their alcohol consumption decreased during child-rearing years, especially within the home environment. At the time of referral both spouses had developed predictable patterns of daily alcohol consumption.

Mr. L. consumed two or three double vodka martinis in an extended $1\frac{1}{2}$-hour lunch period. Later in the day, two or three drinks were consumed on the $1\frac{1}{2}$-hour train ride home and were followed by continued drinking at home. Drinks were usually "straight" and consumed in large sips in approximately 15 minutes. Based on the first 2 weeks of self-monitoring data and body weight (165 lb.), Mr. L. exceeded the legal limit of intoxication (100 mg%) on 12 of 14 days. A peak BAL of 200 mg% was recorded in Week 2, when Mr. L. consumed 12 drinks in 4 hours.

Other high-probability drinking situations for Mr. L. included: sales meetings; social gatherings with heavy drinkers; lunch or dinner with his boss, who drank excessively ("I just can't say no to him!"); sports events on television; arguments with his spouse; difficult or frustrating workdays; successful workdays. Examples of concurrent mood states or thoughts included: "A drink would help me to relax"; "What does he think of me?" "Is this (marital relationship) all I have to look forward to?" "He (the boss) really let me have it today . . . it wasn't my fault"; "I accomplished a lot today . . . I deserve a drink." Positive consequences included: "the blotto" (i.e., forgetting the problems); decreased anger; feelings of relaxation; tastes good (alcohol); avoidance of spouse at home. Negative consequences included: financial (over $300 a month in bar tabs); hangover and stomach pain; intensified arguments with spouse; decreased productivity and fatigue at work (e.g., after heavy drinking lunches); increased frequency of "down" or depressed mood; blackouts; and poor sleep patterns.

Mrs. L. began drinking in the late afternoon, consuming two or three standard drinks in the first hour (2 or 3 oz. of 90-proof beverage mixed with $1\frac{1}{2}$ oz. of tonic). Her rate of consumption then decreased typically to one drink per 30 or 45 minutes until she retired. Based on the first 2 weeks of self-monitoring data and body weight (120 lb), Mrs. L. exceeded the 100 mg% BAL on 6 of 14 days, A peak BAL of approximately 160 mg% was recorded in Week 1 when Mrs. L. consumed seven drinks in 3 hours. Alcohol consumption was higher for both spouses on weekends when drinking usually began earlier in the day.

Additional high-probability drinking situations for Mrs. L. included: bridge with heavy-drinking friends; watching television with her spouse while he drinks; social gatherings with heavy-drinking friends; home alone following an argument with her spouse; sitting in the kitchen at 5:00 P.M. waiting for her husband who was late and had not called. Mood states or thoughts which accompanied drinking centered on marital problems, the prospect of life without the children home, and general feelings of anxiety. Positive consequences included: forgetting the family situation; decreased tension when approaching spouse for sex; avoidance of spouse. Negative consequences included: hangover on occasion; lack of energy; decreased productivity at home and on the job; negative comments from children on her alcohol use; intensification of marital problems; weight gain.

3.5. Summary

No history of alcohol-related problems was identified in either spouse's family. Likewise, neither spouse nor any one in their immediate family had been hospitalized for a psychiatric disorder (e.g., manic depression; major depressive order) that might have had an impact on the etiology or subsequent treatment of their problem drinking. In addition, medical reports indicated that both spouses were in good health, with liver function indices falling in the normal range. Both spouses had been heavy drinkers prior to their marriage, but their intake levels had decreased during child-rearing years. During the 5 years prior to their self-referral, alcohol use and marital distress had increased steadily and appeared to be functionally related (drinking behavior intensified marital conflict and decreased the possibility of effective problem solving). Marital conflict served as an antecedent for increased alcohol consumption. Their increased alcohol intake also had impact on job performance, family relations, finances, mood state and, potentially, their health.

Based on assessment data, a controlled or nonproblem-drinking goal seemed appropriate. The "rule-out" procedure suggested by Miller and Caddy (1977) was followed, and no contraindications for a nonproblem-drinking treatment goal were identified for either spouse. Since each partner's drinking behavior intensified arguments and limited effective problem resolution, a decrease in alcohol intake to nonproblem levels was targeted as the first priority for treatment. Once alcohol intake stabilized at nonproblem levels, marital therapy with an emphasis on effective methods of communication and problem solving was begun.

4. ALCOHOL TREATMENT PROCEDURES

4.1. Session 3: Establishing Treatment Goals

Session 3 was of critical importance to the successful treatment of this couple. As in all the subsequent sessions, self-monitoring data were reviewed and graphed, and information relevant to the functional analysis was recorded. The clients were given detailed feedback on the results of the assessment process.

Prior to this session a functional analysis sheet was developed by the therapist for each client. The sheets listed antecedents that had been identified as triggers for drinking. In addition, they outlined drinking-response characteristics and the specific consequences related to each antecedent. These sheets were given to each client for their input. This feedback process was facilitated by drawing individual drinking-behavior chains on a blackboard and explaining the role of antecedent factors, the drinking response, intervening thought patterns, and the immediate versus delayed, positive versus negative, nature of the consequences. Sample drinking behavior chains for Mr. and Mrs. L. are presented in Table 1.

The couple was also given detailed feedback on the problem areas within their relationship that had been identified during assessment. This feedback, however, stressed the high level of agreement between spouses on the areas that should be targeted for change. At this point, the relationship between their current increased levels of alcohol consumption and their marital problems was discussed. A treatment plan was outlined which emphasized changed in both their drinking behavior and marital relationship. With Mr. and Mrs. L.'s input and consent, the first goal of treatment was to bring alcohol consumption to nonproblem levels. The therapist's reasons for considering a controlled-drinking goal were presented, with the stipulation that this goal could be renegotiated by the therapist or by either of the clients. (In some cases I have found that an initial 3-month abstinence period helps clients ultimately achieve nonproblem-drinking levels.) The therapist emphasized the importance of regaining control of drinking behavior before attempting modifications in marital-interaction patterns.

Table 1. Drinking Behavior Chains

Antecedents	Mood and thoughts	Drinking behavior	Consequences	
			Immediate	Delayed
Mr. L.				
Situation/time: "Working lunch"	Tense: "I need this sale ... a drink would help me unwind."	Vodka martinis, three doubles in 90 minutes	(+) Avoided offending boss who drinks	(−) Lost afternoon and decreased productivity
Place: Cocktail lounge			(+) "More persuasive seller"	(−) Guilt: "I said I would not drink at lunch anymore."
Person: Perspective buyer; boss			(+) Decrease tension level	(−) Fight with spouse on phone
			(−) Customer was a nondrinker: "I wonder if he thinks I drink too much."	(−) Bar tabs $300 per month
			(−) Stuck with the tab again	
Mrs. L.				
Place: Kitchen, watching television	Bored/angry: "I work all day ... make dinner and he doesn't care enough about me to call."	5–6 P.M.: 3 oz. alcohol, 2 oz. tonic	(+) Decreased anger: "I don't care if he comes home or not."	(−) Depressed "down" mood
Time: 5 P.M.		6–6:30 P.M.: 1 SEC	(+) Tastes good	(−) Fight with spouse
Person: Alone		6:30 P.M.: Same	(+) More assertive when he does come home	(−) Lost evening
			(−) Guilt/anxiety: "Why am I doing this?"	(−) Sleep problem, wake up at 4 A.M.

Mr. and Mrs. L. were told that their treatment program for problem drinking would contain four major components. The first step would be to analyze their drinking habits. The second would be modification of their current drinking patterns and the establishment of nonproblem-drinking goals, followed by progressive decreases in consumption to meet those goals. The third step would focus on rearranging and modifying conditions in their environments which cued or maintained problem drinking. The final step would be to learn positive alternatives (new ways to handle old antecedents) to alcohol use. A 10-session treatment contract was signed which specified both client and therapist behaviors. Mr. and Mrs. L. were then asked to choose 2 days in the coming week and commit themselves to decreasing their alcohol consumption on these days. Mr. L. choose to eliminate "liquid lunch" on 2 days. His plan was to eat with colleagues who did not drink at lunch. Mrs. L. decided to decrease consumption around the dinner hour on these 2 days by moving out of the kitchen and structuring her time. This homework assignment was given to begin the downward titration of alcohol consumption and to encourage client- rather than therapist-imposed contingencies on drinking behavior.

4.2. Sessions 4 and 5: Altering the Drinking Response

Sessions 4 and 5 covered the following topics: blood-alcohol level discrimination training (external and internal); instruction in rate control procedures; goal setting; an *in vivo* practice session. The discussion of these topics was prefaced by a general statement on the importance of setting reachable goals and shaping toward ultimate drinking goals. Mr. L.'s self-monitoring had indicated a five-drink increase from Week 3 to Week 4. In the previous session, he had been quite adamant about decreasing his alcohol intake substantially in "just one week." After failing to meet a self-imposed goal of 2 abstinent days, Mr. L. reported that he had become angered over his lack of control and increased consumption. Mrs. L. met her goal.

BAL discrimination training (external) had actually begun when Mr. and Mrs. L. started self-monitoring and graphing their respective alcohol intakes. Beginning in this session, self-monitoring data were translated into actual blood-alcohol levels attained. Each client was given an Alco-Calculator (Rutgers University Center of Alcohol Studies, 1982). This slide-rule device allowed the computation of the percentage of alcohol in the blood based on drinks consumed, body weight, and hours since the start of drinking. To reinforce the connection between BAL achieved, body weight, and drinks consumed, the clients were asked to complete a work-sheet which charted BAL achieved for their body weight over a 4-hour period given various consumption rates. The clients were given a BAL fact card, listing various blood-alcohol levels with the expected physical, motor, cognitive, and psychological impairments at each level.

Rate control procedures emphasized counting drinks, slowing down, modifying the drinking response (e.g., varying the type and alcohol content of the beverage, decreasing sip volume, and spacing drinks, etc.), and setting and maintaining drinking goals. Drinking limits were set for the next week. These limits were specified in terms of the maximum number of drinks consumed on a particular day (i.e., if drinking occurred) and the maximum BAL allowed. The Alco-Calculator and BAL tables were used to determine the number of drinks that could be consumed in the first hour, second hour, third hour, etc. and still maintain the specified limit.

Goals were selected that the clients and therapist believed were attainable. Mrs. L. decided to decrease her consumption to 25 standard drinks per week. A daily maximum of five standard drinks was set, with her BAL not to exceed 70 mg% (five drinks over a 4-hour period). Mr. L. set his weekly consumption goal at 45 standard drinks. A daily maximum of seven standard drinks was specified, with his BAL not to exceed 80 mg% (seven drinks over a 4-hour period).

To help them meet these decreased consumption goals, Mr. and Mrs. L., with therapist input, modified their drinking responses. Mr. L. decided to substitute beer for his usual double martini as often as possible. Likewise, Mrs. L. shifted to a 4-oz. glass of table wine instead of her usual potent mixed drink. In addition, both clients were asked to make a conscious effort to space their drinks, increase the number of sips per drink, decrease sip volume, and try to drink only on a full stomach. Self-monitoring data had indicated that the first hour of consumption was a critical period for both Mr. and Mrs. L. Typically, they achieved blood-alcohol levels during the first drinking hour that either approached or exceeded their new limits. From the therapist's clinical experience, the rapid achievement of a high BAL in the early stages of consumption decreases the probability of the drinker maintaining control. Consequently, Mr. and Mrs. L. were asked to alternate alcohol and nonalcohol beverages during the first hour.

Mr. and Mrs. L. learned these procedures during Sessions 4 and 5. Their homework for Session 4 was to implement their first limits and practice the rate control procedures. Both clients were also asked to concentrate on the added enjoyment of drinking slowly as well as focusing on the internal feelings related to various blood-alcohol levels. Internal blood-alcohol level training was the focus of Session 5, in which both clients consumed one standard drink during the hour session. This quasi *in vivo* procedure provided the therapist with valuable data on their individual drinking responses and provided them with an opportunity to discuss problems related to altering their drinking response. The internal-training homework assignment from Session 4 was repeated for Session 5. In addition, new drinking goals were determined (both clients had decreased consumption below the preceding week's limits): for Mr. L. 40 standard drinks per week, a maximum of 6 drinks in one day, with a BAL maximum of 70 mg%; for Mrs. L. 20 standard drinks per week, a daily maximum of 4 standard drinks, with her BAL not to exceed 50 mg%. Occasional limits, the highest BAL achieved on any occasion (Miller & Muñoz, 1976) were not specified, since both the clients felt that their daily limits encompassed a broad enough range.

4.3. Session 6: Self-Management Planning—Stimulus-Control Procedures

The session began with a review and discussion of the self-monitoring data. Mr. and Mrs. L. had maintained the lower consumption limits they had targeted for Session 6. Drinking goals for the subsequent week were negotiated: Mr. L.—35 standard drinks per week, daily maximum of 5 drinks, with a BAL maximum of 50 mg%; Mrs. L.—20 standard drinks per week, a daily maximum of 3 drinks, with a BAL maximum of 30 mg%. For Mrs. L. this drinking goal did not represent an overall planned decrease in the total number of drinks consumed but rather a decrease in the number of drinks consumed per day and in maximum BAL.

During the previous sessions Mr. and Mrs. L. had learned to view drinking behavior as triggered by specific antecedents and maintained by specific consequences. The objective of Session 6 was to teach the clients how to alter the antecedents that had been identified, in order to decrease the likelihood of drinking in response to these cues. Mr. and Mrs. L. were told that a major goal of treatment was to break up the "automatic" relationship between these antecedent events and drinking behavior. They were also told that there were two ways to accomplish this: (1) to learn methods of modifying or rearranging these antecedents (Sessions 6 and 7); (2) to learn alternative, more effective methods of handling these antecedent conditions (Sessions 8 and 9). Session 7 focused on rearranging the consequences for problem drinking.

Self-management plans were developed for each antecedent. These antecedents were chosen from the functional analysis which had been updated weekly with the addition of relevant information from self-monitoring data. For each antecedent, one of the following management strategies was planned: avoidance; rearrangement; creative behavioral alternative. In some cases both short-term and long-term management strategies were developed (i.e., some plans can be implemented with minimal environmental modifications, while others may require a short-term avoidance strategy followed by a long-term plan calling for the learning of a new behavior). Clients were asked to weigh the positive and negative consequences of each plan and rate the predicted difficulty of each strategy. Mr. and Mrs. L. were instructed to choose two antecendents and the corresponding plans and to implement the self-management plans over the coming week. They were encouraged to select antecedent-plan combinations which had a high probability of success and to move gradually to plans with higher difficulty ratings.

4.4. Session 7: Self-Management Planning—Rearranging Behavioral Consequences

Self-monitoring data indicated that both spouses had met their drinking goals. New drinking goals were negotiated: Mr. L.—30 standard drinks per week, with a daily maximum of 5 drinks and a BAL of 50 mg%; Mrs. L.—15 standard drinks, a daily maximum of 3 drinks, with a BAL of 30 mg%. Problems in implementing the antecedent self-management plans during the preceding week were discussed and additional antecedent-plan combinations were selected for implementation.

The goal of Session 7 was to teach Mr. and Mrs. L. two consequence-control procedures. The first procedure emphasized the covert rehearsal of both the positive consequences of achieving and maintaining a nonproblem-drinking goal and the negative consequences of problem drinking. Both sets of consequences were listed on index cards, and suggestions were given on methods for increasing the amount of time each client reviewed the consequences (e.g., reading the card prior to a high-frequency activity like drinking coffee or looking at a watch). In addition, the use of the list was acted out, with an emphasis on learning new thinking habits. Each spouse was asked to imagine one or two high-probability drinking situations and notice that their first thoughts would be related to the perceived immediate, positive consequences that used to maintain their drinking. They were asked to review their respective consequences lists (i.e., practice a new thinking habit), to describe how they would handle the situation and state the positive consequences related to nonproblem drinking.

Contingency management (contracting) was also introduced during this session as another method of rearranging the consequences of drinking (see Mahoney & Thorenson, 1974). Individual weekly commitment contracts were drawn up specifying both individual drinking goals to be met in the following week and the consequences for meeting or failing to meet these goals. Mr. L. found the contracting procedures extremely helpful and continued this procedure on a weekly basis during treatment and, sporadically, during the follow-up period. Mrs. L., however, reacted quite negatively to the contract and, in fact, did not meet her projected drinking goal.

4.5. Sessions 8 and 9: Training in Creative Behavioral Alternatives

As noted above, Mrs. L. did not meet her drinking goal for this session. From the discussion at the beginning of Session 8, it became evident that Mrs. L. had expected changes in the marital relationship as a result of the couple's involvement in treatment. In addition, she considered the contract as "artificial" and wondered if the marital treatment would include similar procedures. The rationale for the intervention sequence was reviewed, and the therapist stressed the necessity of decreasing drinking behavior, since assessment had indicated that high alcohol intake interfered with successful communication and problem solving. In addition, the therapist reiterated the fact that major changes in the relationship would await a shift in treatment focus to the development of effective communication and problem-solving skills. Both spouses stated that they had seen minimal improvement in their relationship and that drinking less had made them more cognizant of their communication problems. After each spouse had been given an opportunity to discuss their concerns about the relationship, a decision was made by the therapist and both clients to continue alcohol treatment for three more sessions.

Topics covered in Session 8 included muscle relaxation training and cognitive self-management procedures. These topics had been designed to maximize the use of feedback between partners during both the learning and practice phases. Mr. and Mrs. L. learned the relaxation procedures conjointly and helped each other identify tension indicators (actual muscle tension and stressors in home or work environments). Quite fortuitously, the muscle relaxation procedures also provided a structured, nonthreatening vehicle for encouraging communication between them. Mrs. L. subsequently reported that their ability to work constructively together on something boosted her morale at this point in treatment. Clients were given detailed instruction in progressive relaxation procedures (Goldfried & Davison, 1976), and each client received a cassette tape made during session. As part of their weekly assignment they were asked to practice this new alternative to tension and stress-related drinking antecedents. Mr. and Mrs. L. practiced together daily, rating tension levels before and after using the tape.

Mrs. L. was coached on how to express her anger at Mr. L. for being late or not calling (anger-related thoughts were concurrent with late-afternoon drinking) and both spouses were asked to act out the situation and monitor the other partner's reactions.

4.6. Session 10: Maintenance Planning

During treatment Weeks 8 and 9, Mr. and Mrs. L. met or drank less than their drinking goals. A review of the self-monitoring data at the beginning of Session 10 indicated that he had consumed approximately 20 standard drinks during the preceding week and that she had consumed 16 standard drinks.

Session 10, the final alcohol treatment session, was devoted to maintenance and relapse strategies. The array of self-control procedures that Mr. and Mrs. L. had learned was reviewed, and their continued use reinforced. A cognitive-behavioral model of relapse, modified to refer specifically to non-problem versus abstinence treatment goals, was presented to both clients (Marlatt, 1978). This model emphasized the situational determinants of relapse. High-risk situations (high risk for excessive drinking to occur) were identified and placed into five relapse categories: frustration and anger; social pressure; interpersonal temptation; negative emotional state; miscellaneous other (Chaney, O'Leary, & Marlatt, 1978). Clients took turns acting out how they would reestablish control if a problem-drinking episode occurred. Various coping responses were considered and acted out. Mr. and Mrs. L. were encouraged to use each other as resources and sources of support (i.e., reinforcing each other for maintenance of drinking goals). The final objective of the session was to draw up maintenance planning sheets for each client. These sheets, which were to be filled in weekly, allowed specification of weekly drinking goals and self-control procedures to be practiced.

5. MARITAL TREATMENT PROCEDURES

Marital treatment in Sessions 11 through 18 focused on enhancing the couple's communication and problem-solving abilities and increasing the number and reinforcement value of their shared activities. The clinical procedures utilized were drawn from social-learning approaches to marital therapy. These procedures have been described in two recent texts (Jacobson & Margolin, 1979; Stewart, 1980). Consequently, only the major topic areas covered in these eight sessions are presented below. Interested readers are referred to the comprehensive texts for details.

The status of the marital relationship was reviewed in Session 11. The fact that both spouses had learned and maintained new drinking patterns was presented as an example of the ability of each spouse to change. The current severity of problem areas identified during the initial assessment was evaluated. The consensus of the therapist and both spouses was that some improvement had occurred in spouse communication patterns (probably resulting from Sessions 8–10), but that severe problems in the marriage were still evident.

Sessions 11 through 13 focused on communication change. Since each partner exhibited the requisite behaviors necessary for effective communication in areas outside of their relationship (e.g., occupational), they were asked to view and assess their own behavior on the problem-solving videotapes recorded in Session 2. This feedback procedure involved an element of risk. In this case, broad-spectrum assessment procedures had indicated that both spouses had effective communication behaviors but were not exhibiting these behaviors in their marital relationship. The problem was one of stimulus control, rather than a deficit or absence of the requisite behaviors. The differential assessment of a stimulus-control problem versus a deficit problem is important, since videotape feedback to a couple where one or both partners have limited skill could exacerbate problems and promote a feeling of hopelessness. Over these four sessions each spouse was asked to read specific chapters in a book (Gottman, Notarius, Gonso, & Markman, 1976) and complete the exercises at home. These chapters reinforced the communication procedures practiced in each session. The communication skills program emphasized training in the ability to improve understanding by evaluating the intent and impact of messages, effective listening skills, the ability to give and receive feedback, and the ability to make requests for behavior change constructively. In brief, the basic components of effective communication in other environments were reviewed and introduced into marital communication. Behavior rehearsal, therapist coaching, modeling, and role reversal were mainstays during these sessions.

Once the foundation for clear and effective communication was prepared, the focus of Sessions 14 and 15 became training in problem solving (i.e., effective problem negotiation and resolution skills). In this regard, the reader is referred to Chapter 7 in Jacobson and Margolin (1979) and Chapter 9 in Stewart (1980).

Communication and problem-solving training had taught each partner how to decrease the number of negatives in their marriage by resolving rather than constantly "reliving" problem situations. Mr. and Mrs. L. learned methods to increase the number and quality of the positive behaviors they exchanged in Sessions 16 and 17. The caring-days technique was used (Stewart, 1980) to facilitate the initial exchange of positive feelings and behaviors. A variant of the usual behavioral contracting procedure (e.g., *quid pro quo*) was also introduced during these sessions. Mrs. L. had voiced opposition to contracting procedures in an earlier session. Many clients react negatively to contracting procedures, objecting to the absence of spontaneity and the need for external motivation rather than a "genuine" personal commitment to change. Recent evidence has indicated that such negative reactions may be more pronounced in couples who have been married longer with more engrained exchange patterns (O'Leary & Turkewitz, 1978). With therapist support, behavior change lists were prepared for each spouse; responses from the Areas of Change questionnaire were helpful. These parallel lists indicated changes in behavior that each spouse desired in the other spouse. Each spouse agreed to do as many of the behaviors requested by the other spouse as frequently as possible (at least three or four times weekly).

Session 18 was devoted to conflict containment and maintenance strategies. Mr. and Mrs. L. were asked to use role play to find solutions to a number of potential conflict situations. The reasons for entering therapy were reviewed, as were the therapeutic skills they had learned and the major changes each partner had made during treatment. A strategy for conflict containment was developed and acted out (Gottman et al., 1976; Stewart, 1980). At the end of this session, the Marital Adjustment Scale (Locke & Wallace, 1959) was readministered to assess changes in marital satisfaction following treatment.

6. FOLLOW-UP PROCEDURES

Mr. and Mrs. L. were seen at 3 months, 6 months, and 1 year following the termination of treatment. Prior to each follow-up session, Mr. and Mrs. L. were contacted by the therapist and asked to self-monitor alcohol consumption and marital happiness for approximately 2 weeks. Mr. L. self-monitored his alcohol consumption on a daily basis throughout the entire year; Mrs. L.'s self-monitoring was more sporadic. Mrs. L. did record consistently, however, the total number of standard drinks consumed each week. Alcohol-consumption and marital-happiness ratings for each of these 2-week periods are summarized in Figure 1 and Figure 2. In addition, intake interviewing procedures were repeated in each follow-up session to insure that data from these 2-week assessment "windows" were representative. A portion of the first follow-up meeting was used to assist the couple in solving a situation related to their 18-year-old daughter.

7. RESULTS OF TREATMENT

7.1. Alcohol Consumption

At the end of the first 10 weeks of treatment (the alcohol treatment phase), Mr. L.'s alcohol consumption (see Figure 1) had decreased from an intake level of approximately 60 standard drinks per week to slightly less than 20 standard drinks per week. This reduced consumption pattern was maintained during the next 9 weeks (the marital treatment phase), with the exception of Week 13, when 22 standard drinks were consumed. Mr. L.'s con-

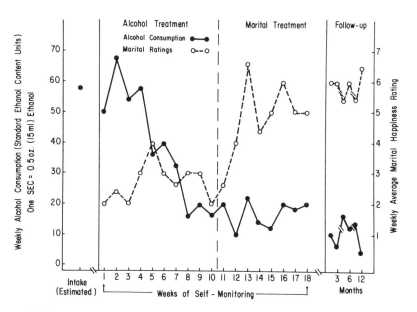

Figure 1. Weekly alcohol consumption in Standard Ethanol Content units and weekly average marital-happiness rating for Mr. L.

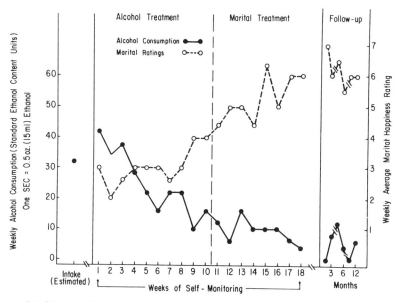

Figure 2. Weekly alcohol consumption in Standard Ethanol Content units and weekly average marital happiness rating for Mrs. L.

sumption in the 2-week periods prior to the 3, 6, and 12-month follow-up sessions is also presented in Figure 1. Mr. L. maintained and eventually lowered his weekly alcohol consumption over the course of follow-up to an average of 10 standard drinks per week at twelve months.

In addition, self-monitoring and interview data indicated that Mr. L. had exceeded his self-imposed limit of 20 drinks per week (maximum BAL of 50 mg%) on only three occasions during the first 3 months of follow-up. This limit was exceeded on only one more occasion (during Month 7). The maximum 50 mg% BAL goal was exceeded twice during the first 3 months of follow-up. In each case the peak BAL achieved was approximately 70 mg%. These data differ dramatically from Mr. L.'s first 2 weeks of self-monitoring, when he exceeded the legal limit, 100 mg%, on 12 of 14 days and achieved a peak BAL of nearly 200 mg%.

At intake Mrs. L. was consuming approximately 30 standard drinks per week. Self-monitoring data during Weeks 1 and 2 suggested consumption levels closer to 40 standard drinks per week (see Figure 2). Mrs. L.'s alcohol consumption decreased from intake levels to approximately 15 standard drinks per week at Session 10. As noted earlier, consumption increased between Sessions 6 and 7 after a steady decrease during the previous four sessions. This increase resulted from Mrs. L.'s disillusionment with the absence of change in the marital relationship and her negative reaction to contract procedures. Consumption continued to decrease during Sessions 11 to 18, marital treatment, to approximately five standard drinks at Session 18. Further, this substantial reduction in consumption was maintained throughout follow-up. Alcohol consumption did not exceed the specified limits (15 drinks per week with a maximum BAL on any drinking day of 30 mg%) at any time during follow-up. Mrs. L. did not maintain a daily drinking record (like her spouse) but did record total drinks per week.

7.2. Marital Status

The results of initial marital assessment procedures (i.e., interviewing, videotaped role playing and standardized marital-happiness questionnaires) indicated a severely distressed relationship. Mr. and Mrs. L. rated their marital happiness daily throughout treatment and during the 2 weeks prior to each follow-up session. These ratings are presented in Figure 1 for Mr. L. and Figure 2 for Mrs. L.

Mr. L.'s happiness ratings remained consistently low during Weeks 1 to 10 (alcohol treatment). This trend was reversed during Sessions 11 to 18, which focused on relationship change and communication. As Figure 1 indicates, marital happiness rating's increased abruptly in the early stages of marital treatment and stabilized at the 5 to 6 range. Ratings remained above

5, ranging between 5 and 7 at each follow-up interval. Visual inspection of Figure 1 suggests little apparent relationship between Mr. L.'s reduction in alcohol consumption in the first 10 weeks of treatment and marital-happiness ratings.

For Mrs. L. a different pattern of marital happiness ratings developed. These ratings are graphed in Figure 2. A gradual trend towards higher ratings is evident following Session 8 (i.e., prior to marital treatment). Up to this session Mrs. L.'s ratings had been consistently low. Mrs. L. exceeded her drinking goal for Session 8. As noted earlier, however, Session 9 and 10 provided structured opportunities for both spouses to engage in nonthreatening communications and to aid each other in reaching their individual drinking goals. Mrs. L. stated that their ability to talk and work together during these sessions was "a turning point" in their relationship. Changes in marital ratings and the concurrent reduction in Mrs. L.'s alcohol consumption were related, therefore, at least from her report. The positive trend in ratings continued throughout marital treatment, with 6 ratings for Sessions 17 and 18. Ratings ranged between 5½ and 7 across the follow-up intervals.

Marital Adjustment Scale scores are summarized in Table 2. The Area of Change Questionnaire was not readministered because of its strong correlation with the MAS ($r = -.70$) (Weiss, Hops, & Patterson, 1973). At intake Mr. L.'s score of 55 and Mrs. L.'s score of 53 on the MAS indicated significant marital distress and low levels of marital satisfaction. MAS scores range from 2 (high marital distress) to 161 (high marital adjustment), with 100 as the accepted cutoff score between distressed and nondistressed couples. Posttreatment MAS scores of 115 for Mr. L. and 129 for Mrs. L. indicated substantial improvements in the marital relationship. As Table 2 indicates these positive changes were maintained throughout the follow-up period.

8. DISCUSSION

Mr. and Mrs. L. reduced their alcohol consumption to nonproblem levels during the initial 10-week treatment period and nonproblem alcohol

Table 2. Marital Adjustment Scale Scores

Time	Mr. L.	Mrs. L.
Intake	55	53
End of treatment	115	129
3-month follow-up	123	132
6-month follow-up	117	125
12-month follow-up	123	130

consumption levels were maintained throughout the 1-year follow-up period. Mr. and Mrs. L. reported positive changes in their marital relationship
beginning during the marital treatment period, Weeks 11–18, and these
changes were also maintained throughout follow-up. Although cause-and-
effect relationships cannot be inferred from a case study format, these results
suggest strongly that the reductions in alcohol consumption and increases in
marital satisfaction were related to the implementation of specific behavioral
treatment procedures.

In the case of Mr. and Mrs. L., as in any case where marital difficulties
and excessive alcohol consumption coexist, the importance of a broad-spectrum assessment strategy cannot be overstated. The pioneering work of the
Sobells and their colleagues (e.g., Sobell & Sobell, 1978) and the recent Rand
report (Polich, Armor, & Braiker, 1981) underscore the necessity of this
broad-spectrum approach. In both instances, these investigators have
demonstrated that drinking behavior should no longer be viewed in isolation
but rather in the context of its interaction with behavioral patterns in multiple life areas. The traditional narrow focus on drinking behavior alone may
not accurately reflect patient status following treatment (Nathan & Hay,
1980). Specifically, drinking disposition may change substantially (e.g., the
client is abstinent or attains a nonproblem-drinking status) while serious
problems in other life areas continue or perhaps intensify.

In the case of Mr. and Mrs. L. dramatic reductions in individual alcohol
consumption patterns did not result in substantial improvements in overall
marital happiness. In the author's clinical experience, the degree and nature
of the relationship existing between alcohol abuse problems and marital
problems varies with the individual couple. For 10 other couples treated
recently with the same procedures, the degree of relationship noted between
changes in alcohol consumption and improvements in marital happiness
varied greatly (Hay, 1982). Only one spouse in each of these couples reported a drinking problem. For three couples, the results were similar to the case
of Mr. and Mrs. L., in that reductions in alcohol consumption and improvements in marital satisfaction were independent. For three other couples,
improvements in marital satisfaction were noted during the alcohol treatment period, prior to any marital intervention procedures. The four remaining couples did not undergo marital treatment, but initial assessment indicated substantial levels of distress in their marital relationships. After the
alcohol treatment period, these couples were followed for 1 year. No significant improvements in marital happiness were noted during follow-up. One
couple separated and subsequently initiated divorce proceedings.

One conclusion that can be drawn from the results of the case of Mr.
and Mrs. L. and the other cases mentioned above is that the successful
application of behavioral assessment and treatment procedures requires a

hypothesis-testing model of clinical intervention. During assessment, hypotheses must be generated concerning the impact of other life areas (e.g., marital, occupational, etc.) on drinking behavior. Treatment decisions should be based on these hypotheses and include consideration of these questions: Which life areas must be modified to alter the contingencies cueing or maintaining abusive drinking behavior? In what sequence should treatment progress? And, at what inclusion level (e.g., family, marital, occupation) should intervention be aimed to increase the probability of treatment success? For example, assessment information may isolate antecedents and consequences in both occupational and marital areas. Further analysis of the interaction, however, may indicate that marital conflict is a consequence of work-related problems, which also trigger drinking. Such an analysis would suggest a treatment program aimed at modification of the occupational area as well as modification of drinking behavior and continued monitoring of marital status as treatment progresses. In the case of Mr. and Mrs. L. assessment information indicated that problem-drinking consumption levels had intensified existing marital communication difficulties and were related to the transitional status of the relationship. The treatment program, therefore, included the modification of specific marital interaction patterns as well as the modification of drinking behavior.

The case of Mr. and Mrs. L. also underscores the fact that behavioral assessment and treatment procedures cannot be applied in a vacuum. The behavior therapist must not lose sight of the impact of individual client characteristics on compliance to the proposed treatment regimen and consequently to subsequent treatment success. Mr. and Mrs. L. were asked to maintain a variety of records and to complete assignments between sessions. The development of a positive, trusting relationship was essential to the treatment process. A flexible clinical approach was especially important in the case of Mr. and Mrs. L., where a number of special clinical issues had to be dealt with, including their age and consequent reactions to some behavioral procedures (e.g., contracting), and the fact that they both were drinking excessively.

COMMENTARY

Peter E. Nathan

Both Mr. and Mrs. L. are very heavy drinkers. The only couple reported on in this book who are both problem drinkers, they clearly presented author Bill Hay with special problems. Not only did treatment goals have to be established for the two as a couple, but separate consumption reduction goals and individualized behavior change goals had to be set for each spouse. As well, the predictable consequence of a reduction in consumption by one or both spouses, inducing other individual or interpersonal problems, had to be anticipated. As difficult as is treatment of a couple with an alcoholic spouse, a couple who are both problem drinkers is that much more so.

As befits a person whose training emphasized behavioral assessment techniques and strategies, Bill Hay places heavy emphasis here on both initial and continuing assessment. Continuous self-monitoring of drinking by both spouses and functional assessment following the SOR model describea elsewhere are supplemented by a technological innovation, namely, videotaped sequences of marital interaction. The advantages of the technology of the television age—immediacy, greater validity, the opportunity to undertake detailed analysis free from time constraints—recommend its use, though it requires more preparation of patients and expenditure of time, energy, and funds than traditional methods. Notable, too, is Hay's continuous, intensive assessment throughout the course of the entire therapy relationship. Here, then, assessment is used not simply to reflect on the success or failure of the therapeutic intervention; it is employed, as well, to provide the therapist with ongoing guidance, through the therapy, on changes in emphasis, techniques, goals, and methods.

Some might ask why Hay's assessment of Mr. and Mrs. L. was separated into alcohol-specific and marital-specific components, since the SOR assessment model has three elements: (1) accurate definition of target behaviors; (2) identification of stimuli and responses to the target behaviors; and (3) delineation of interactions among these three SOR elements. To separate marital- and alcohol-related target behaviors, as Hay has done, then, would seem to defeat the purpose of an interaction analysis. On reflection, however, it is clear that this assessment sequence simply recognizes that their excessive drinking and marital dysfunction merit independent attention. The implication, as well, is that marital dysfunction might well have developed without precipitating drinking problems and vice versa. Though the narrative also illustrates the interdependence of the two target behaviors, their separate identities as basic problems are nonetheless important to recognize, which Hay does effectively by assessing them separately.

The failure of an employee assistance program counselor to deal with Mr. L. with sensitivity and understanding was revealed in the process of assessment. The counselor's almost-immediate insistence that Mr. L. was an alcoholic who required abstinence and total immersion in AA made it more difficult for Mr. L. to seek help elsewhere. We have some familiarity with such employee programs and hear similar stories too often from persons whose help seeking was sidetracked by of a counselor who was committed to a single point of view and came across as indifferent and insensitive. Techniques and procedures for directing such energetic, well-intentioned people into more effective helper modes must be developed.

Bill Hay's decision to focus first on his clients' maladaptive drinking before attempting to help them work on their disturbed marriage harkens back to decisions made by others in this book. Others have decided to work on a troubled marriage before *tackling the drinking that created or worsened the marital problems. There are no hard-and-fast rules governing this decision. The amount and consequences of drinking clearly play an important role; if drinking is out of control, the marital problems it affects cannot be treated unless or until the drinking lessens. By the same token, if marital distress seems at the root of a marked increase in abusive drinking, it probably ought to be addressed first. It would seem to be time to develop guidelines for goal setting when alcohol and marital disharmony interact to bring a couple to treatment.*

9. REFERENCES

Chaney, E. F., O'Leary, M. R., & Marlatt, G. A. Skill training with alcoholics. *Journal of Consulting and Clinical Psychology,* 1978, *46,* 1092–1104.

Goldfried, M. R., & Davidson, G. C. *Clinical behavior therapy.* New York: Holt, Rinehart & Winston, 1976.

Gottman, J., Notarius, C., Gonso, J., & Markman, H. *A couple's guide to communication.* Champaign, Ill.: Research Press, 1976.

Hay, W. M. *The behavioral treatment of the alcoholic marriage: The relationship between drinking status and marital happiness.* Manuscript in preparation, 1982.

Hay, W. M., Hay, L. R., Angle, H. V., & Ellinwood, E. H. Computerized behavioral assessment and the problem-oriented record. *International Journal of Mental Health,* 1977, *6,* 49–63.

Hay, W. M., Hay, L. R., Angle, H. V., & Nelson, R. O. The reliability of problem identification in the behavioral interview. *Behavioral Assessment,* 1979, *1,* 107–118.

Hay, W. M., Hay, L. R., & Nelson, R. O. The adaptation of covert modeling procedures to the treatment of chronic alcoholism and obsessive compulsive behavior: Two case reports. *Behavior Therapy,* 1977, *8,* 70–76.

Jacobson, N. S., & Margolin, G. *Marital therapy: Strategies based on social learning and behavior exchange principles.* New York: Brunner/Mazel, 1979.

Locke, H. J., & Wallace, K. M. Short marital adjustment and prediction tests: Their reliability and validity. *Marriage and Family Living,* 1959, *21,* 251–255.

Mahoney, M. J., & Thorenson, C. E. *Self-control: Power to the person.* Monterey, Calif.: Brooks-Cole, 1974.

Marlatt, G. A. The Drinking Profile: A questionnaire for the behavioral assessment of alcoholism. In E. J. Mash & L. G. Terdal (Eds.), *Behavior therapy assessment: Diagnosis, design and evaluation.* New York: Springer, 1976.

Marlatt, G. A. Craving for alcohol, loss of control, and relapse: A cognitive behavioral analysis. In P. E. Nathan, G. A. Marlatt, & T. Løberg (Eds.), *Alcoholism: New directions in behavioral research and treatment.* New York: Plenum Press, 1978.

Miller, W. R. Behavioral treatment of problem drinkers: A comparative outcome study of three controlled drinking therapies. *Journal of Consulting and Clinical Psychology,* 1978, *46,* 74–86.

Miller, W. R., & Caddy, G. R. Abstinence and controlled drinking in the treatment of problem drinkers. *Journal of Studies on Alcohol,* 1977, *38,* 986–1003.

Miller, W. R., & Muñoz, R. F. *How to control your drinking.* Englewood Cliffs, N.J.: Prentice-Hall, 1976.

Nathan, P. E., & Hay, W. M. Invited comments on the Rand report on patterns of alcoholism over four years—with apologies to Huxley and Shaw. *Journal of Studies on Alcohol,* 1980, *41,* 777–779.

O'Leary, K. D., & Turkewitz, H. T. Marital therapy from a behavioral perspective. In T. J.

Paolino, Jr., & B. S. McCrady (Eds.), *Marriage and marital therapy: Psychoanalytic, behavioral and systems theory perspectives.* New York: Brunner/Mazel, 1978.

Polich, J. M., Armor, D. J., & Braiker, H. B. *The course of alcoholism: Four years after treatment.* New York: Wiley, 1981.

Reyes, E., & Miller, W. R. serum gamma-glutamyl transpeptidase as a diagnostic aid in problem drinkers. *Addictive Behaviors,* 1980, 5, 59–65.

Rutgers University Center of Alcohol Studies. *Alco-Calculator.* New Brunswick, N.J.: Available from the author, 1982.

Sobell, M. D., & Sobell, L. C. *Behavioral treatment of alcohol problems.* New York: Plenum Press, 1978.

Stuart, R. B. *Helping couples change: A social learning approach to marital therapy.* New York: Guilford Press, 1980.

Stuart, R. B., & Stuart, F. *Marital pre-counseling inventory.* Champaign, Ill.: Research Press, 1973.

Weiss, R. L., & Cerreto, M. *Marital status inventory.* Unpublished manuscript, University of Oregon, 1975.

Weiss, R. L., Hops, H., & Patterson, G. R. *A framework for conceptualizing marital conflict, a technology for altering it, some data for evaluating it.* In L. A. Hammerlynck, L. C. Handy, & E. J. Mash (Eds.), *Behavior change: Methodology, concepts and practice.* Champaign, Ill.: Research Press, 1973.

Weiss, R. L., & Margolin, G. Marital conflict and accord. In A. R. Ciminero, K. S. Calhoun, & H. E. Adams (Eds.), *Handbook for behavioral assessment.* New York: Wiley, 1977.

III

Specialized Behavioral Assessment and Treatment Procedures

The three chapters in Part III detail specialized applications of behavioral technology still in their experimental stages. Chapter 8, by Roger E. Vogler, describes three novel procedures which require the administration of alcohol to problem drinkers. Chapter 9, by Ray J. Hodgson and Howard J. Rankin, and Chapter 10, by Rankin alone, introduce us to the use of cue exposure and response-prevention procedures with severely disordered chronic alcoholics.

8

Successful Moderation in a Chronic Alcohol Abuser

The Case of Bob S.

ROGER E. VOGLER

1. INTRODUCTION

Developing better methods for the diagnosis and treatment of alcohol abuse has been the focus of our clinical and research efforts for the past 15 years. The case of Bob S. is fairly typical of our clients. In describing his case I present the essential nature of what we do when we bring to bear what we have learned from our research and clinical experiences in working with an individual alcohol abuser. I discuss one aspect of our most recent research on diagnosis which uses acute tolerance as a measure of degree of abuse and an aid in selecting moderation versus abstinence as the treatment goal. Bob's case also describes the present clinical use of treatment techniques which have been modified and refined from our earlier research, such as the videotaping and replay of drinking behavior and sensitivity training for the effects of alcohol. Bob's case describes the combination of techniques which I believe to be most effective at the present time. Continued research, of course, is necessary to validate and improve the effectiveness of these techniques.

ROGER E. VOGLER ● Department of Psychology, Pomona College, Claremont, California 91711. Partial support for the preparation of this report was provided by Grant 1–RO1–AA03155 from the National Institute on Alcohol Abuse and Alcoholism, Department of Health, Education, and Welfare.

2. REASON FOR REFERRAL

Bob S. was referred by his defense attorney and by the district attorney of the county in which he recently had been arrested for the second time for driving under the influence of alcohol. Bob had been driving home alone on the freeway after having stopped at a bar for drinks after work. The California Highway Patrol stopped him because he was driving erratically, and when he failed the Field Sobriety Test, he was handcuffed and taken to the police station for a blood-alcohol level test. His BAL was 190 mg% and he was kept in jail overnight. His arrest was a profound humiliation, which he shared with no one other than his attorney, the legal authorities, and his wife. The circumstances of Bob's referral are fairly typical.

Bob appeared for his first visit with considerable apprehension. He was a well-dressed 47-year-old successful businessman whose lifestyle reflected his upper-middle-class affluence. Bob was profoundly humiliated over his arrest. He said he was aware of the nontraditional treatment available at our facility and had been seriously considering for some time scheduling an appointment. His current legal problem had precipitated doing so. Bob's wife, his two daughters, and a few intimate colleagues had expressed their concern about his drinking, and actually many people knew of his heavy drinking and had witnessed his intoxicated behavior socially. Bob preferred to play down his social reputation as a drinker; yet it was evident that he was embarrassed and chagrined by his reputation and very much wanted to change it. Thus, he was reasonably well motivated to do something about his drinking from the start but had not succeeded in doing so on his own and felt that he would need professional help in order to make a lasting change. He was skeptical of therapists in general, as are many clients similar to Bob, and it was clear that developing confidence and trust would be essential for an effective working relationship.

3. HISTORY OF DRINKING PROBLEM

We arranged for Bob's wife and older daughter to join us for the second visit. A more complete drinking history and current status are usually obtained when other family members are present. Also, their alliance in implementing subsequent therapeutic strategies is important to cultivate early on. One of them had to agree to chauffeur the client to and from any drinking sessions during the course of his training. Thus, the purpose of a session or two with supportive relatives is not only to obtain more complete information but to give them an opportunity to ask questions and to be reassured that we are dealing with the drinker's problem realistically and with commitment. His younger daughter was not included because of the poor relationship Bob had with her and his discomfort in sharing details of his drinking with her. It became evident that Bob's older daughter was very supportive of her father; his wife was more skeptical of any success with Bob's drinking, and, as was later confirmed, feared losing control over Bob if he were to make any significant changes in his lifestyle. This, too, is a rather frequent reaction of client spouses. Their acceptance of therapeutic change usually takes considerable time and seems to depend on discovering that such changes will not be detrimental to their relationship. In most cases spouses eventually find that such changes are beneficial to both partners.

Bob began drinking as a teenager, but not until his tour of duty in the U.S. Army near the end of the Korean War did his drinking become occasionally excessive. His drinking in the Army was largely motivated by a desire to be accepted by his comrades, a recurrent psychological theme. They typically socialized while drinking together, and since drinking to excess was sanctioned and even encouraged in the service, episodes of drunkenness were not construed as indicative of a problem. Bob was apparently quite susceptible to his fellow servicemen's influence and, as a result, drank to excess in their company on many occasions.

After his discharge from the Army in 1955, Bob married and attended college on the GI Bill of Rights for the next 4 years. His older daughter was born during this time and, despite multiple commitments to school, job, and family, he reports he was very happy. During this period his drinking was light to moderate and, in Bob's opinion, was not a problem. Over the next 10 years, however, his drinking gradually became greater in frequency and amount. Also during this period his second daughter was born. Of particular significance was his employment in sales with a small, developing industry. The pressures of the job, coupled with the expectations of other salespeople to drink, led to a daily, and frequently excessive, drinking pattern. This pattern continued for the next decade and became more of a problem as personal and business matters worsened. Drinking was a significant factor in his poor relationship with his first wife and was at least partially responsible for the ultimate dissolution of their marriage. Following the divorce, his former wife developed cancer and died within a relatively short period of time. Extreme guilt over his wife's death and the financial responsibility for her medical expenses exacerbated his excessive consumption. Daily consumption was in excess of 1 pint of hard liquor or its equivalent in other alcoholic beverages. During this low period in his life, one condition of a relationship with any woman was that she accept his excessive drinking without protest. It was during this time that he met the woman who was to become his second wife.

A somewhat more moderate pattern of consumption developed as Bob resigned from his sales position and became a partner in a local business that was just beginning but was destined for success. His ability to perform on the job depended upon sobriety at least during working hours. Bob was able to accomplish this even with occasional drinking at lunchtime with clients and others. Only rarely did he become too intoxicated to conduct business during regular working hours. When he did, it was usually a social event at the office which began mid- to late afternoon and extended into the evening. On these occasions his associates apparently witnessed his excessive drinking and its consequences and were somewhat embarrassed by them. Vodka was Bob's drink of choice at the time and continued to be so until about three years prior to his referral, at which time he decided that he would be able to maintain relative sobriety if he drank only wine. Bob's attempt at self-regulation by changing to a beverage with a lower alcohol content is fairly common. Typically such attempts are not very successful. Bob's usual evening consumption of wine was sufficient to give him a BAL of between 170 mg% and 250 mg%. He frequently drank in his car and often with a BAL in excess of 100 mg%, the minimum BAL regarded as driving under the influence in the State of California. Bob had rationalized that his first drunk-driving offense was unique and could happen to anyone. Not until his second arrest and conviction was he forced to acknowledge the seriousness of his drinking. As is usually the case, his drinking after the arrest was less than it had been before the arrest. He still drank every day, however, and usually to excessive BALs.

Bob came from a middle-class family of French and Scotch-Irish extraction in which drinking was an acceptable form of behavior. The incidence of drinking problems among relatives and family was low but included an aunt who was regarded by the family as an alcoholic. Bob occasionally witnessed his father drinking to excess, but this was the exception rather than the rule. While nearly everyone drank to some extent, no one besides his aunt was regarded as having a problem with alcohol. Bob reported that his mother had experienced some depression and had received psychiatric care when he was a child. Bob himself had never received treatment for any personal problems, including drinking.

4. RECENT DRINKING HISTORY AND CURRENT STATUS

Prior to his recent conviction for driving under the influence, Bob's daily consumption was about 45 to 61 oz. of table wine. Since his arrest, however, his drinking decreased to about 34 to 45 oz. of wine per day. Bob was concerned that his consumption would gradually increase to previous levels as the unpleasantness of his legal experience began to diminish. An important motivation for consulting us, rather than another treatment resource, was his awareness of moderation as a possible treatment goal for some drinkers. Medical treatment or the social coercion and religious philosophy of Alcoholics Anonymous were aversive to Bob.

Bob reported significant gaps in his memory for episodes of drinking on previous nights. He was aware that his behavior at certain social functions, especially those related to his business, was embarrassing and unacceptable to others. He was also aware of how much he looked forward to drinking at the end of the day, and that he almost never passed a day without some drinking. Bob reported that routine physical examinations had revealed no pathology of significance, and he manifested no particular physiological problems associated with the heavy use of alcohol other than occasional gastritis and diarrhea. He did not experience much hangover effect, even when he drank to considerable excess, and he rarely missed a day of work as a result of drinking. At the time of entering into treatment, he was asked to have a complete medical workup and to tell his personal physician that he was seeking treatment for alcohol abuse. His physician was to advise him on his physical capacity to continue to drink. Bob's physician found him to be in essentially good health with no gross pathology, even in those organ systems which are most susceptible to the toxic effects of alcohol. Since he was functioning within normal limits and there was no history of diabetes or other diseases known to be incompatible with the consumption of alcohol, his physician advised him that he could continue to drink alcohol in moderate amounts.

Consequences of drinking in areas other than physical, vocational, and legal, which are discussed above, include economic, social, marital, and personal. Evaluation of these consequences is an important part of assessment and the selection of treatment goal, which will be discussed again later on. Bob's drinking had very little economic impact. He could easily afford the liquor purchases, and only his legal problem, with subsequent treatment costs, resulted in any other expenses. Socially, however, Bob was indeed quite limited by his desire to drink most of the time when he was not working. He rarely socialized with anyone who did not also drink, and usually to excess. Persons or activities which did not include drinking, of which there were virtually none at the time of his entry into treatment, had been gradually eliminated from his lifestyle over the years. These social consequences are typical of most of our clients. The consequences of Bob's drinking have already been discussed for his first marriage but not his current one. Bob reported that his current wife also drank to excess, although not as abusively as he did. Most of what they did together involved drinking, whether together at home in the evenings, out to dinner, or traveling. Although the probability of a marital dispute was higher when the two of them had been drinking excessively, drinking was not regarded otherwise as a particular problem. His wife was only occasionally embarrassed by him socially when he was more intoxicated than usual. As became increasingly evident, Bob's wife was threatened by the prospect of his becoming a controlled drinker. Not only would she be unable to justify her own excessive consumption, she might lose some degree of control over him. Bob was particularly acquiescent to her demands on days after a heavy-drinking episode.

The remaining important consequence of Bob's drinking was his personal concern about its destructiveness. He had not shared his private distress with anyone. Most of his family and other intimates were reluctant to mention their occasional embarrassment about his public intoxication, so the subject was usually avoided, even though several people were tacitly aware of it. Yet Bob himself knew that he was drinking too much and that it was having a detrimental effect on his sense of self-control, perhaps on his physical health, and occasionally on his job performance. But since Bob had not wished to give up drinking altogether, which he had expected would be required of him in any treatment program until he had become aware of ours, he had put off dealing with it. He continued to worry about it privately, especially after a greater than usual episode of excess.

Bob's disposition about participating in treatment is typical of many clients who ultimately are treated by us. With no other acceptable treatment modality known to them, they avoid dealing with the problem at an earlier and more treatable stage, even though their personal concern and anguish mount over the years. Since Bob knew about our treatment for several years but had not availed himself of it, it is clear that his recent legal problem precipitated referral and may even have been essential for his participation despite his stated intention to come in entirely on a voluntary basis. We estimate that only about one-third to one-half of our clients self-refer without a legal reason or a compelling marital or vocational problem. We speculate that the stigma of the disease model of alcohol abuse inhibits early-stage self-referral. Stigma and referral are discussed in more detail in other papers (Vogler, Compton, & Weissbach, 1976; Weissbach & Vogler, 1977).

5. ASSESSMENT PROCEDURES AND FORMULATION OF TREATMENT GOALS

Assessment takes place across many sessions and has no discrete time limits. Standardized instruments are only occasionally used in evaluating clients' drinking or any other aspect of their background and personality, and none were used in Bob's case. Clinical hunches are sometimes derived from the self-administered Rotter Incomplete Sentences Blank and the MMPI, and sometimes the WAIS is used with clients who need help in establishing realistic educational or professional goals.

5.1. Monitoring Consumption

During the first visit Bob S. was asked to begin recording and graphing his consumption of alcohol. The obvious purpose of this procedure is to obtain one measure of the quantity and frequency of his drinking. Because self-reported drinking data are subject to distortions, they are not regarded as highly reliable until a solid rapport of trust has been established. Also, some decrease in drinking often occurs as a result of the therapeutic attention itself. However, *relative* changes in amount and frequency of drinking seem to remain intact, so that setting events for excessive drinking can still be determined from self-recorded drinking data. A less obvious function of this procedure is to sensitize clients to their drinking, that is, to heighten their awareness of how much, how often, with whom, and in what situations they tend to drink acceptably or excessively. Clients are instructed in the use of the Alco-Calculator so that they can calculate their own BAL for any drinking occasion. Clients also estimate their pretreatment drinking. These estimates are often much higher than current drinking.

An occasional problem is clients who come to their first few appointments somewhat intoxicated; in such cases BAL readings are obtained on a Mark IV Intoximeter to establish honesty as an essential component of the relationship.

Bob S.'s data revealed a consumption pattern of frequent lunchtime drinking and excessive evening and weekend drinking unrelated for the most part to specific precipitating events or a particular emotional disposition. We noted that drinking at home in the evening and any time during a Saturday or Sunday were the setting events for excessive drinking. Weighing 180 lb., his pre-arrest estimates of 45 to 61 oz. of wine daily usually resulted in BALs of between 170 mg% and 250 mg% over a 3-hour drinking period. On weekend days Bob usually drank more but over longer periods of time, so that these peak levels were maintained for several hours. His first 2 weeks of self-recorded drinking data indicated total daily amounts of between 34 and 45 oz. of wine, which resulted in daily peak BALs of about 120 mg% to 170 mg% over 3 hours. It appeared that alcohol accompanied almost all nonwork activities and that feeling good or bad at the end of the day had little influence on the amount or probability of his drinking.

Interviews with family members tended to corroborate these two sources of information. Other important consequences of Bob's drinking (vocational, social, personal, etc.) were previously discussed and are an integral part of assessment. Some aspects of these consequences were also discussed with family members.

5.2. The Acute Tolerance Test

The most important drinking assessment procedure is a test of acute tolerance to the subjective effects of alcohol. This test is derived from several years of clinical experimentation and subsequent systematic research on acute tolerance (Banks, Vogler, & Weissbach, 1979; Benton, Banks, & Vogler, in press; Vogler, Banks, & Benton, 1981).

Both moderate and abusive drinkers report that a given BAL has a greater subjective effect when the BAL is ascending than when it is descending. However, the time-course of magnitude estimates (MEs) of the subjective sense of intoxication compared with BALs reveals significant differences between moderate drinkers and abusers. Overall, the subjective effects of alcohol are much less for the abuser. The abusers' MEs typically begin to descend sooner, fall more rapidly, and reach zero sooner and at higher BALs as compared with moderate drinkers. We assume that a primary motivation for drinking is to achieve an altered state of consciousness (and not the corresponding perceptual-motor or cognitive impairments), and that the propensity of the abuser for consuming greater amounts of alcohol is largely determined by his or her degree of adaptation or acute tolerance, as it is also called. Thus, differences in degree of acute tolerance to the subjective effects of alcohol serve as a diagnostic indicator of degree of abuse. We use the client's degree of acute tolerance in the selection of moderation versus abstinence as an attainable treatment goal. Drinkers who are highly insensitive to the effects of alcohol at moderate BALs are unlikely to succeed in moderation because they are not experiencing the subjective changes which presumably motivate their drinking. Clients whose time-course of ME and BAL data provide functions similar to those of abusers in our research are advised to commit to abstinence. Those drinkers who are more sensitive to lower BALs are more likely to be accepted for moderation training.

At the beginning of the session for determining acute tolerance, Bob was instructed in the use of magnitude estimation, a direct psychophysical measurement technique (Banks, Vogler, & Weissbach, 1979; Ekman, Frankenhaeuser, Goldberg, Bjerver, Jarpe, & Myrsten, 1963; Stevens, 1958). He was told that when he first felt an effect from the drink to examine carefully, by introspection, his feeling of intoxication at that time and to assign it a number of his choosing, with 0 representing a feeling of complete sobriety. Using the initial feeling and its assigned number as a reference, he was asked to assign numerical values to subsequent estimates of intoxication through introspection and comparison. Thus, if he later felt twice as intoxicated, he reported a number twice as great, or if his subsequent level of intoxication felt half as intense as the initial reference point, he reported a number half as large.

Bob was instructed to fast from midnight of the previous night and to use no drugs or alcohol for at least 24 hours before the session. Sessions always begin at 9:00 A.M. for the purpose of standardization. His BAL was checked to be certain it was 0. Bob ingested 1.5 ml of ethanol per kg of body weight mixed with fruit juice and ice within 10 minutes. This amount of ethanol quite reliably results in peak BALs of about 70 mg%. Immediately after consuming the drink Bob rinsed his mouth for 5 minutes and then began providing breath samples, which he continued to do at approximately 7-minute intervals over the next 3 hours. Before each sample Bob estimated his level of intoxication using his initial reference point for comparison. In Figure 1, Bob's data are plotted along with data of severe abusers (13.3 oz. of absolute alcohol per day) and moderate drinkers (1.4 oz. per day) derived from Experiment 1 in the Vogler *et al.* (1981) study. The Vogler *et al.* data are presented for the purpose of illustrating Bob's degree of acute tolerance. Therefore, only one BAL curve is plotted which closely approximates all three BAL curves, and smooth-fitting curves have been drawn through ME data points.

In our experience Bob's data are characteristic of moderate abusers of alcohol. His reduced sensitivity to lower BALs suggests that he may not be satisfied with drinking small amounts of alcohol. Bob reported sobriety, an ME of 0, at 50 mg%, whereas the moderate drinkers did not report a loss

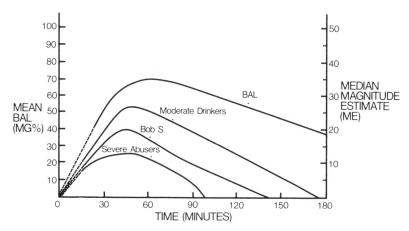

Figure 1. Comparison of time course of Bob S.'s blood-alcohol level and magnitude estimate of intoxication data, with the mean data from severe abusers and moderate drinkers derived from Experiment 1 in Vogler, Banks, & Benton (1981).

of subjective effects until their BALs fell to a mean of 36 mg%. However, Bob demonstrated greater sensitivity than the severe abusers, who reported sobriety at a mean BAL of 65 mg%. In borderline cases I err on the conservative side and recommend abstinence. However, the final decision on treatment goal is usually deferred in borderline cases until after the video and replay sessions. These two sessions combine assessment and treatment.

5.3. Videotaping Procedure

The two main purposes of the videotape and replay sessions are to acquire valuable clinical information rapidly and to motivate the client to change. They often aid as well in the selection of treatment goal (moderation or abstinence) with borderline clients. Because the videotaping session involves consumption of alcohol to excess (usually BALs of between 150 mg% and 250 mg%) and facilitates personal disclosure, it is fraught with practical and ethical problems which must be discussed. The drinking session lasts for at least 4 hours, and the therapist must be prepared to have his or her patience and endurance taxed considerably. And unless the drinker becomes sufficiently intoxicated to demonstrate obvious impairment in psychological and motor functioning, a useful tape will not be obtained. In my opinion the risks and problems associated with the videotaping procedure are far outweighed by the benefits of valid and complete clinical information, a heightened motivation to change, and an honest and accepting rapport which, in my experience, the procedure provides better than any other.

Medical clearance is required before participation and the procedure is never used with currently abstinent clients. Family members are advised as to the care and transportation of the client. The client is advised to eat only a light meal prior to the beginning of the session and to drink no alcohol for at least 24 hours beforehand. The latter requirement came about as the result of finding measurable, and sometimes excessive, BALs at the beginning of sessions for some clients. Even though they may not have drunk anything on the day of the videotaping, their consumption the day before has been found to result in residual BALs ranging from 30 mg% to over 200 mg%.

Clients have had one to three prior visits in which the details of this session have been explained to them. Almost all clients are very apprehensive about their participation and are often ambivalent about following through. Reassurance is usually only partially successful in mitigating their anxiety. Their primary reluctance seems to be the fear of personal disclosure which, they correctly perceive, may not be fully under their control when they become intoxicated. Indeed, one purpose of the session and its replay is to demonstrate to them that personal intimacies will be treated with respect and sympathy.

If too many visits have occurred before the videotaping session, there appears to be a role conflict for many drinkers. Most clients have a well-practiced sober role and well-rehearsed verbal repertoires for discussing their drinking and their intentions to change. The videotaping must occur before they become too invested in establishing this sober-role relationship with the therapist. One example of a role conflict would be that of a drinker who has been seen for several sessions and who has consistently presented a controlled, courteous, and concerned disposition. If their videotaping reveals, for example, hostile, dependent, highly emotional, or antisocial tendencies of which they may be only partially aware, they are often very uncomfortable and sometimes angry about integrating these aspects of themselves, which are so graphically revealed by the videotape, into the therapeutic relationship. On the other hand, early disclosure and integration of this material into the overall clinical picture usually facilitates and hastens therapeutic progress. Most clients experience full disclosure of themselves with relief when they discover acceptance by the therapist despite lifelong efforts to disguise or hide their shortcomings from everyone, including themselves sometimes. In this regard, the videotaping and replay sessions might be viewed as a shortcut to the kind of acceptance and unconditional positive regard considered by Carl Rogers as so essential to therapeutic change.

Should there be any lingering tendencies to deny their drinking problem, undeniable examples of their tolerance and loss of control provide irrefutable evidence of the profound nature of their abusive drinking.

Occasionally, other problems must be dealt with. For example, clients with a history of aggressiveness when intoxicated are required to have relatives or friends available in the reception room. In addition to the psychology assistant who is operating the videotaping equipment, family members or friends have very infrequently been used in calming an emotional or aggressive client.

On the day of the videotaping Bob and his wife and daughter were first taken into my office to answer any further questions and to allay their anxiety. Bob had already signed a consent form and obtained medical clearance. He was then taken into the drinking room and introduced to the psychology assistant who was operating the videotape equipment. He was asked to pour himself a glass of wine, the alcoholic beverage which he typically consumed to excess, and to begin drinking right away. There is considerable variation between clients in the initial rate of consumption. Particularly anxious or highly defensive clients often drink very slowly and may have to be encouraged to drink faster. Others have to be slowed down lest they consume so much alcohol so quickly that little useful tape can be obtained. Bob drank two 5-oz. glasses of wine in the first hour and greater amounts subsequently.

Insofar as possible a relaxed and casual atmosphere was created. After two or three drinks Bob, like most clients, became oblivious to the television cameras and microphone.

Taping is intermittent for about the first 3 hours and becomes more continuous toward the end of the session, resulting in a 2-hour tape. At various points throughout the session elements of a standard field sobriety test used by law enforcement officials were administered, along with procedures for assessing orientation and mental functioning. Components of these tests which best reflect changes in intoxication include: (1) standing on one foot with both arms outstretched, eyes closed, and head tilted backwards, (2) walking a straight line heel to toe and turning around to come back after a given number of steps, (3) holding one hand steady and repeatedly and rapidly clapping the other against it first on one side and then on the other, (4) writing out the alphabet, especially starting in the middle of it, (5) tongue twisters (e.g., Peter Piper picked a peck of pickled peppers), and (6) subtracting from 100 by units of 7 or 3.

Bob was typical in proceeding from an initial phase of apprehension and guardedness, up to about 50 mg% BAL, through a more loquacious and relaxed disposition associated with a BAL of between 50 mg% and 150 mg%, and then through a period of increasing emotionality and impairment of psychological and motor functioning. The latter varies with clients' tolerance to alcohol. Most clients—and particularly those whose treatment goal is or will be abstinence—who do not freely disclose intimacies or behave with sufficient impairment to motivate them to change are allowed to drink above 200 mg% when their drinking history indicates the frequent use of alcohol to a BAL in this range. Rather than taking breath samples, which require 15 minutes of no drinking, the Alco-Calculator is used to estimate BAL. Breath samples are taken near the end of the session. Bob's tolerance and emotional control were great enough to permit him to drink beyond 200 mg%.

During the first 2 hours of the session Bob was free to discuss any subject of his choosing. Besides fostering a more relaxed atmosphere, the relatively free discussion often reveals clients' strategies of avoidance and defensiveness. Bob told me about his military experiences, his college days, and his present business activities. He responded informatively and nondefensively to my inquiries about alternative activities to drinking, family and social background, more details of his drinking history, social relationships, and future plans. During the last 2 hours more emotional material emerged. We discussed candid feelings about his present marriage and his two daughters, his sexual experiences, feelings of inadequacy because he never did as well as he thought he should, and residual feelings of frustration and failure in his earlier sales career. Bob became tearful in discussing his life with his first wife and expressed considerable guilt over divorcing her shortly before her death. Bob rationalized the divorce from his first wife by focusing on their many disputes and emphasizing her inability to provide him with emotional support. At one rather emotional point, Bob remorsefully admitted that he had been having an affair with another woman during the last year of their marriage, and that his wife correctly attributed their marital problems mainly to his drinking. He confessed that he had never admitted this much responsibility for the divorce to anyone before. Her death intensified his feelings of guilt and responsibility. The latter is material which might not become evident for some time in typical psychotherapy sessions.

Another important topic was his anger and lack of control in dealing with his 18-year-old daughter's sexual activities. Bob felt guilty about not spending more time with his daughters as they were growing up and was especially regretful that he did not have a better relationship with his younger daughter.

No attempt was made at obtaining complete information or closure on any of these issues, since the replay and subsequent therapy sessions would provide ample opportunity for dealing with them. Besides, Bob's intoxicated condition precluded constructive discussion beyond disclosure.

Near the end of the fourth hour I asked Bob if he would drive a car and would remember our conversation during this period of the session. He answered yes to both questions. Typical of most clients, however, he did not remember. A breath sample showed his final BAL to be 213 mg%. He said that he had frequently drunk to this level of intoxication. Bob asked for another drink at the end of the session but was not demanding about it. Clients who repeatedly ask for another drink seem to have a poor prognosis for moderation.

5.4. Reply and Analysis of the Videotape

Both therapist and client take notes for later discussion as they watch the 2-hour videotape. Occasionally the tape is stopped or a particular section is analyzed, but most discussion is reserved for the hour after viewing the tape. Allowing sufficient time to discuss the tape after viewing it is important so that the client is not left so distraught and upset at the conclusion of the session that drinking is precipitated. During that hour advantage is taken of the heightened motivation of the client to do something about his or her drinking. It is important to provide immediate structure and guidelines for change.

Before and during the replay I had made a list of clinical hypotheses or areas to be explored with Bob in later sessions. I knew a great deal about him at this time and had to exercise patience and skill in using this information to facilitate therapeutic change. Too much feedback at once might overwhelm

Bob and make him either defensive or depressed and withdrawn. Since Bob presented with drinking as the primary problem, I began with that.

Bob was indeed aroused from viewing the tape and was very eager to make a change in his drinking and related behavior. From the start Bob had made it clear that he preferred moderation as the treatment goal. I told him that in the long run I thought his chance for success in abstinence was greater than it was for moderation. His history of abuse and his tolerance for alcohol suggested a relatively poor prognosis for success in moderation. In support of moderation as a possible treatment goal were his success in stopping smoking several years before, his history of self-discipline and being goal-oriented, his general competence and determined lifestyle, his successful career change, paying off his first wife's considerable medical expenses, his present financial success, and his susceptibility to the approval of others and to reporting to me. After much discussion, we agreed to work towards moderation for 3 months. It was decided that should he not succeed in achieving a stable pattern of moderate drinking in 3 months, defined as no more than 19 oz. of 12% wine daily, consumed over a $1\frac{1}{2}$-hour period (representing a peak BAL of about 70 mg%), then abstinence would have to follow.

In Bob's case we began by focusing on his drinking during evenings and weekends because of the high probability of excessive drinking at these times. Bob had been making a list of reinforcing activities which might successfully compete with drinking, or at least excessive drinking, and it was decided that he should consistently attempt to occupy his evenings and weekends as often as possible with bicycling, tennis, golf, concerts, and plays, all of which had been pleasurable activities at some time in his life. He would move his dinner hour from 7:30 to 6:30 and not start drinking until 1 to $1\frac{1}{2}$ hours before dinner. Dinner would terminate his drinking because eating attenuated his desire for more alcohol. Bob agreed to eliminate lunchtime consumption as often as possible and to attempt abstinence on 1 or 2 days of each week. He was given a book on assertiveness, in his case mainly for extricating himself from situations where others expected him to mediate for them. He was also provided with a cassette tape recording of exercises for deep-muscle relaxation (Marquis, 1982). Bob agreed to practice refusing drinks assertively, particularly at lunchtime, and to substitute often nonalcoholic beverages in restaurants and at home. He was told that personal pleasures including food, travel, sex, recreation, and adult toys (e.g., boats, motorcycles) were to be indulged freely in.

Bob was provided with alcohol education material, which included an Alco-Calculator and several papers (Vogler & Weissbach, 1976; Vogler, Weissbach, & Compton, 1977; Weissbach & Vogler, 1977). His understanding and use of this information became an ongoing part of therapy. Bob was also to bring his recorded drinking data to every session. He agreed never to drive when his BAL was estimated to be at or above 50 mg% and ascending.

In general, a no-nonsense approach, coupled with definitive guidelines for change and some degree of optimism, should they commit themselves wholeheartedly, usually works best. By this time I am usually confident about abstinence versus moderation as a treatment goal. In a direct and candid manner I tell clients what I think they must do about their drinking. I strongly suggest that they become abstinent, or moderate, immediately. If they cannot agree to this then I recommend that we decide on a date for doing so. Setting events for excessive drinking and their alternatives are discussed in detail. Other problem areas which can be worked on right away, because they do not result in defensiveness and because they often have immediately reinforcing consequences, are assertiveness, relaxation training, and alternatives training. More sensitive material, such as distortions in self-perception of which the client may be only partially aware, are usually dealt with later on. It is important to bear in mind that nearly all clients will be taking a look at themselves in a way that they have never done before. Threatening material must be presented in a gradual, gentle manner, usually over many sessions in order to facilitate its constructive integration into the treatment plan. This session is usually closed on an optimistic note, and the client is scheduled for two visits per week for the next 3 months.

5.5. Sensitivity Training for Alcohol

Another aspect of Bob's moderation treatment was two training sessions to heighten awareness to the effects of lower BALs. These sessions were scheduled at monthly intervals after the videotape replay session. During these 2- to 3-hour sessions, Bob consumed an amount of alcohol which brought his BAL to about 70 mg%. During the first half-hour or so of these sessions alcohol education was a primary topic. Discussion of adaptation was useful in providing a rational basis for limiting consumption. The main purpose here was to make it clear to Bob that his maximum pleasure from alcohol would be experienced as the BAL is rising. The same BAL on the descending curve would not be experienced as intensely. Hence, the logical conclusion—and the one Bob reached on the basis of the data obtained in this session—was that he enjoyed the effects of alcohol far more when his BAL was rising than when it was falling. Thus, to get the maximum benefits from drinking with a minimum of negative consequences, he should only drink for about 45 minutes to an hour and terminate his drinking with another pleasurable activity. Once his BAL has peaked, to maintain a subjective sense of intoxication, much less to increase that sense of intoxication, would require an amount of alcohol which is incompatible with his health and well-being. As in the acute tolerance test described earlier, BAL and magnitude estimation data were collected and plotted on a graph. Any cues, external or internal, which might serve to help discriminate a BAL range of 30 mg% to 70 mg%, are identified and noted by the client on paper. Other topics include alcohol equivalencies between different kinds of beverages, the metabolism of alcohol, and the effects of alcohol on sleep. Other issues, often clinical ones, are also followed up.

Like other moderation clients, Bob reported these sessions to be useful to him in heightening his awareness of the subjective effects of alcohol and in providing tangible guidelines for limits to his consumption.

5.6. Psychological Evaluation

The videotape and replay sessions provided a wealth of information which I introduced over many sessions to allow ample opportunity to confirm, modify, or disconfirm my clinical hypotheses about Bob. The following clinical picture emerged. Bob S. was a highly energetic, driven man with extreme tendencies in work, play, sex, and drink. Far too much of what he did was product-oriented or "constructive." His nonwork or "play" activities were such things as equipment repair, remodeling, and yardwork. He rarely relaxed except with the ingestion of a considerable amount of alcohol. Alcohol appeared to facilitate shifting gears to a more relaxed evening mood. Without it, however, he was not able to adopt a nonwork disposition. Bob's self-insight and his insight into others was limited. He tended to deal with superficialities and to solve best those problems external to himself. In this regard he was an excellent mediator and was much used in this capacity by others. He was highly dependent on the approval and acceptance of others, which made him too susceptible to their influence. The mediator role had too frequently caused Bob unhappiness insofar as he often accepted blame for problems he had little or nothing to do with, except for attempting to solve them, which sometimes failed. Key people in his life, particularly his wife and his business associates, manipulated Bob to meet their own needs. Bob was only partially aware of this aspect of his relationship with them. He had failed to accept his personal inadequacies and failures, which occasionally resulted in a lack of genuineness, secretiveness or defensiveness in some areas, frequent attempts to impress others, and difficulty in accepting the faults of some of his subordinates. He showed what Julian Rotter calls "high minimal goals," in that he rarely felt reinforced or satisfied with the results of his efforts. Much guilt was in evidence about failing to spend more time with his daughters and to establish a better relationship with his younger daughter, and the circumstances of the divorce and death of his first wife. The nurturant relationship with his father and the lack of friendships with girls as he grew up apparently set the stage for better friendships with men than with women. His lack of knowledge and ease with his own needs and emotions, and his limited self-acceptance, precluded a more open emotional expressiveness. Efforts were made to deal with these various personal issues over several months. The high-risk videotaping session provided strong motivation to change accompanied by a wealth of clinical material, which could be systematically integrated into sessions designed to train Bob, primarily with behavioral methods.

6. CONTINUED TREATMENT

In subsequent sessions I routinely inquired about Bob's drinking. We analyzed his drinking data and any episodes of excess. Assertive refusals of drinks, alternatives to drinking, and so forth were often briefly discussed. Gradually we explored the personal concerns mentioned above. In most of his important relationships, particularly with his wife and business associates, we determined that their interests usually came before his own. We speculated that without more personal satisfactions he may have been seeking relief from the stress of always working conscientiously for others, leaving him predisposed to an easy escape, such as by drinking. This tendency was compounded by high-minimal goals. When Bob began to question the nature of his important relationships and stopped the many things he had been doing for these people, they protested and questioned his reasons for continued therapy when he had so obviously attenuated his consumption of alcohol. Reestablishing these relationships on a more equitable, give-and-take basis took several months to accomplish. During this time Bob reacquired some recreational activities which were not so product-oriented, such as bicycling and golf. I repeatedly gave Bob "permission" to play and actively encouraged him to give himself permission to do so. Existential concerns about the meaningfulness of various pursuits, and the balance between work and play, became significant areas of therapeutic attention. Better insight into himself and his guilt about perceived transgressions toward others helped allay his guilty reactions. Ample evidence of his success and accomplishments were used to help him accept his achievements as sufficient. We also focused upon Bob's tendency for self-chastisement and a better understanding of why others value him. Whenever Bob reported an episode of excessive drinking his self-punishment was adequate motivation for renewed effort.

After 3 months of semiweekly sessions, Bob's visits were cut to once a week. Bob was shown elements of his videotape once again, 4 months after it was made. In his case the purpose was to maintain his motivation and to underscore personal problems and changes in them which we had been working on in therapy.

Focusing on Bob's success and sensitizing him to the advantages of sobriety was a maintenance strategy. Bob became aware that he felt much better physically, slept better, was more competent sexually, could conduct business at any hour of the day or night, and had a new sense of self-control which was particularly gratifying to him. After 3 months of daily recording of alcohol consumption this procedure was modified to include only weekly samples every 3 weeks, and discontinued altogether after 6 months. However, Bob was to note any exceptional drinking behavior whenever it occurred.

Since I regard changes in personal problems as requisite to lasting changes in drinking behavior, these too were given extensive attention over the course of many months of treatment. A word of caution should be given about the utility and ethics of using some of the procedures described in this chapter. The video, replay, and psychotherapy sessions in particular obviously require clinical skills and should not be used by persons who are untrained in clinical work. Individual assessment or treatment procedures, such as the acute tolerance test, alcohol education, or sensitivity training for alcohol, might be used to advantage by nonclinical personnel. However, the most effective treatment combines all of the techniques.

7. TREATMENT RESULTS

Bob drank to excess on the average of about once a month for the first 3 months of treatment. However, he did so with circumspection and concern and without compromising the welfare of others. He was able to follow the one absolute rule about never driving when his blood alcohol was above 50 mg%. Each occasion of excess was in his own home, the setting event with the highest probability of excess in his history. Except for these three events, Bob's drinking data suggested steady improvement. He rarely passed a day without drinking some, and his eventual pattern became very stable. His daily consumption changed from 45–61 oz. of 12% table wine before treatment to 25 oz. during the first 3 months of treatment, eventually reaching and stabilizing at about 19 oz. of table wine per day. Bob was particularly gratified from the praise and encouragement he received from his family and his business partners as his drinking came under self-control. Because Bob's drinking consistently decreased over time to within moderate limits, it was not necessary to change our treatment goal to abstinence.

After 15 months I am now reasonably confident that Bob's success will last. He continues to drink every day. About once every 3 months Bob drinks to a BAL of between 150 mg% and 200 mg%. These rare occasions occur at home, usually alone, and have not resulted in any significant negative consequences. Presently his normal daily consumption is about 15 to 20 oz. of wine in a 1½-hour period, which brings him to a BAL of about 50 mg% to 70 mg%. Over the past 6 months he has had one therapy session every two to three weeks. He will continue to have intermittent contact with me for another year or so, although the frequency may be reduced to as little as one visit every other month. With a heightened motivation for change, successful alternatives training, ways to relax without chemical aids, assertiveness skills, definitive guidelines for moderate drinking, and clinical insight, Bob has the tools to deal with new stressors. He has learned that he can function effectively and solve problems without resorting to excessive alcohol use. Bob is well aware of the importance of continued vigilance with regard to any increase in his consumption of alcohol over time. He is keenly aware of how much he drinks. Continued contact provides an opportunity to intervene with corrective measures before any significant increase occurs. Given the progress Bob has made in resolving personal problems and his diligence in following moderate drinking guidelines, his prognosis for continued success as a controlled drinker is favorable.

COMMENTARY

William M. Hay

This chapter by Roger Vogler describes the behavioral assessment and treatment of a court-referred chronic alcohol abuser. The chapter provides an excellent overview of the therapeutic skills necessary to deal with the unique problems of the court-referred client. The chapter also describes the integration of standard behavioral treatment components for problem drinking with three specialized assessment and treatment procedures—acute tolerance testing, videotape replay and analysis, and alcohol sensitivity training.

As clinicians, we are aware of the importance of tailoring our treatment procedures to the individual client. At the present time, however, we have few diagnostic aids available to us when we are deciding on the most appropriate treatment goal for a particular client. In this chapter, acute tolerance testing to the subjective effects of alcohol serves as a measure of degree of abuse and provides the clinician with an empirically based diagnostic tool for treatment goal decisions. Vogler hypothesizes that drinkers who are insensitive to the subjective effects of alcohol at moderate blood-alcohol levels are unlikely to succeed at moderation, since the subjective effects of alcohol have been found to be attenuated for the alcohol abuser. A high degree of adaptation or acute tolerance to the subjective effects of intoxication may, according to Vogler, account for the excessive consumption of alcohol abusers. In our own work on BAL discrimination ability, we have consistently found that individuals who consume large amounts of alcohol over prolonged periods are poor estimators of blood-alcohol level as compared to social drinkers. In both cases increased tolerance to the effects of intoxication may alter or attenuate the feedback from regulatory mechanisms and result in continued drinking.

Vogler deals with the issue of moderation or abstinence as a treatment goal in a direct manner; he serves as a good model for other clinicians. In this case the client entered therapy seeking an alternative to abstinence. Based on assessment data, however, Vogler felt that the client's best chance was for abstinence. A realistic trial period of 3 months to achieve a specified level of consumption was set, with the stipulation that abstinence would be required unless the target goal was met. The client, however, was not placed in a "lose-lose" situation. Vogler capitalizes on the assets of his client, works on developing positive expectations for success, and gives the client every opportunity to reach the goal. This conservative, goal-oriented approach is echoed throughout the text. The reader will notice that in a number of the chapters a period of abstinence is required before a controlled or moderate-drinking goal is considered. I second these conservative approaches and frequently require at least a 3-month period of abstinence before embarking on a drinking retraining program. Initially, clients are resistant and, as Peter Nathan points out in one of his commentaries, some clients may terminate treatment. The value of the assessment data gathered during this abstinent period may outweigh this termination risk. Also, clients who successfully abstain are elated over their control and subsequently express positive feelings concerning the experience.

Vogler's use of videotape replay and analysis procedures with this client is particularly interesting. A 2-hour videotape was made of the client drinking to a rather heroic blood-alcohol level. The client was given the opportunity to view the tape and analyze its content. The Sobells and their colleagues have also reported on the use of videotaping-feedback procedures in some of their earlier work. Based on the quantity of relevant data gathered via this procedure, it has great potential as an adjunct to other assessment instruments. It is apparent, however, that the feedback and analysis aspects of the procedure must be carefully monitored both in terms of rate and content. The goal is not to overwhelm the client and perhaps trigger a drinking episode but rather to use the experience as a motivation to change unproductive drinking habits. The reader should take note of the fact that the videotaping and replay procedures, as well as acute tolerance testing and alcohol sensitivity training, were all carried out in controlled environments, and only after careful medical screening and extensive client preparation.

Treatment programs which include procedures where individuals with drinking-related problems ingest alcohol remain extremely controversial. As clinicians we are bound ethically to monitor the impact of our treatments and to minimize the possibility of a treatment procedure actually triggering excessive alcohol consumption. Once we have established that a moderate or controlled goal has a reasonable probability of success, however, the regulated ingestion of alcohol by the client has a number of advantages. As noted above, ingestion of alcohol during a prolonged videotaping session can provide important assessment data in a number of areas (e.g., changes in mood or

*thoughts with increasing intoxication; specification of drinking response parameters).
Similarly, the alcohol sensitivity training procedures described by Vogler and in my
chapter can help to reestablish an effective regulatory system for the client. These comments are speculative, however, and require careful empirical validation.*

9. REFERENCES

Banks, W. P., Vogler, R. E., & Weissbach, T. A. Adaptation of ethanol intoxication. *Bulletin of the Psychonomic Society*, 1979, *14*, 319–322.

Benton, R. P., Banks, W. P., & Vogler, R. E. Carryover of tolerance to alcohol in moderate drinkers. *Journal of Studies on Alcohol*, in press.

Ekman, G., Frankenhaeuser, M., Goldberg, L., Bjerver, K., Jarpe, G., & Myrsten, A. Effects of alcohol intake on subjective and objective variables over a five-hour period. *Psychopharmalogia*, 1963, *4*, 28–38.

Marquis, J. N. Deep muscle relaxation, 1982. Self-Management Schools, 745 Distel Drive, Los Altos, Calif. 94022.

Stevens, S. S. Problems and methods of psychophysics. *Psychological Bulletin*, 1958, *55*, 177–196.

Rutgers University Center of Alcohol Studies *Alco-calculator* Rutgers University, New Brunswick, N.J.: Publications Division, 1982.

Vogler, R. E., & Weissbach, T. A. *Alcohol education.* Unpublished manuscript, 1976.

Vogler, R. E., Compton, J. V. & Weissbach, T. A. The referral problem in the field of alcohol abuse. *Journal of Community Psychology*, 1976, *4*, 357–361.

Vogler, R. E., Weissbach, T. A., & Compton, J. V. Learning techniques for alcohol abuse. *Behavior Research and Therapy*, 1977, *15*, 31–38.

Vogler, R. E., Banks, W. P., & Benton, R. P. *Subjective report of intoxication as a measure of tolerance in moderate and abusive drinkers.* Manuscript submitted for publication, 1981.

Weissbach, T. A., & Vogler, R. E. Implications of a social-learning approach to the prevention and treatment of alcohol abuse. *Contemporary Drug Problems*, 1977, *6*, 553–568.

9

Cue Exposure and Relapse Prevention

RAY J. HODGSON and
HOWARD J. RANKIN

1. INTRODUCTION

Compulsions and addictions are very similar in many respects. In both, there is a strong urge to do something which is difficult to resist. They often lead to a reduction in anxiety but are sometimes difficult to stop, and then, if prolonged, they are associated with an increase in anxiety and a feeling of helplessness. Frequently, both compulsions and addictions are so powerful that family or work responsibilities are ignored, and both, when severe, involve repetitive stereotyped actions. Both addictions and compulsions are prime examples of the irrational self-destructive behavior which is part of the human condition, and both are generally considered to be among the most intractable of problems. If they are similar in so many ways, then there may be some advantage to be gained from applying a "compulsion model" to alcoholism, especially since there have been recent advances in the treatment of compulsive disorders (e.g., Meyer, 1966; Rachman & Hodgson, 1980; Rachman, Hodgson, & Marks, 1971). It has been clearly demonstrated in a number of studies that compulsions can be modified by an extinction procedure involving prolonged exposure to those cues which trigger, or at least influence, the compulsive ritual. The compulsive hand washer is per-

RAY J. HODGSON and HOWARD J. RANKIN ● Addiction Research Unit, Institute of Psychiatry, Maudsley Hospital, London, England.

suaded to touch "contaminated" objects and then resist the urge to wash so that the imaginary contamination is spread to all and sundry. A person who feels compelled to check and recheck gas taps after cooking or before retiring will be encouraged to practice switching them off as quickly as possible without checking. Obsessional ruminating about causing harm, accompanied by a desire to check that everything is alright, has been successfully treated by exposing the person to situations which provoke the ruminations while encouraging them to resist the urge to check. Research carried out in the United Kingdom, the United States, Germany, Greece, and Australia has shown that cue exposure can be a very powerful method of breaking up compulsive behavior (Rachman & Hodgson, 1980).

Which processes are at work in cue exposure treatment is still an open question, but it would appear that reality testing is involved to some extent (Meyer, 1966; Rachman & Hodgson, 1980). Clients comment during treatment that "I didn't enjoy that at all, but it wasn't as bad as I thought it would be," and "I thought that the rumination would be with me for days, but it seems to have disappeared."

Rachman, de Silva, and Roper (1976) provide very convincing evidence that under certain conditions the compulsive urge will decline during a single cue exposure session. On the left of Figure 1 the effect of a ritual on the compulsive urge is displayed, and on the right we can see that there is a gradual reduction during a 3-hour period of response prevention. As predicted by an extinction model, Likierman and Rachman (1980) have also demonstrated a gradual reduction *across* repeated cue exposure sessions. Putting together the evidence on processes and on treatment outcome, there is now no doubt that cue exposure can be an effective way of modifying obsessional-compulsive complaints. But is such an approach of any relevance to other compulsive and addictive behaviors?

In 1974 we decided to use the same approach with a client who was severely dependent on alcohol, and 2 years later we published our findings up to the 6-month follow-up period (Hodgson & Rankin, 1976). The following description covers the original treatment, a series of booster sessions after 18 months, and a progress report up to 5 years.

2. MR. M. AND HIS PROBLEMS

On admission to hospital, Mr. M. was a 43-year-old manual worker. He believed that he had inherited two things from his father, namely, his alcoholism and a passionate support for the Irish Republican Army. He started to drink moderately at the age of 17, after coming to the United Kingdom from Ireland, but very quickly he was regularly consuming about 4 pints of beer

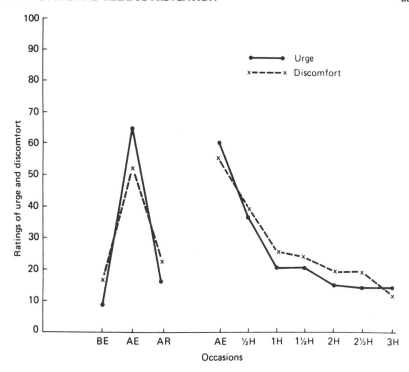

Figure 1. The decline of obsessional-compulsive urges as a result of ritual performance (left) and response prevention (right). Mean ratings of urge and discomfort ($n = 11$) before cue exposure (BE), after exposure (AE), after ritual performance (AR), after reexposure (AE), and at 1½-hour intervals during response prevention (Rachman *et al.*, 1976).

every day. At the age of 21, while he was in the Army, he would frequently consume a bottle of liquor in a day. Heavy drinking continued with a few breaks and fluctuations, but he began to worry that he had a problem when he was 39 and started to experience severe shakes, sweating, and blackouts.

His infancy and childhood were relatively normal, but he did get into trouble for fighting and truancy. He left school at the age of 12 and spent 3 years working as a milkman and then a few years as a builder's laborer. At the age of 14 he spent 2 years in hospital with spinal tuberculosis. After 3 years in the Army he then returned to laboring and painting. When he was 24, he served time for breaking and entering.

Between 1970 and 1975, he had twice received traditional inpatient treatment with group therapy, and abstinence as the stated treatment goal, but on each occasion he relapsed within a month of discharge. During the 2 years prior to his 1975 admission, he had been employed only sporadically, and his wife had been on the point of leaving him on at least 6 occasions. In the last few months before this admission, Mr. M.

had threatened his wife with a knife; she also reported a number of occasions when he would roll screaming on the floor and several incidents when he had injured himself in falls. At this time his wife described him as "helpless." He reported blackouts and a number of withdrawal symptoms including "sweats" and "shakes." His favorite drink was vodka, although he would drink anything alcoholic, including methylated spirits if nothing else was available.

When first considered as a possible candidate for cue exposure treatment, Mr. M. was being seen regularly in the Maudsley Hospital outpatient clinic. He was severely dependent and clearly believed that once he started to drink, it would be difficult for him to stop. Sometimes he could curtail his drinking for 2 or 3 days after a fortnight of heavy drinking, but only with the help of Valium. Since a few drinks appeared to act as a cue for further drinking, it appeared that cue exposure could be of some help in breaking the compulsion. He was therefore approached and was happy to volunteer for this "untested form of treatment."

He had many other problems which could have been the focus of treatment, but he was very willing to take part in a program, which had the simple aim of "breaking the compulsion to drink and developing your willpower." In fact, he was thankful that somebody would at last pay attention to his compulsion because he was sick and tired of talking about his other problems.

These other problems were dyslexia, sexual impotence, and depression, as well as aggressive thoughts and impulses toward his wife. His wife was just about at the end of her tether, and he had no other social activities or support; furthermore, he was frequently unemployed.

It was decided, with his agreement, that after treatment we would give him some brief counseling for these problems, but most of our effort would go into the cue exposure treatment. We emphasized that although our aim was to help him with his drinking problem, we also wanted him to help us test out the cue exposure approach. He was very clearly informed that he could opt out at any time, and we would then switch to another approach or refer him back to another member of the treatment team.

3. DRINKING PRIOR TO TREATMENT

Mr. M. and his wife were interviewed independently by an experienced psychologist in November 1974, just before our involvement in the case. They provided the following description of his drinking at that time.*

* Quoted with permission from Dr. Jim Orford's notes.

Neither were able to describe any recent controlled or moderate drinking. Mr. M. described drinking at least half a bottle of spirits (usually vodka) daily, and usually more like one and a half to two bottles, and his wife described how he drank until he was drunk, collapsed or fell into bed and later recovered to start drinking again. She thought that he drank at least one large bottle of spirits per day. She described his drinking as secret and lately as "defiant." He would hide drink under the bedclothes when he was in bed, and in numerous other places. She felt his drinking was worse now than ever in the past. He was "stupid drunk" for days and days, had been crawling about the floor recently and threatened her with a knife, tried to strangle her on another occasion, and had started to act very strangely, for example, by hiding trivial things like tickets under the carpet. She tried to get him to stay in bed when he was like this, but he often refused and had fallen downstairs several times. He was telling lies repeatedly and had exchanged his watch for drink in the off-licence recently. These were all things he would never have done before. She felt that he had become "desperate."

His wife, when asked about the details of drinking over the last 12 months, explained that Mr. M. had been in hospital (Bethlem) for 3 months earlier in the year, and she felt that he had two separate periods of abstinence of a month each at other times. Otherwise she thought that he had a bout lasting from late on a Thursday until Monday, approximately once a fortnight. On the Thursday, at the start of these bouts, he might have only two drinks or so, but this was not normal drinking—he was just getting prepared for the next day's drinking. The last 3 weeks he had been off work, and other than 2 days to come up to the hospital, he had been drinking every day. This works out at a rough estimate of 30 weeks (roughly 85 days in toto) "drunk," and the rest abstinent (plus roughly 15 days, contained in the 30 weeks, of just a few drinks prior to a drinking bout).

It seems likely that this, if anything, is an underestimate, as Mr. M. admitted that much of his drinking was secret. He did not recall periods of abstinence other than 3 months in hospital and admitted that once he had gone back to work, following an accident, a few weeks after coming out of hospital and he had been drinking throughout the week. This included Mondays to Wednesdays, when he would be at work but would have a drink early in the morning and then surreptitiously (e.g., nipping out to the toilets) swig drink during the day. He thought his wife didn't know of this. Previously he would abstain at least on Tuesdays and Wednesdays, but his bout (weekly not fortnightly according to him) would finish on the Monday morning with a final quarter of a bottle of spirits to relieve "the shakes." At that time he took Valium on Tuesdays and Wednesdays to calm him down. This makes a rough estimate of around 40 weeks of this kind of drinking, all over the 100 gm per day mark and most of it well over (approximately 200 days in toto over the last 12 months, plus approximately 25 days of less than 100 gm, but again not definable as "normal drinking" because it is simply the end of a bout).

Mr. M. also felt that his drinking was worse than ever before. He described the urge to drink as "chronic" now. He was drinking 24 hours a day in effect because he was even waking up in the night to drink and drinking first thing in the morning. He felt he was "losing control" even more than ever.

When asked when Mr. M. last drank "normally," his wife said it was at least 2 years ago. Then he might have gone out in the evening with a couple of friends (now he didn't drink with people—nearly all his drinking was at home). He would ask her if she minded before he went but even then would drink a lot and go on to a club afterward, coming home at 3:00 or 4:00 in the morning. They had rows over that. Even in those days, he would be "a bit merry"—he had always been a drinker—he had been "drunk" ever since she could remember. There had been a time, even longer ago, when she had gone out to have the odd drink with him. She had stopped that because it was embarrassing. He always wanted to go to the pub—he had a one track mind even in those days. When Mr. M. was asked the same question, he put it at 6 or 7 years ago. He had then been able to enjoy himself but even then had drunk heavily, perhaps a pint or two of lager and 10 or 12 shorts.

Mr. M. strongly agreed with statements like "I know the best thing is for me to abstain from alcohol permanently," "I shall never be able to drink like most people," "I can never stop at one or just a few drinks," "I would be very happy to start treatment to help me become a total abstainer," "Once you get to my state you can never be a normal drinker again," and "I wouldn't mind at all giving up drinking completely." On the other hand, he disagreed strongly with statements like "Ideally, I would prefer to drink normally than to abstain," "I think I could learn to drink in a normal controlled way," and "I should hate to give up drinking altogether." He also disagreed with the statement "I would be very happy to start treatment to help me to become a more controlled drinker," adding that this was, for him, "impossible." His wife also stated that he "cannot drink in moderation—he knows it himself—he's got to stop—he's trying to prove to himself that he can, but he can't—once he starts drinking he's finished then."

When asked if he had ever been advised to abstain from drinking totally by anyone, Mr. M. said that he had, by a whole variety of people, starting with his general practitioner 6 years ago, including two periods of inpatient treatment at the Bethlem unit, outpatient attendances at the Maudsley, and at Lambeth Hospital on two occasions when he was admitted briefly after overdoses. He was also told to abstain totally by his wife, both brothers, all three sisters, friends at work, and Alcoholics Anonymous, which he had first been to 5 years ago but very infrequently since, feeling that he couldn't get very much out of it. He didn't know why, he felt that there was just nothing there that would work for him. He felt that the advice that all these people had given him—to stop drinking—was very good advice, if only he could take it. Everything they said was true. No one had ever advised him to cut down his drinking or drink less, rather than cut it out altogether, and if he had been given this advice he would not think it was particularly good advice. He knows he couldn't do it.

Of the various self-descriptions which we offered, Mr. M. rated the following three as "completely right" for him: an uncontrolled drinker, a compulsive drinker, and an alcoholic. Of these he preferred "a compulsive drinker," the second best being "an uncontrolled drinker." He said he could think of no better expression than a "compulsive drinker" but proceeded to draw an analogy with drug addiction. He felt his present state was simply due to a buildup of heavy drinking over the years to a point at which he was addicted and uncontrolled and getting worse all the time. He agreed the term "an addictive drinker" would be just as suitable as "a compulsive drinker."

4. TREATMENT PLANS

Over 95% of alcoholics passing through the Maudsley outpatient department will have some alcoholic drink during a 3-year follow-up period

(Orford, Oppenheim, & Edwards, 1976). This also appears to apply to treatment units in the United States, since the Rand 4-year follow-up report (Polich, Armor, & Braiker, 1980) came up with a very similar figure. If, in addition, we bear in mind that Mr. M. had not been able to maintain abstinence for very long in recent years, then it is very realistic to present the following rationale:

> We know that you would like to be totally abstinent for life, but our knowledge of alcoholics generally and of you in particular suggests that however hard you try, you are likely to drink on some occasion or occasions after you leave hospital. This is not being pessimistic, but simply realistic. We are not suggesting that your task is hopeless—far from it—but we do want you to anticipate future events and work out ways of coping. We have already told you that some drink will be given to you during your stay in hospital and that your aim is to stop after a certain amount when you feel like continuing. In this way we believe that you will gradually break the compulsion to continue and will develop your willpower. This should have two effects when you leave hospital. First, when you attempt to drink, your experience of resisting temptation in hospital will give you greater control. Second, if you do drink you will find it easier to pull out before you explode into a heavy-drinking binge. So you see, the idea really is very simple. Remember that although we are teaching you to have greater control, we are not advising a goal of controlled drinking. We agree with you that for the next year, probably for a few years, you should aim for total abstinence. Whether you should be totally abstinent for life is a question that you can consider again in a few years' time. Let us first of all concentrate on the next 6 months.

Of course, our functional analysis would suggest many other ways of attacking the problem. We could have focused, for example, on his employment, his dyslexia, or his depression. But with limited time and resources to focus on one patient, we decided to keep the treatment relatively simple.

5. HOSPITAL TREATMENT

During the first few days in hospital, Mr. M. was almost discharged for continuing his drinking, but then he managed to stay sober for 7 days and treatment began. Several cues were identified with a desire for drink, but the strongest of these was drink itself. The consumption of one large vodka was enough to set up a considerable desire for further drinking. It was therefore decided that, as our rationale dictated, we should give Mr. M. a priming dose of alcohol to raise desire and then encourage him to resist. Since one parameter we wanted to observe was the strength of the priming dose, there were two treatment conditions in which our patient received either a priming dose of one double vodka neat (40 ml 65.5% proof) or four double vodkas neat. Mr. M. weighed 150 lb. Figure 2 shows the average BAL during the 4 hours after the consumption of the priming dose.

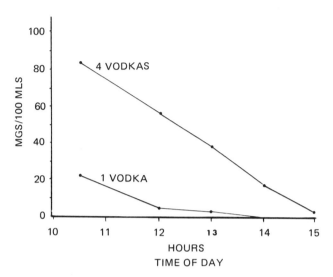

Figure 2. Mean blood-alcohol levels during the 4-hour response prevention period after consuming 1 or 4 double vodkas.

The procedure was as follows. Throughout treatment, Mr. M. was an inpatient on a mixed psychiatric ward, which included a couple of other alcoholics receiving more conventional treatment. He spent most of the day in the research unit and was returned to the ward in the late afternoon. He was always supervised. Mr. M. would arrive from the ward at 10:00 A.M., and we would spend half an hour in measurement. Measures of mood were taken by use of an adapted Lorr-McNair scale, and we also elicited subjective estimates of tremor and desire to drink. Pulsemeter measures were taken and BAL recorded by breath analysis using an evidential fuel-cell alcolmeter.* Each morning, after having been told how much he would be drinking, Mr. M. rated the degree to which he felt his particular withdrawal symptoms (e.g., "My stomach feels knotted") would be present in the evening. All the measures, with the exception of the BAL and heart rate, were taken four times in the morning, three times in the afternoon, and twice in the evening. BAL and heart rate were only taken in the morning and afternoon. After the initial testing at about 10:30 A.M., Mr. M. was given his first drink. This was given as a priming dose, and he was encouraged to drink it as quickly as possible. For Mr. M. the cognitive and physiological effects of the drink were cues which triggered a compulsion to continue. Having consumed his drink (which he was able to do with the utmost speed), Mr. M.

* Lion Laboratories Ltd., Pearl Street, Cardiff, Great Britain.

then retired to a room where he entertained himself by reading, listening to the radio, and assisting the psychologist each hour in measurement taking. During this period there was always available drink within reach. Response prevention was thus very gentle and involved no physical coercion. The nursing staff provided similar supervision when Mr. M. returned to the ward, where he was, of course, not confined to just one room.

6. RESULTS OF INITIAL TREATMENT

First, the predicted extinction of Mr. M.'s desire for a drink across treatment days was confirmed. Second, we obtained confirmation of our prediction, that initially Mr. M. would *expect* the response prevention period to be a very distressing experience, and that this expectation would be modified by the cue exposure treatment. Finally, the subjective measures that we took seemed to have some reliability and validity.

First, consider the data we collected on Mr. M.'s desire for a drink. Just before the priming dose and at hourly intervals thereafter, Mr. M. was asked to rate his desire for a drink on a 0 to 10 scale. Initially, Mr. M.'s reported desire was raised immediately after the consumption of one large vodka. If the hypothesized extinction process is operating at all, one would expect that across sessions the desire for a drink would gradually diminish. Figure 3 shows that this is indeed what happens.

Another measure of some interest was Mr. M.'s expectation of unpleasant consequences after having drunk the priming dose. We elicited from him typical physical feelings associated with drinking cessation. These included such sensations as "My stomach is knotted," "I feel completely drained," and "My whole body is shaking." Before drinking each day, but with knowledge of the day's program, Mr. M. rated how severe he expected these symptoms to be at 8:00 that evening. Once again, a 0 to 10 scale was used, in which 10 represented maximum severity. Scores for each condition are plotted in Figure 4 and show that although initially Mr. M. anticipated severe unpleasant consequences some 10 hours after drinking, these expectations change markedly across treatment sessions. This suggests that cue exposure involved a learning experience that modifies expectations.

An interrater reliability of 0.77 between the patient's and the psychologist's subjective estimates of Mr. M.'s tremor, based on 90 recordings, was obtained. On the same number of readings, a correlation of 0.52 was obtained between Mr. M.'s desire for a drink and his estimate of hand tremor.

The final stage of treatment was the consumption of 8 vodkas (320 ml) in an hour, resulting in feelings of intoxication which would normally have been cues for further drinking. Breath analysis showed a BAL of 165 mg%,

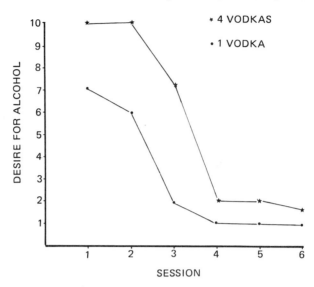

Figure 3. Desire for a drink 4 hours after the priming dose across 6 high-dose and 6 low-dose sessions.

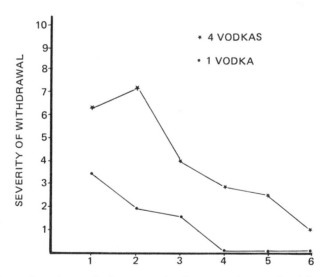

Figure 4. Mean ratings given at the beginning of each session of expected withdrawal symptoms 10 hours after the priming dose.

and although craving did increase slightly, it returned to baseline within 4 hours, much to Mr. M.'s surprise. The behavioral analysis and treatment was completed in 4 weeks.

7. SIX-MONTH FOLLOW-UP

Mr. M. reported the following progress during the 6-month follow-up. First, he remained dry over Christmas for the first time in many years. Second, his wife reported a great improvement in their relationship. She confirmed that he had been off work for only 2 days with a bout of flu, and both his wife and the patient believed that treatment had increased his control over drinking.

During this period, Mr. M. drank on six occasions, despite his abstinence goal. On a couple of occasions the drinking was excessive, although he did manage to stop the next day. He was not considered to be a cured alcoholic, since on these occasions, stopping was difficult; nevertheless, there was no doubt in his mind that his behavior had been modified by the treatment. This was also the view of his wife. They both confirmed that the six occasions of drinking and then stopping were atypical and had never occurred during the previous 3 years.

It should be pointed out that his craving for a drink in his home environment was much greater than that experienced within the hospital environment. With any other behavioral problem, our first thought would have been how to attack the problem of generalization, and a graded series of homework assignments would have been planned, involving drinking and then stopping. After discussing such an approach with our colleagues, we concluded that in our state of knowledge at the time, such a policy could have been dangerous. Many awful consequences were depicted, the worst being murder, suicide, or a fatal accident while under the influence of drink *prescribed by his therapists.* Fortunately, his regular uuncated drinking sessions could be construed as *in vivo* cue exposure practice, so we deliberately reinforced this view by telling him:

> Although you feel that you failed, we would like you to look at your lapses in rather a different way. What you are proving to yourself is that when you do start drinking, you are no longer totally helpless. You are now able to stop even after a heavy drinking session, so that 'one drink, one drunk' no longer applies to you.

Another interesting point of some clinical and theoretical importance is his description of the way in which the treatment experience was used as a cognitive coping strategy. When craving for a drink in the real world, he would say to himself, "I know from those sessions in the Maudsley that the craving will slowly pass away if I can sit it out." Each time he successfully curtailed his drinking, the experience was used to help him on future occasions. He was therefore gradually building up his confidence or his "perceived self-efficacy" and eliminating negative thoughts linked with "learned helplessness."

8. EIGHTEEN-MONTH FOLLOW-UP

Mr. M. was seen about every 2 months throughout the first year, in order to give him continuing support and to keep track of his drinking. He continued to have sporadic heavy-drinking sessions, but he was able to stop after 1 or 2 days (15 sessions during the first year). On two occasions, he did go "over the brink" and found that he could not stop. One of these heavy-drinking sessions began after Mr. M. had won £22 on the football pools and appeared also to be linked to his worry about starting work. He consumed eight bottles of vodka during a 2-week period, and in a drunken state he had threatened his wife with a carving knife. At this point, 14 months after treatment, he was therefore readmitted for a series of booster sessions.

During this admission, we decided that an attempt should be made to simulate a 1-day binge in order to cope with his difficulty in resisting drink the morning after the night before. In order to analyse the processes going on during this treatment, we gave him low doses (L) and high doses (H) in a balanced order (L L L, H H H, L L L, L L L, H H H, L L L). One day of abstinence was interspersed between the drinking days, with additional days of abstinence at the weekend. The low dose involved the consumption of 40 ml of vodka in the evening. In the high condition, Mr. M. was allowed to drink one bottle of vodka during the day up until 10:00 P.M. Figures 5 and 6 show the subjective ratings of desire for a drink as well as an objective measure of hand tremor at 10:00 A.M. on the day after each drinking day; hand tremor was measured by an accelerometer attached to the index figure of the right hand. Also included in Figure 5 are the ratings made *before* each drinking day of expected desire for a drink the following morning. These

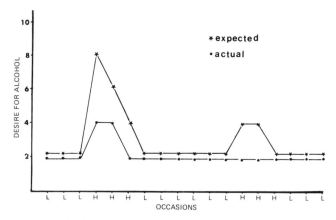

Figure 5. Desire for a drink and expected desire the morning after low dose and high dose across 18 sessions of tests (L = 40 ml vodka; H = 760 ml vodka).

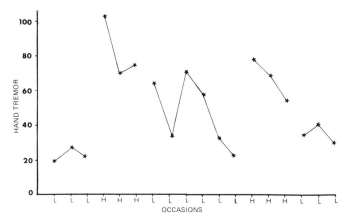

Figure 6. Hand tremor across the 18 occasions of testing.

data suggest, first of all, that tremor is raised the morning after just 1 day of heavy drinking. This conclusion was later reinforced by the results of a more controlled investigation (Stockwell, Hodgson, & Rankin, 1982). Desire for a drink was also raised after the high-dose day but only at the beginning of treatment. On the other hand, expected desire did not decline to the low-dose level until the final treatment session and was always above the rating of actual desire.

These flimsy data are not strong proof that our ideas are following the right lines, but we can claim that the data, along with our client's comments, are at least consistent with the following hypothesis:

> Cue exposure can prime the urge to drink, even within a hospital environment. When the urge is primed by a heavy-drinking session, then the associated cues tend to be "psychophysiological" in nature, since they involve a cognitive component (e.g., "What will happen if I don't drink?") and a physiological component (e.g., tremor). Repeated cue exposure leads to extinction of craving and subsequent reality testing until expectations match up with reality. As treatment progresses, there is a gradual dissociation or discordance between disposition to drink (which decreases) and the underlying physiological state involving minimal withdrawal symptoms (which still appears to be raised after the six sessions).

After leaving hospital, Mr. M. had another good 6-month period, during which he was able to curtail his drinking on about eight occasions, even when feeling ill and shaky the morning after a couple of days of heavy drinking. At this time, he was interviewed by an independent psychologist who reported that "amazingly, there seems to be a split between craving and withdrawal. He can experience withdrawal symptoms with no apparent desire for a drink." With hindsight, we believe that this type of discordance probably occurs naturally as a function of various cognitions and contingencies. Nevertheless, Mr. M. has always maintained that it was unusual for him and that it was a direct result of our treatment program.

9. THE NEXT FIVE YEARS

From June 1976 to April 1981, Mr. M. was seen by one of us at least every 6-months in order to give support and advice, keep a record of heavy-drinking sessions, and examine the relationship between his many problems and his truncated binges. Usually Mr. M. and his wife were seen together, and both agreed that although he was still a man with problems, his excessive drinking had been curtailed. Figure 7 gives some indication of the amount of heavy drinking during each year from 1974 to 1980. The reduction from 200 days per year to about 30 days per year after cue exposure would appear to be partly a function of treatment, since there were many occasions throughout the 6-year period when Mr. M. managed to cut short a binge; however, a number of other factors were also responsible. First, the number of days in hospital fluctuated during the 6-year period. The length of admission was not at all related to the drinking problem per se but appears to have been a function of depression, changing admission policies, and

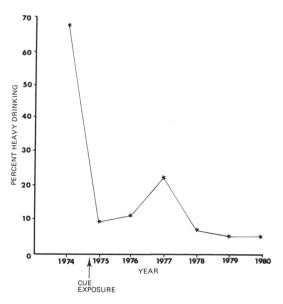

Figure 7. Heavy drinking during the years 1974–1980. Number of days per year during which more than 100 gm of alcohol was consumed expressed as a percentage of days spent outside hospital.

concern for the well-being of the patient's wife. At one stage, the doctor in charge of this patient wrote in the case notes, "Mr. M. is to be admitted if his wife finds his behavior frightening," (provided, of course, that Mr. M. himself consented to a period in hospital). Another factor which has to be taken into account is Mr. M.'s tendency towards excessive use of other substances when feeling stressed. In the last few months of 1980, he was obtaining Valium from his doctor and from other sources. During his worst period, he consumed 2,500 mg of Valium during a 3-week period. During 9 months in 1979, he used a Benzodrex inhaler about once a week to relieve his depression and boredom and was frequently making use of antidepressants throughout the whole 6-year period. It is possible, therefore, that the major change in his consumption levels, which coincided with treatment, actually had nothing at all to do with the cue exposure procedures. It is possible but not probable. Mr. M. certainly attributed the change to cue exposure, since there were rapid changes in his beliefs and expectations during the two treatment periods. Furthermore, on the 80 occasions during the 6-year period when he was able to curtail a binge, he frequently brought to mind, as a self-control procedure, the success that he had experienced during and just after treatment. It is unlikely that these changes in self-control strategies and perceived self-efficacy actually had no influence at all on his pattern of consumption. Mr. M. still has marital and family problems, sexual impotence, depression, and dyslexia. In 1979 his depression was so severe that he was admitted to hospital after taking an overdose of Imipramine, along with a bottle of vodka. During this period, his wife reported: "I feel as if I am living with someone who isn't there. He is just a shell." Mr. M. believes that a major part of his problem was the hopeless employment situation. He had applied for more than 40 jobs during the period from 1977 to 1979 but still remained unemployed. Our strategy of giving support and simple advice, along with antidepressant medication, did not produce a radical change in these problem areas. Whether he would benefit from a more intensive cognitive-behavioral approach (Beck, 1976), along with a basic strategy of community reintegration (e.g., Azrin, 1976), is an open question which we are about to put to the test.

10. DISCUSSION

When dealing with a wide spectrum of drinkers from the heavy social drinker through the early problem drinker to the severely dependent alcoholic, one important question cries out for an answer. What psychological and physiological changes take place as consumption and dependence increase? In a number of questionnaire studies a dimension usually labeled "alcohol dependence" has been identified, which is characterised by tremors, drinking to escape and avoid withdrawal symptoms, the subjective experience of compulsion or loss of control, and long periods of continued drinking (Chick, 1980; Polich *et al.*, 1980; Polich & Orvis, 1979; Skinner, 1981; Stockwell, Hodgson, Edwards, Taylor, & Rankin, 1979).

This dimension has to do with the strength of the urge to drink and should not be considered simply a continuum of increasing physical dependence. The experience of a severe withdrawal state is both a sign of dependence and a strong motivation for further drinking, but physical dependence is just one component of the so-called dependence syndrome (Edwards, 1977).

In our published research on the dependence continuum, using a validated psychiatric rating of dependence, we have demonstrated that increasing dependence is associated with a priming effect after the consumption of a few drinks (Hodgson, Rankin, & Stockwell, 1979) and also with craving the morning after the night before (Stockwell *et el.*, 1979). Mr. M.'s treatment was based upon the hypothesis that priming effects and cravings are, in part, learned phenomena which can be unlearned through repeated cue exposure. In other words, dependence is a reversible learned compulsion rather than an irreversible disease.

Important cues for Mr. M. were the cognitive and physiological effects of consuming moderate amounts of alcohol (4 double vodkas) as well as his psychophysiological state the morning after a day of heavy drinking (one bottle of vodka in 12 hours). The data that we have presented, along with Mr. M.'s attributions, suggest that cue exposure did have the effect of breaking the link between these cues and the compulsion to continue. Cue exposure altered Mr. M.'s expectations about the consequences of going without drink after a period of drinking. He learned that minimal withdrawal symptoms and craving will rapidly subside and this reality testing had the effect of reducing his "abstinence phobia."

The cue exposure approach can be viewed as one method of preventing relapse (e.g., Marlatt, 1978) and also as a way of changing perceived self-efficacy (Bandura, 1977). Bandura differentiates between outcome expectancies (e.g., "Giving up smoking will increase health and wealth") and efficacy expectancies (e.g., "I am able to give it up"), but Mr. M.'s experience of cue exposure suggests that a change in perceived self-efficacy is, to a large extent, a function of changes in outcome expectations. Mr. M. was able to stop because he altered his outcome expectations vis-à-vis minimal withdrawal symptoms and craving.

Our further experience of cue exposure suggests that consuming drink in a hospital environment is a potent cue for the severely dependent, but not for the moderately dependent, alcoholic. Also, craving is difficult to prime even in the severely dependent alcoholic if there is no available alcoholic beverage. The most effective instructions for a cue exposure session appear to be:

> Here is some more drink which you may be tempted to consume. Your aim should be to increase your self-control by resisting temptation. We will not stop you drinking if you really want to, but, of course, that will not help you in the long run and will not increase your willpower.

This method was used in a further controlled investigation of the cue exposure approach (Rankin, Hodgson, & Stockwell, 1981), which demonstrated that within a hospital environment craving can be extinguished. This controlled investigation of craving over a 6-week period in hospital, together with Mr. M.'s experiences during 6 years in his home environment, strongly supports the cue exposure approach as an adjunct to treatment.

Mr. M.'s experiences clearly show that even if dependence is reversed to some extent, we cannot assume that other problems will magically disappear. The 5 years after cue exposure were better than the similar period before treatment, but he was still unemployed and depressed after treatment, and he still attempted to take his own life. During the 6-year follow-up period, he attended the outpatient clinic regularly, was an inpatient for 18 months, and received counseling, psychotherapy, and group psychotherapy from various helpers, but most of his problems were still not ameliorated.

It could be argued that Mr. M. will be more inclined to drink heavily because he now knows that he is able to stop. This is certainly not the case. He believes that aiming for total abstinence is the only way and that he could easily become severely dependent again as a result of a few very heavy drinking sessions. Furthermore, he knows that he can be violent when drunk, and in the past he has come very close to stabbing his wife. He therefore has very good reasons to remain abstinent. On the other hand, he has never been able to maintain total abstinence and uses the analogy of a man walking a tightrope but repeatedly falling off. He still believes that he is walking a tightrope and will be for the rest of his life, but he maintains that the cue exposure treatment has given him a better sense of balance and has also provided him with a very strong safety net.

COMMENTARY

Peter E. Nathan

With the exception of Seamus, the patient described in Chapter 10 by Howard Rankin, Ray Hodgson's friend and colleague at the Addiction Research Unit, Mr. M. displays a consumption pattern nowhere else demonstrated in this volume. Although all too many alcoholics in the United States drink as much as Seamus and Mr. M.—and are as violent and self-destructive—the behavioral clinicians in the United States who have written for this book have not reported on such clients. One reason may be that such persons are often dismissed as untreatable in this country. For that reason, the Maudsley group's cue exposure and relapse prevention program may well be of special interest to clinicians who work with severely addicted chronic alcoholics.

Other authors of chapters in this book have focused initial therapeutic administrations on marital or vocational rather than alcohol problems. Ray Hodgson chooses to focus on Mr. M.'s drinking, alongside which even his grossly dysfunctional marriage looks adequate. When alcohol and its consequences have taken a person over body and soul, the therapist has little choice but energetic exorcism of the ethanol specter.

Hodgson, like Rankin, offers an appealing model of how to integrate rigorous continuing measurement with effective, sophisticated clinical intervention. The provision made for regular assessment of autonomic responses to cue exposure, for example, is such that it does not interfere with ongoing therapy while it provides regular feedback on the effectiveness of the intervention.

Although cue exposure is a very different technique from those employed by others in this book, Hodgson's treatment of Mr. M. does emphasize efforts to enhance self-esteem and build a sense of self-efficacy. To the extent that Mr. M. was able to withstand feelings of craving, control his drinking at home, and refrain from violence or verbal abuse directed at his wife, he could feel himself in greater control of himself and, accordingly, in possession of greater self-efficacy. Hodgson makes clear that this change in his patient's cognitions about his ability to manage his life better was not only an effect but a cause of the changes in his drinking.

One of the real strengths of Hodgson's report lies in the more than 6-year follow-up of treatment it provides. No other chapter in this book approaches this length; few, in fact, go beyond 6 months. Long-term follow-up is almost certainly easier when one is working in an institutional setting, especially one like Hodgson's, which is public, inpatient, and available whenever the patient needs a brief period of hospitalization. But the value of long-term follow-up remains, regardless of the ease or difficulty in bringing it off. One knows less than one wants to about the efficacy of one's interventions with short follow-ups because problem drinking is often characterized by periods of both improvement, abstinence, and nonproblem drinking, and deterioration, heavy drinking, and loss of control. Hence, one is hard put to know whether an improvement is associated with therapy, a natural cycle of the patient's, an increase in the patient's desire to do something about his or her drinking problem, or something else. In the case of Mr. M., though, one can be rather sure that his drinking pattern 6 years into treatment is very different from the way it was before treatment began.

The continuing availability of the addiction research unit at the Maudsley Hospital to patients like Mr. M. and Seamus, who require periodic "booster" reconditioning, contrasts sharply with the absence of such provisions in either private practice or other outpatient settings. In our zeal to document the benefits of outpatient as against inpatient treatment for a variety of psychiatric and psychological disorders, we sometimes forget the real virtues of the inpatient facility as a haven for the oppressed, the violent, and the out-of-control alcoholic like Mr. M.

11. REFERENCES

Azrin, N. H. Improvements in the community reinforcement to alcoholism. *Behaviour Research & Therapy*, 1976, *14*, 339–348.

Bandura, A. Self-efficacy: Toward a unifying theory of behavioural change. *Psychological Review*, 1977, *84*, 191–215.

Beck, A. *Cognitive therapy and the emotional disorders* New York: International University Press, 1976.

Chick, J. Is there a unidimensional alcohol dependence syndrome? *British Journal of Addiction*, 1980, *75*, 265–280.

Edwards, G. The alcohol dependence syndrome: Usefulness of an idea. In G. Edwards & M. Grant (Eds.), *Alcoholism: New knowledge and new responses*. London: Croom Helm, 1977.

Hodgson, R. J., & Rankin, H. J. Modification of excessive drinking by cue exposure. *Behavior Research & Therapy*, 1976, *14*, 305–307.

Hodgson, R. J., Rankin, H. J., & Stockwell, T. R. Alcohol dependence and the priming effect. *Behaviour Research & Therapy*, 1979, *17*, 379–387.

Likierman, H., & Rachman, S. J. Spontaneous decay of compulsive urges. *Behaviour Research & Therapy*, 1980, *18*, 387–394.

Marlatt, G. A. Craving for alcohol, loss of control, and relapse: A cognitive-behavioral analysis. In P. E. Nathan, G. A. Marlatt, & T. Løberg, (Eds.), *Alcoholism: New directions in behavioral research and treatment*. New York: Plenum Press, 1978.

Meyer, V. Modification of expectations in cases with obsessional rituals. *Behaviour Research & Therapy*, 1966, *4*, 273–280.

Orford, J., Oppenheim, E., & Edwards, G. Abstinence of control: The outcome for excessive drinkers two years after consultation. *Behaviour Research & Therapy*, 1976, *14*, 409–418.

Polich, J. M., & Orvis, B. R. *Alcohol problems: Patterns and prevalence in the U.S. Air Force*. Santa Monica: Rand Corporation, 1979.

Polich, J. M., Armor, D. J., & Braiker, H. B. *The course of alcoholism: Four years after treatment*. Santa Monica: Rand Corporation, 1980.

Rachman, S., Hodgson, R. J., & Marks, I. M. Treatment of chronic obsessive-compulsive neuroses. *Behaviour Research & Therapy*, 1971, *9*, 237–247.

Rachman, S., de Silva, P., & Roper, G. The spontaneous decay of compulsive urges. *Behaviour Research & Therapy*, 1976, *14*, 445–453.

Rachman, S., & Hodgson, R. J. *Obsessions and compulsions*. Englewood Cliffs, N.J.: Prentice-Hall, 1980.

Rankin, H. J., Hodgson, R. J., & Stockwell, T. R. *Modification of craving for alcohol through cue exposure*. Unpublished manuscript, 1981.

Skinner, H. A. Primary syndromes of alcohol abuse: Their measurement and correlates. *British Journal of Addiction*, 1981, *76*, 63–76.

Stockwell, T. R., Hodgson, R. J., Edwards, G., Taylor, C., & Rankin, H. J. The development of a questionnaire to measure severity of alcohol dependence. *British Journal of Addiction*, 1979, *74*, 79–87.

Stockwell, T. R., Hodgson, R. J., & Rankin, H. J. Tension reduction and the effects of prolonged alcohol consumption. *British Journal of Addition* 1982, *77*, 65–73.

10

Cue Exposure and Response Prevention in South London

HOWARD J. RANKIN

1. CASE HISTORY

I saw him first on a Wednesday. A colleague of mine who had been seeing him had run out of ideas and in some desperation referred him to me. Although the case notes were thick, I had not read them yet. I seldom do until after I have seen the client and got his side of the story. He certainly had a lot to tell. He was a two-volume man, a privilege reserved for those who seem to have been around Maudsley Hospital since the Great Fire of London. There was more information in his files than in a scouting report on the Dallas Cowboys.

He shuffled in apologetically. How many interviews like this must he have been through, I thought to myself. I tried to keep it as relaxed and as informal as possible. But he did not need much encouraging, this sad, short, round man. Looking up every now and again over his National Health spectacles, he started to tell his story, his ruddy cheeks seemingly reddening by the moment. Occasionally, his words were carried across the room on a cloud of whiskey vapor, perceptible enough to reassure me that he was not successfully carrying out his abstinence program. The story was not an unfamiliar one for those of us who have been working in this particular South London establishment.

HOWARD J. RANKIN • Addiction Research Unit, Institute of Psychiatry, Maudsley Hospital, London England.

Seamus was born in Ireland early in the 1920s, the eldest of six children. A normal delivery, his infancy was apparently uncomplicated by any unduly neurotic traits or milestone delays. As other siblings arrived, Seamus went about his business of growing up on the farm that was his home.

Seamus remembers himself as a rather moody lad, often worrying about small, inconsequential things. This broodiness may well have been a function of the atmosphere at home and, in particular, the relationship between his mother and father. His father was apparently too fond of alcohol. The extent and consequences of the heavy drinking can really only be guessed at, but it did seem to strain the family budget—and this around the time of the Wall Street crash. Seamus's mother was a very straight, hard-working country girl: Uninhibited behavior of any sort was certainly out. Indeed, given her personality and the context of the time, masochistic puritanism was probably the only thing in. Still, if longevity is the criterion by which these things are judged, puritanism wins hands down. She is still going strong at aged 90. Her husband, died of a heart attack at the age of 76. Whatever their particular outlooks, their specific parental skills did not apparently lead to psychopathology in any of the remaining siblings, none of whom have a history of psychological difficulties or problematic alcohol use.

Seamus went to school—occasionally. His school attendance was highly correlated to climatic conditions: Generally, he would show up when the weather was bad, but on fine, dry days Seamus helped his father around the farm. Such an arrangement is not conducive to a satisfactory education, even given the Irish climate. So Seamus stayed at home stacking, chopping wood, and participating in other similarly agricultural activities. Every now and again his father would shout at him to move himself or stop chasing butterflies, while his mother managed her domestic affairs with capability. If she ever had regrets that the boy was being deprived of a ticket to a brighter future, they were quickly buried under a blanket of practical necessity. For above all she was a practical woman—almost cold, in fact—and that is what Seamus has always found difficulty with, to the present day. His father, despite his strictness, was far more approachable and demonstrative, even if, or perhaps because, he drank heavily.

Seamus did not so much leave school as stop going on the wet days. Perhaps there were a series of fine, sunny, dry years. In any event, he stayed on the farm until he was 18 years old. Then he left home for a larger community and a job in a local store.

Although Ireland remained officially neutral in World War II, it did undergo some social changes. The town in which Seamus lived rapidly became overpopulated by men who were employed in war-related work. The town's major leisure activities consisted of gambling and drinking. Exposed to this atmosphere and freed from direct parental influence, Seamus started indulging in both these pastimes. It did not take long before he was drinking 7 to 8 pints each night, as well as some at lunchtime. While this lifestyle had much to commend it to a country boy making his way in more populous surrounds, Seamus had great ambitions. He wanted to progress and make a good living and felt that to do this, he really needed to go to London. As soon as the war was over, Seamus set out, like so many of his compatriots before and after him, to make his future in the great capital.

Whatever ambitions he harboured when he set off, Seamus had to start at the bottom, as a residential staff member of a large pub. Here the affable young Irishman worked hard, and no doubt his common sense and sociability made him likable to both customers and staff alike. Both groups bought him drinks for his labors and let him sit in on after-hours drinking sessions. Gradually, his drinking habits changed. Soon spirits, particularly whiskey, were added to increasing amounts of beer. That is not to say that drinking was a problem—it certainly was not seen as such. Indeed, Seamus was about to embark on perhaps the most successful state of his life. Step by step he moved up the ladder from pub to hotel, gaining experience in catering, portering, and general hotel administration. Within a few years he had reached head porter status in one of London's finest hotels. Although salaries were poor, there was much money to be made in tips and other sidelines. Someone in his position could earn a lot, and before too long Seamus had taken full advantage of his position. At the height of his success, he owned five properties in the Central London area. He enjoyed his work. Much of it centered on the bar and providing services for people who were known internationally, and whose glamor was infectious. Hours were erratic and although that did not bother Seamus, it did bother his wife, a shy Irish girl, not unlike his mother. Although initially happy, they had few similar interests and rather opposite personalities. He was ambitious and sociable, while she was introverted, with more limited aspirations.

Gradually, the cracks of disenchantment grew into rifts of disaffection. The marriage has foundered ever since on a San Andreas fault of unease and dissension which, surprisingly perhaps, has never developed into a catastrophic quake. The ground has shaken a few times, but never wrenched open. The arrival of five children probably helped to stabilize matters, but sizeable rumblings can still be measured on the Richter Scale today.

At one point Seamus sold off his properties in Central London; now, quite rightly from a pure financial viewpoint, he regrets this move and blames his wife for pressuring him to do it and himself for listening to her. The episode seemed to mark the start of the downward trend. Although he was able to support his large family adequately, alcohol was taking more of the domestic finances. In his early forties, he was drinking as much as three bottles of liquor a day. His work performance deteriorated, although he was cushioned against this by certain factors. First, this sort of drinking problem was well-known and well tolerated in the hotel business. Second, the hotel trade in the swinging London of the 1960s was flush with success, and if Seamus lost a job at one hotel, he could simply go to his friends at another and be employed almost immediately. The merry-go-round which Seamus was now on revolved faster and faster, and it was only a matter of time before he was flung off. After a particularly heavy drinking episode in 1967, he was referred to the Maudsley Hospital Alcoholism Clinic.

The records show that Seamus settled quickly on the ward after experiencing nonproblematic withdrawal and was discharged after 6 weeks with a resolve to maintain abstinence, a commitment to find less tempting employment, and a prescription for Antabuse. Four weeks later he was drinking heavily again, and after failing to keep appointments at the hospital and Alcoholics Anonymous, he was readmitted. The pattern of his hospitalization was being established. Over the next 11 years Seamus had more than a dozen hospital admissions, half of which were in alcoholism units, the others in units treating him for the physical consequences of excessive drinking.

All but one of his admissions for alcoholism *per se* were at the Maudsley and Bethlem hospitals. On each occasion, he would come into hospital following a prolonged drinking period. Each admission was characterized by withdrawal, which increased with severity on successive occasions. He often claimed to be anxious and forlorn about his career and life prospects. However, except for one occasion when he left the hospital and went on a drinking binge, he was always cooperative and helpful. On some of these admissions, alcoholic hallucinosis was documented. The main features of this were his preoccupation with death, guilt about his drinking, and, in particular, worries and concerns about his aged and infirm mother in Ireland. Each admission found slight memory impairment and general slowing of cognitive function. His intelligence was rated as average. However, despite the problems caused by his drinking, he rarely got into difficulties with the police and certainly never had any criminal record. His major clash with the police was when he lost his license for drunk driving on one occasion, but he just was not the sort of person that would end up in a pub brawl.

On each admission, Seamus was detoxified and then spent 6 to 12 weeks in the supposedly therapeutic milieu of the ward, with access to group therapy, occupational therapy, and general counseling. Each time he was diagnosed as alcoholic, each time abstinence was the goal of treatment, each time he would leave with the best of intentions, and each time he relapsed within a matter of weeks.

Although he had been admitted to hospital for physical complaints (mild diabetes, hypertension, pleurisy, dislocated shoulder), there was no evidence of gross abnormality in liver function. Finally, in the late summer of 1979, after being unemployed for 2½ years, faced with some financial problems and racked with guilt and regret, Seamus overdosed. However, he survived this attempt and returned to the Maudsley Hospital. On this occasion he was supported by a social worker and attended the Bethlem as a day patient during the week. For 3 months he struggled, successfully, to stay off the alcohol, but he was still very miserable. Sobriety was gained at a price. In the New year he returned to Ireland to visit his mother; learning of the death of two close friends and deprived of the supportive atmosphere of the Bethlem alcoholism program, Seamus started drinking again. Dejected and helpless, he returned to the Maudsley; he was seen once again by the social worker who, having heard of my program, referred him to me. Finally, the music had stopped, and he was now in my care.

2. ASSESSMENT

Naturally, the first level of involvement in the case necessitated an adequate assessment of his drinking behavior: the context in which it occurred and its consequences.

2.1. Drinker Behavior

Seamus gave the impression of a very stable drinking pattern in the recent past. Day-by-day consumption in the past 2 weeks showed that he had drunk between 1 and 1½ bottles of scotch a day, as well as 3 to 6 pints of stout. The least that he had drunk was ¾ of a bottle of scotch and no beer, and the most 3 pints of scotch. Further self-reports, corroborated subsequently by family members with whom he lived, suggested a typical consistent consumption of between 1 and 1 ½ bottles of 66° British proof scotch and 3 to 6 pints of stout daily. This works out to a range of 315 to 460 gm of absolute alcohol daily. At this time Seamus weighed 196 lb. In short, he was drinking between 3.6 and 5.3 gm per kg of absolute alcohol daily. Seamus would drink first thing in the morning before he did anything else. He would start the day with about ½ bottle of scotch and 2 beers. This would last until lunchtime, when he would adjourn to the pub to drink mainly beer and a little scotch. In the evening he would either return to the pub or go to bingo, where more beer would be consumed. On his return home, he would sit in his own lounge when everyone had gone to bed and consume more whiskey. This pattern had been fairly typical of his drinking, not only in the recent past but during his drinking spells over the past 3 years. The longest he had been off alcohol during that time was the 3 months after the overdose when he was a day patient at Bethlem. Over the last 10 years, his longest period of abstinence had been 14 weeks.

2.2. Effects of Alcohol

Because Seamus would often drink throughout the day, he rarely got drunk. At home, he would generally sit slouched in a chair in front of the television after everyone had gone to bed. Eventually, he would make his way to his bedroom and "crash." Occasionally, when drinking outside the home, he would get drunk, but he was rarely abusive or aggressive. Under these circumstances, he would talk incessantly about past experiences and generally become more garrulous. After heavy alcohol intake, funereal fears and worries would overcome him. He would "see" dead friends returning from the past and images of his mother chastening him for his behavior. On two occasions, while withdrawing from a heavy-drinking session, he actually "heard" his mother's voice, but this is interpreted as mild alcoholic hallucinosis rather than indication of any more sinister underlying affective disorder. He had, when drunk, fallen down on a couple of occasions, once dislocating his shoulder. He also reported occasional blackouts and memory loss during his heavy-drinking spells.

2.3. Questionnaire Assessment

Two initial questionnaires were completed. The Severity of Alcohol Dependence Questionnaire (SADQ) is a questionnaire devised to rate the client's degree of physical dependence. It has 20 items concerning the frequency and intensity of withdrawal symptoms (Stockwell, Hodgson, Edwards, Taylor, & Rankin, 1979). This questionnaire showed that Seamus reported frequently experiencing severe sweating and shaking as well as heavy morning drinking. Based on this data, Seamus is best described as severely dependent in the terms used by this writer and his colleagues (see, for example, Hodgson, Stockwell, Rankin, & Edwards, 1978, for further discussion).

The second questionnaire is a so-called Cue Questionnaire devised by this author as part of his Ph.D. research requirements. The cue questionnaire called for subjects to make ordinal judgments on the potency of influence of particular physiological, social, and psychological situations. Research (Rankin, Hodgson, & Stockwell, 1982) has shown that severely dependent subjects score highly on those situations specifically related to alcohol and its immediate effects, whereas less dependent groups do not. Seamus was typical of a severely dependent person, in that he reported to be heavily influ-

enced by the immediate effects of the alcohol as well as its psychophysiological consequences.

As well as these two questionnaires, informal behavioral analysis suggested the following cues were important in his drinking behavior:

1. Drinking to relieve boredom.
2. Drinking to be able to get to sleep.
3. Drinking in order to be "sociable."
4. Compulsive drinking after drinking had begun, particularly after a
   couple of doubles.

All these cues were considered to be important, but particularly those
which related to the psychophysiological effects of alcohol. This analysis did
show that the cue-exposure response-prevention treatment about to be described was suitable for this particular client.

2.4. Family and Domestic Factors

As previously described, the marital relationship was one of passive
acceptance of differences and, to some extent, incompatibility. However,
despite this, it was seen as a stable relationship. Particularly supportive were
his daughters, one living at home and the other living nearby, who took
particular care of their father and often inquired about his well-being. On
the employment front, Seamus has been out of work for 3 years, a reflection
of the economic climate as well as his particular psychophysiological condition.

3. TREATMENT

The history of alcoholism treatment has not been one of success. Close
analysis shows that traditional programs typically involve taking clients out
of their drinking environments and placing them in a hospital, where purely
verbal advice rather than *behavioral training* occurs. After a fairly lengthy time,
clients are then returned to the same environment which maintains heavy-
drinking behavior. There are several things wrong with this approach. First,
procedures used in hospital are not of proven efficacy and generally are
limited to mere "advice." Second, such procedures are often used without
regard to the specific client problems. More important, though, such procedures generally occur in a vacuum, and little attempt is made either to take
into account specific environmental variables or, more importantly, endeav-
or to change them. An ideal program is one that identifies critical variables
and successfully trains the client to cope with them. At the very least, one of

these goals should be sought. Cue-exposure response-prevention attempts to change a person's ability to cope with some of the critical influential variables, namely, the psychophysiological effects of alcohol itself, which is shown to be a cue of fundamental importance in at least those alcoholics designated as severely dependent.

3.1. Cue-Exposure Response-Prevention Methods

Cue-exposure response-prevention methods have been used with success in the treatment of compulsive disorders (e.g., Rachman, Hodgson, & Marks, 1973), and the applicability of this conceptual model to the field of alcoholism treatment is discussed elsewhere in this book (see Chapter 9). Following a successful early case study (Hodgson & Rankin, 1976) and further promising work (Rankin & Hodgson, 1977), more recent process research on modified and updated cue-exposure methods shows considerable promise (Rankin & Hodgson, in preparation). The rationale for the theory is that heavy alcohol consumption, characterized by the desire to relieve and avoid withdrawal, is considered to be a discriminated operant. Under these circumstances, response prevention in the presence of influential cues is thought to reduce the potency thereof. Of course, there are many cues impinging on the alcoholic's behavior. One could, for example, expose the alcoholic to the boredom of a lonely afternoon while preventing alcohol consumption. The current program, however, uses alcohol and its effects (smell, taste, blood-alcohol level) as a potent cue to be "defused" by response prevention. The program consists of several phases, most of which take place in the hospital setting. Criteria demarking the suitability of particular clients are shown in Table 1. The program consists of several phases, most of which take place in hospital.

Table 1. Criteria for Admission into Cue Exposure Program

1. Subjects were rated as severely dependent by the following criteria: There was evidence of frequent withdrawal symptoms and drinking in order to escape or relieve those withdrawal symptoms.
2. Subjects reported a strong priming effect that manifested itself as a difficulty in stopping drinking after taking the first couple of alcoholic drinks.
3. There was no evidence of dangerous or debilitating physical disorder, particularly no evidence of brain damage or severe liver injury.
4. No evidence that subjects would be unmanageable or violent after a moderate amount of alcohol.
5. Subjects were willing to cooperate in the inpatient program of approximately 7 to 8 weeks' duration.
6. Subjects gave their full informed consent to participating in the experimental regime.
7. There was no evidence of other debilitating psychiatric illness.

3.2. Experimental Phase

Following a period of withdrawal from alcohol and a settling-in period lasting about 10 days, the first therapeutic phase begins. This involves a test session in which, following a series of subjective and physiological measures, clients are given 1 gm per kg of absolute alcohol in their preferred beverage. In this case, it was scotch whiskey 66° proof. Clients are then asked to drink this in their own time, with an informal limit set of about 20 minutes. This typically produces blood-alcohol levels between 75 and 100 mg%, and after drinking, clients sit quietly in the experimental room. In the particular procedure described here, every 15 minutes, subjective and physiological measures are taken. After 45 minutes in this test session, subjects are asked to drink 2 glasses of 30 ml of their favorite alcoholic beverage. They are told to drink this in their own time, and the purpose of this is to derive estimates of the rated pleasantness of taste of each drink. The real purpose is to record the speed at which the client consumes the two drinks. Such a measure has been shown to be a correlate of craving or disposition to drink (Rankin, Hodgson, & Stockwell, 1979). It should be pointed out here that the choice of subjective measures is an arbitrary one in this procedure, dictated to some extent by other research considerations. However, it is important for therapists to get ratings of desire and difficulty in resisting available alcohol, or something like that which will serve as a guide to see how well treatment is progressing.

After this test session, clients return to the ward and are kept under close staff supervision. Although clients can leave the ward at any time, they must not leave the hospital grounds. They are encouraged to report any strong craving or other ill effects to the staff. Following the initial test session, the main treatment phase begins. This starts 2 days after the test session and continues for about 6 sessions on alternate days, but not weekends. The treatment sessions are similar to the test sessions but differ in some important respects.

3.3. Treatment Phase

After the initial measures are taken and alcohol consumed, clients are asked to do the following. They are sat at a table on which there is a bottle of their preferred beverage and a glass of the same. For three 15-minute phases, divided only by a few minutes in which the usual range of measures are taken, clients are asked—for consecutive periods of about 3 minutes' duration—to hold the glass in their hand, maintain eye contact with it as much as possible, and finally hold it up to their mouth so that they can smell the alcohol. They are given the following instructions: "The idea of treatment is to resist this drink. However, if you find it impossible to resist, then you can drink it—the idea is to resist it if you can."

After the three 15-minute phases, unlike in the test session, clients are not provided with further alcohol but are returned to the ward where the described conditions of close supervision obtain. A flow chart of the therapeutic proceedings is given in Figure 1.

In Seamus's case, following the 6 treatment sessions a further test session occurred. Performance on the two tests obviously allows a comparison of before and after therapeutic intervention and tests for specific treatment effects.

Following a further 10 days in hospital, in which the client had no further alcohol but was exposed to the general ward milieu, he was discharged under close supervision. This set up the next phase of treatment involving homework assignments.

3.4. Homework Assignments

With the full knowledge of his wife and family, Seamus was given cue-exposure response-prevention tasks to do in the home. These included, not unnaturally, exposure to those cues which were previously influential in his alcohol consumption. In this case, they involved the following:

1. Sitting in the lounge watching television with a bottle in front of him, having no more than 1 double scotch.
2. Going into a pub and having just 1 double or a pint of beer.
3. When feeling tense, going into a bar and ordering a nonalcoholic drink.

Seamus was asked to do at least one of these tasks once a day and to keep a record of performance as well as a simple rating on a 1–10 scale of the difficulty of each task. He was seen three times during the first month after discharge, twice during the next, and approximately once a month thereafter. After 6 months attendance was reduced to about once every 2 months. The

Subjective Ratings: physiological measures	→	ALCOHOL CONSUMPTION	→	Subjective Ratings: physiological measures	→
CUE EXPOSURE: eye contact; holding; sniffing	→	Subjective Ratings: physiological measures	→	CUE EXPOSURE: eye contact; holding; sniffing	→
Subjective Ratings: physiological measures	→	CUE EXPOSURE: eye contact; holding; sniffing	→	Subjective Ratings: physiological measures	→

Figure 1. Flow chart of therapeutic procedures (inpatient phase).

homework assignments in this case were not supervised but on other occasions could be, particularly in cases where clients feel less confident about being able to carry them out. As will be discussed later, the tasks are self-paced, and clients are encouraged to push themselves hard enough to do the task, but not so much that they are likely to fail. Clients are warned that initially they may find the tasks very difficult and they may have some failures. In the event of a dramatic failure, they are told to contact the therapist at the earliest opportunity. In this particular case, homework assignments were, in general, very successful and were gradually faded out after a few weeks. After a while, the line between homework assignments and normal drinking behavior becomes very obscure, particularly in this case where there was a goal of controlled drinking.

3.5. Goal of Treatment

The cue-exposure response-prevention methodology's main purpose as described is to rob critical cues, in this case the psychophysiological consequences of having some alcohol, of their influence, thus tackling the crux of the problem for this particular group of severely dependent people. While this undoubtedly can be seen as providing good training in controlled drinking and thus suitable where that goal is the desired one, cue-exposure response prevention of this sort can be justified as a suitable treatment where abstinence is preferred. The rationale runs as follows. Since we know that a large majority of clients undertaking abstinence take alcohol after discharge from hospital (Orford & Edwards, 1977), clients for whom stopping is a problem will require skills to tackle this. Under these circumstances, cue-exposure response prevention acts as just that—a sort of fire drill which, by defusing critical cues and giving people more confidence in their ability to stop, prevents *extensive* relapse and minimizes its disruptive effects. Where abstinence is the desired goal, homework assignments would not include drinking, for obvious reasons.

One further interesting point concerns the relevance of this treatment with the choice of goal. Although there are many successful reports of controlled-drinking programs, many of these have focused on the less dependent person or problem drinker. Clearly, this has proved a great advance in the treatment of alcohol problems. Theoretically, however, severely dependent subjects will have difficulty following a controlled-drinking program *unless* specific training such as cue-exposure response prevention is offered which tackles the heart of the problem—difficulty in stopping. Indeed, there is evidence to show that the severely dependent subject is more likely to have difficulty attempting a controlled-drinking goal (Orford, Oppenheimer, & Edwards, 1976).

In this particular case, however, a controlled-drinking goal was deemed suitable for the following reasons. First, following the successful inpatient phase, it was felt that Seamus could drink limited amounts of alcohol in a nonproblematic fashion. Second, this particular client never successfully came to terms with an abstinent goal after many opportunities. Although he had tried informally to control his drinking with a similar lack of success, this would be expected, given the previous analysis which predicts that specific training of the sort offered by cue-exposure response prevention is the only way severely dependent clients will achieve successful control. Third, there were no serious contraindications to this choice of goal. Thus, following full discussion with both Seamus and his wife, a controlled-drinking goal was adopted. This does not preclude modification or abandonment of the approach if it was subsequently thought advisable.

After discussions with Seamus, the following guidelines for his controlled drinking were written down.

1. No more than 2 pints of beer or 2 doubles on any one day (approximately 30 gm absolute alcohol)
2. Such drinking to occur no more than 5 times a week
3. No carry-over of day's allowances
4. No drinking for medicinal purposes or to alleviate anxiety or depression

It was stressed to Seamus that these were allowances, and if he did not wish to drink he need not do so! The guidelines could be modified at any time by mutual agreement.

4. RESULTS

Seamus was very cooperative throughout the program. Although subsequently he admitted that "I didn't think it would work at first," he complied with all the rules and did all that was asked of him. Following an uneventful withdrawal, the first treatment phase began. Figures 2 and 3 show the significant improvement made by Seamus on subjective measures of "desire" and "difficult to resist" after consuming alcohol. These are simple subjective measures which run on a scale from 1 to 10, where 10 equals a maximum and 1 a minimum. While initially it can be seen that maximal levels on these two subjective measures were reported, within a couple of sessions these scores decline rapidly. Equally, scores on the before-and-after behavior tests (Figures 4 and 5) on these measures, like the within-session readings reported above, show the same dramatic effects. Similar dramatic reductions were found on subjective measures of "frustration" and "temptation."

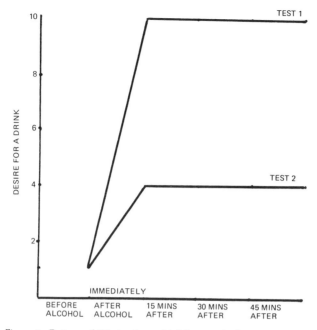

Figure 2. Ratings of "desire for a drink" across both test sessions.

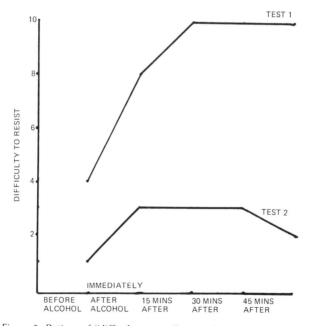

Figure 3. Ratings of "difficult to resist" across both test sessions.

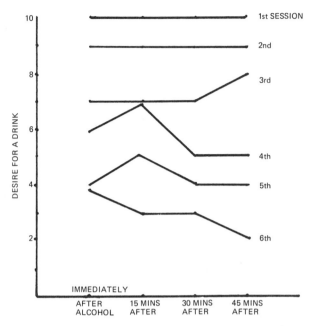

Figure 4. Ratings of "desire for a drink" across experimental sessions.

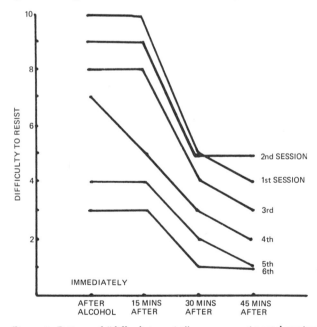

Figure 5. Ratings of "difficult to resist" across experimental sessions.

Furthermore, speed to consume the test doses of alcohol in the before-and-after behavior test show significant differences. In the first test the time to consume the alcohol was a total of 592 seconds, whereas at the end of the second behavior test, after the treatment sessions, that time rose to 999 seconds. In short, these data support anecdotal and informal information and observation that the inpatient treatment phase substantially altered Seamus's response to a moderate dose of alcohol. Indeed, whereas at the beginning of the program, ambivalence, agitation, and discomfort were evident, by the end of the inpatient phase of the program, these had largely disappeared, to be replaced by confidence and tempered optimism.

Following the successful inpatient phase and subsequent rest period, the external phase of homework assignments also proceeded very successfully. Figure 6 shows the reported difficulty of one of the homework assignments over the first 6 occasions. This was the assignment where Seamus had to sit at home in the lounge after everyone had retired with a bottle of his favorite whiskey in front of him and consume no more than 1 double scotch. Despite a little expected discomfort to begin with, he quickly adjusted to this assignment and soon had no difficulty at all in performing it. Seamus did do at least one of the homework assignments daily for the first 3 weeks but thereafter

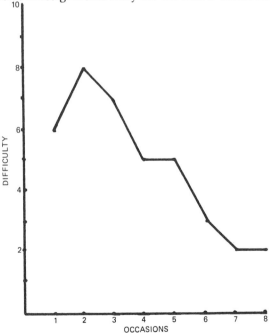

Figure 6. Rated difficulty of homework assignment across eight occasions.

felt less need to carry them out. There were only minor problems in the homework assignments. One of these was that the opportunity to practice one of the situations, namely, when tense, go into a bar and buy a nonalcoholic drink, was limited due to his increased activity in the home and his experiencing less tension. There was one other problem. Seamus had been given a limit of not more than 30 gm absolute alcohol per day for no more than 5 days a week, as listed previously. A glance at Figure 7 shows that in only 2 weeks following treatment (New Year and Christmas) Seamus did have more than 200 gm per week, and this with the previous knowledge and consent of the therapist. However, it will be noted that in Week 6 after discharge, Seamus did have 2 consecutive days of heavier drinking than was allowed, when he met an old friend, but he was able to stop subsequently and resume the program without further damage.

In the early phases of treatment, Seamus settled into the habit of having about 4 pints a week with the occasional scotch in two or three weekly trips to the bar, mostly on weekends. Subsequently, this has reduced considerably to the point where he only drinks at lunchtime on Sundays in the pub, and at most 2 pints of beer. At 9-month follow-up Seamus is satisfactorily controlling his drinking and, more importantly, reports no desire to increase consumption whatsoever.

In other areas of his life, Seamus is doing well. His rated appetitite, mood, and sleep have all improved dramatically. For example, where his

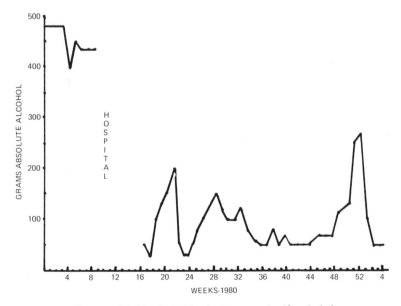

Figure 7. Weekly alcohol intake in grams absolute alcohol.

previous estimates had shown that even with the aid of 1 sleeping tablet he had averaged 4 hours sleep a night, he now reported 7 hours or more as normal.

His family relationships have improved. Clearly, his wife and he still have certain difficulties, but these are no longer being accentuated by alcohol. His family in general, and his daughters in particular, report a much more relaxed atmosphere at home.

Unfortunately, Seamus is still out of work. This, however, is seen more of a reflection of the current economic problems in Britain than of any deficiencies in the client. As an indication of this, it is now clear that Seamus is doing a lot more around the house, as well as redecorating his own and one of his daughter's houses. He generally makes the evening meal for his family and helps out in other domestic chores. In fact, it is one of the strong points of his posttreatment performance that he continues to be so well and to be able to control his drinking in the face of continued unemployment.

It was previously mentioned that his alcohol consumption at Christmas was controlled, even if a bit higher than usual. But Christmas was a good time for Seamus. He was reunited with his brother, from whom he had been estranged for a long time. This made him feel considerably better toward his family and reduced his guilt about upsetting his aged mother over the feud. It will be recalled that this was the theme that haunted him both prior to and during previous heavy drinking episodes. Christmas also served to highlight the general improvement in the family situation. In Seamus's own words:

> For the first time my children could bring back friends without being ashamed of me. We did have alcohol in the house. For once it was normal. They had confidence that I could control myself and were much more relaxed. It was the best Christmas that I could remember.

5. DISCUSSION

The main conclusion that can be drawn from this case study is that cue-exposure response-prevention treatment can be a useful clinical tool. Although the follow-up period here is at the present time only 9 months, which is rather shorter than should normally be used, comparisons with previous treatment attempts show that his performance to date shows considerable improvement over previous efforts.

Several things stand out about this case study. First, it is difficult to see what other factors are responsible for Seamus's current well-being. No other form of treatment was offered. The client did not suddenly seek or get other institutional help, such as Alcoholics Anonymous. There were no changes in his domestic or financial circumstances. No new or wonder drugs were administered. Indeed, the observed improvements occurred in the face of continuing unemployment. Other physical or psychiatric problems do not seem to have unduly influenced the improvement; rather continued improvement in areas such as mood, sleep, and appetite are seen as a result of the specific treatment. Whatever the reason for the improvement in drinking behavior, this case does seem to amply illustrate the effect of the treatment of alcohol problems on other life areas.

At least two factors about the specific treatment regime stand out. First, the treatment does seem to have effected some changes, both specific and general. Despite initial pessimism, within the hospital situation Seamus did show marked changes, not only on key subjective variables but also on the behavioral measurement of "craving," which indicated the efficacy of the inpatient phase. While it could be argued that subjective measures are susceptible to methodological factors and that this particular subject told the therapist what he wanted to hear, this is unlikely for a number of reasons. First, improvements occurred on the unobtrusive behavioral measure as mentioned, and second, at an anecdotal level there were perceptible differences in the client's reaction to successive treatment sessions. Confidence clearly increased as treatment progressed. Quite how this treatment might effect change, bearing in mind the short time scale, is a matter discussed in detail elsewhere (Rankin & Hodgson, in preparation). Suffice to say here that changes in cognitions brought about by the disconfirmation of negative expectancies that are purported to occur in the successful resistance to alcohol are influential. Clearly, coping strategies are effected and engender new confidence and optimism.

Of course, it is one thing to demonstrate such effects in hospital, quite another to generalize these to the client's natural environment. The confidence gained by the client in hospital in this case clearly transferred to the homework assignments. He was also fortunate in having a supportive family, and close contact with the therapist is deemed essential. It may be that in other cases where confidence is lower, therapist-assisted homework is indicated to ease clients into this critical phase of treatment. Clearly, initial success in homework assignments is vital, and no doubt "luck" (i.e., nonspecific factors) plays a sizable part in this early success. The critical part of homework assignments is that they are self-paced. Like any other part of the cue-exposure response-prevention treatment, one has to strike the right balance between pushing the client to the limits of therapeutic usefulness but not pushing them beyond them into failure. What should not be overlooked is the fact that the client was on a controlled-drinking goal for the first time. Clearly, goals and treatment do not exist as independent entities but form a dynamic reciprocal arrangement. The fact that Seamus was on a controlled-drinking goal made a significant contribution. He had spoken of abstinence as "a life sentence," and even when successful, struggled miserably with it. That does not mean to say that abstinence is not appropriate with cue-exposure response prevention—merely that in this case, at least to date, the treatment-goal combination has brought great rewards.

Interestingly, Seamus's pattern of consumption, even after treatment, has changed. Following the phasing out of formal monitoring and home-work, Seamus has now settled into a pattern of drinking 2 pints of beer on Sunday at lunchtime. He now claims to be able to "take it or leave it" and clearly has an acceptable degree of control over his intake. Not only is he controlling his intake, but, more importantly, he no longer feels the need to drink. For what it is worth, when questioned on these matters, he attributes his success to the confidence engendered by his successful experiences in resisting alcohol both in the hospital and at home, although it is hard to judge how much this is merely a therapist-pleasing statement.

The reader will no doubt be struck by the fact that this treatment procedure is not a standard approach, and that there are—or could be—many difficulties with its implementation.

First, it does require the administration of moderate doses of alcohol to persons designated alcoholic. Fortunately, the powers of this particular hospital agree that such a practice is ethically acceptable. As shown in Table 1, reasons do exist for excluding people from such a program, and each prospective case is fully discussed with all team members. Moreover, it is essential that clients be aware of exactly what will happen to them when in hospital and the full implications of treatment. Treatment does not go ahead without the full signed, informed consent of each client and, where possible, discussion with the spouse and relatives. Moreover, the client has, of course, a right to withdraw from the program at any time.

Naturally, the all important inpatient phase of treatment could not take place without the full cooperation and support of the supervisory nursing staff. Owing to present arrangements, the client involved in this program was in the same ward with other "alcoholics" not undergoing this program. Under these circumstances, it is important to warn the client not only that this is the case but that certain jealousies or other feelings may arise. It is equally important to keep the other patients fully aware of what is going on, why they are not in the program, and so forth. In general, it has been my experience that if two patients are in the program together, they can support each other, share experiences, and indeed learn from each other. Having said that, intragroup problems have been rare and confined to the odd case.

As for the cue-exposure response-prevention methodology itself, several other considerations need to be noted. Readers are no doubt wondering what happens if clients do not resist the available alcohol during the treatment sessions. As far as inpatient treatment is concerned, the rule here is to terminate the session in a nonjudgmental fashion, while making the usual supervisory arrangements when the client is back on the ward. If this should happen on more than two occasions, it might be best to abandon the treatment altogether, although this is purely arbitrary. This has happened so far in just one case treated in this way. Equally important is the fact that on some days, the treatment session, although planned, may be inadvisable. Clients may be under undue stress or unduly preoccupied with other events. Under such circumstances, the therapist has the discretion to postpone the treatment for a day. It is hoped that subsequent research may reveal predictive factors which will permit a more rational and satisfactory assignment to this form of treatment.

Finally, the strictness of supervision required clearly varies from case to case. Generally, clients on this program gladly submit to being given firm rules about not leaving the hospital, or even the ward. In this program, if clients do go out and break the rules (for example, drink), they are subject to the usual consequences, which generally mean discharge.

The cue-exposure response-prevention methods as described here tackle a particular cue complex involving the psychophysiological consequences of drinking which are important for the severely dependent person. Giving alcohol in this way obviously needs to be done in the security and under the supervision of the inpatient setting. However, the cue-exposure response-prevention principles could, theoretically, be extended to cover other cues not overtly psychophysiological or related to the effects of alcohol. Under such circumstances and where alcohol did not need to be administered, such treatment might not require an initial stage of hospitalization but might begin in the community setting with homework assignments.

COMMENTARY

William M. Hay

The assessment and treatment of the severely dependent alcoholic present the clinician with a number of problems. This chapter, by Howard Rankin, describes the assessment and successful treatment of a modern-day Dickens character, named Seamus, a severely dependent alcohol abuser with an extensive history of unsuccessful hospitalizations for treatment of alcoholism. Rankin hypothesizes that severely dependent individuals like Seamus are heavily influenced by the direct or immediate stimulus effects of alcohol (i.e., smell, taste, blood-alcohol level). Consequently, he suggests that treatment for the severely dependent individual should include a cue-exposure and response-prevention component.

As Rankin and his colleague Ray Hodgson note, cue-exposure response-prevention procedures have been used successfully in the treatment of compulsive disorders. For the severely dependent alcohol abuser the treatment entails systematic unreinforced exposure to the cues or situations which have been found to be the most consistently related to alcohol abuse. The treatment in this case was divided into three phases. During the experimental phase, Seamus was given a priming dose of alcohol that resulted in a blood-alcohol level of between 75 and 100 mg%. Forty-five minutes after this dose, Seamus was asked to consume two glasses of his preferred alcoholic beverage. The rate at which these two drinks are consumed has been found by Rankin and his colleagues to be a correlate of "craving." This unique measure may eventually provide the clinician with an empirically based measure of craving. As behavioral clinicians, we are committed to the operational definition and measurement of what we target for change rather than a reliance on loosely defined constructs such as "craving" or "loss of control." These procedures were repeated after the treatment phase to assess the impact of the treatment procedures on both subjective and behavioral (i.e., rate of consumption of preferred beverage) measures of craving.

During the treatment phase, Seamus was asked to hold a glass of alcohol in his hand, maintain eye contact, and smell the contents. This procedure was accompanied by instructions which emphasized that he could resist the drink. This phase was completed in the hospital to prevent any extratreatment contact with alcohol. The inpatient program was followed by a series of graded homework assignments, designed to facilitate generalization, which required Seamus to consume prescribed amount of alcohol in situations where he previously consumed excessively.

To aid in the assessment of the severely dependent alcohol abuser, Rankin et al. have developed two questionnaires, the Severity of Alcohol Dependence Questionnaire (SADQ) and the Cue Questionnaire. The SADQ contains 20 items and measures the frequency and intensity of withdrawal symptoms. The Cue Questionnaire asks the drinker to judge the differential impact of specific physiological, social, and psychological cues on the subsequent probability of excessive drinking behavior. These questionnaires were developed by Rankin for use in his clinical research program. The results of that research indicated that severely dependent alcohol abusers were more heavily influenced by the direct effects of alcohol then less dependent groups and, therefore, might benefit from cue-exposure response-prevention procedures. As such, the use of these questionnaires in this case study represents a promising integration of experimental measurement and clinical work.

Treatment success in this case appeared to be related to a number of factors. One factor, the selection of a controlled rather than an abstinence treatment goal for Seamus, is certainly worth noting. Rankin reminds us of the crucial importance of shaping treatment goals to the individual client. Seamus had been repeatedly unsuccessful in achieving abstinence and viewed abstinence as a "life sentence." Treatment success in this case also appeared related to the fact that the cue-exposure response-prevention procedures changed Seamus's negative expectations concerning his ability to resist alcohol. Rankin cautions us, however, that we must be very conservative in our use of this *treatment modality, since reliably predictive indices of who would be successful in this form of treatment have not yet been clearly identified.*

6. REFERENCES

Hodgson, R. J., & Rankin, H. J. Cue exposure in the treatment of alcoholism. *Behaviour Research & Therapy,* 1976, *14,* 305–307.

Hodgson, R. J., Stockwell, T., Rankin, H., & Edwards, G. Alcohol dependence: The concept, its utility and measurement. *British Journal of Addiction, 1978, 73, 339–342.*

Orford, J., & Edwards, G. *Alcoholism.* London: Oxford University Press, 1977.

Orford, J., Oppenheimer, E., & Edwards, G. Abstinence or control: The outcome for excessive drinkers two years after consultation. *Behaviour Research & Therapy,* 1976, *14,* 409–418.

Rachman, S., Hodgson, R., & Marks, I. The treatment of obsessive-compulsive neurotics by modelling and flooding in vivo. *Behaviour Research & Therapy,* 1973, *11,* 463–471.

Rankin, H. J., & Hodgson, R. J. Cue exposure: One approach to the extinction of addictive behaviours. In M. Gross (Ed.), *Alcohol intoxication and withdrawal* (Vol. 3). New York: Plenum Press, 1977.

Rankin, H. J., & Hodgson, R. J. *Cue exposure and response prevention with severely dependent alcoholics.* Manuscript in preparation.

Rankin, H. J., Hodgson, R. J., & Stockwell, T. The Concept of craving and its measurement. *Behaviour Research & Therapy,* 1979, *17,* 389–396.

Rankin, H. J., Hodgson, R. J., & Stockwell, T. Cues for drinking and alcohol dependence. *British Journal of Addiction,* 1982.

Stockwell, T., Hodgson, R., Edwards, G., Taylor, C., & Rankin, H. The development of a questionnaire to measure severity of alcohol dependence. *British Journal of Addiction,* 1979, *74,* 79–87.

IV

Conceptualization and Treatment of Alcoholism: Two Models

Part IV consists of chapters by E. Mansell Pattison and Glenn R. Caddy. These two chapters make an appropriate final section for this text. The range of assessment and treatment procedures which fall under the rubric of the behavioral approach are described, and the authors present two models and discuss their impact on treatment-related decision making.

11

Decision Strategies in the Path of Alcoholism Treatment

E. MANSELL PATTISON

1. INTRODUCTION

The selection of treatment methods for alcoholism has been singularly advanced in the past decade (Pattison, 1977). In large part this is due to the reformulation of alcoholism treatment in terms of specific target behaviors in multiple areas of life dysfunction rather than the notion of one specific treatment for a global and unitary phenomenon termed "alcoholism." I have called this reformulation a "multivariate approach" (Pattison, 1974, 1976, 1980a; Pattison, Sobell, & Sobell, 1977). Although there have been seeming polarities between "medical models" and "behavioral models" of alcoholism treatment, both may be subsumed under the basic epidemiologic model of treatment that has long been employed in the public health model theorem, which can be stated thus: "what alcoholism syndromes at which stage of their development in what patients will respond in what short- and long-range ways to what measures administered by whom?" (Pattison, 1966, p. 25).

The above theorem assumes that there is variation in the manifestation of the alcoholism syndrome, which will therefore present with different clusters of target behaviors and and will require treatment intervention varying according to individual patient characteristics, treatment settings, and treat-

E. MANSELL PATTISON ● Department of Psychiatry, Medical College of Georgia, Augusta, Georgia 30912.

ment personnel. The concept of alcoholism as a multivariate syndrome has now been widely accepted as a paradigmatic approach to alcoholism treatment selection (Caddy, 1978; Costello *et al.*, 1976; Davis & Schmidt, 1977; Edwards, 1974; Horn, 1978; Kissin, 1977; Larken, 1974; Pomerleau, Pertschuk, & Stinnet, 1976; Replogle & Haim, 1977).

However, we *cannot* assume that this approach implies that we need only seek one better treatment method among others. Rather, it is my intent to illustrate how *multiple* treatment decisions are involved in the career path of treatment of the alcoholic. Or, to state the issue specifically, there are *multiple treatment decisions* which may involve *multiple treatment interventions* over time.

2. ALCOHOLISM AS A SYNDROME

There is no question but that there are "alcoholics," for the label refers to a certain social reality for which there is consensual validity. But the fact that we can describe, denote, and diagnose a person as "alcoholic" does not logically imply that there is a specific entity, "alcoholism." Rather, the person *presents* with a *syndrome of alcoholism*.

The medical dictionary states that a syndrome is "a group or set of concurrent symptoms which together can be considered a disease." Thus, the fact that a specific disease entity, alcoholism, does not exist neither vitiates labeling alcoholism a disease nor engaging in differential diagnosis and differential treatment of the syndrome—for health care in general deals with many syndromes which are not specific diseases (Pattison, 1980b).

Miller (1976) has recently pointed out that the *utility* of diagnosis of alcoholism as a syndrome lies in the description of consistently interrelated sets of signs and symptoms with *predictive* implications for etiology, prognosis, treatment, and prevention. There are several major issues imbedded in this perspective.

First, a simple binary diagnostic decision as to whether the person does or does not have the syndrome is inadequate for the utilization of syndrome diagnosis. As Miller (1976) comments:

> A large amount of information is lost when the data regarding various aspects of the problem are reduced to a binary nomenclature. Certainly this reduction cannot improve our prediction of such complex events as treatment outcome. (p. 650)

Second, a syndrome does not imply that there is just *one* pattern of signs and symptoms in the syndrome; rather, there may be various combinations of patterns of signs and symptoms which represent *subsets* of the syndrome.

Third, different sign and symptom sets may have different predictive utility, depending upon whether one attempts to predict etiology, treatment, outcome, or prevention. Thus, *no one set* of interrelated items may be usefully predictive for all dependent variables.

Fourth, the collation of items in a syndrome diagnosis from a research perspective is a statistical maneuver. The clinical application of such derived typologies must be done with care. The problem here is noted by Finney and Moos (1979):

> It should be kept in mind that their main strength and weakness are two sides of the same coin: a simplification of reality. A typology may allow efficient assignment of patients to general methods of treatment. Treatment programs will have to remain flexible, however, to be responsive to individual differences that inevitably obtain among persons within types. (p. 37)

Thus, a syndrome diagnosis can hopefully provide the clinician with a general lifestyle categorization within which to place a patient, which will generate guidelines for treatment; but individuation to a much finer degree must be implemented at the clinical level (Garitano & Ronall, 1974).

3. SELECTION AND MATCHING OF TREATMENT

A discomfiting recent trend is found among scientists who acknowledge and accept the multivariate-syndrome model yet, because of sparse research evidence, have questioned the utility of treatment selection; they even go so far as to suggest to clinicians that the cheapest and simplest treatment be offered indiscriminately to all.

Examples of skepticism about differential treatment are shaded in their degrees of doubt. Armor, Johnson, and Stambul (1976), in their national survey of NIAAA-supported programs, found little evidence for the differential effectiveness of treatment modalities, although significant improvement was produced by most; the same was reported by Emrick (1975) for psychological methods of treatment. Both concluded there was little *evidence* to support differential-treatment efforts. In a different vein, Edwards *et al.* (1977) reported that patients who were seen diagnostically and received no treatment did as well at follow-up evaluation as a control group who received active treatment. This report was taken by some to indicate that treatment might well be just ineffectual—thus, differential diagnosis and treatment would be considered superfluous. Two other recent studies on *untreated* alcoholics also report similar improvement but found that the areas of improvement varied considerably from *treated* alcoholics (Imber *et al.,* 1976; Tuchfeld *et al.,* 1976) Nonetheless, this data lends weight to skepticism about differentiated treatment. Ogborne (1978) recently reviewed patient characteristics as predictors of treatment outcome. He found that patient characteristics were so dominant a variable that he wondered if different treatments made much difference.

> But what is by no means clear is whether or not different patients are more or less likely to remain with or be helped by different treatment modalities. The literature provides only limited evidence relevant to this issue and the results are inconclusive. (p. 351)

More critical was a study by Levinson and Sereny (1962) which compared an intensive structured treatment experience with a generic unstructured treatment approach; they were equally effective. He, therefore, questioned the value of the effort and the expense of more specific treatment methodologies. Finally, Stinson *et al.* (1979) recently compared four systems of care and found no differences between intensive selective treatment and generic low-input approaches. They conclude:

> No particular system of care demonstrated superior effectiveness.... The study was unsuccessful in delineating a rationale for differentially assigning particular patients to any particular treatment approach. (p. 538)

Thus, we see that although the *concept* of treatment selection has been widely accepted, there are many caveats about the *application* thereof.

The essence of the selection problem is to optimize treatment effectiveness by matching the characteristics of patients with the most appropriate treatment facilities, which will provide the most appropriate treatment methods, administered by the most appropriate personnel. Thus, we seek to match clientele with facility with treatment with personnel. So we may ask: What evidence is there that matching occurs, what evidence is there of mismatching, and what evidence is there of the consequences thereof?

First, let us consider evidence for matching processes. The most clear-cut data come from an analysis of types of alcoholics who enter different treatment facilities. Comparisons of the clientele of skid-road facilities, halfway houses, and hospital and outpatient clinics reveal striking homogeneity of each within-group clientele and major between-group differences (Bromet *et al.*, 1977a; Delahaye, 1977; English & Curtin, 1975; Kern, Schmelter, & Fanelli, 1978; Pattison, Coe, & Rhodes, 1969; Pattison, Coe, & Doerr, 1973). This data suggests a covert social process of linking, in which different types of alcoholics seek out a facility congruent with their alcoholism pattern or lifestyle. This process is highlighted in studies of the same *type* of facility, but with differences in programs and personnel, which in turn offer the image of differences. Again, we find different types of alcoholics attracted to different kinds of hospitals (Edwards, Kyle, & Nicholls, 1974), halfway houses (Otto & Orford, 1978), and outpatient clinics (Gerard & Saenger, 1966). Finally, we must note the reverse, where apparent facility differences reflect the *same* covert social-program process. In this case, skid-road facilities of jail, clinic, and mission, all superficially different, offer the same "social shelter" to an identical skid-road clientele (Wiseman, 1970).

A second set of evidence is negative in content. These are studies which demonstrate that treatment personnel ignore the spectrum of problems associated with alcoholism, as well as individual goals, needs, and expectations of clientele. Two studies found that although program personnel acknowledged the existence of emotional, social, vocational, and physical rehabilitation problems, they focused solely on emotional problems and treatment (Einstein, Wolfson, & Gecht, 1970; Pemper, 1976). Another study of 10 different facilities reported that the personnel in each program did not offer consistent treatment in accord with program intent but provided idiosyncratic treatment based on personal proclivity (Hadley & Hadley, 1972). Two recent studies found that treatment staff ignored client needs and expectations and made no attempt to offer treatment based on client needs. (Hague, Donovan, & O'Leary, 1976; Martin, 1979). And finally, in a major monograph, Schmidt, Smart, and Moss, (1968) report an elegant study of a treatment program where differential diagnosis for treatment was made at admission, but when the alcoholic clientele entered the actual treatment program, needs assessments were ignored, and the alcoholics were treated in accord with generic social-class biases. This negative data raises the question of treatment efficacy when treatment is not being directed to even identified major areas of disability.

Part of the problem here is the legacy of the folk-science unitary model of alcoholism, which assumed that abstinence was the major and primary goal of treatment and, corollary to this, if abstinence were achieved, then the person was rehabilitated. Thus, specific program efforts aimed at intervention and rehabilitation in the spheres of emotional, social, vocational, and physical function were often ignored as irrelevant. Thus, there is neither differential diagnosis of disabilities in each sphere of function, nor differential treatment intervention directed to each area of disability, nor recognition and assessment of possible treatment gains in each area of disability. Just on the face validity of clinical logic, it does not seem plausible that treatment efficacy can be optimized by generic, global, diffuse, and nonspecific treatment of such singularly different dimensions of change as drinking behavior, psychological function, social interaction, physical function, and vocational competency. Pattison et al. (1977) have extensively explicated data which demonstrate that the outcome covariance between changes in drinking emotional, social, vocational, and physical function is low. Similarly, Stein and Bowman (1977) and Bowman et al. (1975) have found that drinking measures per se have a low correlation with social behavior. A good example of the issue is provided by Lowe and Thomas (1976) who evaluated treatment outcome on three variables. In their follow-up population, 70% had achieved vocational rehabilitation, 62% psychosocial behavioral rehabilitation, and 34% abstinence.

Third, what evidence suggests that matching is effective or makes a difference? In a review of the generic characteristics of treatment programs and methods, Costello (1975a, b) found that the more specific and individualized treatment programs had lower dropout rates and higher success rates. In a different vein, Kissin, Platz, and Su (1968) found that successful participants in drug, milieu, and psychotherapy treatment had significantly different personality and social patterns. Trice, Roman, and Belasco (1969) similarly reported different social and psychological patterns for successful AA affiliators versus psychotherapy attenders. Vannicelli (1979) reported higher satisfaction in treatment where the patient chose the specific contract content for treatment. In matching patients by level of conceptual capacity, McLachlan (1974) reported that when patient was matched to both therapy and aftercare environments, 77% recovered; when matched to aftercare or therapy environments alone, 61% and 65% recovered; and when mismatched to both therapy and aftercare, only 38% recovered. Two studies by Pattison *et al.* (1969, 1973) evaluated the relationship between treatment facility programs and methods and patterns of treatment outcome. They found substantial evidence that matching does affect outcome. A similar clinical correlation of matching is reported by Kern *et al.* (1978). More elegant multivariate statistical-analysis studies have separated the effects of patient and treatment variables. Although patient variables do account for major portions of outcome variance, the direct effects of treatment variables alone account for up to 30% of outcome variance (Cronkite & Moos, 1978; Smart & Gray, 1978). Finney and Moos (1979) have reported matching processes similar to Pattison *et al.*, although they found considerably more "looseness" in natural matching. Further, they confirm the major contribution of treatment variables to outcome variance but were unable to find specific correlations with specific treatments.

In sum, the face validity of the matching concept appears sound. There is a handful of different empirical studies which support both the existence of social matching processes and the efficacy of treatment matching. From a clinical point of view, the value of matching is supported, but there is only modest research demonstration of the efficacy of matching in available rigorous studies.

4. METHODOLOGICAL STRATEGIES

Techniques of data collection and analysis can provide "good" data to the extent that the technical operations are based on "good" conceptual models. Thus, the construction of models of alcoholism and models of treatment systems necessarily impact on the adequacy of methodologies. In brief, we can review the concepts behind a variety of methods for differential diagnosis of alcoholism, to determine the assets and liabilities of different technical approaches.

First, the vast majority of "diagnostic alcoholism" instruments are based on the binary-decision concept. Such diagnostic instruments may be useful for certain epidemiological survey purposes or for screening and initial triage decisions. However, all such binary-decision diagnostic methods fail to provide an adequate methodology for differential diagnosis (Jacobson, 1976; Neuringer & Clopton, 1976).

A second strategy has been the use of multivariate analyses of personality variables to construct predictive typologies for treatment prescription and outcome prediction (Costello, 1978a,b; Moger, Wilson, & Helm, 1970; Partington & Johnson, 1969). Similar typologies have been derived for sociodemographic variables (Hart & Stueland, 1979a,b). These typologies do describe meaningful clinical subtypes of alcoholics and may have some predictive value. However, they focus on limited sets of preexisting "exogenous" treatment variables.

A third strategy is just the reverse; it uses simple correlational or complex multivariate analyses of treatment variables, yet does not account for preexisting background variables or their interaction with treatment variables (Backeland, 1977: Backeland, Lundwell, & Kissin, 1975).

A recent review by Gibbs and Flanagan (1977) failed to reveal any consistent or even consensual data on prognostic indicators of alcoholism treatment outcome, much less prediction for treatment methods. The problems with both types of studies noted above are clinical and methodological. The clinical problem is that most of these studies are based on populations at one alcoholism facility, immediately skewing the predictability of any typology as well as its generalizability. Potent typologies must encompass a broad spectrum of variations on the alcoholism syndrome. The methodological problem is that such studies generate predictive measures derived from *individual differences* (which ignore the joint and interactive effects of different variables) or produce higher-level abstract data which is difficult to interpret back in clinical terms.

A fourth strategy is the use of multivariates scales to assess background and current-status variables, which in turn can generate typologies. The work of Marlatt (1975) and Wanberg, Horn, and Foster (1977) is distinctive here. This strategy can sample numerous populations and assess multiple background variables and degrees of disability in various current life functions associated with alcoholism. However, the application of these sophisticated methods is somewhat limited by a *linear* analysis of treatment processes, which precludes statistical analysis of the interactional effects of exogenous and endogenous variables.

This leads us to a fifth strategy, which I consider the most promising methodology, termed "causal pathway analysis." The exemplary work of R. H. Moos and R. M. Costello is pioneering in alcoholism. In brief, data sets are accumulated for each major block of variables in the treatment sequence. Empirical typologies can be derived for subpopulations of alcoholics entering any given treatment system. Subsequent analysis of the interaction of block variables for each typology can then be conducted in relation to treatment variable blocks and discrete outcome variables. In this manner, one can determine the extent to which preexisting variables in each typology interact with and influence the effect of various treatment variables. Further, one can separate the indirect (interactional) effects which combine to influence outcome from direct (noninteractional) effects on outcome. Finally, one can determine different pathways of direct and indirect influence on specific outcome variables. In a pictorial sense, we are taking a moving picture of a similar group of people walking through a sequence of treatment scenarios, and by the end of the film we can now observe how the different outcomes were the result of the interaction between different types of people and specific treatment experiences. This begins to approximate a *research methodology* for differential diagnosis. However, it is, at the same time, a limited method for *clinical* differential diagnosis.

Some of the preliminary findings from the Costello (1978) research are of great interest. For example, *preexisting* psychosocial variables do not exert a direct effect on treatment outcome but rather have an indirect influence through the current status and disabilities of the alcoholic or treatment difficulty measure (TDS). In turn, the TDS directly interacts with treatment participation and outcome. Clinically, this suggests the importance of evaluation of current status and disabilities, rather than a major focus on the past history, in making differential treatment recommendations. However, since the prior development of psychosocial competence indicates potential for treatment change, it cannot be ignored. Thus, initial differential diagnosis must assess both current level of dysfunction and potential for improvement, based on prior competency attainment.

Costello also found that aftercare participation significantly influenced treatment outcome, which calls attention to the importance of both the active and the aftercare treatment period in a sequential model of rehabilitation.

Finally, Costello found that simple direct links between pretreatment status and outcome status on discrete variables were potent. That is, despite many complex interactional effects, the most potent predictor on specific outcome variables was pretreatment status on the same variable. Thus, vocational status at entry was the most potent predictor of posttreatment vocational function, marital interaction at entry the best predictor of marital interaction at follow-up, and so forth. Again, in clinical perspective, this finding suggests the value of discrete assessments of specific areas for specific treatment intervention, but it also may generally indicate what *levels* of rehabilitation can reasonably be set as goals for treatment.

The work of Moos and his colleagues has focused more on the interactional issues (Bromet & Moos, 1977; Bromet *et al.*, 1977b; Moos & Bliss, 1978; Moos, Bromet, Tsu, & Moos, 1979). They found that their typologies account for only 13% of the outcome variance, although the typologies correlate .44 and .52 with outcome. Thus, the conceptual simplicity of their typologies leads to significant decrement in predictive utility. Clinically, this highlights the importance of using typologies only for general guidelines in treatment selection, which must then be clinically individualized.

Pursuing the interactions, the Moos group found that although both social background and intake symptoms are relatively strong predictors of outcome, most of the total effect of the *intake symptoms* was *directly* on outcome, whereas the *social-background* variables acted *indirectly* upon treatment participation. The effect of *unique* program-treatment variables on outcome, up to 33%, was almost as strong at patient variables. But more importantly, most of the explained outcome variance (23%–40%) is *shared by interaction* between patient and treatment variables. Or, 28% to 72% of the patient variable effects are shared in interaction with treatment variables. Alcohol consumption and behavior patterns at outcome were most directly influenced by treatment variables, but other variables such as marital function and occupational function were directly related to intake status. Yet program selection, program perceptions, and program participation were most strongly influenced by social background, rather than intake symptoms. In summary, this work suggests that social-background variables influence the choice of treatment programs and participation, while disability status at intake is directly linked to level of rehabilitation at outcome. Treatment experience significantly influences outcome *per se,* but that effect is strongly influenced by interaction with patient variables.

In sum, I find these two sets of studies strongly indicative of the value of differential diagnosis and differential treatment selection, which can produce more precise treatment outcomes on specific variables.

5. PATHWAYS OF TREATMENT

It is easy to assume that differential diagnosis and differential treatment selection mean *one* assessment. However, I propose that there are a *series* of differential decisions that must be made throughout the sequence of the *system of rehabilitation.* In Figure 1, I have set out a systems perspective of the *sequence of movement* through different facilities and stages of rehabilitation. In each phase there are decisions to be made. In consonance with the terminology of causal-pathway analysis, I shall consider each of these phases as a "block" which contains a set of variables. I am deliberately setting out a *clinical* model of the pathways of treatment here, so that we can more firmly establish what variables exist in which blocks in the sequence. This is important clinically, and just as important for further methodological application of causal-pathway analysis. As Magoon (1978) has commented:

> A different and more profound weakness is the lack of good description of the modeled situation; many path analysts simply do not spend sufficient time carefully examining the phenomena they model statistically. Good applications of path analysis will often have to await the patient accumulation of case study data, longitudinal studies, and ethnographic accounts in order to be reasonably useful as statistical accounts of the whole interrelated phenomenon. (p. 95)

So with this as the springboard of justification, let us examine the sequence in the pathway of treatment, as shown in Figure 1.

The treatment of the alcoholic is not a single event or set of events but rather a process that involves a series of decision points throughout an entire community system. Thus, I view selection of treatment in both longitudinal and cross-sectional perspective. The alcoholic enters this system through multiple community ports, proceeds through the treatment system, and reenters the community. As a heuristic device, I have identified seven phases of treatment, each of which involves treatment selection decisions. However, I also must emphasize that there are three *types* of decision processes involved (Pattison, 1978, 1979).

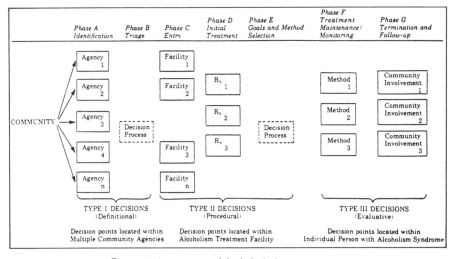

Figure 1. A system model of alcoholism treatment.

Type 1 decisions are *definitional*. These decisions involve criterion for denoting a person as alcoholic, defining a need for treatment, and deciding where, when, and how to make a referral.

Phase A is community identification which occurs in various agencies of entry throughout the community. Note that not all possible candidates for definition as alcoholic may be so denoted. Or if defined as alcoholic, the person may not be defined as in need of treatment or considered for referral. These decision processes may, in a given agency entry port, result in actual definition of only high-risk or low-risk cases for referral.

Phase B is a triage, or the process of referral from the entry port agency to a treatment facility. Here decision processes involve how, when, and where to refer the alcoholic. Again there are potential and real-life discrepancies. The triage process may be desultory or definitive. Alcoholics may be triaged indiscriminately to all facilities or selectively to only one facility.

Next are Type 2 decisions, which are *procedural*. Here the decision process revolves around general clinical operations that will effectively promote facility entry and induction into the general treatment program; select immediate interventions required to meet physical, social, and psychological crises of the patient; and finally proceed to individual assessment for ongoing definitive treatment method selection.

Phase C is the entry process. Here the procedural decisions involve methods to reduce personal anxiety, isolation, and alienation of the alcoholic, resolve denial and rationalization, provide initial hope and positive expectation, and provide socialization into the treatment milieu. Note that these are generic operations, although the application will vary somewhat with each individual entry.

Phase D involves initial treatment. Again the procedural decisions do not involve definitive treatment but address general treatment problems presented by the alcoholic patient. We might consider these treatment interventions for complications of the current lifestyle but not treatment of the "alcoholism." Here we are concerned with immediate problems of detoxification, medical complications of chronic alcoholic use, immediate disabling psychological symptoms such as ambient anxiety or depression, transitory neuropsychological impairment, lack of clothes, food, or shelter, or social crises with the immediate family, legal, or social agencies.

Phase E involves the selection of goals and methods for definitive treatment of the alcoholic person on an ongoing basis. This would include evaluation of *degrees of deficit* and *potential for change* in specific target areas of behavior. This may involve the selection of multiple interventions in the areas of drinking behavior *per se*, psychological function, social behavior, vocational function, and physical dysfunction.

Finally, there are Type 3 decisions which are *evaluative*. Here we are concerned with decisions that evolve from ongoing and regular review of the patient's progress toward specific treatment goals, appropriate utilization of specific treatment procedures, and individual progress toward treatment termination based on goal attainment. This is followed by evaluation of individual plans for community reentry and planned reinvolvement in community life.

Phase F, then, is treatment maintenance and monitoring. Evaluation decision will involve review and assessment of treatment involvement, treatment participation, and goal attainment.

Phase G is termination and follow-up. This will involve evaluation of maximum treatment benefit, remaining functional deficits, suitable levels of community function, and assessment of appropriate methods for community reentry.

In summary, the model of system flow described identifies decision points at each stage of the treatment process. Note that the decision points in Type 1 (definitional) are located externally in multiple community agencies. These types of decisions are most generic. The Type 2 decisions (procedural) are located within each alcoholism treatment facility. While these decisions are generic in terms of program operation, they must be modified to meet individual variation in presenting condition. These decisions will lead in Phase E to specific individualized treatment plans. Type 3 decisions (evaluative) are points located within each individual and are the most specific of the treatment decisions.

6. BLOCK VARIABLES

As indicated, treatment selection proceeds from the most general treatment decisions in the community to the most specific decisions with each alcoholic. Yet each decision point does not exist in isolation but is imbedded in the prior decision processes and their consequences. It is therefore inadequate to simply evaluate the effect of a specific treatment decision in terms of the immediate consequence, since decision outcomes are influenced considerably by prior variables and events in the pathway of treatment. The possible significance of these variables in the pathway of treatment can be illustrated by consideration of the variable sets which exist in "blocks" at each phase of treatment, as illustrated in Figure 2.

6.1. Psychological Background

Variables here include age, sex, ethnicity, vocational skills and competence, education, and marital and social history. Taken together they comprise a level of *psychosocial competence.*

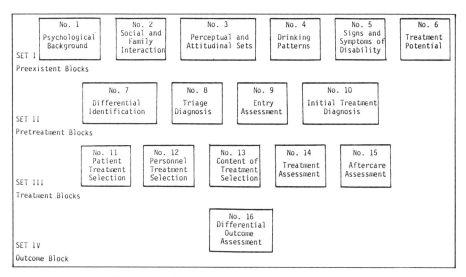

Figure 2. Block variables in the pathway of treatment.

6.2. Social and Family Interaction

This involves the *current* level of social function and interaction with spouse, family, relatives, and significant others in the community. It includes the alcoholic's social standing, degree of social deviancy, and the extent of social support either for treatment or for continued alcoholism. These factors influence entry into treatment, program participation, aftercare participation, and ultimate treatment outcome (Moos & Bliss, 1978; Moos & Bromet, 1976; Moos *et al.*, 1979; Orford *et al.*, 1976; Rae, 1972; Smith, 1967; Webb *et al.*, 1978; Wright & Scott, 1978).

6.3. Perceptual and Attitudinal Sets

This includes similarities and differences in the perceptions of the alcoholic and significant others about the definition of the alcoholism, need for treatment, motivation for change, perceived needs, and perceived goals (Henry & Zastowny, 1978).

6.4. Drinking Patterns

This involves measures of consumption (Khavari & Farber, 1978; Little, Schultz, & Mandell, 1977); the severity of the consequences of drinking behavior (Hilton & Lokare, 1978; Shelton, Hollister, & Gocka, 1969); the meaning, involvement, and investment in drinking (Gillies *et al.*, 1975); and possible assessment of the stage of development of the alcoholic process (Mulford, 1977, 1979; Stallings & Oncken, 1977).

6.5. Signs and Symptoms of Disability

This involves the degree of dysfunction and loss of competence due to alcoholism. It includes physical disabilities; neuropsychological disabilities, which may limit the degree of program participation, and may or may not be reversible (Berglund, Leijonquist, & Horlea, 1977; Tarter, 1976); vocational disabilities; and social and family disabilities.

6.6. Treatment Potential

This component is derivative from data in Blocks 1 to 5. A good-risk alcoholic with many assets and few disabilities might respond equally well to a variety of treatments; whereas a poor-risk alcoholic, like the skid-row stereotype with few assets and many liabilities, might respond poorly to any treatment intervention. Between these extremes are different types of alcoholics, who vary in their prognosis for improvement in specific areas of disability.

6.7. Identification

This includes definitions of who is alcoholic, information imparted, attitudes and expectations generated, social constraints on entry (probation, jail, divorce, treatment fees), and the context of identification (welfare, police, medical).

Several recent studies have reemphasized the difficulty in linking the alcoholic from the identification agency to the treatment agency (Corrigan, 1972; Vogler, Compton, & Weissbach, 1976). This process may skew the type of alcoholic who enters treatment or the degree to which a "good match" is obtained so that the alcoholic actually enters a suitable treatment program.

6.8. Triage

Variables include criteria for referral, method of referral, mechanisms of referral, participation of the index alcoholic in the referral process, availability of referral resources, and degree of objective and subjective suitability and acceptance of referral.

This is a critical phase, for most dropouts occur right here. This is undesirable, of course, from a clinical standpoint, and certainly biases predictive research efforts. Baekland and Lundwall (1977) report that dropouts from inpatient programs range from 13% to 40%, and in outpatient programs from 52% to 75%. Here patient motivation, attitudes, expectations, and perceptions of the program become initial interactive variables (Moos & Bromet, 1976; Pratt et al., 1977). In addition, the "social climate" of the program is an immediate determining variable (Bromet, Moos, & Bliss, 1976).

6.9. Entry Assessment

This includes prior negative treatment experience, self-expectations and perceptions, significant-other expectations and perceptions, social climate, waiting time for entry, degree of immediate support and reduction of anxiety, degree of immediate symptom relief, provision of necessary immediate life support (food, clothes, shelter), degree of entry mechanics such as paperwork and financial evaluation, and participation of significant others in the entry phase. Immediate physical assessment in terms of need for detoxification, immediate major physical impairments, and maintenance of daily-life patterns are paramount here (Feldman et al., 1975). Reports indicate the importance of providing socialization with other clientele (Gallant, Bishop, Stoy, Faulkner, & Paternostro, 1966), immediate involvement of the family and significant others (Catanzaro, Pisani, Fox, & Kennedy, 1973; Pattison 1965; Pattison, Courlas, Patti, Mann, & Mullan, 1965), and the provision of education about alcoholism and information about further treatment alternatives (John 1976).

6.10. Initial Treatment Diagnosis

Variables include needs for medical, welfare, and social intervention, degree of socialization, involvement of family and significant others, and methods and mechanisms for transition into intermediate phases of treatment.

6.11. Patient Treatment Selection

First are individual expectations and goals of treatment (Canter, 1972; O'Leary, Rohsenow, & Chaney, 1979); second is the degree of patient participation in the evaluation and selection of treatment alternatives (Ewing, 1977; Vannicelli, 1979); and third is the interaction of patients with other patients, which provides a specific gestalt of treatment experience (Price & Curlee–Salisbury, 1975).

6.12. Personnel Treatment Selection

This would include the attitudes, values, and interests of treatment personnel; their levels of training and competency; congruency and collaboration between team personnel; and congruency and interaction between treatment personnel and the patient (Pattison 1973).

6.13. Content of Treatment Selection

Specific types of treatment would be the first variable, second would be more generic aspects of treatment implementation, including frequency, intensity, and levels of interaction; third would be singularity of treatment or combinations of treatments; and fourth would be the variables of who is involved in the treatment process, as for example, individual, marital, family, peer, and social network members of the treatment process (Bromet et al., 1976; Bromet, Moos, Bliss, & Wuthman, 1977a,b).

6.14. Treatment Assessment

Variables here might include degree of patient participation in selection of methods and goals, the congruence of methods and goals with prior status and potential for change, the methods and mechanisms of assessment, and the degree of feedback utilization of such clinical assessment (Bean & Karasievich, 1975).

6.15. Aftercare Assessment

Variables include linkage to the treatment program, methods and mechanisms of transition, linkages between clients, linkages to family, significant others, and community social network, level of participation and significant other response. This has been a neglected dimension until recently in the sequence of treatment. But recent evaluative studies provide modest support for the value of aftercare programs (Chavpil, Hymes, & Delmastro, 1978; Dubourg, 1969; Kirk & Masi, 1978; Pittman & Tate, 1969; Pokorny et al., 1973; Sands & Hanson, 1971; Vannicelli, 1978). Perhaps more important is the issue of community reentry and the reinvolvement of the alcoholic in community life and structure with family, significant others, and community relations, which have been shown to be significant factors in subsequent outcome (Bromet & Moos, 1977; Finlay, 1966; Simpson & Webber, 1971).

6.16. Differential Outcome Assessment

The first set of variables in this block concerns biases in sampling as outlined by Miller et al. (1970). A second set are different sources of information which can provide convergent validity of outcome measures, as indicated by Sobell and Sobell (1978). Third are the variables associated with the location of and cooperation of subjects. Moos and Bliss (1978) found that difficult-to-locate and uncooperative subjects were generally in the poor-outcome category.

7. SUMMARY

The selection of treatment for alcoholics has been described here in terms of a system flow model. There is no single treatment decision, but rather a series of treatment decisions as the patient proceeds through the system of treatment. Evaluation of the effectiveness of treatment methods and treatment selection decision is embedded in the complex of variables associated with the entire system of treatment. These variables are briefly set forth in 16 blocks of variables throughout the treatment system.

Finally we must distinguish between the research process and the clinical process. Obviously I have set forth an immensely complicated decision system. For the clinician a much more simplified operational schemata must be developed. Further, a highly rigorous individualized assessment process may not be clinically necessary. In fact, we need to explore in much more detail the limits of specificity of treatment. On the other hand, this analysis may illustrate the pitfalls of treatment selection and evaluation, as observed from only one point along the pathway of treatment.

COMMENTARY

Peter E. Nathan

Mansell Pattison was one of the first psychiatrists to argue that a range of treatment approaches and more than one treatment outcome ought to be available to the alcoholic. He has also been influential in urging that specific treatments be provided specific patients in specific treatment settings. Hence, he comes to the multivariate thrust of his remarks naturally.

Mansell Pattison has moved public and professional understanding of alcoholism along, in part, by being controversial, thought provoking, and intentionally out of step with prevailing views. He assumes this role of agent provocateur *easily and convincingly; it is a constructive role. Perhaps the role is best illustrated in this chapter by Pattison's strong position that syndromes of alcoholism can predict effective treatments. In fact, I think this position is still more a wishful thought—a hope—than a fact. Those of us who work intensively with alcoholics must lament the comparative ineffectiveness of many of our most energetic interventions and the discouraging tendency of some of our favorite patients to drink abusively after our best therapeutic efforts. Syndromes of alcoholism cannot be effective predictors of successful treatment until or unless we develop robust treatments, a goal which still remains beyond our reach. The pitfalls awaiting the syndromal predictor are further complicated by the plethora of divergent etiologies, etiologic theories, and signs and symptoms of alcoholism. The diversity in etiologic conceptions portrayed in this book (including genetic, familial, stress-induced, depression-induced, marital dysfunction—induced, and psychosis—induced) is striking; in a volume written from a single underlying etiologic position, this diversity gives one a sense of the virtually limitless range of current etiologic conceptions. I take this range of opinion on etiology to signify that the etiology of alcoholism remains uncertain. This being so, the use of syndromes for better understanding of etiology and more accurate prediction of outcome is seen as a hope, not yet a reality.*

Pattison is generous in his appraisal of current levels and optimistic about future levels of success of behavioral intervention for alcoholism. While I share his optimism for the future, I am not so sanguine about current success rates. I also question Pattison's view that it is by matching specific patients to specific treatment settings that the best success rates will be achieved because, according to him, specific intervention modes work best for specific syndromes. While I heartily endorse the importance of matching, I do so for very different reasons—reasons reflective of my somewhat greater caution in accepting current assessments about treatment success. I believe that the best way to ensure therapeutic success is to select patients whose motivation to acquire a nonproblem-drinking pattern or to establish and maintain abstinence is very high. Treatment approaches and facilities which can ensure this level of motivation do best; the composition of their treatment package may be, correspondingly, less important than the patients they succeed in attracting. Thus, the requirements set down by Caddy, the Sobell group, Hay, and others that patients who aspire to nonproblem drinking first establish and maintain a lengthy period of abstinence ensures high motivation, a strong desire to change, and a willingness to undergo certain challenges along that path. Similarly, the success rates of the Raleigh Hills group of alcoholism treatment facilities likely stems, at least in part, from the rigors of the chemical-aversion treatment, around which its treatment package is organized. Patients who are not highly motivated to do something about their drinking are not likely to subject themselves to hours of conditioned nausea and vomiting otherwise. Accordingly, I conclude that patients who are treated successfully at facilities with substantial records of successful treatment are (1) more highly motivated to begin with than the average substance abuser, or (2) more highly motivated by the facility or its staff than is usual, or (3) both.

The virtue of the differing positions Mansell Pattison and I take on this issue is that both are amenable to empirical study. Studies relating patients' treatment motivation at a variety of treatment facilities to estimates of outcome could serve to link initial and continuing motivation levels with outcome, with patients' demographic data as a covariate.

I believe that Pattison's Type 1, Phase B, triage is a most important treatment element, at least as important as the kind of treatment offered, the training and experience of the clinicians offering the treatment, or the philosophy of the facility. Granted, all of the latter influence and are influenced by the kind of patients treated, but motivation and motivational tests bulk larger, in my view, in anticipating treatment outcome. Hence, the decision on where to send the patient who needs treatment, because it reflects a choice among facilities which vary in the prevailing motivation of patients seen at them, may be the most important decision made. Similarly, when Pattison traces the block variables in the Pathway of Treatment, he convinces me that Block 6, Treatment Potential, which builds on Blocks 1 to 5, is of supreme importance; it seems to determine most of what follows, including what happens in Block 8, Triage. Treatment Potential includes those personal, historical, and interpersonal variables that determine motivational level—which, so far as I am concerned, is the bottom line as far as treatment outcome is concerned.

8. REFERENCES

Armor, D. J., Johnson, P., & Stambul, H. *Alcoholism and treatment.* Santa Monica, Calif.: Rand Corporation, 1976.

Baekeland, F. Evaluation of treatment methods in chronic alcoholism. In B. Kissin & H. Begleiter (Eds.), *The biology of alcoholism* (Vol. 5). New York: Plenum Press, 1977.

Baekland, F., & Lundwall, L. K. Engaging the alcoholic in treatment and keeping him there. In B. Kissin & H. Begleiter (Eds.), *The biology of alcoholism* (Vol. 5). New York: Plenum Press, 1977.

Baekeland, F., Lundwall, L. K., & Kissin, B. Methods for the treatment of chronic alcoholism: A critical appraisal. In Y. Israel, R. J. Gibbins, H. Kalant, R. E. Popham, W. Schmidt, & R. G. Smart (Eds.), *Research advances in alcohol and drug problems* (Vol. 2). New York: Wiley, 1975.

Bean, K. L., & Karasievich, G. O. Psychological test results at three stages of inpatient alcoholism treatment. *Journal of Studies on Alcohol,* 1975, *36,* 838–852.

Berglund, M., Leijonquist, H., & Horlea, M. Prognostic significance and reversibility of cerebral dysfunction in alcoholism. *Journal of Studies on Alcohol,* 1977, *38,* 1761–1770.

Bowman, R. S., Stein, L. I., & Newton, J. R. Measurement and interpretation of drinking behavior. *Journal of Studies on Alcohol,* 1975, *36,* 1154–1172.

Bromet, E., & Moos, R. H. Environmental resources and the post-treatment functioning of alcoholic patients. *Journal of Health and Social Behavior,* 1977, *18,* 326–338.

Bromet, E., Moos, R. H., & Bliss, F. The social climate of alcoholism treatment programs. *Archives of General Psychiatry,* 1976, *33,* 910–916.

Bromet, E., Moos, R. H., Bliss, F., & Wuthmann, F. Treatment experiences of alcoholic patients: An analysis of five residential treatment programs. *International Journal of the Addictions,* 1977, *12,* 953–958. (a)

Bromet, E., Moos, R. H., Bliss, F., & Wuthman, C. Post-treatment functioning of alcoholic patients: Its relation to treatment participation. *Journal of Consulting and Clinical Psychology,* 1977, *45,* 829–842. (b)

Caddy, G. R. Toward a multivariate analysis of alcohol abuse. In P. E. Nathan, G. A. Marlatt, &

T. Løberg (Eds.), *Alcoholism: New directions in behavioral research and treatment.* New York: Plenum Press, 1978.

Canter, F. M. Treatment participation related to hospitalization goals of patients and their families. *Psychiatric Quarterly,* 1972, *46,* 81–87.

Catanzaro, R. J., Pisani, V. D., Fox, R., & Kennedy, E. R. Familization therapy. *Diseases of the Nervous System,* 1973, *34,* 212–218.

Chavpil, M., Hymes, H., & Delmastro, D. Outpatient aftercare as a factor in treatment outcome: A pilot study. *Journal of Studies on Alcohol,* 1978, *39,* 540–544.

Corrigan, E. M. Linking the problem drinker with treatment. *Social Work,* 1972, *17,* 54–60.

Costello, R. M. Alcoholism treatment and evaluation: I. In search of methods. *International Journal of the Addictions,* 1975, *10,* 251–272. (a)

Costello, R. M. Alcoholism treatment and evaluation: II. Collation of two-year follow-up studies, *International Journal of the Addictions,* 1975, *10,* 857–868. (b)

Costello, R. M. Programming alcoholism treatment: Historical trends. In J. S. Madden, R. Walker, & W. H. Kenyon (Eds.), *Alcoholism and drug dependence.* New York: Plenum Press, 1977.

Costello, R. M. Evaluation of post-hospital adjustment: Path analysis of causal chains. *Evaluation and the Health Professions,* 1978, *1,* 83–93.

Costello, R. M., Giffen, M. B., Schneider, S. L., Edginton, P. W., & Manders, K. B. Comprehensive alcohol treatment planning, implementation, and evaluation. *International Journal of the Addictions,* 1976, *11,* 553–570.

Costello, R. M., Biever, P., & Baillargen, J. G. Alcoholism treatment programming: Historical trends and modern approaches. *Alcoholism Clinical and Experimental Research,* 1978, *4,* 311–318. (a)

Costello, R. M., Lawlis, G. F., Manders, K. R., & Celistino, J. F. Empirical derivation of a partial personality typoligy of alcoholism. *Journal of Studies on Alcohol,* 1978, *39,* 1258–1266. (b)

Cronkite, R. C., & Moos, R. H. Evaluating alcoholism treatment programs: An integrated approach. *Journal of Consulting and Clinical Psychology,* 1978, *46,* 1105–1119.

Davis, C. S., & Schmidt, M. R. (Eds.). *Differential treatment of drug and alcohol abuses.* Palm Springs, Calif.: ETC Publications, 1977.

Delahaye, S. An analysis of clients using alcoholism agencies in a community service. In J. S. Madden, R. Walker, & W. H. Kenyon (Eds.), *Alcoholism and drug dependence.* New York: Plenum Press, 1977.

Dubourg, G. O. Aftercare for alcoholics: A follow-up study. *British Journal of Addiction,* 1969, *64,* 155–163.

Edwards, G. Drugs, drug dependence, and the concept of plasticity. *Quarterly Journal of Studies on Alcohol,* 1974, *35,* 176–195.

Edwards, G. The alcohol dependence syndrome: Usefulness of an idea. In G. Edwards, & M. Grant (Eds.), *Alcoholism: New knowledge and new responses.* Baltimore: University Park Press, 1977.

Edwards, G., Kyle, E., & Nicholls, P. Alcoholics admitted to four hospitals in England. *Quarterly Journal of Studies on Alcohol,* 1974, *35,* 499–522.

Edwards, G. Orford, J., Egert, S., Gutherie, S., Hawker, A., Hensman, L., Mitcheson, M., Oppenheimer, E., & Taylor, C. Alcoholism: A controlled trial of "treatment" and "advice." *Journal of Studies on Alcohol,* 1977, *38,* 1004–1031.

Einstein, S., Solfson, E., & Gecht, P. What matters in treatment: Relevant variables in alcoholism. *International Journal of the Addictions,* 1970, *5,* 295–307.

Emrick, C. D. A review of psychologically oriented treatment of alcoholism: II. The relative effectiveness of different treatment approaches and the effectiveness of different treatment approaches and the effectiveness of treatment versus no-treatment. *Journal of Studies on Alcohol,* 1975, *36,* 88–108.

English, G. E., & Curtin, M. E. Personality differences in patients at three different alcoholism treatment agencies. *Journal of Studies on Alcohol,* 1975, *36,* 52–68.

Ewing, J. A. Matching therapy and patients: The cafeteria plan. *British Journal of Addiction,* 1977, *72,* 13–18.

Feldman, D. J., Pattison, E. M., Sobell, L. C., Graham, T., & Sobell, M. B. Outpatient alcohol detoxification: Initial findings on 564 patients. *American Journal of Psychiatry,* 1975, *132,* 407–412.

Finlay, D. G. Effect of role network pressures on the alcoholics approach to treatment. *Social Work,* 1966, *11,* 71–77.

Finney, J. A., & Moos, R. H. Treatment and outcome for empirical subtypes of alcoholic patients. *Journal of Consulting and Clinical Psychology,* 1979, *47,* 25–38.

Gallant, D. M., Bishop, M. P., Stoy, B., Faulkner, M. A., & Paternostro, L. The value of a "first contact" group intake session in an alcoholism clinic: statistical confirmation. *Psychosomatics,* 1966, *7,* 349–352.

Garitano, W. A., & Ronall, R. E. Concepts of life style in the treatment of alcoholism. *International Journal of the Addictions,* 1974, *9,* 585–592.

Gerard, D. L., & Sarnger, G. *Outpatient treatment of alcoholism.* Toronto: University of Toronto Press, 1966.

Gibbs, L., & Flanagan, J. Prognostic indicators of alcoholic treatment outcome. *International Journal of the Addictions,* 1977, *12,* 1097–1111.

Gillies, M. C., Aharan, C., Smart, R. G., & Shain, M. The alcoholic involvement scale: A method of measuring change in alcoholics. *Journal of Alcoholism (London),* 1975, *10,* 142–148.

Hadley, P. A., & Hadley, R. G. Treatment practices and philosophies in rehabilitation facilities for alcoholics. *Proceedings of the American Psychological Association,* 1972, *80,* 779–780.

Hague, W. H., Donovan, D. M., & O'Leary, M. R. Personality characteristics related to treatment decisions among inpatient alcoholics: a nonrelationship. *Journal of Clinical Psychology,* 1976, *32,* 476–479.

Hart, L., & Stueland, D. Relationships of sociodemographic and drinking variables to differentiated subgroups of alcoholics. *Community Mental Health Journal,* 1979, *15,* 47–57. (a)

Hart, L. S., & Stueland, D. An application of the multi-dimensional model of alcoholism: Differentiation of alcoholics by mode analysis. *Journal of Studies on Alcohol,* 1979, *40,* 283–290. (b)

Henry, J. D., & Zastowny, J. R. Perceptual differences in alcoholics and significant others. *Alcohol Health and Research World,* 1978, *3,* 36–39.

Hilton, M. R., & Lokare, V. G. The evaluation of a questionnaire measuring severity of alcoholism dependence. *British Journal of Psychiatry,* 1978, *132,* 42–48.

Horn, J. L. Comments on the many faces of alcoholism. In P. E. Nathan, G. A. Marlatt, & T. Løberg (Eds.), *Alcoholism: New directions in behavioral research and treatment.* New York: Plenum Press, 1978.

Imber, S., Schultz, E., Funderbuck, F., Allen, R., & Flamer, R. The fate of untreated alcoholics. *Journal of Nervous and Mental Disease,* 1976, *162,* 230–247.

Jacobson, G. R. *The alcoholisms: Detection, diagnosis, and assessment.* New York: Human Sciences Press, 1976.

Kern, J. C., Schmelter, W., & Fanelli, M. A comparison of three alcoholism treatment populations. *Journal of Studies on Alcohol,* 1978, *39,* 785–792.

Khavari, K. A., & Farber, P. D. A profile instrument for the quantification an assessment of alcohol consumption: The Khavari alcohol test. *Journal of Studies on Alcohol,* 1978, *39,* 1525–1539.

Kirk, S. A., & Masi, J. Aftercare for alcoholics: Services of community mental health centers. *Journal of Studies on Alcohol,* 1978, *39,* 545–547.

Kissin, B. Theory and practice in the treatment of alcoholism. In B. Kissin& H. Begletier (Eds.), *The biology of alcoholism (Vol. 5). Treatment and rehabilitation of the chronic alcoholic.* New York: Plenum Press, 1977.

Kissin, B., Platz, A., & Su, W. Social and psychological factors in the treatment of chronic alcoholism. *Journal of Psychiatric Research,* 1968, *8,* 13–27.

Larkin, E. J. *The treatment of alcoholism: Theory, practice, evaluation.* Toronto: Addiction Research Foundation, 1974.

Levinson, T., & Sereny, G. An experimental evaluation of "insight therapy" for the chronic alcoholic. *Canadian Psychiatric Association Journal,* 1969, *14,* 143–146.

Little, R. E., Schultz, F. A., & Mandell, W. Describing alcohol consumption: A comparison of three methods and a new approach *Journal of Studies on Alcohol,* 1977, *38,* 554–562.

Lowe, W. C., & Thomas, S. D. Assessing alcoholism treatment effectiveness: A comparison of three evaluative measures. *Journal of Studies on Alcohol,* 1976, *37, 883–889.*

Magoon, A. J. Path analysis and evaluation models. *Evaluations and the Health Professions,* 1978, *1,* 94–99.

Marlatt, G. A. The drinking profile: A questionnaire for the behavioral assessment of alcoholism. In E. J. Mash & L. G. Terdahl (Eds.), *Behavior therapy assessment: Diagnosis, design, and evaluation.* New York: Springer, 1975.

Martin, P. Y. Client characteristics and the expectations of staff in half-way houses for alcoholics. *Journal of Studies on Alcohol,* 1979, *40,* 211–221.

McLachlan, J. F. C. Therapy strategies: Personality, orientation, and recovery from alcoholism. *Canadian Psychiatric Association Journal,* 1974, *19,* 25–30.

Miller, W. R. Alcoholism scales and objective assessment methods: A review. *Psychological Bulletin,* 1976, *83,* 649–674.

Miller, B. A., Pokorny, A. D., Valles, J., & Cleveland, S. E. Biased sampling in alcoholism treatment research. *Quarterly Journal of Studies on Alcohol,* 1970, *31,* 97–107.

Mogar, R., Wilson, W., & Helm, S. Personality subtypes of male and female alcoholic patients. *International Journal of the Addictions,* 1970, *5,* 99–113.

Moos, R. H., & Bliss, F. Difficulties of follow-up and alcoholism treatment outcome. *Journal of Studies on Alcohol,* 1978, *39,* 473–490.

Moos, R. H., & Bromet, E. Relation of patient attributes to perception of treatment environment. *Journal of Consulting and Clinical Psychology,* 1976, *46,* 350–351.

Moos, R. H., Bromet, E., Tsu, V., & Moos, B. Family characteristics of the outcome of treatment for alcoholics. *Journal of Studies on Alcohol,* 1979, *40,* 78–88.

Mulford, H. A. Stages in the alcoholic process: Toward a cumulative, nonsequential index. *Journal of Studies on Alcohol,* 1977, *38,* 563–583.

Mulford, H. A. Treating alcoholism versus accelerating the natural recovery process: A cost-benefit comparison. *Journal of Studies on Alcohol,* 1979, *40,* 505–513.

Neuringer, C., & Clopton, J. R. The use of psychological tests for the study and identification, prediction, and treatment of alcoholics. In G. Goldstein & C Neuringer (Eds.), *Empirical studies of alcoholism.* Cambridge, Mass.: Ballinger, 1976.

Ogborne, A. C. Patient characteristics as predictors of treatment outcome for alcohol and drug abuse. In Y. Israel, F. B. Glaser, H. Kalant, R. E. Popham, W. Schmidt, & R. G. Smart, (Eds.), *Research advances in alcohol and drug problems* (Vol. 4). New York: Plenum Press, 1978.

O'Leary, M. R., Rohsenow, D. J., & Chaney, E. F. The use of multivariate personality strategies in predicting attrition from alcoholism treatment. *Journal of Clinical Psychiatry,* 1979, *40,* 190–193.

Orford, J., Oppenheiner, E., Egert, S., Hensman, D., & Gutherie, S. The cohesiveness of alcoholism-related marriages and its influence on treatment outcome. *British Journal of Psychiatry,* 1976, *128,* 318–339.

Otto, S., & Orford, J. *Not quite like home: Small Hostels for alcoholics and others.* New York: Wiley, 1978.

Partington, J. T., & Johnson, F. G. Personality types among alcoholics. *Quarterly Journal of Studies on Alcohol,* 1969, *30,* 21–34.

Pattison, E. M. Treatment of alcoholic families with nurse home visits. *Family Process,* 1965, *4,* 75–94.

Pattison, W. M. A critique of alcoholism treatment concepts, with special reference to abstinence. *Quarterly Journal of Studies on Alcohol,* 1966, *27,* 49–71.

Pattison, E. M. A differential view of manpower resources. In G. E. Staub & L. M. Kent (Eds.), *The paraprofessional in the treatment of alcoholism.* Springfield, Ill.: Charles C Thomas, 1973.

Pattison, E. M. Rehabilitation of the chronic alcoholic. In B. Kissin & H. Begleiter (Eds.), *The biology of alcoholism* (Vol. 3). New York: Plenum Press, 1974.

Pattison, E. M. A conceptual approach to alcoholism treatment goals. *Addictive Behaviors,* 1976, *1,* 177–192.

Pattison, E. M. Ten years of change in alcoholism treatment and delivery systems. *American Journal of Psychiatry,* 1977, *134,* 261–266.

Pattison, E. M. The Jack Donovan Memorial Lecture, 1978: Differential approaches to multiple problems associated with alcoholism. *Contemporary Drug Problems,* 1978, *9,* 265–309.

Pattison, E. M. The selection of treatment modalities for the alcoholic patient. In J. H. Mandelson & N. K. Mello (Eds.), *The diagnosis and treatment of alcoholism.* New York: MrGraw-Hill, 1979.

Pattison, E. M. Differential treatment of alcoholism. In W. E. Fann (Ed.), *Phenomenology and treatment of alcoholism.* New York: Spectrum, 1980. (a)

Pattison, E. M. The N.C.A. Diagnostic Criteria: Critique, Assessment, alternatives. *Journal of Studies on Alcohol,* 1980, *41,* 965–980. (b)

Pattison, E. M., Courlas, P. G., Patti, R., Mann, B., & Mullan, D. Diagnostic-therapeutic groups for wives of alcoholics. *Quarterly Journal of Studies on Alcohol,* 1965, *26,* 605–615.

Pattison, E. M., Coe, R., & Rhodes, R. J. Evaluation of alcoholism treatment: Comparison of three facilities. *Archives of General Psychiatry,* 1969, *20,* 478–488.

Pattison, E. M., Coe, R., & Doerr, H. O. Population variation among alcoholism treatment agencies. *International Journal of the Addictions,* 1973, *8,* 199–229.

Pattison, E. M., Sobell. M. B., & Sobell, L. C. *Emerging Concepts of Alcohol Dependence.* New York: Springer, 1977.

Pemper, K. Dimensions of change in the improving alcoholic. *International Journal of the Addictions,* 1976, *11,* 641–649.

Pittman, D. J., & Tate, R. L. A comparison of two treatment programs for alcoholics. *Quarterly Journal of Studies on Alcohol,* 1969, *30,* 888–899.

Pokorny, A. D., Miller, B. A., Kanas, T., & Valles, J. Effectiveness of extended aftercare in the treatment of alcoholics. *Quarterly Journal of Studies on Alcohol,* 1973, *34,* 435–443.

Pomerleau, O., Perschuk, M., & Stinnet, J. A critical examination of some current assumptions in the treatment of alcoholics. *Journal of Studies on Alcohol,* 1976, *37,* 849–867.

Pratt, R., Linn, M., Carmichael, J., & Webb, N. The alcoholic's perception of the ward as a predictor of after care attendance. *Journal of Clinical Psychology,* 1977, *33,* 915–918.

Price, R. H., & Curlee-Salisbury, J. Patient-treatment interaction among alcoholics. *Journal of Studies on Alcohol,* 1975, *36,* 659–669.

Rae, J. B. The influence of wives in the treatment outcome of alcoholics: A follow-up study at two years. *British Journal of Psychiatry,* 1972, *120,* 601–613.

Replogle, W. H., & Haim, J. F. Multivariate approaches to profiling alcoholism subtypes. *Multivariate Experimental Clinical Research,* 1977, *3,* 157–164.

Sands, P. M., & Hanson, P. G. Psychotherapeutic groups for alcoholics and relatives in an outpatient setting. *International Journal of Group Psychotherapy,* 1971, *21,* 23–33.

Schmidt, W., Smart, R. G., & Moss, M. K. *Social Class and the Treatment of Alcoholism.* Toronto: University of Toronto Press, 1968.

Shelton, J., Hollister, L. E., & Gocka, E. F. The drinking behavior interview: An attempt to quantify alcoholic impairment. *Diseases of the Nervous System,* 1969, *30,* 464–467.

Simpson, W. M., & Webber, P. W. A field program in the treatment of alcoholism. *Hospital and Community Psychiatry,* 1971, *22,* 170–173.

Smart, R. G., & Gray, G. Multiple predictors of dropouts from alcoholism treatment. *Archives of General Psychiatry,* 1978, *35,* 363–367.

Smith, C. G. Marital influences on treatment outcome in alcoholics. *Journal of the Irish Medical Association,* 1967, *60,* 433–434.

Sobell, L. C., & Sobell, M. B. Convergent validity: An approach to increasing confidence in treatment outcome conclusions with alcohol and drug abuse. In L. C. Sobell, M. B. Sobell, & E. Ward (Eds.), *Evaluating alcohol and drug abuse treatment effectiveness: Recent advances.* New York: Pergamon Press, 1978.

Stein, L. I., & Bowman, R. S. Reasons for drinking: Relationship to social functioning and drinking behavior. In F. A. Seixas (Ed.), *Currents in alcoholism* (Vol. 2). New York: Grune & Stratton, 1977.

Stallings, D. L., & Oncken, G. R. A relative change index in evaluating alcoholism treatment outcome. *Journal of Studies on Alcohol,* 1977, *38,* 457–464.

Stinson, D. J., Smith, W. G., Amidjaya, I., & Kaplan, J. M. Systems of care and treatment outcome for alcoholic patients. *Archives of General Psychiatry,* 1979, *36,* 535–539.

Tarter, R. E. Neuropsychological investigations of alcoholism. In G. Goldstein & C. Neuringer (Eds.), *Empirical studies of alcoholism.* Cambridge, Mass.: Ballinger, 1976.

Trice, H. M., Roman, P. M., & Belasco, J. A. Selection for treatment: A predictive evaluation of an alcoholism treatment regime. *International Journal of the Addictions,* 1969, *4,* 303–317.

Tuchfeld, B. S., Simuel, J. B., Schmitt, M. L., Ries, J. L., Kay, D. L., & Waterhouse, G. J. *Changes in patterns of alcohol abuse without the aid of formal treatment: An exploratory study of former problem drinkers.* Final report to NIAAA. Research Triangle Park, N.C.: Research Triangle Institute, 1976.

Vannicelli, M. Impact of aftercare in the treatment of alcoholics. *Journal of Studies on Alcohol,* 1978, *39,* 1875–1886.

Vanicelli, M. Treatment contracts in an inpatient alcoholism treatment setting. *Journal of Studies on Alcohol,* 1979, *40,* 457–471.

Vogler, R. E., Compton, J. V., & Weissbach, T. A. The referral problem in the field of alcohol abuse. *Journal of Community Psychology,* 1976, *4,* 357–361.

Wanberg, K. W., Horn, J. L., & Foster, F. M. A differential assessment model for alcoholism: The scales of the alcohol use inventory. *Journal of Studies on Alcohol,* 1977, *38,* 512–543.

Webb, N. L., Pratt, T. C., Linn, M. W., & Carmichael, J. S. Focus on the family as a factor in differential treatment outcomes. *International Journal of the Addictions,* 1978, *13,* 783–796.

Wiseman, J. P. *Stations of the lost: The treatment of skid-road alcoholism.* Englewood Cliffs, N.J.: Prentice-Hall, 1970.

Wright, K. D., & Scott, T. B. The relationship of wives' treatment to the drinking status of alcoholics. *Journal of Studies on Alcohol,* 1978, *39,* 1577–1581.

12

A Multivariate Approach to Restricted Drinking

GLENN R. CADDY

1. INTRODUCTION

The most significant elements common to persons diagnosed as alcoholic is that they drink too much. Because the range of physiological, psychological, and sociocultural correlates of alcoholism is vast, many authorities in the field reject global etiological theorizing and univariate conceptualizations of alcoholism in favor of a multivariate approach (see, for example, Edwards, 1974; Goldstein & Linden, 1969; Pattison, 1974a,b; Wanberg & Knapp, 1970). The multivariate approach views alcohol dependence not as an entity represented by symptoms but as an array of behaviors and cognitions that collectively produce different types of problems, which are subsequently labeled. To underline this perspective, Horn and Wanberg (1969) have recommended that terms like "alcoholism" and "alcoholic" not be used, for they argue that these terms denote that a specific attribute, "alcoholism," exists in the unitary fashion implied by the terms.

The multivariate approach owes at least some of its conceptual development to the empirically based criticisms of the disease models of alcoholism (see the reviews by Caddy & Gottheil, in press; Sobell & Sobell, 1975), as well as other data addressing the epidemiology of alcohol misuse (Cahalan, 1970; Cahalan & Room, 1974; Knupfer, 1967). The growing appreciation of

GLENN R. CADDY ● Department of Psychology, Nova University, Fort Lauderdale, Florida 33324.

the multivariate nature of alcohol problems has also been facilitated by the application of factor-analytic techniques to clinical data in the field (Horn & Wanberg, 1969, 1970). Perhaps as important as any of these contributions, however, have been the contributions of a relatively small number of clinical pragmatists who have been less concerned with models of alcoholism than with broad-spectrum approaches to the treatment of individuals for whom alcohol use has become a serious problem. The approaches of these investigators have been ideographic in character.

Up until quite recently, the development of a multivariate approach to alcohol dependence has been characterized most accurately as a social-systems approach (see Holder & Stratas, 1972; Nathan, Lipson, Vettraino, & Solomon, 1968; Steinglass, Weiner, & Mendelson, 1971a,b). One such systems approach, that offered by Pattison (1974a,b), suggested that there are several alcoholic populations that may be treated by several different methods leading to different patterns of outcome.

> It may be possible to match a certain type of patient with a certain type of facility and treatment method, to yield the most effective outcome ... treatment programs can maximize effectiveness by clearly specifying what population they propose to serve, what goals are feasible with that population, and what methods can be expected to best achieve those goals. (Pattison, 1974b, p. 59)

This and other systems approaches represent major advances over the still widely held view that there exists essentially one population of alcoholics to be treated by one best method, with primarily one therapeutic outcome, abstinence, in mind.

Subsequently, Pattison, Sobell, and Sobell (1977) have reviewed and summarized the recent evidence bearing on the emerging multivariate approach. These authors proposed that (1) alcohol dependence summarizes a variety of syndromes defined by drinking patterns and the adverse physical, psychological, and/or social consequences of such drinking; (2) alcohol dependence syndromes may be viewed as lying on a continuum from nonpathological to severely pathological; (3) a variety of factors, which do not produce alcohol dependence per se, may contribute to differential susceptibility to alcohol problems and lead to a syndrome of alcohol dependence; (4) the development of alcohol problems follows variable patterns over time and does not necessarily proceed inexorably to severe or fatal stages; and (5) alcohol problems are typically interrelated with other life problems, especially when alcohol dependence is long established.

In an effort to extend the multivariate approach to the assessment and treatment of alcohol abusing or dependent individuals, Caddy (1978) proposed that alcohol-related problems be understood best as behavioral disorders which are established and maintained as a result of the unique, direct,

and reciprocal interactions of behavioral, discriminative, incentive, and social elements, all of which function with varying degrees of cognitive media-
tion. Within the framework of this multivariate approach, it is assumed that
each of these elements or dimensions is interactive and yet each is sufficiently discrete to preserve its own, albeit cognitively mediated, locus of control.
Such a multivariate approach permits an assessment of both the nature and
the extent of the involvement of each of the elements (behavioral, discriminative, incentive, and social), which are variously integrated within the overall cognitive functioning of the individual and which account for that person's "alcoholismic" behavior. From this type of assessment it is possible to
establish operational hypotheses regarding a drinker's unique interactions
with alcohol. Such an assessment also facilitates the development of treatment planning which takes into consideration the many elements that support problem drinking.

The following case example illustrates the manner in which the multivariate approach to assessment and treatment may be employed.

2. THE CASE OF RALPH P.

I first met Ralph P. after a presentation I gave to the patients and staff of
an alcoholism unit in a local psychiatric hospital. My talk had addressed the
various models of alcohol dependence that exist concurrently in our society,
and I had attempted to shed some light both on the advantages and special
problems that stem from the demand by many treatment agencies for a rigid
adherence to the traditional (disease-oriented) perspective of alcoholism.* I
had no sooner completed my presentation and begun to entertain questions
when Ralph rose to his feet. First, he complimented me, but then he turned
to the audience and expressed in angry and abusive tones his lack of respect
for the competence of "the hospital." He concluded his outburst extremely
flushed, and with his voice trembling he mumbled that I was "the first damn
person" who had made any sense to him since he had been "in this goddamn
institution."

Three weeks later I was in my office at the university and Ralph telephoned me. In a voice again filled with emotion but not noticeably slurred by
alcohol, Ralph told me he had left the hospital earlier that week against
medical advice. He was so angry about the way he was being treated, he said,

* My presentation offered a synthesis of much of the recent literature dealing with present-day
  concepts of alcohol dependence and their implications for both prevention and treatment.
  Some of these perspectives may be found in Caddy, 1978; Caddy, Goldman, & Huebner,
  1976a, b; Linsky, 1972; Marconi, 1967; Miller & Caddy, 1977; Siegler, Osmond, & Newell,
  1968.

that if he had not left the hospital he was sure he would have hurt somebody. He was calling me because he "had to find someone" who could help him. He reported feeling extremely anxious, and he presented a sequence of "unreal sensations," which he interpreted as indications of pending insanity. He also advised me that he had been drinking, "but only a little bit," over the past few days.

My first action during this crisis was to communicate a sense of support and to reflect to Ralph that all would be well. I then told him that I would make an immediate appointment for him with a psychiatrist colleague who would likely prescribe some medication to reduce his level of anxiety. Thereafter, and as soon as possible, I would arrange to see him myself.

2.1. The Historical Context

Ralph's fiftieth birthday fell two days before his first session with me. Up until age 17, he had lived with his parents and older brother on the family farm in Virginia. He described his childhood years as generally pleasant, though life on the farm was hard. Ralph's relationship with his mother had always been close, but he described his now-deceased father as a very powerful and controlling man whom neither of his children could ever please. Ralph's brother was 12 years older than he, and they were never particularly close. He described his brother as a drifter and an alcoholic.

Ralph left home at age 17 after a confrontation with his father, who "threw him out of the house." Within a week Ralph had enlisted in the Navy. He enjoyed the security, the comradeship, and the adventure of Navy life; he also enjoyed the prestige he gained as he became skilled as an electronics technician and received steady pay increments.

At age 24 Ralph met and married Joyce who was 4 years his junior. During their early marriage, Joyce perceived Ralph as "larger than life" and a man of great charm and strength of character. He was away at sea a great deal during those early years, and when he was at home Joyce reported him to be very demanding of both her time and her energies. Yet he also was generous of his time and money, and "except when he had had too much to drink," he was a "good husband."

By the time Ralph was 35, he and Joyce had two children, Ralph, Jr., and Catherine, yet largely as a consequence of his continued drinking, their relationship had deteriorated to the point that both Ralph and Joyce looked forward to his sea duty. Increasingly, Joyce perceived herself to be the sole foundation of the family, as well as being the mother of both her children and her husband. Increasingly, too, she began to nag him, first about his drinking, and then about much of his nonalcohol-related behavior as well.

Ralph, in turn, began to vascillate between withdrawal from the family and attempts to control and to demand respect from all concerned.

With few exceptions, Ralph perceived his drinking to be nonproblematic prior to age 38. Joyce, on the other hand, traced Ralph's frequent and sometimes quite heavy drinking from before they were married. Detailed long-term retrospective time-line follow-back assessment (Sobell, Maisto, Sobell, & Cooper, 1979, 1980) indicated that rarely did a day pass without Ralph having at least four to six cans of beer and, perhaps twice weekly, even in the first few years of his marriage, Ralph's alcohol consumption exceeded 9 oz. of absolute alcohol (the approximate volume of alcohol in 180 oz. of beer) per drinking occasion. While these drinking activities were of no concern to Ralph (in fact, he reported them to be enjoyable "social-drinking" events, typically occurring at a club on the base at which he was stationed), they did provoke progressive disillusionment in Joyce, for she began to see her husband as being crude, sexually aggressive, short-tempered, and "impossible to deal with" when he had been drinking.

By age 38, however, the frequency of Ralph's abusive drinking began to increase so that now he was engaged in between four and five heavy drinking episodes each week. His style of drinking was beginning to change, too. Whereas previously he had drunk beer almost exclusively, by age 35 he would begin drinking beer but, after five or six cans, he would change to bourbon. Further, as a consequence of his increase in tolerance for alcohol, Ralph now was capable of consuming the equivalent of 10 to 12 oz. of absolute alcohol over a period of perhaps 6 hours without appearing particularly intoxicated. In so doing, he routinely achieved blood-alcohol levels within the range of 100 to 175 mg%. Additionally, on two or three occasions each month, he would drink enough to become markedly intoxicated. On these occasions it is likely that Ralph drank enough to provoke BALs in excess of 200 mg%.

Yet despite this pattern of routine heavy drinking, together with occasional patterns of drunkenness, Ralph did not perceive himself to be experiencing a serious alcohol problem. He saw his drinking as "heavy," yet not more so than some of his friends and fellow drinkers, and certainly he did not consider his drinking to be beyond his own control. Even after an arrest at age 39 for "driving under the influence" (BAL 220 mg%), Ralph did not perceive himself to be experiencing a serious alcohol problem; rather, he regarded his arrest as simply an indication of bad luck. Certainly, he admitted that his drinking was expensive, and he agreed that the money expended on alcohol could have been put to good use in other ways. But he also asserted that it was he who had earned the money, and that, provided his family was "adequately supported," he had the right to spend some of it as he saw fit. The only significant crack in the shield that he had created to protect his drinking image was occasioned by worry over memory lapses following some of his heavier drinking episodes. Yet even these "blackouts," which he had experienced occasionally since his mid-20s, were not unduly distressing to him; he had experienced them over a number of years, and he viewed them as the result of excessive drinking (which he could choose to alter), not an indication of an emerging serious drinking problem.

Between the ages of 40 and 45, however, the continued deterioration in Ralph's relationships with Joyce and the children forced him to recognize that it was primarily his drinking that had provoked much of the family conflict and the loss of respect which he was experiencing. All too often Ralph reacted to this conflict by attempting to control activities within the household. This reaction, especially because it typically was punitive in nature, provoked even greater resistance in the family and led to even greater familial conflict. In turn, Ralph would react to this building conflict by further drinking; he also began deliberately to distance himself emotionally from the family.

Ralph's retirement from the Navy occurred at age 45. Notwithstanding his years of heavy drinking, Ralph apparently had functioned competently in his career with the Navy. In the years immediately preceding his retirement, however, Ralph had become increasingly disenchanted with the Navy and was looking forward to civilian life. He was planning to attend college and study electrical engineering. Retirement, however, brought even more family conflict and a period of even more excessive and now solitary drinking. During the first 2 years of his retirement, Ralph was fired from or chose to leave five different jobs. He also undertook but failed a series of introductory-level college courses. Joyce, who had been working for 4 years as a telephone operator, began taking tranquilizers to help deal with the stress she experienced in response to Ralph's drinking and in order to cope with the anger which she had come to feel over her husband's unwillingness to maintain employment adequate to ensure the economic security of the family.

At about this time, at age 47, Ralph was again arrested for driving under the influence (BAL 240 mg%). This time he was ordered by the court to attend an alcohol education and treatment program. It was while attending this program that Ralph was first confronted by a mental health worker, who asserted that Ralph was indeed an alcoholic. Ralph rejected this "accusation," though he did accept that his drinking was now becoming a serious problem, and for the first time in his life he initiated a period of abstinence (4 months). Thereafter, following an argument with Catherine and Joyce, Ralph again began drinking. Within a period of 2 months, he was drinking as much as ever before. His consumption now amounted to approximately a dozen

12-oz. cans of beer, together with up to 35 oz. of bourbon drunk over a period of about 12 to 14 hours for intervals ranging from several days to 3 or 4 weeks. Interspersed between these periods of extremely heavy drinking were short periods of abstinence or periods of lesser drinking involving consumption figures perhaps equal to half or less of those observed under the conditions of extreme consumption noted previously.

Ralph continued this on-again, off-again pattern of largely reactive drunkenness against a backdrop of heavy but commonplace drinking for a period of 2 more years, during which time his relationship with his family deteriorated still further, as did his job stability. Then, he was again arrested for driving under the influence, but this time he was charged also with refusal to submit to breath analysis, negligent driving, and assault. (He had been in a minor collision and had initiated a shouting and scuffling match with the driver of the other vehicle.) This outcome really scared Ralph. Almost as disconcerting as the legal charges facing him, however, was the fact that Ralph could not recollect much of the evening prior to his arrest. The distress Ralph began to experience regarding this entire incident led him to 8 days of continuous intoxication, involving the consumption of between 35 and 40 oz. of bourbon daily. Then, in response to threats from Joyce and following the recommendation of his attorney, Ralph decided to admit himself to the alcoholism unit in which I met him.

2.2. Current Status

Given Ralph's emotional state during his telephone plea for assistance, he attended his first therapy session with me in a relatively stable and intact condition. (This state, no doubt, had been facilitated by the fact that he had begun taking Thorazine, 50 mg qid, the day before our appointment.) During the first three sessions (the last of which was split between Ralph and Joyce) the aforestated history was collected in order to provide a framework for the assessment of Ralph's current functioning.

Ralph's BAL at the beginning of his first session with me was 60 mg%. When he left 2 hours later it was 30 mg%.* Fortunately, Ralph had drunk on only about 6 of the days since he left the hospital and had been drinking "only" six to eight 12-oz. cans of beer on each of these days. Thus, given that he would not experience significant withdrawal symptoms by not drinking, I felt reasonably confident in requesting him to commit himself

---

* I require all my alcohol-abusing clients to undergo breath analysis at the beginning of each therapy session. This procedure permits some confirmation of the client's self-report of his or her drinking earlier that day and minimizes the possibility of deceptive practices. Typically, I do not conduct therapy with clients whose BAL exceeds 5 mg% at the time of the appointment.

to abstinence from alcohol until at least our fourth session, by which time the initial assessment would be completed.* (In fact, Ralph did comply with this request.)

3. MULTIVARIATE ASSESSMENT

During the first three sessions, I conducted a detailed behavioral assessment of Ralph's current functioning in accord with the multivariate approach discussed previously: general medical information from the hospital which he had just recently left, and a functional assessment of the discriminative, incentive, social, and cognitive variables that provided a framework for the behavioral dimension which exemplified his difficulties.

3.1. General Behavioral Specification

In addition to the information about Ralph's drinking presented previously, certain specific and noteworthy behavioral elements emerged during the assessment. First, from his earliest drinking experiences, Ralph drank quite substantial quantities of beer. Rarely did he consume only one or two glasses of beer and then stop. Further, he would drink rapidly, typically being one of the first to finish a drink in almost any social context. Additionally, while Ralph always used a glass when drinking spirits, an *in vivo* trial of his pattern of pouring "a drink" indicated that he did not routinely measure the drink; rather, he would pour approximately 4 oz. of bourbon into a glass with ice each time he made a drink for himself. Thus, while the parameters of Ralph's alcohol-related behavior indicated the at-risk nature of his drinking, until these parameters were examined during the assessment phase, Ralph was oblivious of any reasons for concern regarding his drinking behavior *per se*.

3.2. Discrimination Variables

From our first session together, it was clear that Ralph's drinking had become a generalized response to a wide variety of social and other contexts. Further, due to his acquired tolerance for alcohol, Ralph was capable of consuming quite large quantities, but at the same time he failed to discrimi-

---

* I make it a standard practice with alcohol-abusing clients that abstinence during the initial assessment phase is a prerequisite for continued therapy. Not only is the abstinence condition necessary for ensuring an adequate initial evaluation of the client, it also communicates to clients that I consider them both capable of and responsible for regulating their behavior.

nate minor changes in his internal alcohol related state.* In fact, given that Ralph typically drank about 4 oz. of bourbon in 5 to 15 minutes, and that he would drink at least 8 oz. of bourbon in the first hour of a spirits consumption sequence, it is little wonder that he would experience difficulty in accurately discriminating his BAL (for it would be changing so rapidly). Finally, and within this same general context, like many alcohol-abusing individuals, Ralph appeared not to be particularly cognizant of the early indices of his intoxication and was not debilitated by them. Thus, he did not consider himself "intoxicated" on many occasions when his BAL clearly must have been considerably in excess of 100 mg%.

3.3. Incentive Variables

Although the incentives for Ralph's current drinking were multiple, the primary elements provoking his use of alcohol appeared to be (1) the negative reinforcement that came from his attempts to alter his psychological state, (2) the reinforcement associated with the psychopharmacological properties of alcohol, and to a lesser extent, (3) the positive reinforcement associated with the social aspects of his drinking. Until his mid-30s, the euphoria, relaxation, and comradeship which Ralph experienced when drinking, and the expectation of these positive consequences, seemed to be the major factors promoting his drinking. Thereafter, however, the desire to reduce anxiety, to increase his feelings of self-worth and influence, and, in particular, to counteract the anger and frustration that he so often experienced in his interactions with Joyce and the children became the primary incentives for him to drink.

3.4. Social Variables

The assessment of social influences on drinking behavior is difficult, for it is the individual drinker's unique perception of his or her social context that, in many cases, provides the effective social-stimulus components for the act of drinking. Ralph began drinking in a social context in which the range of acceptable drinking was considerable. As a young sailor, his persistent and excessive patterns of alcohol consumption were seen both by himself and by many of his drinking companions as socially acceptable and even

---

* This observation is in keeping with the suggestions by Caddy (1977) that the apparent inability of alcoholics (by comparison with nonalcoholics) to discriminate their BALs from internal cues may be a function of the increase in alcohol tolerance which parallels the development of alcoholismic drinking. According to this hypothesis, alcohol-tolerant drinkers are minimally effected by low BALs, so they have difficulty formulating accurate BAL discriminations, especially at low BALs (see also Huber, Karlin, & Nathan, 1976).

socially reinforcing. In essence, he drank in a social context which both condoned and supported drinking that was, from the outset, abusive. With the passage of time, however, and especially following his retirement, Ralph became involved in the process which Bacon (1973) referred to as "dissocial-ization." This process involved, first, a reduction in the number and variety of Ralph's social activities and, then, a movement into social groups more tolerant of his drinking. According to this formulation, alcohol is used repeatedly to ease difficulties so that drinking becomes individually rather than socially motivated. In fact, by the time of our first consultation, Ralph's drinking was only partially motivated by positive social contacts or social pressure to drink. The negative social interactions which he experienced within his family and the lack of any positive social reinforcement from the family when he limited his drinking, however, became major factors, which required particular therapeutic attention.

3.5. Cognitive Variables

The extent to which an alcohol-abusing individual is capable of exerting control over his or her drinking is one of the most controversial elements in the current alcoholism literature (Maisto & Schefft, 1977; Marlatt, 1977; Pattison *et al.*, 1977). From the multivariate perspective, drinking—like all other behavior—is "controlled" in that its occurrence is the consequence of the unique interaction of various cognitive, behavioral, discriminative, incentive, and social antecedents. Moreover, it continues because of reinforcement coming from these same dimensions. Such behavior is neither random nor indiscriminant and may involve very stringent controls. From this perspective, the repeated apparent failure of an individual to regulate his or her use of alcohol is seen as somewhat akin to learned helplessness (Seligman, 1972).

For Ralph, and many other alcohol-abusing individuals, the inability to control the use of alcohol (interpreted in terms of a *complete* lack of control) was regarded to be the *sine qua non* of alcoholism. In Ralph's case this cognitive distortion contributed significantly to his failure to appreciate the extent of his own alcohol-related problems, for despite his patterns of drunkenness, he continued to hold to his assertion that he was capable of regulating his drinking. Thus, he was not an alcoholic. It was in large measure this issue that provoked much of the anger which Ralph experienced during his hospitalization, for he perceived the hospital staff as being determined to force him to accept his "alcoholism" (to surrender cognitively to the label) as the first step toward recovery. At that point, by confronting Ralph with a view of himself that he was unwilling to accept, the hospital staff had, in fact, provoked a further expansion of Ralph's all-too-common tendency to react with extreme anger when confronted by others on the topic of his drinking. It was the expansiveness of Ralph's rage reaction, his inability to cope with it, and his uncertainty about how to conceptualize his various difficulties that led to his spiraling pattern of anxiety. This, in turn, culminated in the panic which he was experiencing at the time he sought my services.

By the end of the initial assessment phase, and with psychotherapeutic and medication support, Ralph was no longer experiencing his previous levels of anxiety. Whatever might prove to be the case later in therapy, my initial assessment of Ralph's cognitions regarding his drinking behavior revealed that (1) Ralph viewed himself as being capable of regulating his alcohol consumption, if he chose to do so; (2) he viewed himself as a person with a drinking problem but not an alcoholic; (3) he did not consider abstaining from alcohol throughout the remainder of his life; and (4) he wished to drink in a nonproblematic fashion in the future.

Following an integration of the various elements from the aforestated multivariate assessment, and given also the data from the hospital indicating no appreciable liver or other physiological impairment, I spent the fourth and fifth therapy sessions with both Ralph and Joyce formulating a series of therapeutic objectives to be accomplished over the next several months.

4. THE SETTING OF TREATMENT GOALS

Even though the multivariate approach permits an assessment of the complex dynamic functioning of an individual, this very complexity creates the need to plan and set priorities for the numerous aspects of the therapeutic process very carefully. In the case of alcohol abuse, the multivariate concept dictates that a far greater range of goals and options must be considered in providing alcoholism therapy than is the case when therapy is based on the more traditional concepts of alcoholism.

With respect to the treatment implications of the multivariate approach, Pattison et al. (1977) have proposed that recovery from alcohol dependence bears no necessary relationship to abstinence, although their concurrence is frequently the case, and that the consumption of a small amount of alcohol by an individual once labeled alcoholic does not initiate a physical dependence or the physiological need for more alcohol by that individual. They further propose that (1) treatment services should be multivariate, emphasizing the development of a variety of services in determining which treatment, delivered in which context, is most effective for which persons, with what types of problems; (2) emphasis should be placed on dealing with alcohol problems in the environment in which they occur, because of the strong relationship which has been demonstrated between drinking behaviors and environmental variables; and (3) recovery from alcohol problems typically is a lengthy process, and treatment services should be designed to provide for continuity of care throughout the process.

Although recourse to some prescriptive strategy for initiating the treatment of Ralph and his family would seem highly desirable, it is not yet possible to match clients to a prescribed treatment technology precisely and with confidence. In fact, the multivariate concept of alcohol abuse both permits and recommends that a far greater range of goals and options be considered in providing alcoholism therapy than was the case with therapy based on the more traditional concepts of alcoholism. Inevitably, at this point, sound clinical judgment must dictate the nature, scope, and priority of the services to be rendered. The following set of immediate and short-term therapeutic goals were developed in consultation with both Ralph and Joyce.* The rationale upon which each of these goals was based is also presented.

4.1. Goal 1

To develop a pattern of honest, respectful, and comfortable communication between Ralph and Joyce and among Ralph, Joyce, and myself.

4.1.1. Rationale

The assessment had indicated clearly that Ralph had developed a pattern of deceiving Joyce and the children, as well as others, regarding his alcohol usage. Additionally, Ralph, Joyce, and the children had developed communication patterns reflecting a general lack of courtesy and respect. Given the multiple agendas of the present treatment planning, it was decided to direct an initial and primary focus on improving the communication patterns between the parents. The expectation here was that as these communication patterns improved and the parents began to work more closely together, the communication styles throughout the family would begin to improve. If, in fact, this could be achieved, then Ralph's primary relationships could begin to improve and some major reinforcement from within the social domain could be anticipated. With regard to the relationship between Ralph, Joyce, and myself, the assumption of honesty in the therapeutic relationship was deemed essential to the success of therapy. From the assessment it

* Despite the major difficulties separating Joyce and Ralph, both asserted in private consultation that they wanted to remain married, if possible, and they wanted to make a serious attempt to improve the quality of their relationship. Thus, and because the assessment had shown Joyce to be a major force in precipitating Ralph's patterns of drunkenness, it was deemed advisable, perhaps essential, to include Joyce in all the major phases of Ralph's therapy, including the setting of therapeutic goals.

appeared reasonable to expect that some marked and rapid improvement in some of Ralph's relationships was both possible and necessary. (Recall that even Ralph's drinking had become individually rather than socially motivated, and that he had withdrawn from much social contact.) The expectation that success could be achieved in these social domains of Ralph's functioning led to the high priority of this communication goal.

4.2. Goal 2

To ensure Ralph's abstinence from alcohol for a period of at least 6 weeks.

4.2.1. Rationale

Given that Ralph was not pharmacologically dependent on alcohol at the time of assessment, and given also that during the assessment phase he complied with my demand that he refrain from alcohol and asserted that he could refrain from drinking if he so desired, there was little question in my mind but that Ralph was capable of extending his present state of abstinence. Given also the fact that his use of alcohol had a profound impact on his family and would thereby disrupt the achievement of Goal 1, Ralph's short-term commitment to continued abstinence was deemed to be essential. It was not as important as Goal 1, however, for I regarded its achievement with less confidence than I regarded the success of Goal 1. And my agenda in goal setting was to maximize the probability of reasonable successes, while at the same time conducting a credible therapeutic program.

4.3. Goal 3

To provide Ralph and Joyce with an understanding of his recent emotional state and to establish in him strategies for coping with his emotions in the future.

4.3.1. Rationale

Assessment of the incentive domain indicated that a major element provoking Ralph's drinking came from his attempts to alter his psychological state (reduce anxiety, counteract anger, and increase his feelings of self-worth). Additionally, at the time of the assessment, both Ralph and Joyce were frightened by and did not understand the emotional crisis which Ralph had experienced after he left the hospital. And they were concerned about the prospects of a reoccurrence. The pressing nature of these concerns required relatively rapid attention. Further, because Ralph's generally heightened emotionality at this time made him particularly susceptible to the possibility of additional emotional distress, which in turn might provoke drinking, these incentive-dimension affective elements were given high priority for therapeutic attention.

4.4. Medium-Range Goals

In addition to these short-term goals, four medium-range (i.e., 3–6 month) goals were also outlined at the outset of therapy, as follows: (1) to continue to improve the quality of the relationship among Ralph, Joyce, and the children, thereby ensuring the future stability of the family; (2) to educate Ralph and his family about alcohol and its effects and to train him to drink in a restricted (controlled and nonproblematic) fashion; (3) to continue to aid Ralph in dealing with his impulse control and to further examine some of the family styles that may contribute to difficulties in this area; and (4) to aid Ralph in exploring employment alternatives that would prove rewarding to him, and thereby contribute to a heightening of his self-esteem, as well as the economic stability of the family. While the rationale for the first, third and fourth goals is obvious, some discussion regarding the second medium-range goal would seem necessary.

In examining the drinking-related goals to be set for alcohol-abusing individuals, I have asserted previously with considerable empirical support (see the review by Miller & Caddy, 1977), that without question a number of alcohol-abusing individuals do ultimately restrict their drinking without serious subsequent negative consequences. I also have argued that while abstinence may be a goal of choice for some alcoholic individuals, both abstinence *and* restricted drinking therapies are needed (see also the reviews by Gottheil, 1976; Lloyd & Salzberg, 1975; Sobell, 1978; Sobell & Sobell, 1975). Further, I have proposed that a rationally planned approach be adopted in deciding the appropriate drinking-related goals to be set for a particular individual.

This proposal (Miller & Caddy, 1977) recommended the following contraindications of a controlled-drinking treatment goal: (1) evidence of progressive liver disease, such that any continuing use of alcohol could be life-threatening; (2) evidence of other health problems (e.g., certain cardiac anomalies) or psychiatric disorder (e.g., psychosis) that might seriously be exacerbated by moderate alcohol use; (3) a personal commitment or request of the client for abstinence; (4) strong external demands upon the patient to abstain (e.g., disulfiram treatment or abstinence as a condition of probation or for reinstatement of a driver's license); (5) pathological intoxication, such that the patient consistently or frequently exhibits uncontrolled or bizarre behavior following even moderate alcohol use; (6) evidence of recent physiological addiction to alcohol, because dependence may occur more readily in persons with a history of withdrawal symptoms; (7) use of medication, prescribed or otherwise, that is considered dangerous when taken in combination with alcohol; (8) current successful abstinence from alcohol following a history of severe drinking problems; and (9) prior failure to respond to reputable therapy oriented toward moderation, particularly if previous treatment methods are similar to modalities being considered.

While the contraindications to abstinence were fewer, nevertheless, the following conditions would appear relevant: (1) the client's refusal to consider abstinence; (2) strong external demands upon the client to drink; (3) younger clients with apparent early-stage problem drinking (e.g., no history of physiological addiction; family, employment, and social-support systems intact); or (4) prior failure to respond to reputable therapy oriented toward abstinence, particularly if previous treatment methods are similar to modalities being considered.

Following this approach, in Ralph's case the drinking-related therapeutic goal was obvious, especially given that Ralph was neither convinced about his own alcoholism nor willing to devote serious consideration to lifelong abstinence. Thus, following a period of temporary abstinence, during which several of the immediate goals of therapy would be addressed (and during which time Ralph's willingness to follow the therapeutic directive of abstinence in order to permit his involvement in subsequent restricted-drinking therapy would be assessed), I agreed to provide Ralph with a program which included a restricted-drinking regimen as part of his overall therapy.

5. THE IMPLEMENTATION AND OUTCOME OF THERAPY

Like Yates (1970), I conceptualize therapy in large measure as the systematic application of the experimental method to the management of the individual case; and, like Lazarus (1971, 1976), I espouse a technical eclecticism in therapy. From such a framework, therapy is not simply the implementation of strategies designed to achieve the goals of therapy. Rather, it requires a process of constant and ongoing assessment of the multiple dimensions and dynamics of the case (and not solely the identified client). This dynamic assessment process, in turn, leads to a number of adjustments in, or fine-tuning of, the strategies of therapy. This adjustment, however, must be done in a modulated fashion, so that the goals of therapy continue to be clear and the process of therapy remains structured and ultimately goal-oriented. One of the most significant advantages of the multivariate assessment approach is that it facilitates structure and the establishment of treatment objectives. The approach also highlights and enables priorities to be set for the dynamics to be addressed. Given this clarity, a rather prescriptive approach to the application of the treatment procedures becomes possible.

Turning now to the case at hand, recall that the initial short-term goal in Ralph's therapy was to develop honest and comfortable communication between Ralph and Joyce and among Ralph, Joyce, and myself. Ralph, Joyce, and I reached an agreement about the importance of this goal following a motivational arousal approach to the issue which required nearly half of the fourth session. The procedures used to address the goal required the development of a contingency contracting program within an overall program of behavioral marital therapy. This contracting element included the following components:

Ralph agreed that he would (1) speak politely and quietly to Joyce and would not use vulgar language or raise his voice in discussions; (2) show affection toward Joyce, including giving her backrubs at least three times weekly before they went to sleep; (3) be completely honest with Joyce about his use of alcohol and, in the event that he did drink, to acknowledge his alcohol use; and (4) call me in the event that he was having difficulty with any of the above procedures, and at least once between the weekly therapy sessions, even if no difficulties were being encountered.

In return, Joyce agreed to (1) speak politely and quietly to Ralph and monitor his voice volume and tone by asking him to speak more slowly and quietly if she found his speech becoming stress-laden; (2) respond to Ralph by stating, "I would appreciate it if we could talk about this later" if she felt she was being pressured by Ralph to discuss a matter likely to result in emotional escalation; (3) show courtesy, respect, and affection for Ralph in their daily interactions; (4) initiate sexual behavior or respond to Ralph's sexual overtures at least twice weekly; (5) take a major role in dealing with the children and, in particular, ensure that the children were not permitted to act discourteously to either parent; and (6) call me in the event that she was having difficulty with any of the above procedures, and at least once between the weekly therapy sessions even if no difficulties were being encountered.

For my part, I agreed to (1) see Ralph and Joyce conjointly and separately, as required; (2) provide up to 10 minutes without charge to both Ralph and Joyce during each telephone call I received from them; and (3) accept Ralph's word that he had not been drinking alcohol unless I had good evidence to the contrary. (I told Ralph and Joyce that I would take breath samples from Ralph as a standard procedure at the beginning of *every* therapy session. Also, I indicated that I would expect to speak with Joyce prior to each session with Ralph to gain any knowledge she might have about his possible use of alcohol.)

With this contracting strategy, the relationship between Ralph and Joyce began to show immediate though variable improvement. In addition, both individual and conjoint therapy was begun. Thus, within a period of 6 weeks, the family (with the possible exception of Catherine) was exhibiting a degree of interpersonal caring and mutual support that each member agreed had been almost completely lost in the chaos of the past few years. On a series of 7-point Likert rating scales addressing spousal communication, family communication, frequency of arguments, intensity of arguments, and affectional behavior between spouses, the ratings of both Ralph and Joyce showed marked changes in the positive direction for each dimension scored. Joyce, for example, reported a change in the intensity of arguments from a mean of 7 (very intense) to a mean of 2 within a period of 3 weeks. It should be noted, however, that while improvement in the spousal relationship and communication was set as a relatively immediate goal, the temporary achievement of this goal within the projected period of 4 to 6 weeks should not suggest that thereafter this goal was abandoned for other matters. Rather, the initial success here was used to provide a base for the transition to the longer-term relationship and communication goal involving the entire family.

The second short-term therapeutic goal—ensuring Ralph's abstinence from alcohol for a period of at least 6 weeks—was also successfully achieved. The initial procedure here involved a paradoxical orientation (see Ascher, 1980), in which Ralph was confronted by his own cognitions; namely, he was told that if he was not an "alcoholic," then *not* drinking for a period of 6 weeks should not be a particularly difficult task. In this approach, therefore, abstinence was used symbolically as evidence that Ralph was *not* an alcoholic. The other assertion used to encourage temporary abstinence was that Ralph's drinking inevitably provoked such distress in the family that to drink at that point would greatly risk subverting his stated priority of reestablishing a good relationship with his wife and children. Given these two perspectives, together with the reinforcement and support that Ralph received from Joyce and his son, his commitment to short-term abstinence was established and maintained.* Of course, the fact that Ralph was to be introduced to a program of restricted drinking within a very short period of time no doubt made the notion of his temporary abstinence more acceptable to him than would have been the case if he been asked to commit himself to lifelong abstinence.

---

* Catherine was less willing to commit herself to providing her father or the family with much support. In fact, during the early therapy she was experiencing marked emotional difficulties which she refused to address until considerably later. In the fifth month of Ralph's therapy Catherine began to see me in individual therapy. Thereafter, she participated in family therapy.

In dealing with the third short-term therapeutic goal, (aiding Ralph and Joyce in understanding and coping with his emotional state), the following therapeutic strategies were employed. First, using a didactic approach, both Ralph and Joyce were assured that he was not "going crazy" and that his anxiety, depression, and depersonalization were understandable and controllable. Second, with a series of cognitive-restructuring techniques, Ralph's concepts regarding his self-worth were explored, and he was encouraged to assess his behavior and act in a manner which he valued rather than in a manner he did not respect. Third, using a similar procedure (see also Meichenbaum, 1974), the early strategies of Ralph's control of anger were explored, the self-statements he engaged in regarding his emotional responses to frustration and self-depreciation (which often provoked drinking) were examined in detail, and alternative and more effective self-statements were proposed. In this context, too, and related also to the communication goal, Ralph and Joyce were further introduced to the concept of assertion that would be addressed fully later in treatment. Fourth, both Ralph and Joyce were trained in a breathing-focused muscular-relaxation technique designed to help them cope better with stress and reduce Ralph's tendency to permit an initial stressor to escalate to a panic state, with hyperventilation and extreme trauma. Finally, during this phase of therapy I began to address Ralph's failure to discriminate his emotions and his generalized response of anger and drunkenness following virtually any interpersonal upset. During this early phase of therapy the agenda was simply to aid Ralph in becoming increasingly more aware of his emotional responses to even mild upset and to motivate him to recognize the failure inherent in the emotional coping strategies which he had been using.

In evaluating Ralph's improvement in this area of his therapy, especially during this initial phase, I routinely recorded his observations of the relative success of his various efforts to implement the strategies I had been recommending. I also systematically recorded Joyce's comments regarding his implementation of these strategies. I did not, however, require formal quantifiable ratings of the various relative successes experienced by Ralph regarding the emotional-control goal for, given that chemotherapy support had been introduced and that the assurances I provided in our first session had helped defuse the fear of Ralph's emotional disintegration, I chose initially to concentrate on the interpersonal communication and the alcohol consumption dimensions, for which I did require weekly quantifiable data.

Once the short-term therapeutic goals were achieved, the medium-range goals now became the focus of attention. This change from short- to medium-range goals involved a transition rather than a clear redirection in effort. Thus, the initial endeavor to improve communication between Ralph and Joyce blended into a commitment to improve the quality of the relationship among Ralph, Joyce, and the children. The initial commitment to abstinence blended into a program designed to educate the family about alcohol and train Ralph in the procedures of restricted drinking. The initial focus on communicating an understanding of Ralph's emotional state and bringing this condition under some temporary control continued to be a priority of long-term programming. And finally, in order to facilitate all of the aforestated goals, the issue of Ralph's employment would require some therapeutic examination.

The procedures employed in working toward each of these goals, especially in the case of medium-range Goals 1, 3, and 4, were routine and do not require detailed presentation. Briefly, however, in working toward the goal of continued family stability, I moved from an initial contracting procedure involving conjoint therapy with Ralph and Joyce to a procedure of drawing Ralph, Jr., into several sessions, with the final agenda being the involvement of all members of the household.* (In fact, Ralph, Joyce, Ralph, Jr., and Catherine began a behaviorally oriented family therapy program with me during the sixth month of Ralph's therapy.)

The goal associated with Ralph's emotional stability was addressed by a series of cognitively oriented behavior therapy strategies ranging from the analysis and restructuring of many of Ralph's self-statements to the introduction of both Ralph and Joyce to a detailed program of assertiveness training (focused especially on assertiveness in family interactions). Routine medication support was progressively eliminated during the second month of therapy.

The matter of Ralph's employment involved goals clarification and some realistic assessment of both his skills and his shortcomings. But it also involved training Ralph in job application procedures, and in putting into perspective the notion that not being invited to take a position did not logically equate with the concept of personal failure. Assertiveness issues regarding employment-related interactions were also explored within this goal. Finally, within this goal, therapy oriented Ralph to seek employment that he believed would be satisfying to him rather than simply taking a job in which he had no investment (as he had done ever since he retired). In this regard, at the time Ralph consulted me he was unemployed. Toward the end of the first month of therapy, he interviewed for three different positions,

---

* It is noteworthy that beyond self-report data, no quantitative assessment procedures were used to measure the progress of therapy in the social (interpersonal) domain. Nevertheless, ongoing assessment of family interaction patterns was obtained by requiring Ralph to tape half-hour segments of dinnertime family interactions at least twice weekly using a cassette recorder. After several therapy sessions involving analysis of these tapes, with occasional recommendations for interaction style changes, the family was requested to undertake their own home-based analysis and critique of their taped interaction on at least a weekly basis.

none of which he particularly wanted; following a fair degree of pressure from Joyce, he took one of them, a position as an electrician in a nearby factory. Despite his constant dissatisfaction with this job, Ralph stayed in his position (though emotional outbursts on the job very nearly led to him being terminated on several occasions) until he obtained a satisfactory employment opportunity. (During the sixth month of his therapy, and after a number of frustrations, Ralph was successful in obtaining a position as an instructor for a major weapons-exporting corporation.)

Unlike the above therapeutic procedures, which are relatively straight forward and well-known, the techniques for establishing restricted drinking in the treatment of alcohol abuse are relatively poorly understood as common therapeutic procedures, so these will be presented in greater detail. The procedures used to train Ralph to restrict his drinking were based on the original procedures of Lovibond and Caddy (1970) (see also Caddy & Lovibond, 1976; Miller & Muñoz, 1976; Pomerleau et al., 1978; Sanchez-Craig, 1979; Sobell & Sobell, 1973; and Vogler et al., 1977).

Initially (i.e., during Sessions 9, 10, and 11), Ralph underwent an educational program during which he was given detailed information about alcohol and its effects, including the general parameters relating to alcohol intake, BAL, and the relationship between BAL, alcohol intake, and intoxication. During this program, the emerging concepts of alcohol abuse and the multivariate perspectives were communicated to Ralph, as was the cognitive-behavioral perspective of loss of control and relapse (Caddy, 1979; Marlatt, 1978).

Thereafter, within a psychotherapeutic component, specific training in self-regulation was begun. This procedure included therapy designed to help Ralph accept the concepts presented in the educational component. Thus, for example, Ralph was encouraged to see himself as a person with a behavioral disorder rather than a disease over which he could exert no control. The therapy was geared toward conveying to Ralph the perspective that within certain rather narrow limits, he could drink and yet still exert decisive control over his drinking. I will mention other specific aspects of the psychotherapeutic component subsequently.

The third component of the controlled-drinking approach involved BAL discrimination training, which began in Session 10 (see the review by Caddy, 1977). This component involved training Ralph to discriminate his BAL within the limits 0 to 80 mg%. At the beginning of this training, Ralph was provided with a scale describing the behavioral effects which typically accompany various BALs (Greenberg, 1958). Then, he was required to consume beer (and, in later sessions, bourbon), in small and measured amounts and examine his subjective experiences and behavior as the basis for estimating his BAL. Twenty minutes after the completion of each drink, a sample of Ralph's breath was analyzed on a model 900 Breathalyzer and the results fed back to him. Each time the result was presented, Ralph was encouraged to relate his subjective state with that particular BAL. Additionally, during each drink, Ralph was shaped to drink slowly, to take small sips, to focus on the flavor, and to develop a deliberate style of slowly enjoying the beverage and the very mild effects he was experiencing.

This procedure was repeated within each of the next eight sessions, during which time Ralph's ability to estimate his BAL accurately rapidly approached asymptotic performance, with mean estimation errors after the second session always below 10 mg%. At the point in each of these sessions where Ralph's BAL reached 50 mg%, he was advised that he had reached the BAL beyond which his ability to control his behavior would decrease dramatically. During approximately 50% of these sessions, he was pressed to drink beyong the 50 mg% limit in order to experience in detail and in a controlled environment these higher BALs. When Ralph's BAL exceeded 50 mg%, covert sensitization procedures were administered via graphic presentations of his past drunkenness (see Elkins & Murdock, 1977). During these sessions, also, he was advised about the narrowness of the limits in which moderate (not necessarily social) drinkers engage in alcohol usage. And finally, again during these sessions, Ralph was subjected to drink refusal training (Foy et al., 1976). The primary training phase of the controlled-drinking program lasted for a total of 10 sessions, the latter 4 of which were separated by sessions addressing other aspects of Ralph's treatment.

Ralph's response to the restricted drinking program was most gratifying. As noted previously, he soon became capable of accurately discriminating his BAL, and he also rapidly mastered required changes in the parameters of his drinking behavior. Further, he came to recognize the abusive nature of his previous drinking practices, and he recognized also that if he drank alcohol in the future, he could not take the risk of drinking in the same manner as many "social drinkers" appear to do. In fact, on at least several occasions early in his restricted-drinking program, Ralph raised the question, "If that is all I can drink without serious risk, then is it worth drinking at all?" He concluded that to have several glasses of beer for the taste or the conviviality of a social exchange was an adequate reason to use alcohol. Thus, he set out to establish a new pattern of restricted alcohol use.

At the end of the twelfth month of Ralph's therapy, I tallied the weekly reports from Ralph and Joyce and concluded that Ralph had drunk on approximately 80 days during the year and had exceeded a BAL of 50 mg% on 12 occasions. With the exception of a 2-day period during his fifth therapy month, when Ralph became intoxicated following a confrontation with his employer, these excessive-drinking days rarely resulted in BALs above 100 mg%, and in no instance did his drinking lead Ralph into serious difficulty.

This being the case, and given the marked improvement in many other areas of Ralphs functioning, we agreed to terminate therapy at the end of 14 months (by which time I was seeing Ralph and Joyce only monthly, anyway). Nevertheless, I have remained in routine contact with both Ralph and Joyce, and I have continued to confront them with the need for ongoing attention to the goal of restricted drinking for a person with Ralph's learning history. Perhaps most important of all, I have continued to communicate to all concerned the view that it is reasonable to expect that at least occasionally Ralph may begin to slip back into a pattern of abusive drinking. And in the event that such a pattern emerges, the family should stand firm together against such behavior and should contact me so that I may again be helpful.

Ralph's continued general success with regard to his goal of restricted drinking notwithstanding (it is now $3\frac{1}{2}$ years since he entered therapy with me), I saw Ralph and Joyce for a total of four additional sessions toward the end of his second posttreatment year. Again, they had been experiencing some interpersonal difficulties, and although Ralph did not return to his previous patterns of drunkenness, his pattern of alcohol consumption did increase over a period of 3 to 4 weeks, with intoxication occurring on approximately 5 occasions during that period. With the exception of this period of relative crisis, however, overall, the changes made by Ralph and his entire family during the course of therapy were most impressive. Such results, I consider, reflect the merits of the multivariate perspective of alcoholism and recommend the alternative of restricted drinking as a viable goal in the treatment of at least some abusive drinkers.

COMMENTARY

Peter E. Nathan

Glenn Caddy's call for greater appreciation of the diversity of factors contributing to the development of alcoholism is a timely one. Our individual and collective zeal to offer something new to theory or practice sometimes leads us to admire our own views of a phenomenon too highly and to appreciate too little how others see the same thing. Caddy's multivariate appreciation of the span of factors playing causative roles in alcohol problems, and his consequent insistence that as many treatment modalities as necessary be involved in remediation efforts, reflects the conviction that two unduly narrow views have held sway at this time. Hence, Caddy's call for theories of etiology and treatment that more adequately reflect the multiplicity of factors—biological, psychological, social, and cultural—that underlie alcohol problems.

The multivariate model of mental disorder actually goes back quite a way; with each rediscovery of its virtues, undue focus on a single etiologic or treatment view is revealed—and replaced. Examples abound, from the ancient Greeks to the Islamic physicians of the Middle Ages to the philosopher-psychologists of the 17th and 18th centuries. Of more direct and immediate relevance, Adolph Meyer's psychobiology—a reaction against Kraepelin's single-minded organic focus and Freud's newly popular psychoanalysis—shares a great deal with Caddy's contemporary intent. When examining a patient, for example, Meyer took a complete life history, assessed personality, and examined physical, neurological, genetic, and social status, as well as the manner in which the patient integrated all of these developmental elements. This assessment plan sounds very similar in specifics as well as intent to Caddy's.

In the execution of his multivariate treatment plan, moreover, Glenn Caddy has a significant forebear—pioneering behavior therapist Arnold Lazarus—who wrote of the importance, in the mid–1960s, of providing the alcoholic a full range of therapeutic interventions, from the somatic to the psychological, from techniques that focused on the problem drinking itself to those which confronted associated behavioral deficits and excesses, from individual techniques to those viable for the alcoholic and his or her spouse and children.

Caddy makes a good case for the extensive period of functional analysis that precedes his behavioral interventions with Ralph P. Short- and longer-term goals flow naturally from the assessment. Surprising to nonbehavioral clinicians, perhaps, is Caddy's decision to give first priority to efforts to deal with the patient's marriage and its effects on his drinking before confronting the drinking itself, in the belief both that a continuation of the dysfunctional marriage would make much more difficult any efforts to alter drinking patterns, and that the dysfunctional marriage might be somewhat easier to deal with than the abusive drinking. In other words, behavior therapists do not automatically focus their interventions on abusive drinking, in the naive belief that everything else will fall into line once the drinking is under control or has been stopped. Instead, like other experienced clinicians, behavior therapists recognize the reciprocal nature of marital, vocational, academic, and interpersonal problems and abusive drinking; to fail to recognize the synergism of these elements is to complicate the remediation process immensely.

The specificity of the goals outlined by Caddy might also surprise some. They reflect the disposition of experienced behavior therapists to "target" their interventions. They also further illustrate the value of the functional analysis; in this case, it provides the clinician a clear picture of the issues to be confronted in therapy, their interrelationship, and the order in which they might most appropriately be addressed. While behavioral assessment does not always yield such clear-cut, useful, and effective goals, the process is a valuable one, even when its results are not so worthwhile.

Most surprising to many readers of Caddy's report will be his decision to require a period of abstinence from patients before they attempt to achieve a nonproblem-drinking pattern. Most traditional clinicians view abstinence as a more difficult short-term treatment goal than nonproblem drinking; hence, requiring abstinence before treatment with a controlled-drinking focus would appear to be putting the cart before the horse. *Others would question the readiness of most problem drinkers who choose non-problem drinking as a treatment goal to maintain an initial period of abstinence. Although they would acknowledge its function as a test of motivation, as a screening method to separate the serious from the casual patient, many would question the numbers of alcohol abusers who would participate in the abstinence trial if their real treatment goal is nonproblem drinking (an "easier" goal).*

My own concern at this sequence, which Caddy, Hay, and the Sobell group share, has to do with the ethics of removing someone from the ranks of the sober once he or she has been able to achieve and maintain abstinence for a month or more. The conventional wisdom is that nonproblem drinking ought not be offered an alcoholic who has been abstinent for any length of time; someone who has achieved abstinence and then maintained it for 6 weeks or more, by this logic, is a wholly inappropriate candidate for nonproblem-drinking treatment because it requires a return to drinking. On the other hand, in examining my reaction to Caddy's plan, I had to acknowledge its value as an effective means to separate patients with good from those with poor treatment motivation. I had to conclude that few other approaches would be as robust. I also wish Caddy, Hay, or the Sobells would plan research contrasting the outcome of nonproblem-drinking treatment of patients selected in this way from that without such a rigorous hurdle. I would also like to know how different the treatment outcomes of 6-week abstainers who were provided the agreed-upon nonproblem-drinking treatment would be from those of abstainers asked to maintain abstinence indefinitely. This approach to patient selection and treatment is a most important one to test. That three groups of highly regarded clinicians have adopted it impresses me; the field. though, requires empirical validation.

6. REFERENCES

Ascher, M. Paradoxical intention. In A Goldstein & E. B. Foa (Eds.), *Handbook of behavioral intervention.* New York: Wiley, 1980.

Bacon, S. D. The process of addiction to alcohol: Social aspects. *Quarterly Journal of Studies on Alcohol,* 1973, *34,* 1–27.

Caddy, G. R. Blood alcohol concentration discrimination training: Development and current status, In G. A. Marlatt & P. E. Nathan (Eds.), *Behavioral approaches to the assessment and treatment of alcoholism.* New Brunswick, N.J.: Center for Alcohol Studies, 1977.

Caddy, G. R. Toward a multivariate analysis of alcohol abuse. In P. E. Nathan, G. A. Marlatt, & T. Løberg (Eds.), *Alcoholism: New directions in behavioral research and treatment: New directions in behavioral research and treatment.* New York: Plenum Press, 1978.

Caddy, G. R. *Preventing alcoholic relapse: A comparison of aftercare procedures.* Paper presented at the American Psychological Association Annual Convention, New York, September 1979.

Caddy, G. R. & Lovibond, S. H. Self-regulation and discriminated aversive conditioning in the modification of alcoholic's drinking behavior. *Behavior Therapy,* 1976, *7,* 223–230.

Caddy, G. R., & Gottheil, E. The role of programmed access to alcohol in alcoholism research and treatment. In M. A. Galanter, M. A. Rothschild, & J. Mason (Eds.), *Currents in alcoholism.* New York: National Council on Alcoholism, in press.

Caddy, G. R., Goldman, R. D., & Huebner, R. Relationships among different domains of attitudes towards alcoholism: Model, cost and treatment. *Addictive Behaviors*, 1976, *1*, 159–167. (a)

Caddy, G. R., Goldman, R. D., & Huebner, R. Group differences in attitudes towards alcoholism. *Addictive Behaviors*, 1976, *1*, 281–286. (b)

Cahalan, D. *Problem drinkers: A national survey.* San Francisco: Jossey-Bass, 1970.

Cahalan, D., & Room, R. *Problem drinking among American men.* Monograph No. 7. New Brunswick, N.J.: Rugers Center of Alcohol Studies, 1974.

Edwards, G. Drugs: Drug dependence and the concept of plasticity. *Quarterly Journal of Studies on Alcohol*, 1974, *35*, 176–195.

Elkins, R. L., & Murdock, R. P. The contribution of successful conditioning to abstinence maintenance following covert sensitization (verbal aversion) treatment of alcoholism. IRCS Medical Science: Psychology and psychiatry. *Social and Occupational Medicine*, 1977, *5*, 167.

Foy, D. W., Miller, P. M., Eisler, R. M., & O'Toole, D. H. Social skills training to teach alcoholics to refuse drinks effectively. *Journal of Studies on Alcohol*, 1976, *37*, 1340–1345.

Goldstein, S. G., & Linden, J. D. Multivariate classification of alcoholics by means of the MMPI. *Journal of Abnormal Psychology*, 1969, *74*, 661–669.

Gottheil, E. Advantages and disadvantages of the abstinence goal in alcoholism. *American Journal of Drug and Alcohol Abuse*, 1976, *3*, 13–23.

Greenberg, L. A. Intoxication and alcoholism: Physiological factors. *Annals of the American Academy of Political and Social Science*, 1958, *315*, 22–30.

Holder, H. D., & Stratas, N. E. A systems approach to alcoholism programming. *American Journal of Psychiatry*, 1972, *129*, 32–37.

Horn, J. L., & Wanberg, K. W. Symptom patterns related to the excessive use of alcohol. *Quarterly Journal of Studies on Alcohol*, 1969, *30*, 35–58.

Horn, J. L., & Wanberg, K. W. Dimensions of perception of background and current situation of alcoholic patients. *Quarterly Journal of Studies on Alcohol*, 1970, *31*, 633–658.

Huber, H., Karlin, R., & Nathan, P. E. Blood alcohol level discrimation in non-alcoholics: The role of internal and external cues. *Journal of Studies on Alcohol*, 1976, *37*, 27–39.

Knupfer, G. The epidemiology of problem drinking. *American Journal of Public Health*, 1967, *57*, 974–986.

Lazarus, A. A. *Behavior therapy and beyond.* New York: McGraw-Hill, 1971.

Lazarus, A. A. *Multimodal behavior therapy.* New York: Springer, 1976.

Linsky, A. S. Theories of behavior and social control of alcoholism. *Social Psychiatry*, 1972, *7*, 47–52.

Lovibond, S. H., & Caddy, G. Discriminated aversive control in the moderation of alcoholics' drinking behavior. *Behavior Therapy*, 1970, *1*, 437–444.

Maisto, S. A., & Schefft, B. K. The constructs of craving for alcohol and loss of control drinking: Help or hindrance to research. *Addictive Behavior*, 1977, *2*, 207–217.

Marconi, J. Scientific theory and operational definitions in psychotherapy with special reference to alcoholism. *Quarterly Journal of Studies on Alcohol*, 1967, *28*, 631–640.

Marlatt, G. A. *Craving for alcohol, loss of control, and relapse: A cognitive-behavioral analysis.* (Technical Report No. 7705) Seattle: University of Washington, Alcoholism and Drug Abuse Institute, 1977.

Meichenbaum, D. H. *Cognitive behavior modification.* Morristown, N.J.: General Learning Press, 1974.

Miller, W. R., & Caddy, G. R. Abstinence and controlled drinking in the treatment of problem drinkers. *Journal of Studies on Alcohol*, 1977, *38*, 986–1003.

Miller, W. R., & Muñoz, R. F. *How to control your drinking.* Englewood Cliffs, N.J.: Prentice-Hall, 1976.

Nathan, P. E., Lipson, A. G., Vettraino, A. P., & Solomon, P. The social ecology of an urban clinic for alcoholism. *International Journal of Addictions*, 1968, *3*, 55–64.

Pattison, E. M. Drinking outcomes of alcoholism treatment. Abstinence, social, modified, controlled, and normal drinking. In N. Kessel, A. Hawker, & H. Chalke (Eds.), *Alcoholism: A medical profile*. London: Edsall, 1974. (a)

Pattison, E. M. The rehabilitation of the chronic alcoholic. In B. Kissin & H. Begleiter (Eds.), *The biology of alcoholism* (Vol. 3). New York : Plenum Press, 1974. (b)

Pattison, E. M., Sobell, M. B., & Sobell, L. C. (Eds.). *Emerging concepts of alcohol dependence*. New York: Springer, 1977.

Pomerleau, O. F., Pertschuk, M., Adkins, D., & d'Aquili, E. Treatment for middle-income problem drinkers. In P. E. Nathan, G. A. Marlatt, & T. Løberg (Eds.), *Alcoholism: New directions in behavioral research and treatment*. New York: Plenum Press, 1978.

Sanchez-Craig, M. *Reappraisal therapy: A self-control strategy for abstinence and controlled drinking.* Paper presented at the Taos International Conference on Treatment of Addictive Behaviors, Taos, N.M., February 1979.

Seligman, M. E. P. Learned helplessness. *Annual Review of Medicine*, 1972, *23*, 407–412.

Siegler, M., Osmond, H., & Newell, S. Models of alcoholism. *Quarterly Journal of Studies on Alcohol*, 1968, *29*, 571–591.

Sobell, L. C., Maisto, S. A., Sobell, M. B., & Cooper, A. M. Reliability of alcohol abusers' self-reports of drinking behavior. *Behaviour Research and Therapy*, 1979, *17*, 157–160.

Sobell, M. B. Alternatives to abstinence: Evidence, issues and some proposals. In P. E. Nathan, G. A. Marlatt, & T. Løberg (Eds.), *Alcoholism: New directions in behavioral research and treatment*. New York: Plenum Press, 1978.

Sobell, M. B., & Sobell, L. C. Individualized behavior therapy for alcoholics. *Behavior Therapy*, 1973, *4*, 49–72.

Sobell, M. B., & Sobell, L. C. The need for realism, relevance, and operational assumptions in the study of substance dependence. In H. D. Cappell & A. E. LeBlanc (Eds.), *Biological and behavioral approaches to drug dependence*. Toronto: Addiction Research Foundation, 1975.

Sobell, M. B., Maisto, S. A., Sobell, L. C., Cooper, A. M., Cooper, T. C. & Sanders, B. Developing a prototype for evaluating alcohol treatment effectiveness. In L. C. Sobell, M. B. Sobell, & E. Ward (Eds.), *Evaluating alcohol and drug abuse treatment effectiveness: Recent advances*. New York: Pergamon Press, 1980.

Steinglass, P., Weiner, S., & Mendelson, J. H. Interactional issues as determinants of alcoholism. *American Journal of Psychiatry*, 1971, *128*, 275–280. (a)

Steinglass, P., Weiner, S., & Mendelson, J. H. A systems approach to alcoholism. *Archives of General Psychiatry*, 1971, *24*, 401–408. (b)

Vogler, R. E., Weissbach, T. A., Compton, J. V., & Martin, G. T. Integrated behavior change techniques for problem drinkers in the community. *Journal of Consulting and Clinical Psychology*, 1977, *45*, 267–279.

Wanberg, K. W., & Knapp, J. A multidimensional model for the research and treatment of alcoholism. *The International Journal of the Addictions*, 1970, *5*, 69–98.

Yates, A. J. *Behavior therapy*. New York: Wiley, 1970.

Index

Author Chapter	Patient sex	Treatmen		
		Individual	Group	Conjoint
P. M. Miller *Chapter 1*	Male	X		
M. S. Goldman and Diane K. Klisz *Chapter 2*	Female	X	X	
W. R. Miller *Chapter 3*	Male			
	Female			
N.E. Noel *et al.* *Chapter 4*	Male	X		
	Male	X		
	Male		X	
	Male	X		
	Male	X		
P. E. Nathan *Chapter 5*	Female			X
B. S. McCrady *Chapter 6*	Male			X
W. M. Hay *Chapter 7*	Male			X
R. E. Vogler *Chapter 8*	Male	X		
R. J. Hodgson and H. J. Rankin *Chapter 9*	Male	X		
H. J. Rankin *Chapter 10*	Male	X		
G. R. Caddy *Chapter 12*	Male	X		X